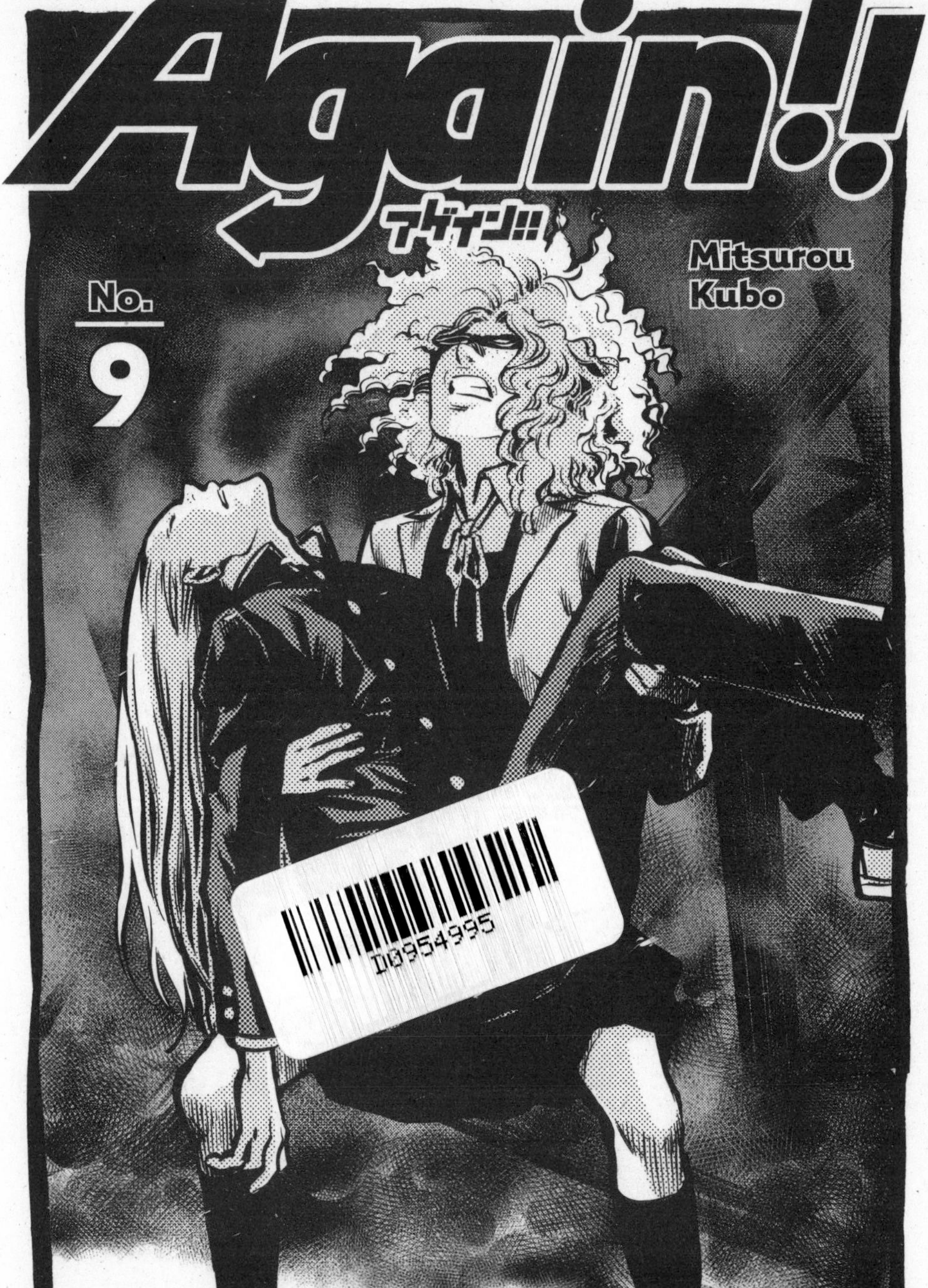
Again!!
アゲイン!!
Mitsurou
Kubo
No.
9

contents

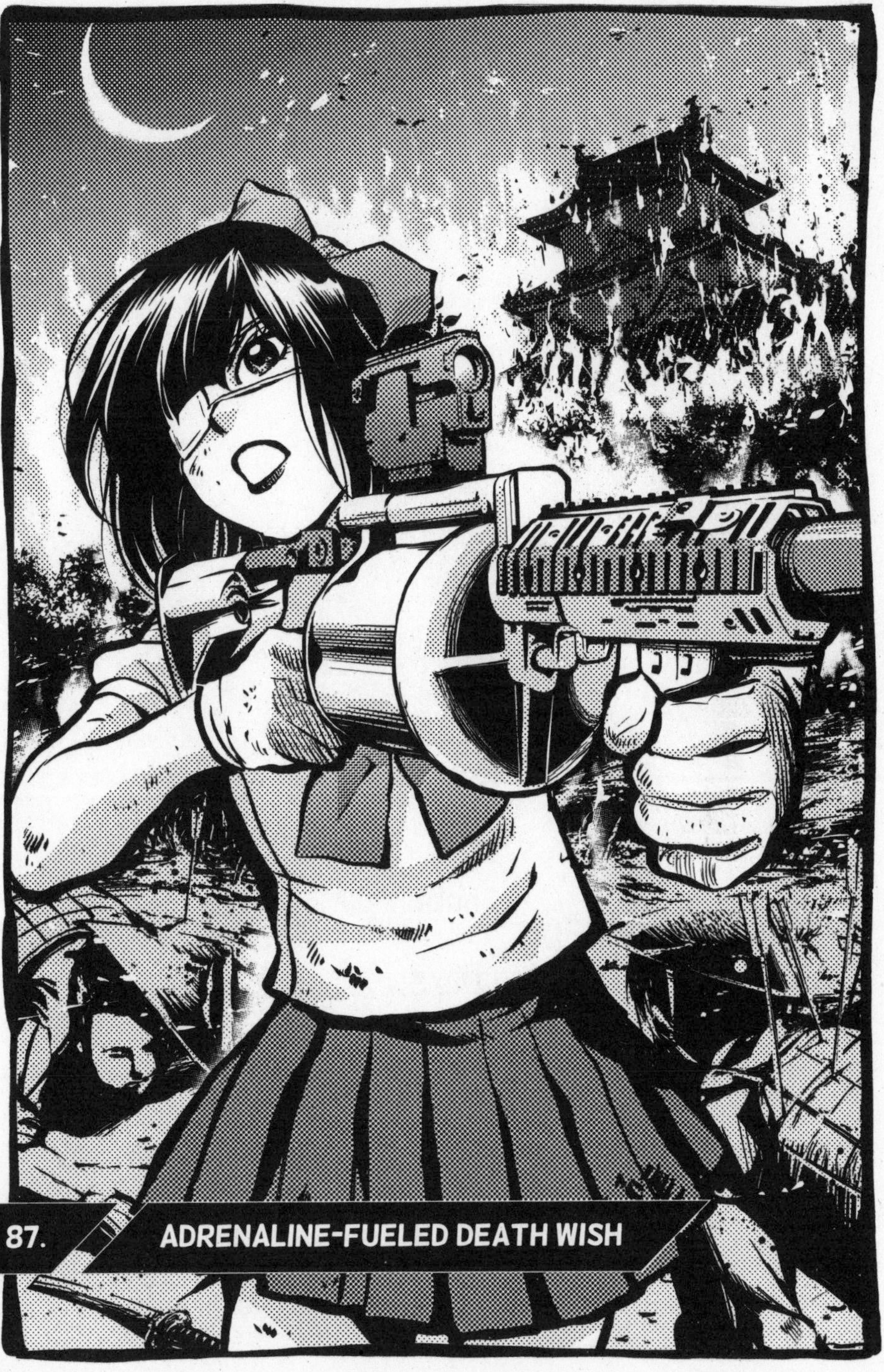

87. ADRENALINE-FUELED DEATH WISH

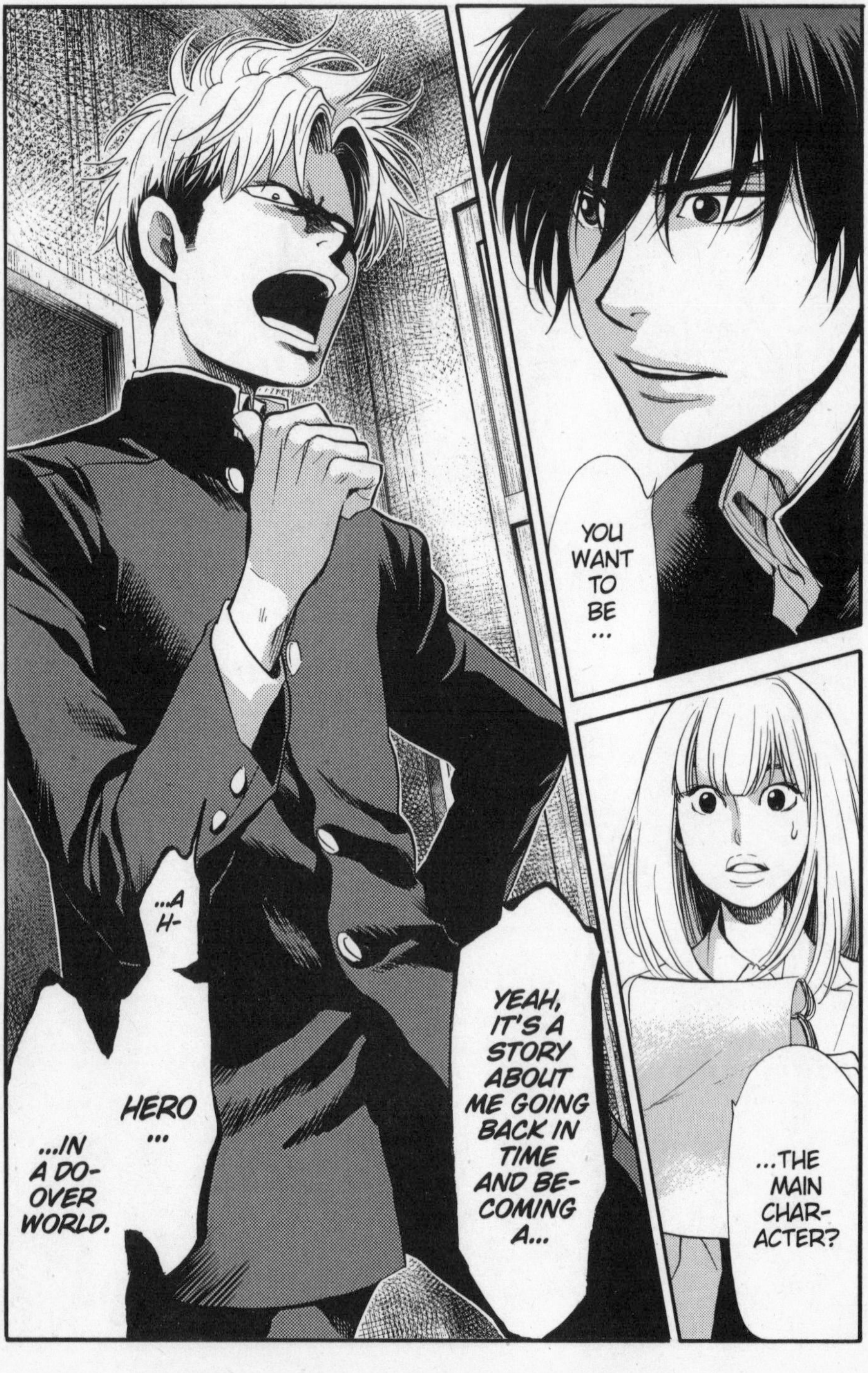
YOU WANT TO BE...
...THE MAIN CHARACTER?
YEAH, IT'S A STORY ABOUT ME GOING BACK IN TIME AND BECOMING A...
...A H-
HERO...
...IN A DO-OVER WORLD.

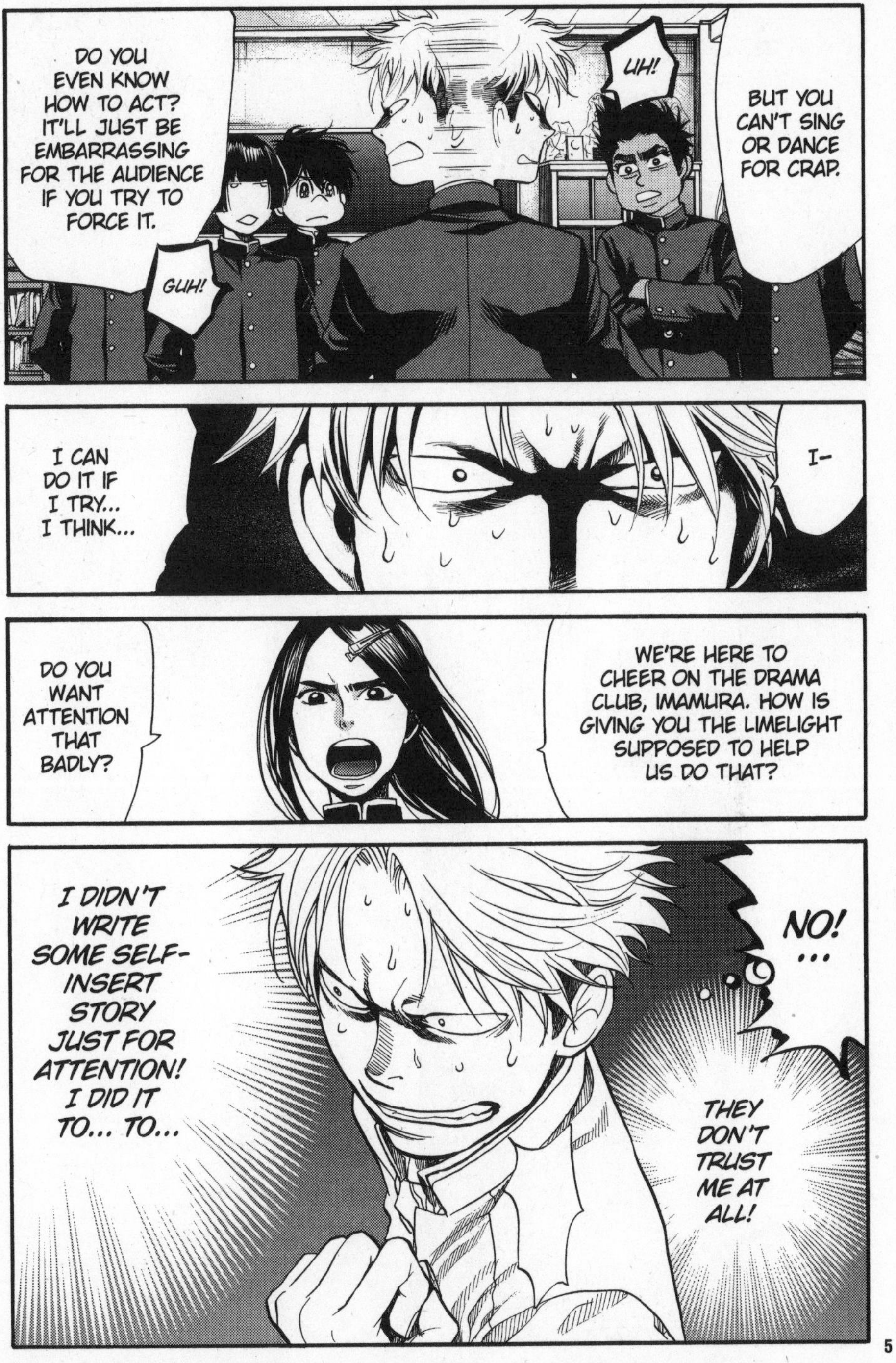
BUT YOU CAN'T SING OR DANCE FOR CRAP.
UH!
DO YOU EVEN KNOW HOW TO ACT? IT'LL JUST BE EMBARRASSING FOR THE AUDIENCE IF YOU TRY TO FORCE IT.
GUH!
I-
I CAN DO IT IF I TRY... I THINK...
WE'RE HERE TO CHEER ON THE DRAMA CLUB, IMAMURA. HOW IS GIVING YOU THE LIMELIGHT SUPPOSED TO HELP US DO THAT?
DO YOU WANT ATTENTION THAT BADLY?
NO! ...
THEY DON'T TRUST ME AT ALL!
I DIDN'T WRITE SOME SELF-INSERT STORY JUST FOR ATTENTION! I DID IT TO... TO...

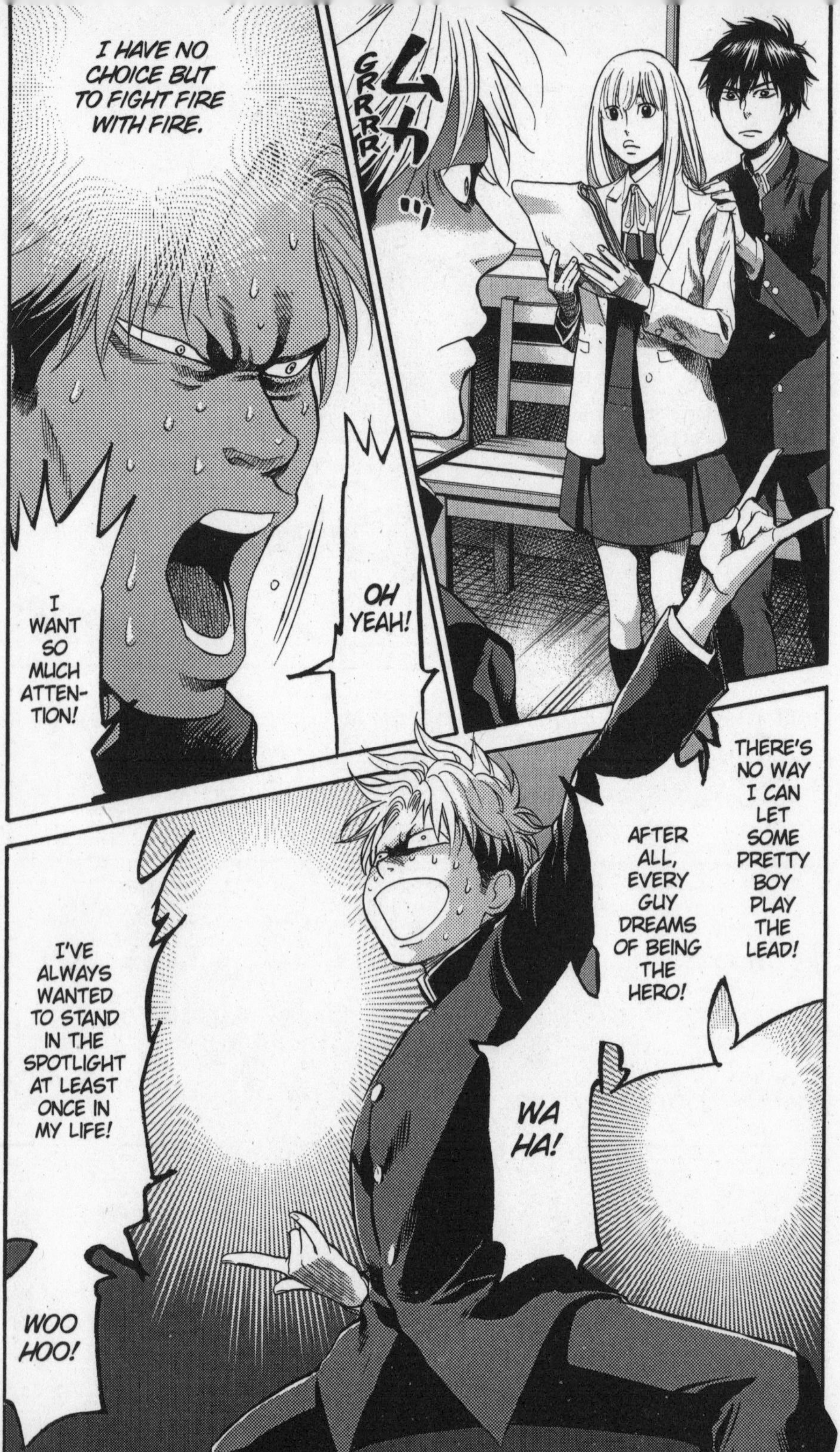
GRRRR
I HAVE NO CHOICE BUT TO FIGHT FIRE WITH FIRE.
OH YEAH!
I WANT SO MUCH ATTEN-TION!
THERE'S NO WAY I CAN LET SOME PRETTY BOY PLAY THE LEAD!
AFTER ALL, EVERY GUY DREAMS OF BEING THE HERO!
WA HA!
I'VE ALWAYS WANTED TO STAND IN THE SPOTLIGHT AT LEAST ONCE IN MY LIFE!
WOO HOO!

HUUUSH

THE ANXIETY OF ATTENTION-SEEKING WITHOUT ANY TALENT TO MERIT IT IS MORE INTENSE THAN I IMAGINED!

I CAN'T BELIEVE THERE ARE PEOPLE OUT THERE WHO BLUSTER LIKE THIS ALL THE TIME!

NOW I REALLY DO FEEL LIKE I WANT TO DIE!

FWIP

HMM
...

A "DO-OVER," HUH?

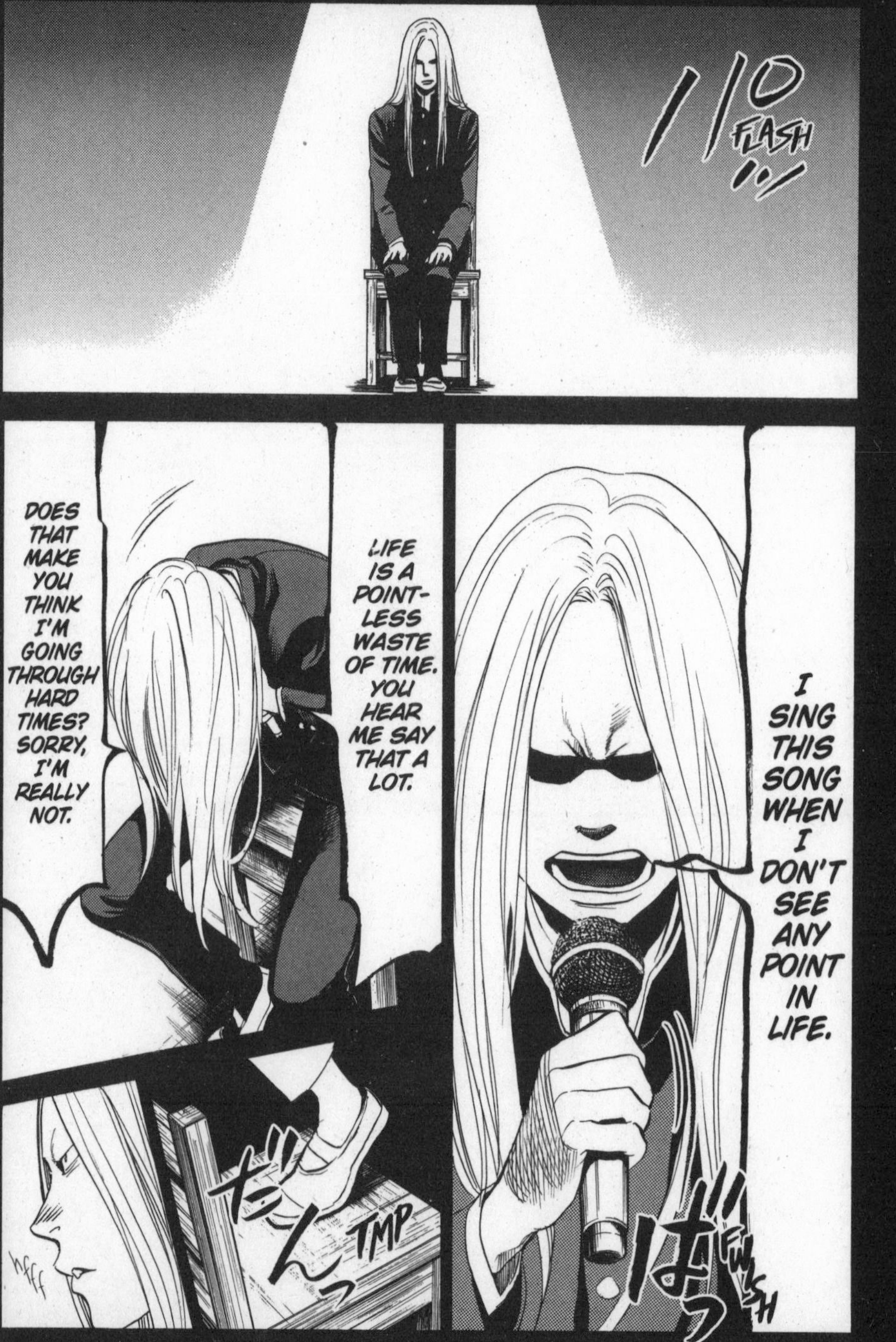
FLASH
I SING THIS SONG WHEN I DON'T SEE ANY POINT IN LIFE.
FWISH
LIFE IS A POINT-LESS WASTE OF TIME. YOU HEAR ME SAY THAT A LOT.
DOES THAT MAKE YOU THINK I'M GOING THROUGH HARD TIMES? SORRY, I'M REALLY NOT.
TMP
hfff

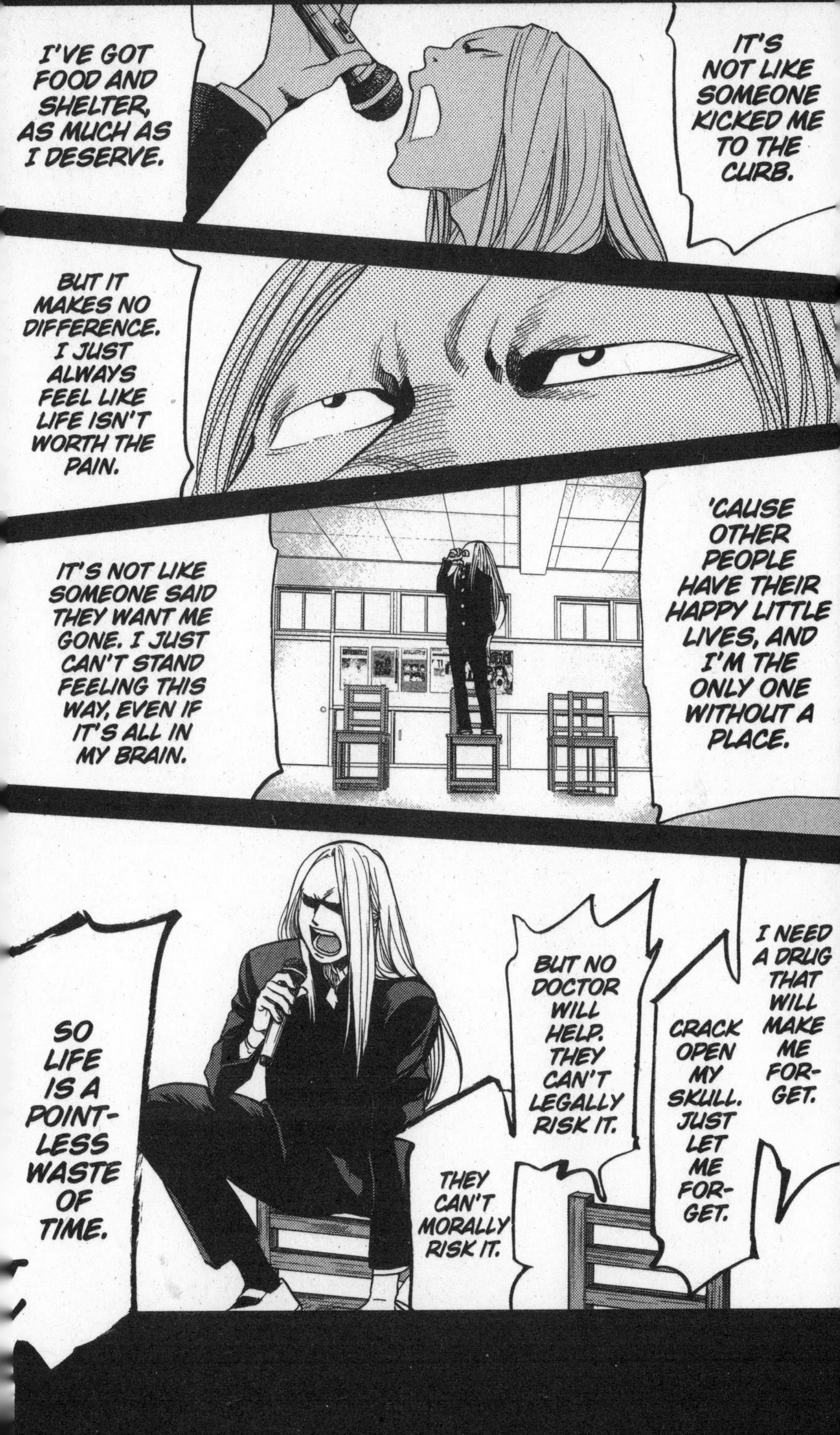
IT'S NOT LIKE SOMEONE KICKED ME TO THE CURB.
I'VE GOT FOOD AND SHELTER, AS MUCH AS I DESERVE.
BUT IT MAKES NO DIFFERENCE. I JUST ALWAYS FEEL LIKE LIFE ISN'T WORTH THE PAIN.
'CAUSE OTHER PEOPLE HAVE THEIR HAPPY LITTLE LIVES, AND I'M THE ONLY ONE WITHOUT A PLACE.
IT'S NOT LIKE SOMEONE SAID THEY WANT ME GONE. I JUST CAN'T STAND FEELING THIS WAY, EVEN IF IT'S ALL IN MY BRAIN.
I NEED A DRUG THAT WILL MAKE ME FOR-GET.
CRACK OPEN MY SKULL. JUST LET ME FOR-GET.
BUT NO DOCTOR WILL HELP. THEY CAN'T LEGALLY RISK IT.
THEY CAN'T MORALLY RISK IT.
SO LIFE IS A POINT-LESS WASTE OF TIME.

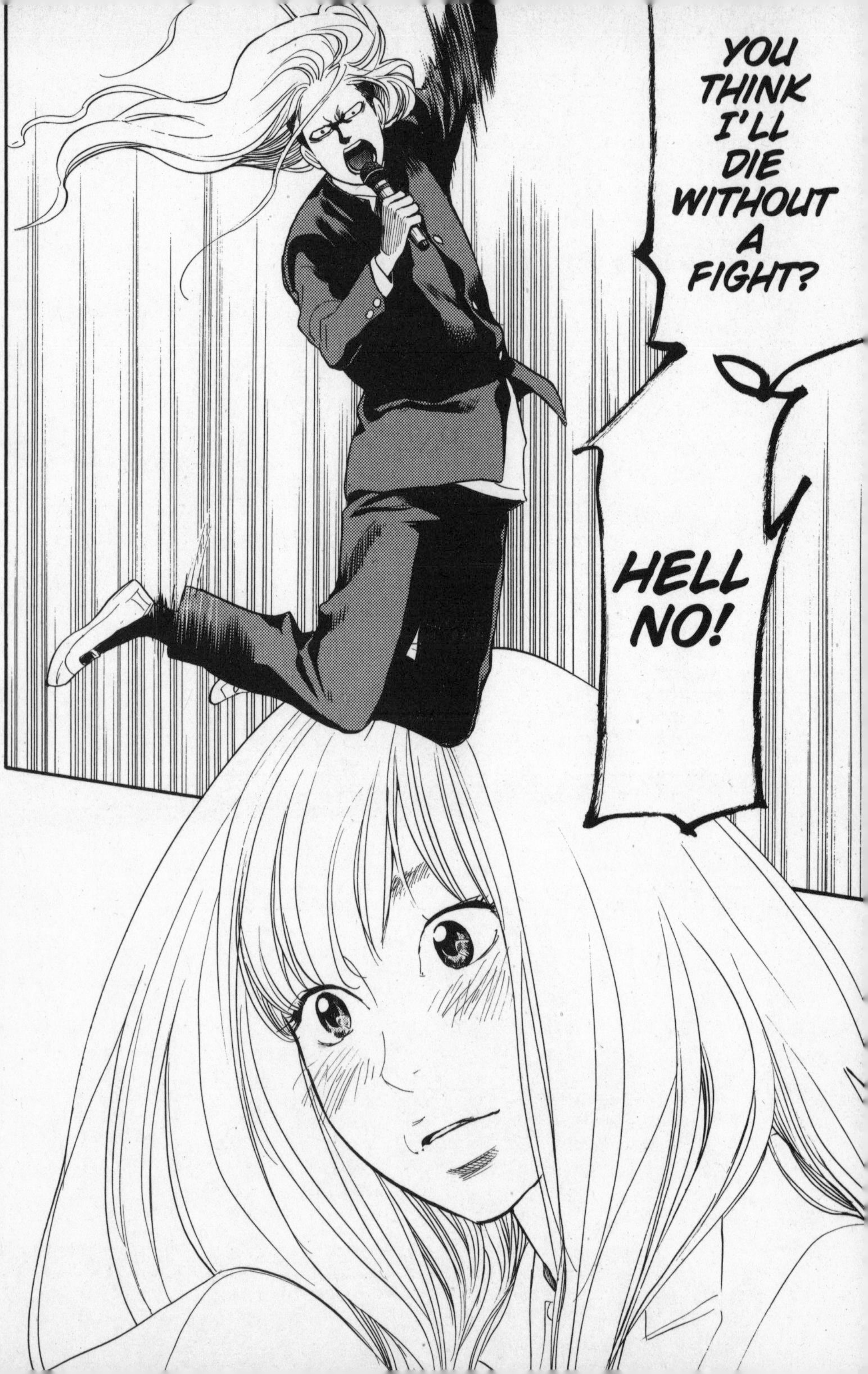
YOU THINK I'LL DIE WITHOUT A FIGHT?
HELL NO!

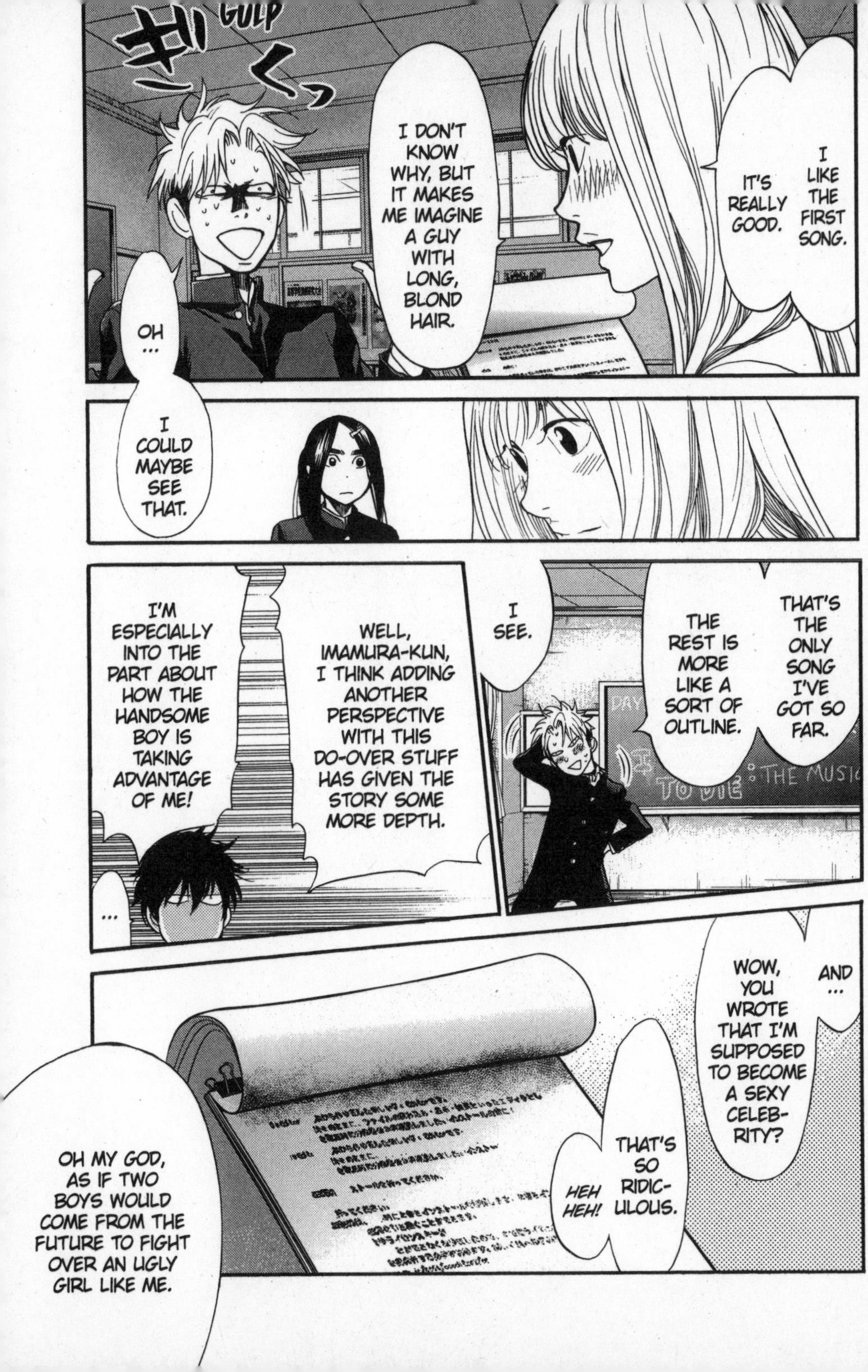
I LIKE THE FIRST SONG.
IT'S REALLY GOOD.
ぎくっ
GULP
I DON'T KNOW WHY, BUT IT MAKES ME IMAGINE A GUY WITH LONG, BLOND HAIR.
OH ...
I COULD MAYBE SEE THAT.
THAT'S THE ONLY SONG I'VE GOT SO FAR.
THE REST IS MORE LIKE A SORT OF OUTLINE.
I SEE.
WELL, IMAMURA-KUN, I THINK ADDING ANOTHER PERSPECTIVE WITH THIS DO-OVER STUFF HAS GIVEN THE STORY SOME MORE DEPTH.
I'M ESPECIALLY INTO THE PART ABOUT HOW THE HANDSOME BOY IS TAKING ADVANTAGE OF ME!
...
AND ...
WOW, YOU WROTE THAT I'M SUPPOSED TO BECOME A SEXY CELEBRITY?
THAT'S SO RIDICULOUS.
HEH HEH!
OH MY GOD, AS IF TWO BOYS WOULD COME FROM THE FUTURE TO FIGHT OVER AN UGLY GIRL LIKE ME.

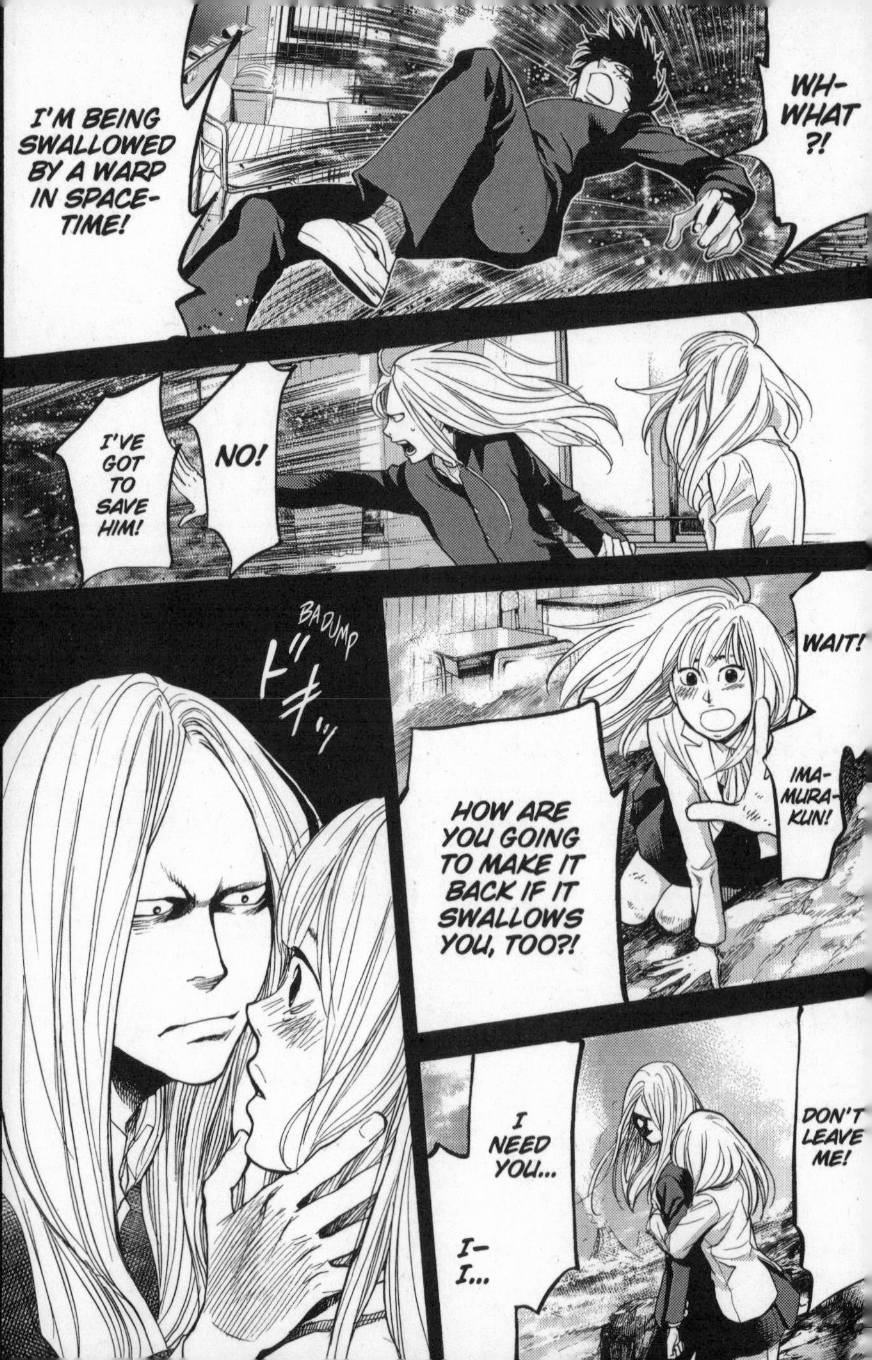
WH- WHAT?!
I'M BEING SWALLOWED BY A WARP IN SPACE-TIME!
NO!
I'VE GOT TO SAVE HIM!
WAIT!
IMAMURA-KUN!
HOW ARE YOU GOING TO MAKE IT BACK IF IT SWALLOWS YOU, TOO?!
DON'T LEAVE ME!
I NEED YOU...
I- I...
BADUMP
ドキッ

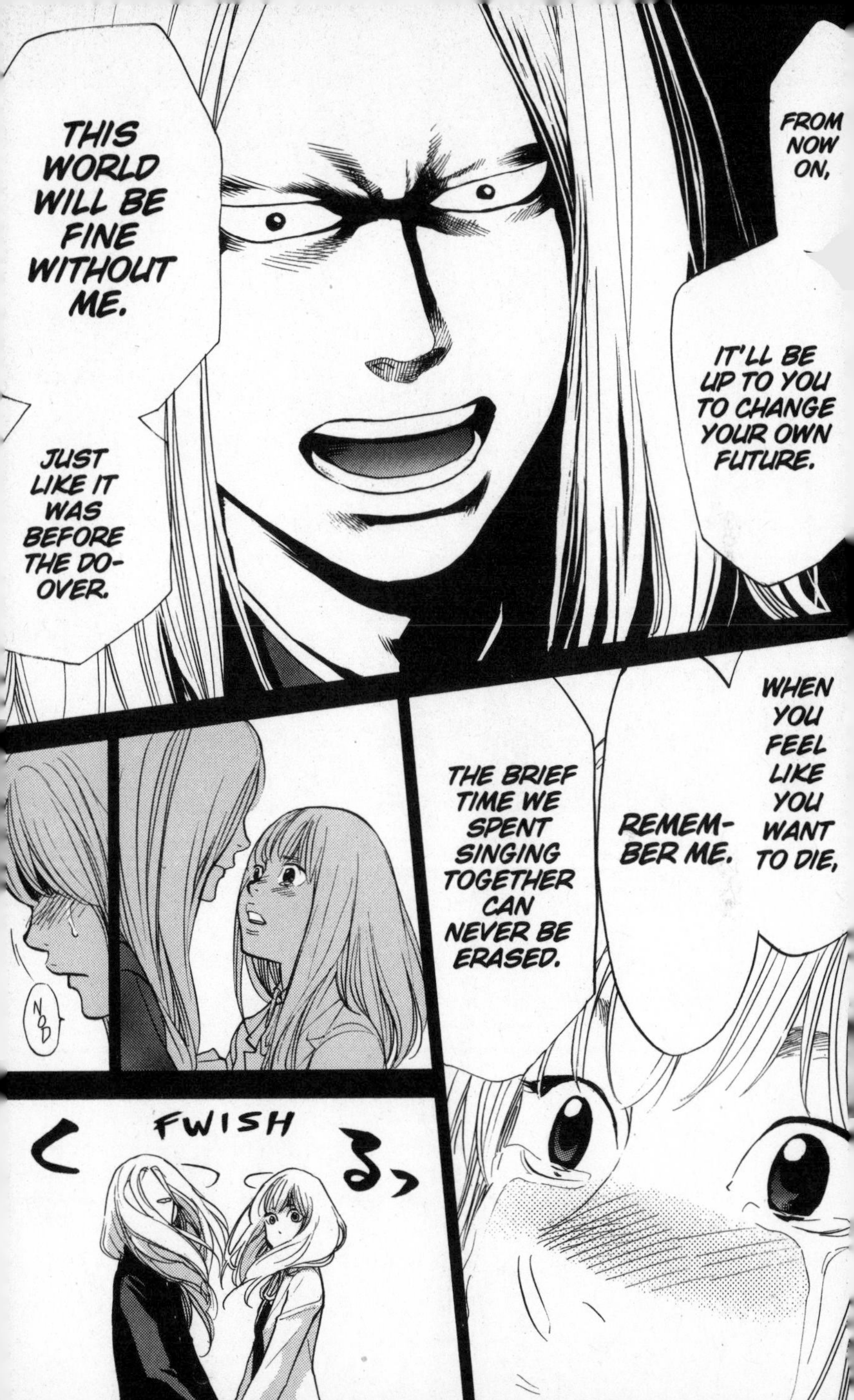
FROM NOW ON,
IT'LL BE UP TO YOU TO CHANGE YOUR OWN FUTURE.
THIS WORLD WILL BE FINE WITHOUT ME.
JUST LIKE IT WAS BEFORE THE DO-OVER.
WHEN YOU FEEL LIKE YOU WANT TO DIE,
REMEMBER ME.
THE BRIEF TIME WE SPENT SINGING TOGETHER CAN NEVER BE ERASED.
NOD
FWISH

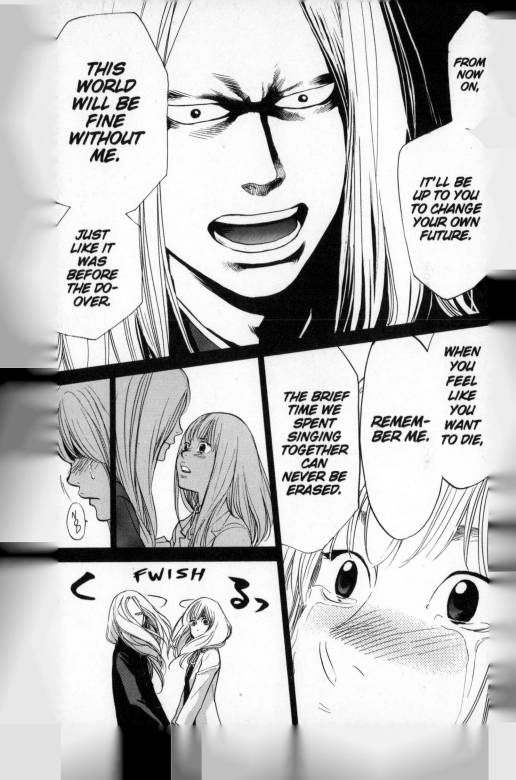

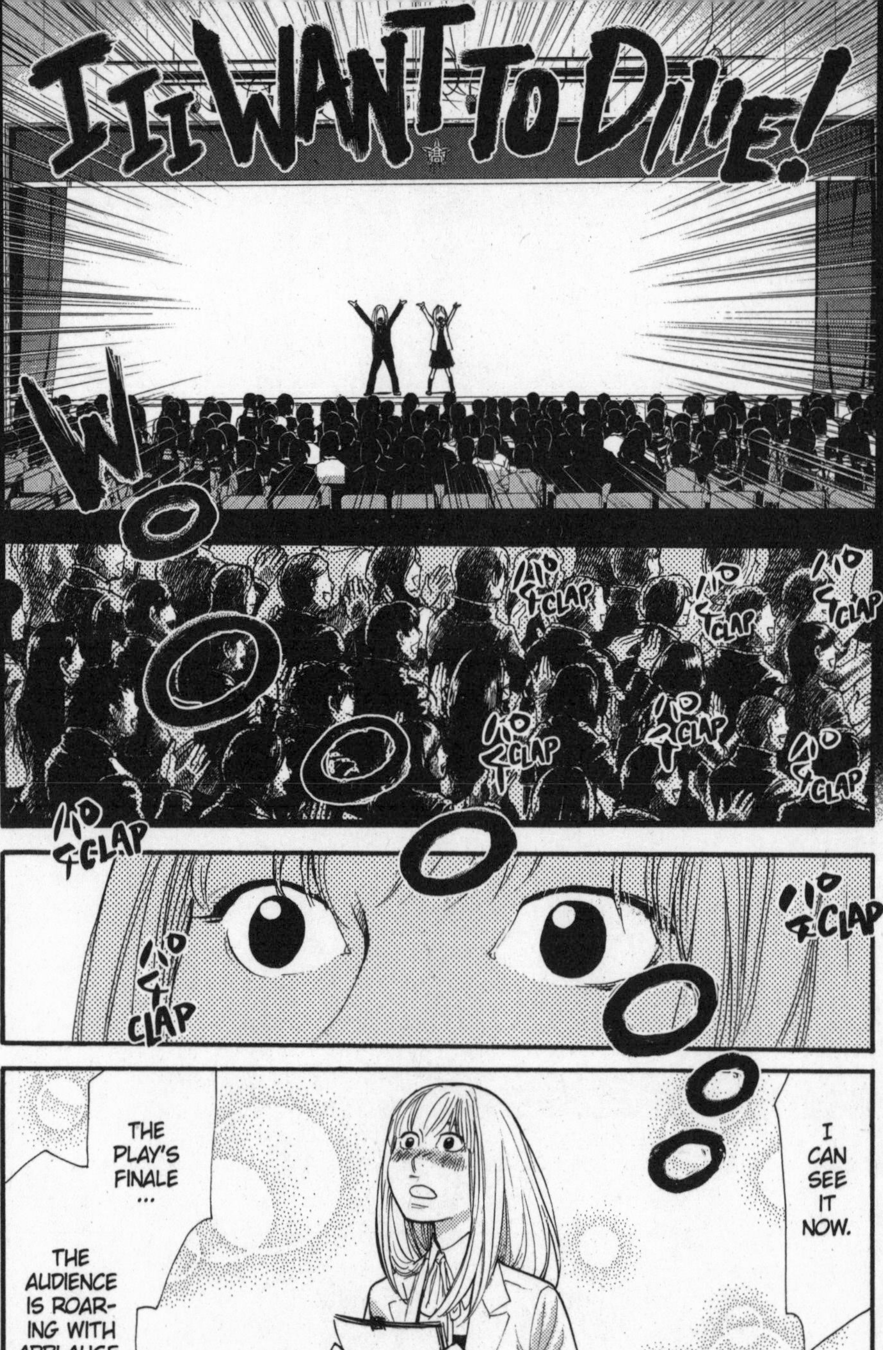

I I WANT TO DI I E!
WOOOOOO
CLAP
CLAP
CLAP
CLAP
CLAP
CLAP
CLAP
CLAP
CLAP
I CAN SEE IT NOW.
THE PLAY'S FINALE...
THE AUDIENCE IS ROARING WITH APPLAUSE.

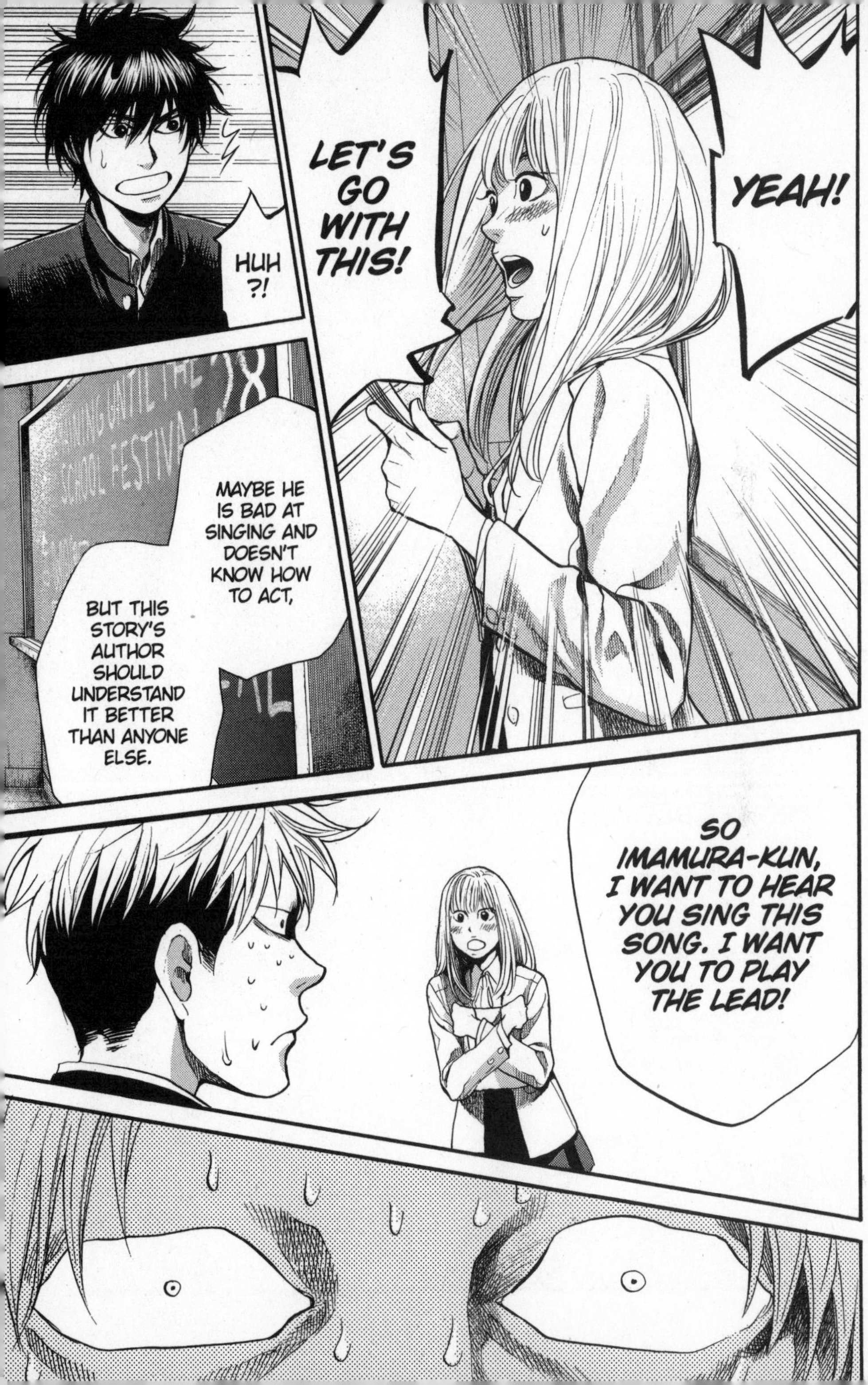
YEAH!
LET'S GO WITH THIS!
HUH ?!
MAYBE HE IS BAD AT SINGING AND DOESN'T KNOW HOW TO ACT,
BUT THIS STORY'S AUTHOR SHOULD UNDERSTAND IT BETTER THAN ANYONE ELSE.
SO IMAMURA-KUN, I WANT TO HEAR YOU SING THIS SONG. I WANT YOU TO PLAY THE LEAD!

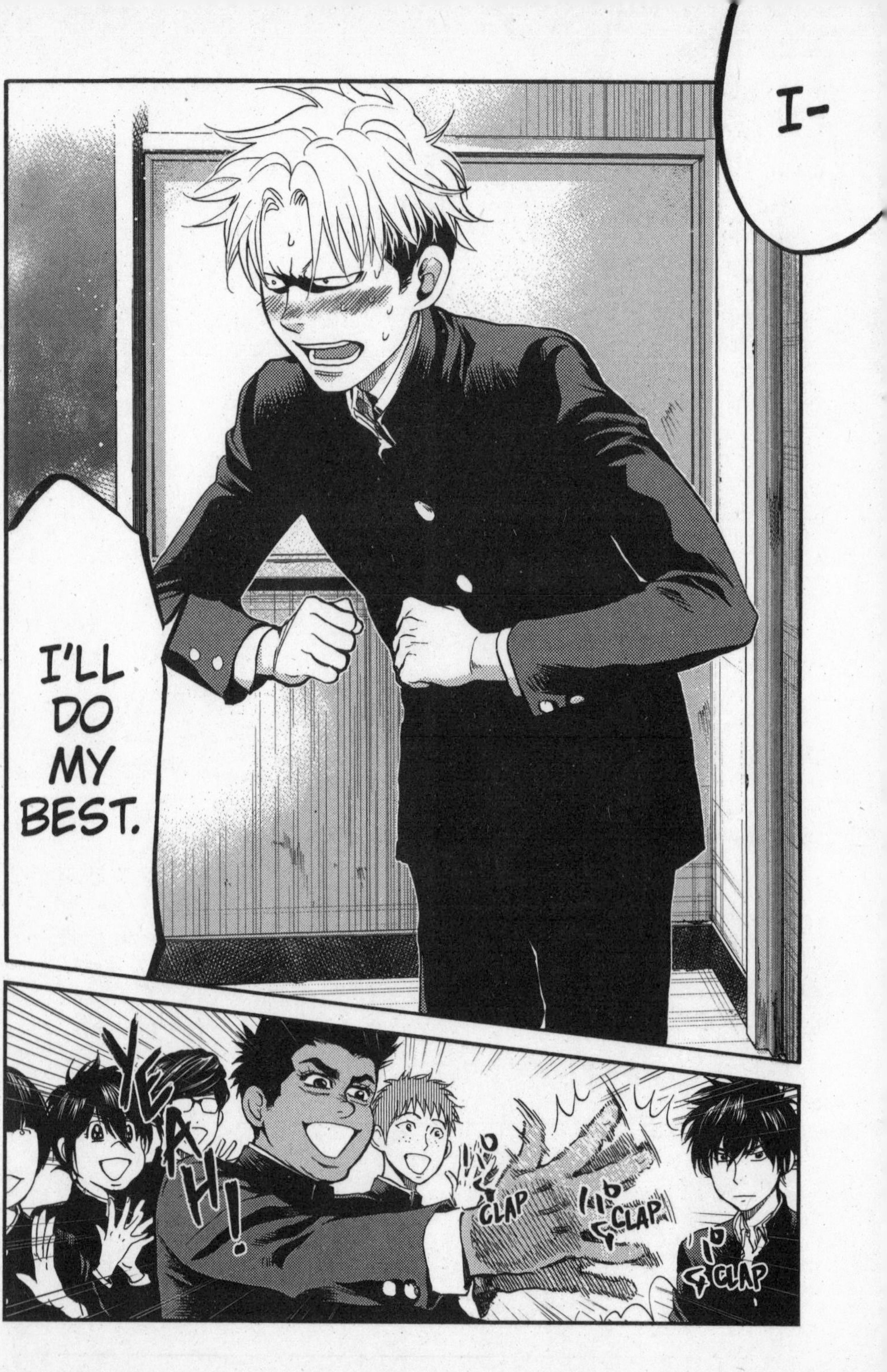
I-
I'LL DO MY BEST.
CLAP
CLAP
CLAP
YEAH!

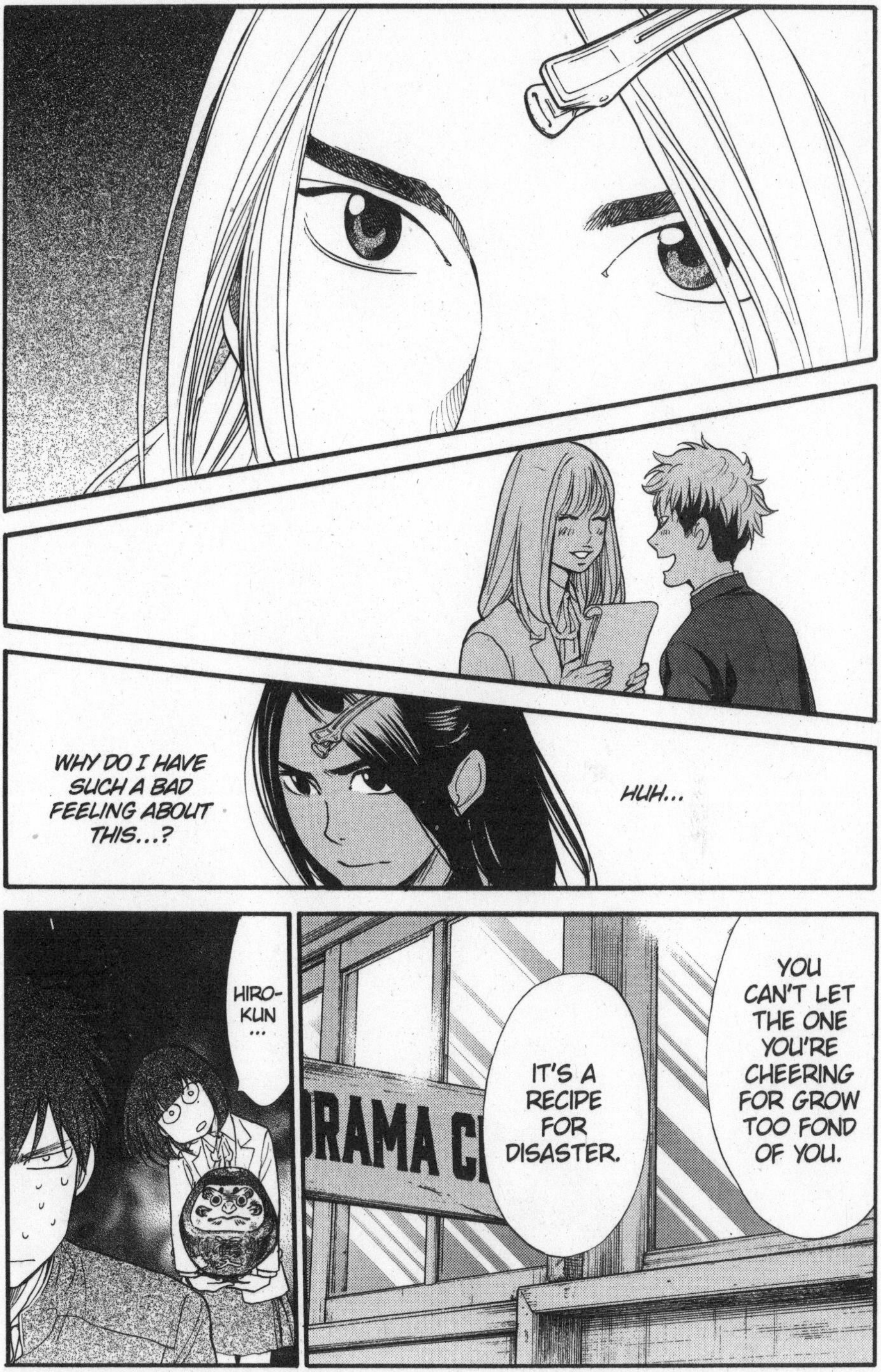
HUH...
WHY DO I HAVE SUCH A BAD FEELING ABOUT THIS...?
YOU CAN'T LET THE ONE YOU'RE CHEERING FOR GROW TOO FOND OF YOU.
IT'S A RECIPE FOR DISASTER.
HIRO-KUN...

Again!!

アゲイン!!

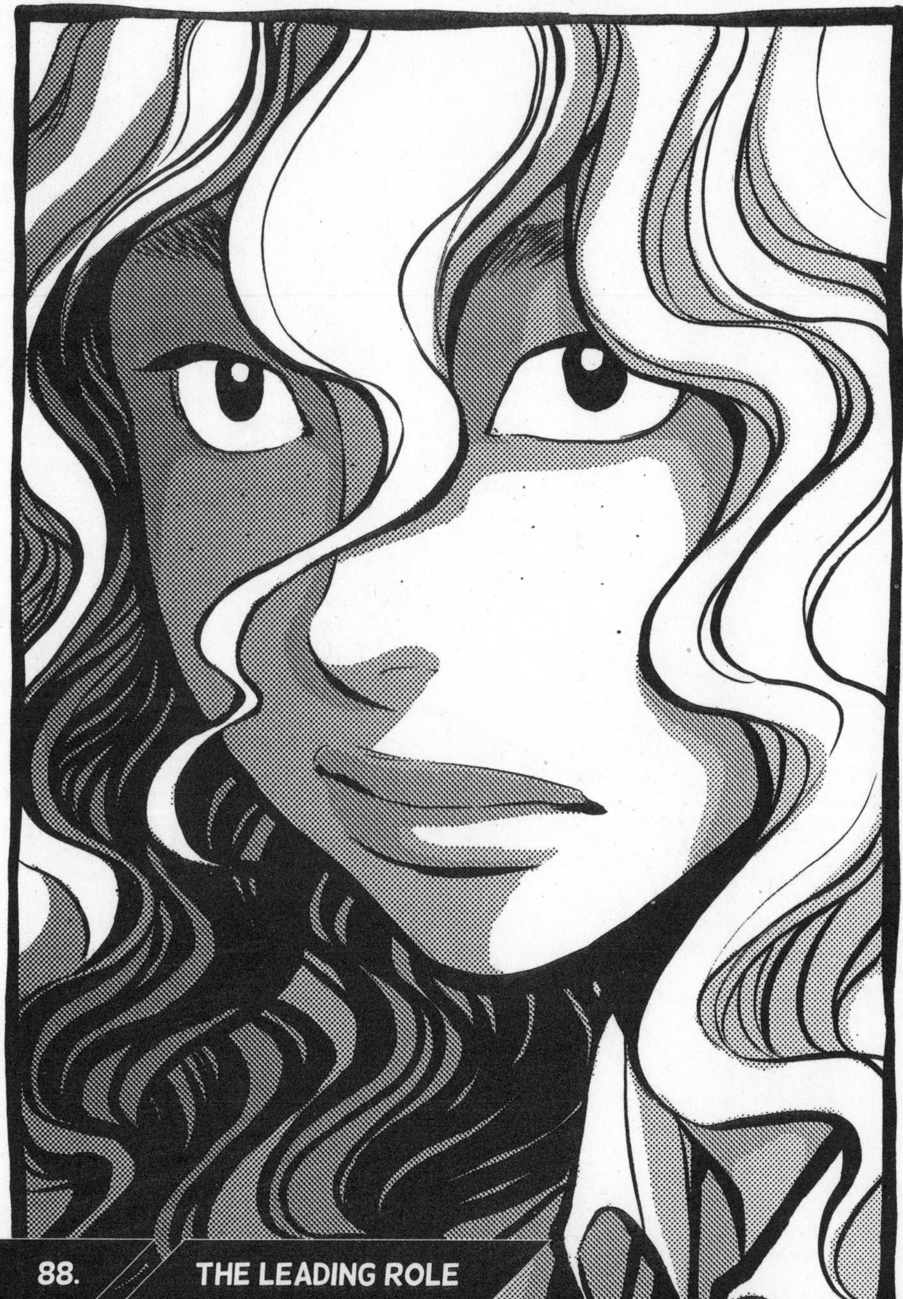

88. THE LEADING ROLE

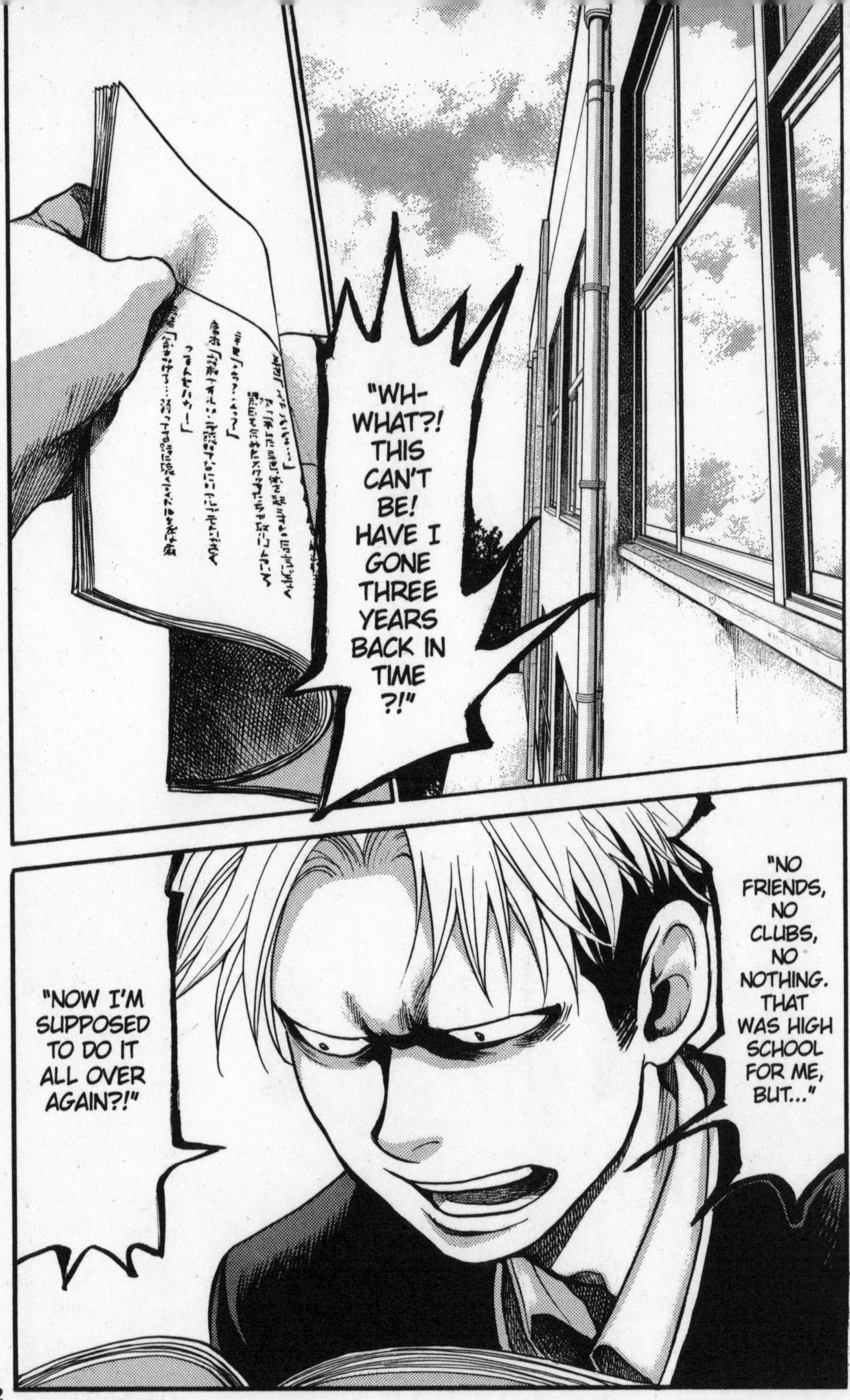
"WH-WHAT?! THIS CAN'T BE! HAVE I GONE THREE YEARS BACK IN TIME?!"
"NO FRIENDS, NO CLUBS, NO NOTHING. THAT WAS HIGH SCHOOL FOR ME, BUT..."
"NOW I'M SUPPOSED TO DO IT ALL OVER AGAIN?!"

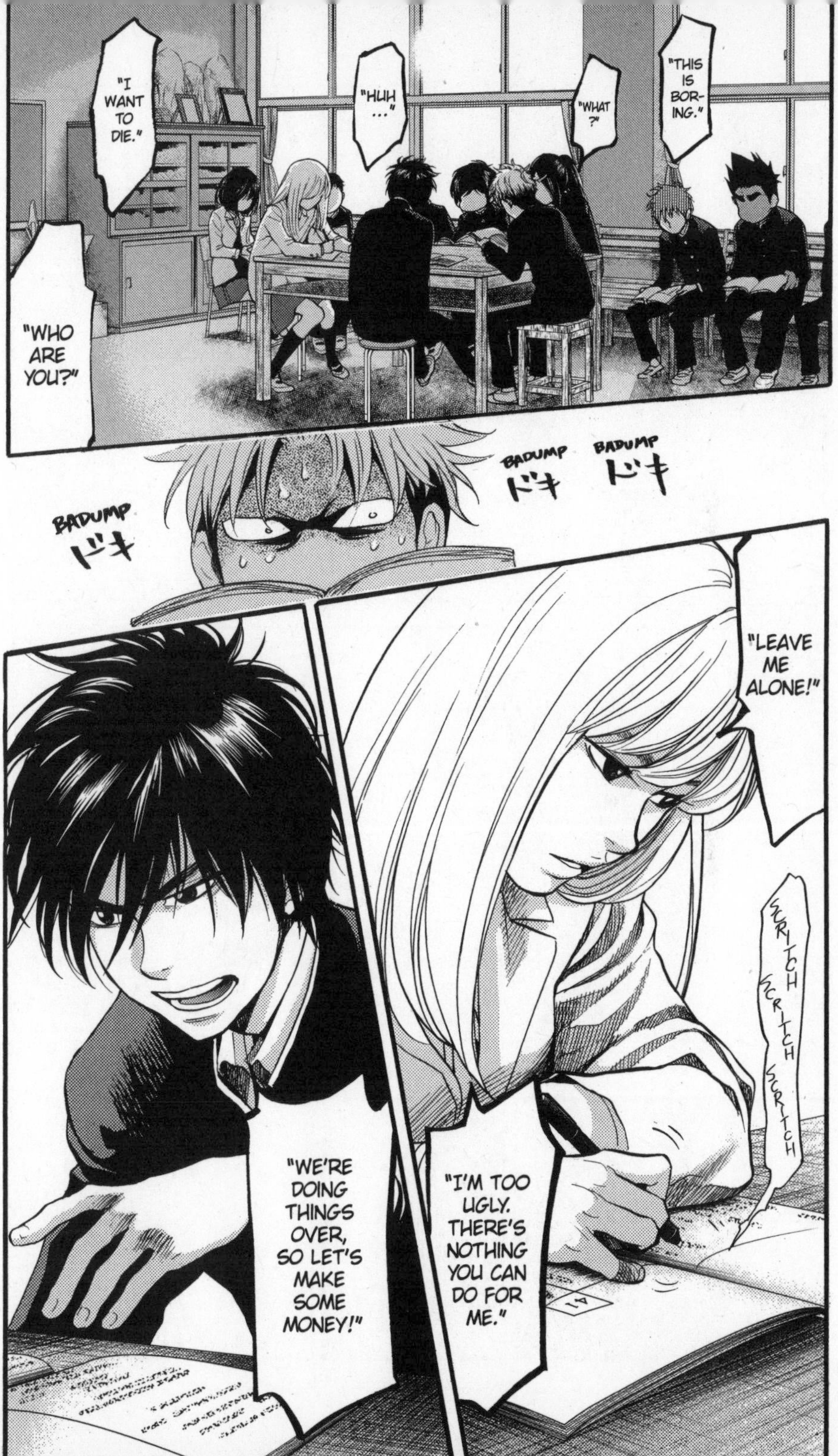
"THIS IS BORING."
"WHAT?"
"HUH..."
"I WANT TO DIE."
"WHO ARE YOU?"
BADUMP ドキ
BADUMP ドキ
BADUMP ドキ
"LEAVE ME ALONE!"
SCRITCH SCRITCH SCRITCH
"I'M TOO UGLY. THERE'S NOTHING YOU CAN DO FOR ME."
"WE'RE DOING THINGS OVER, SO LET'S MAKE SOME MONEY!"

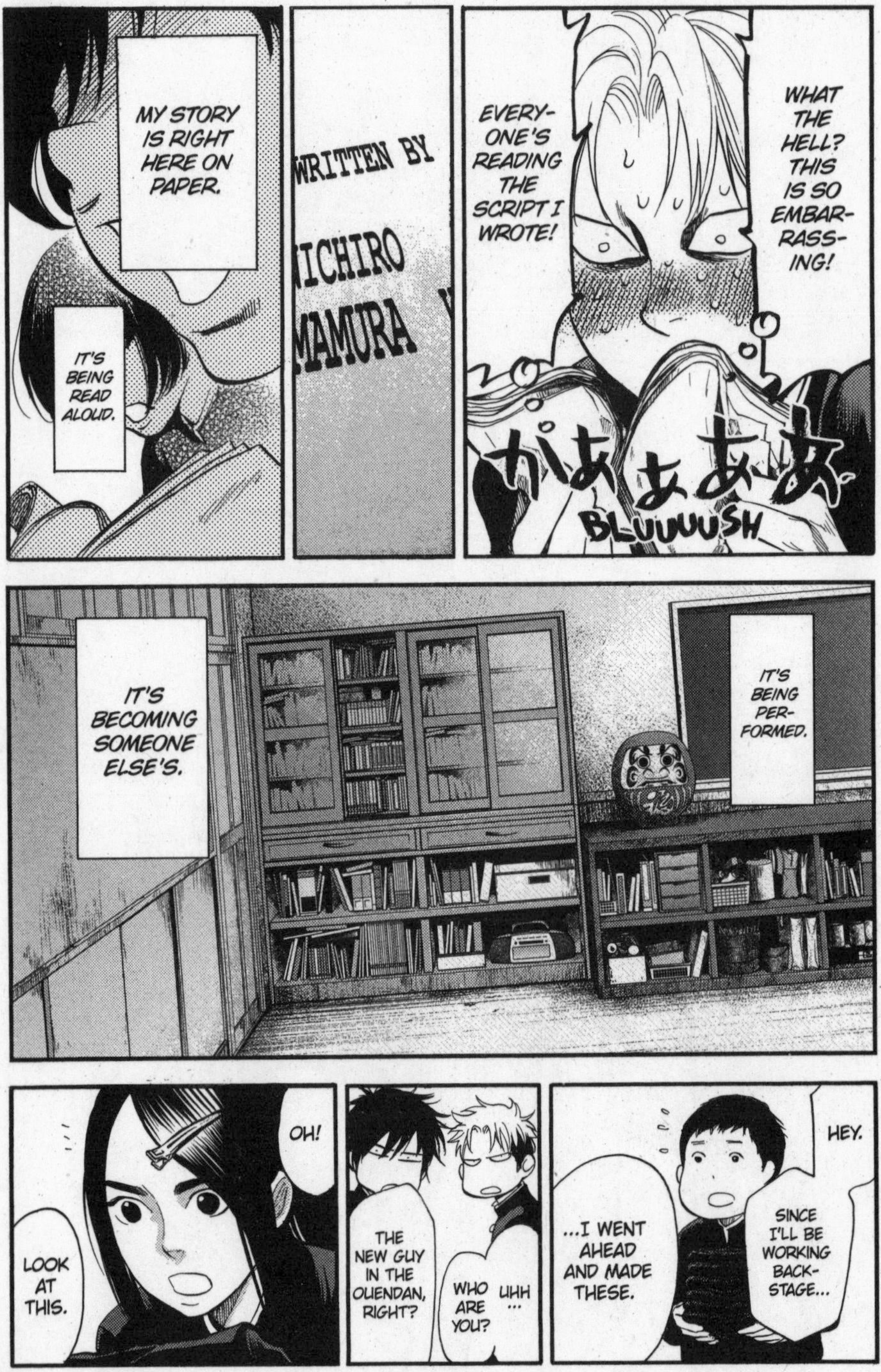
WHAT THE HELL? THIS IS SO EMBARRASSING!
EVERYONE'S READING THE SCRIPT I WROTE!
があぁああ
BLUUUUSH
WRITTEN BY
MICHIRO
MAMURA
MY STORY IS RIGHT HERE ON PAPER.
IT'S BEING READ ALOUD.
IT'S BEING PERFORMED.
IT'S BECOMING SOMEONE ELSE'S.
HEY.
SINCE I'LL BE WORKING BACKSTAGE...
...I WENT AHEAD AND MADE THESE.
UHH...
WHO ARE YOU?
THE NEW GUY IN THE OUENDAN, RIGHT?
OH!
LOOK AT THIS.

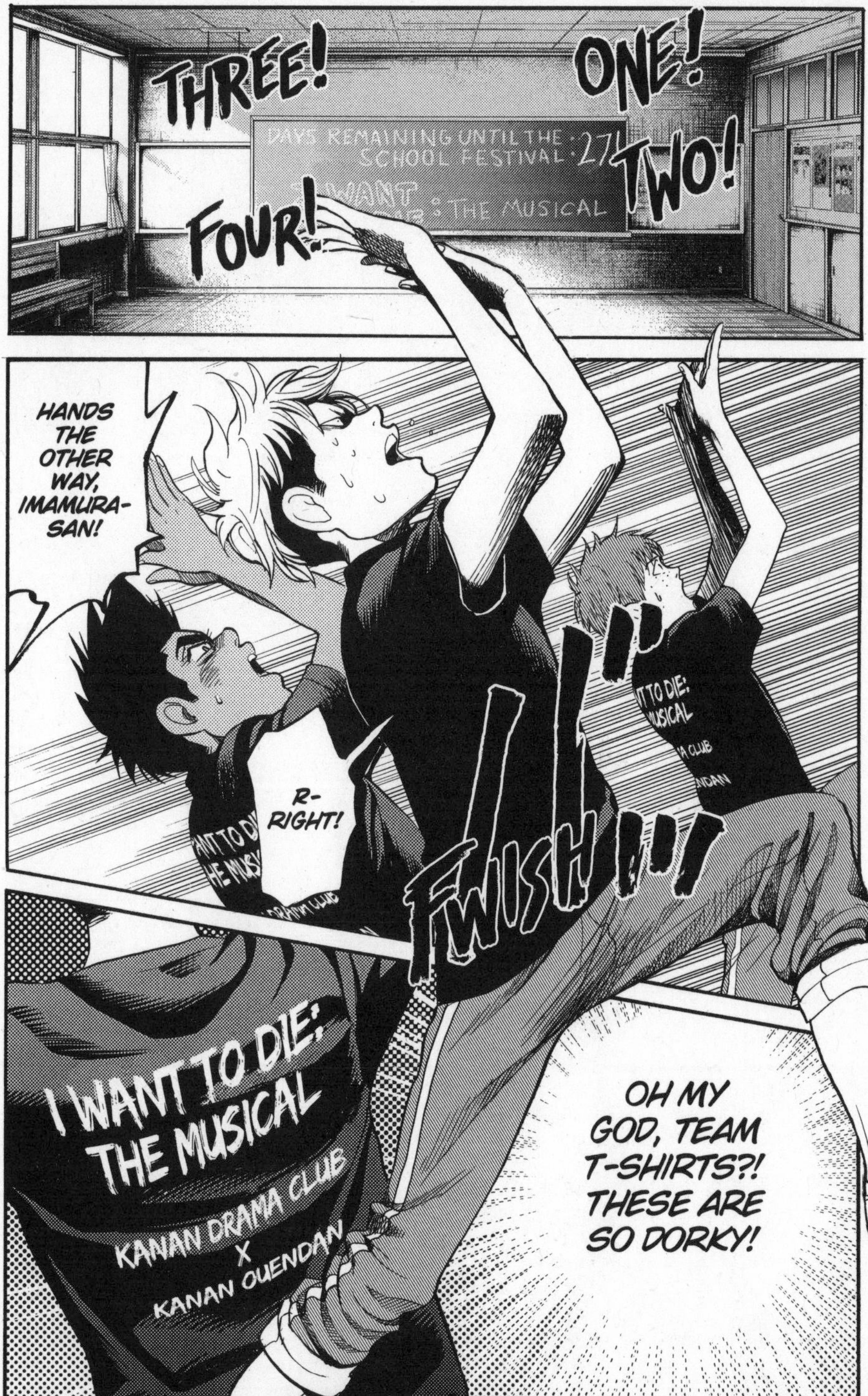
ONE!
TWO!
THREE!
FOUR!
DAYS REMAINING UNTIL THE SCHOOL FESTIVAL: 27
THE MUSICAL
HANDS THE OTHER WAY, IMAMURA-SAN!
R-RIGHT!
FWISH
OH MY GOD, TEAM T-SHIRTS?! THESE ARE SO DORKY!
I WANT TO DIE: THE MUSICAL
KANAN DRAMA CLUB
X
KANAN OUENDAN

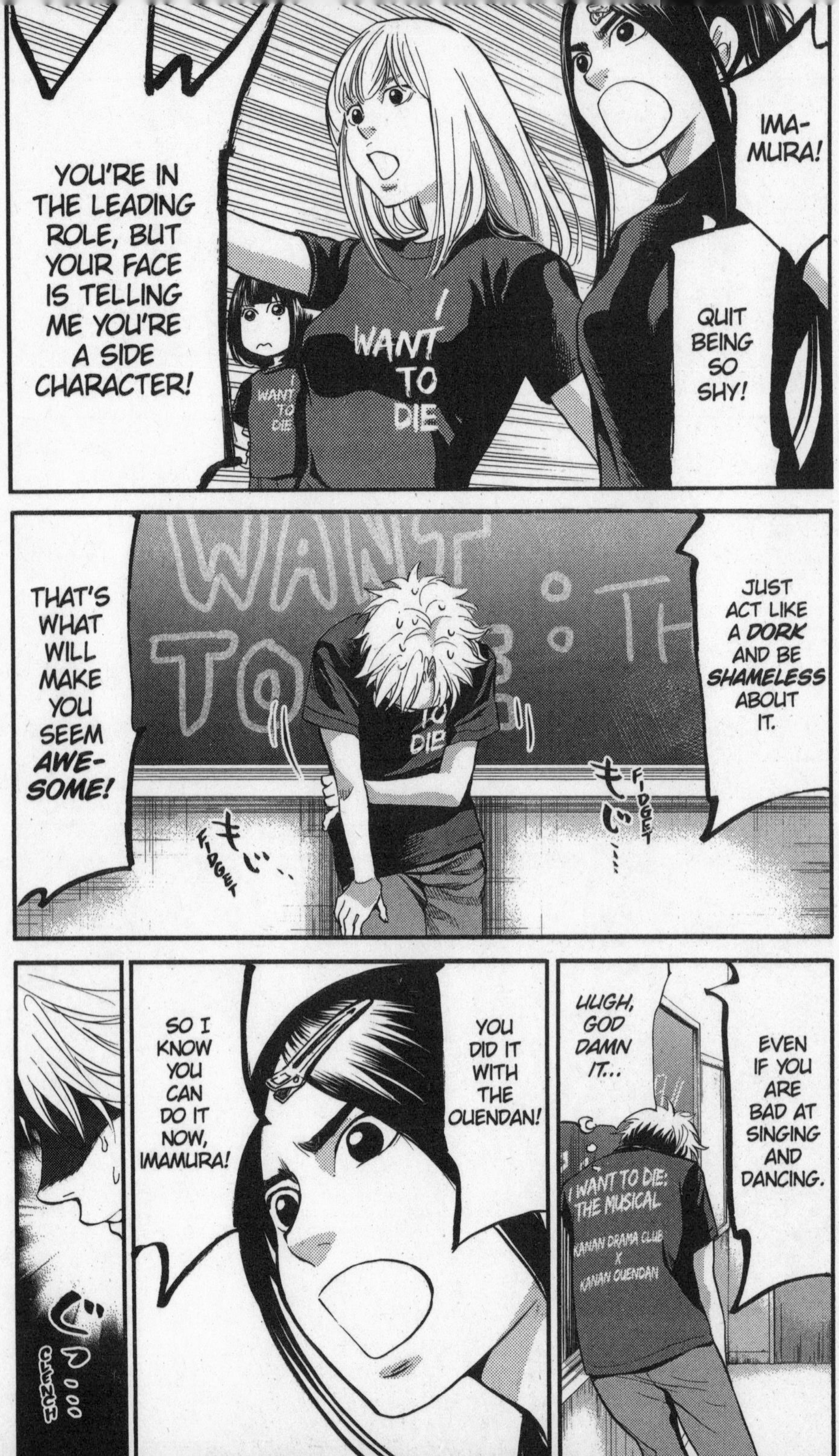
IMA-MURA!
QUIT BEING SO SHY!
YOU'RE IN THE LEADING ROLE, BUT YOUR FACE IS TELLING ME YOU'RE A SIDE CHARACTER!
I WANT TO DIE
I WANT TO DIE
JUST ACT LIKE A DORK AND BE SHAMELESS ABOUT IT.
THAT'S WHAT WILL MAKE YOU SEEM AWESOME!
FIDGET
FIDGET
EVEN IF YOU ARE BAD AT SINGING AND DANCING.
UUGH, GOD DAMN IT...
I WANT TO DIE: THE MUSICAL
KANAN DRAMA CLUB x KANAN OUENDAN
YOU DID IT WITH THE OUENDAN!
SO I KNOW YOU CAN DO IT NOW, IMAMURA!
CLENCH

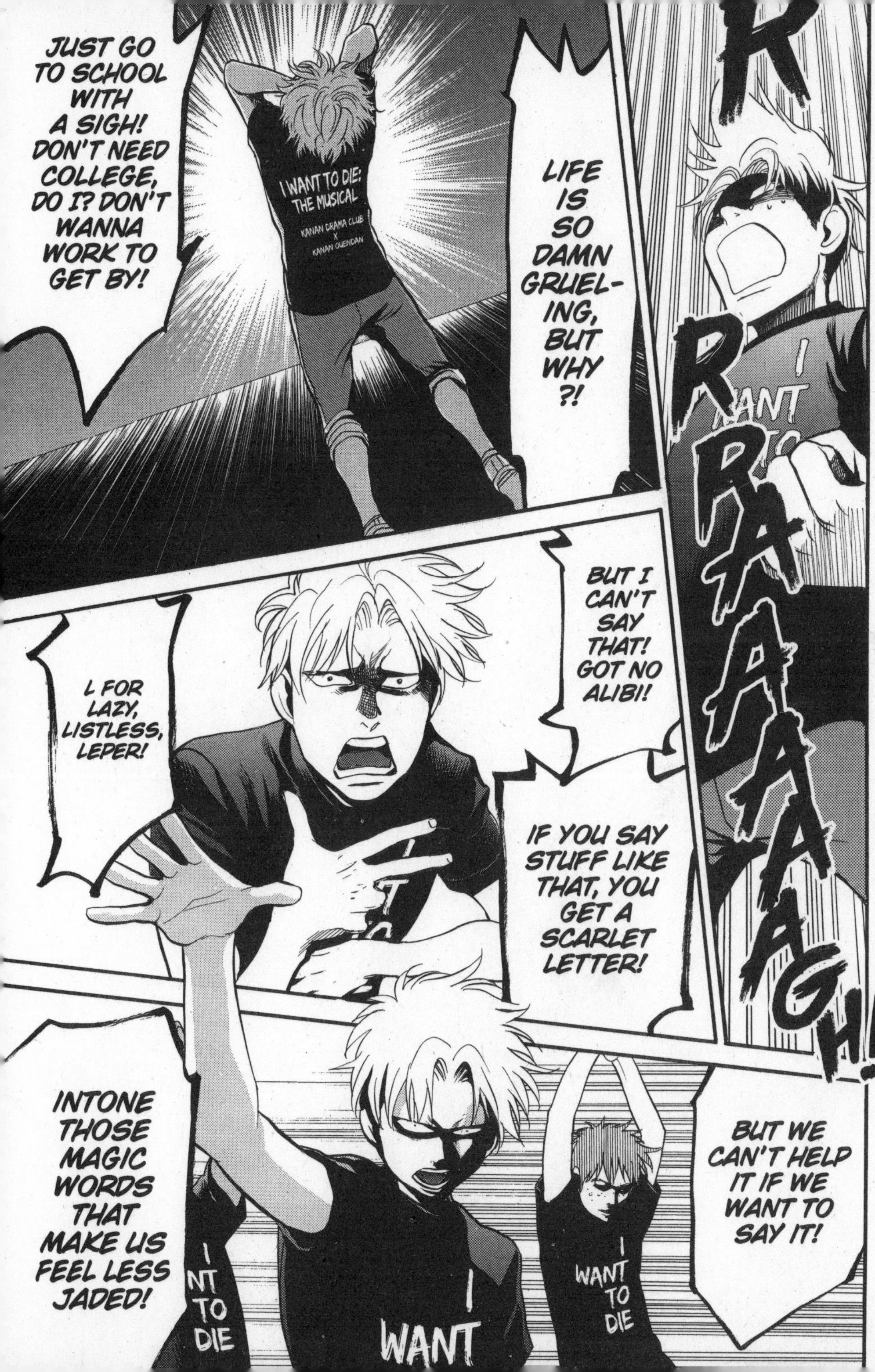
R
RRAAAAAGH!!
I WANT TO DIE: THE MUSICAL
KANAN DRAMA CLUB X KANAN OUENDAN
LIFE IS SO DAMN GRUEL-ING, BUT WHY?!
JUST GO TO SCHOOL WITH A SIGH! DON'T NEED COLLEGE, DO I? DON'T WANNA WORK TO GET BY!
BUT I CAN'T SAY THAT! GOT NO ALIBI!
L FOR LAZY, LISTLESS, LEPER!
IF YOU SAY STUFF LIKE THAT, YOU GET A SCARLET LETTER!
BUT WE CAN'T HELP IT IF WE WANT TO SAY IT!
I WANT TO DIE
I WANT
I NT TO DIE
INTONE THOSE MAGIC WORDS THAT MAKE US FEEL LESS JADED!

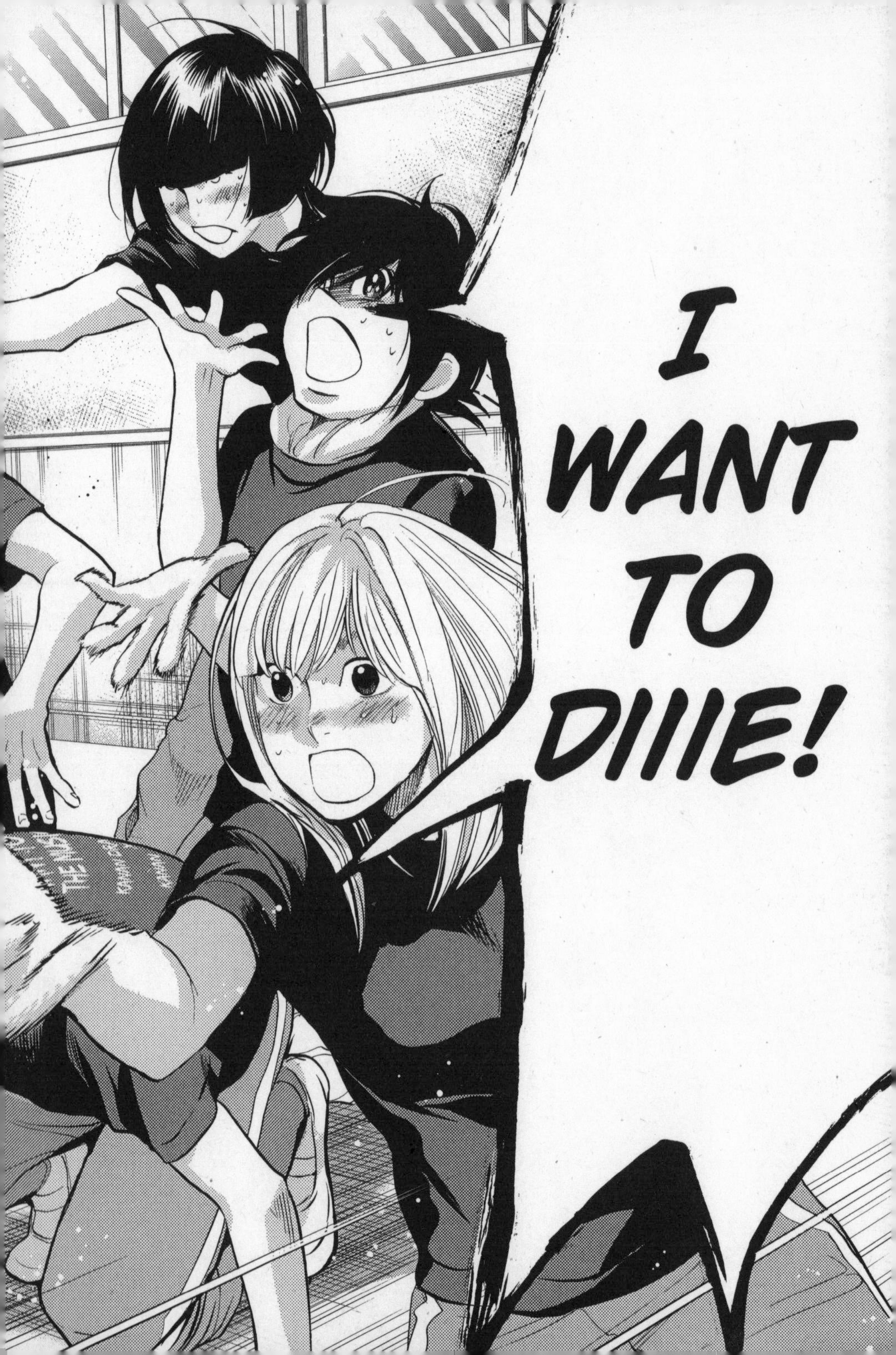
I WANT TO DIIIE!

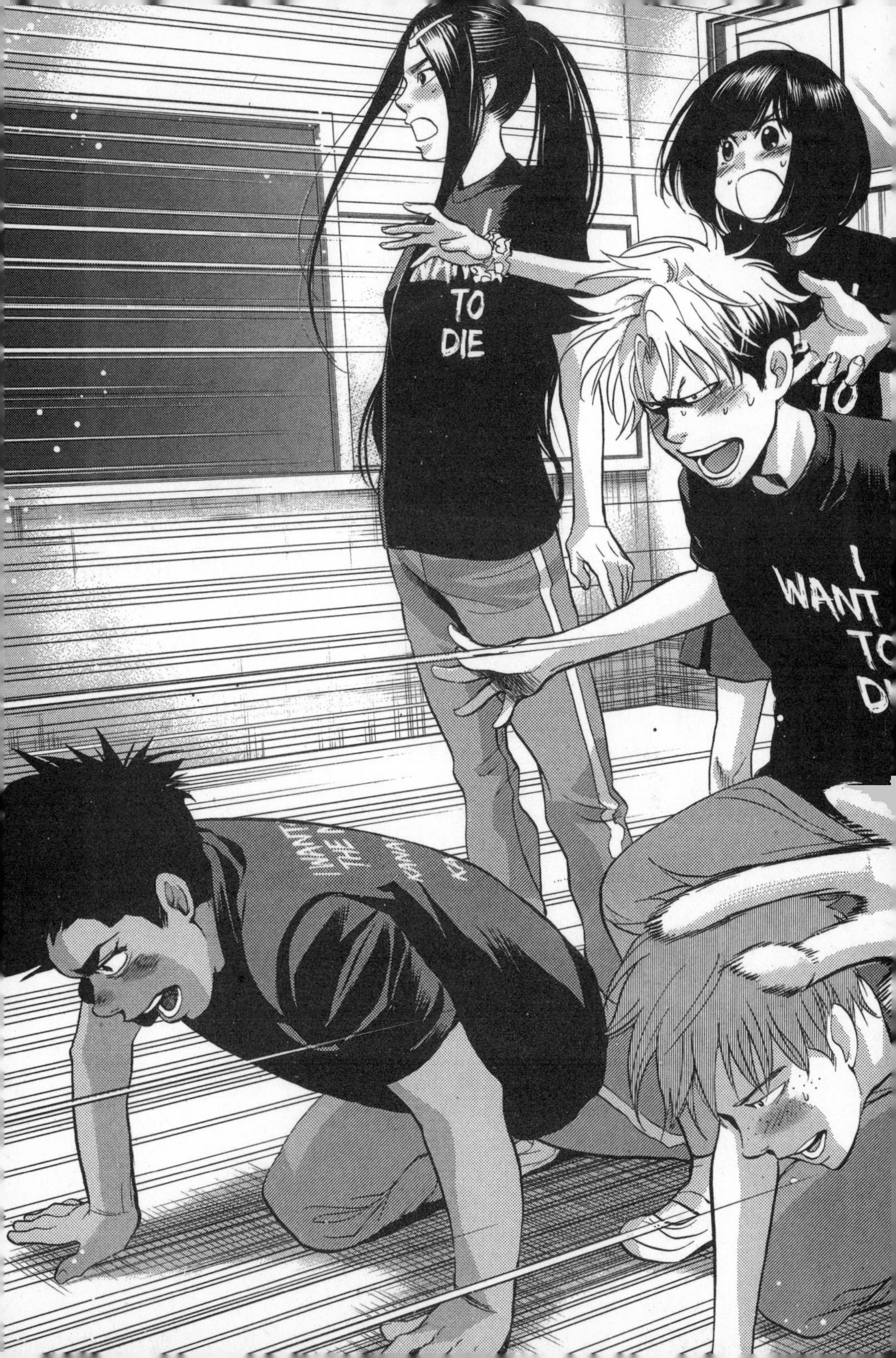
TO
DIE
I
WANT
TO

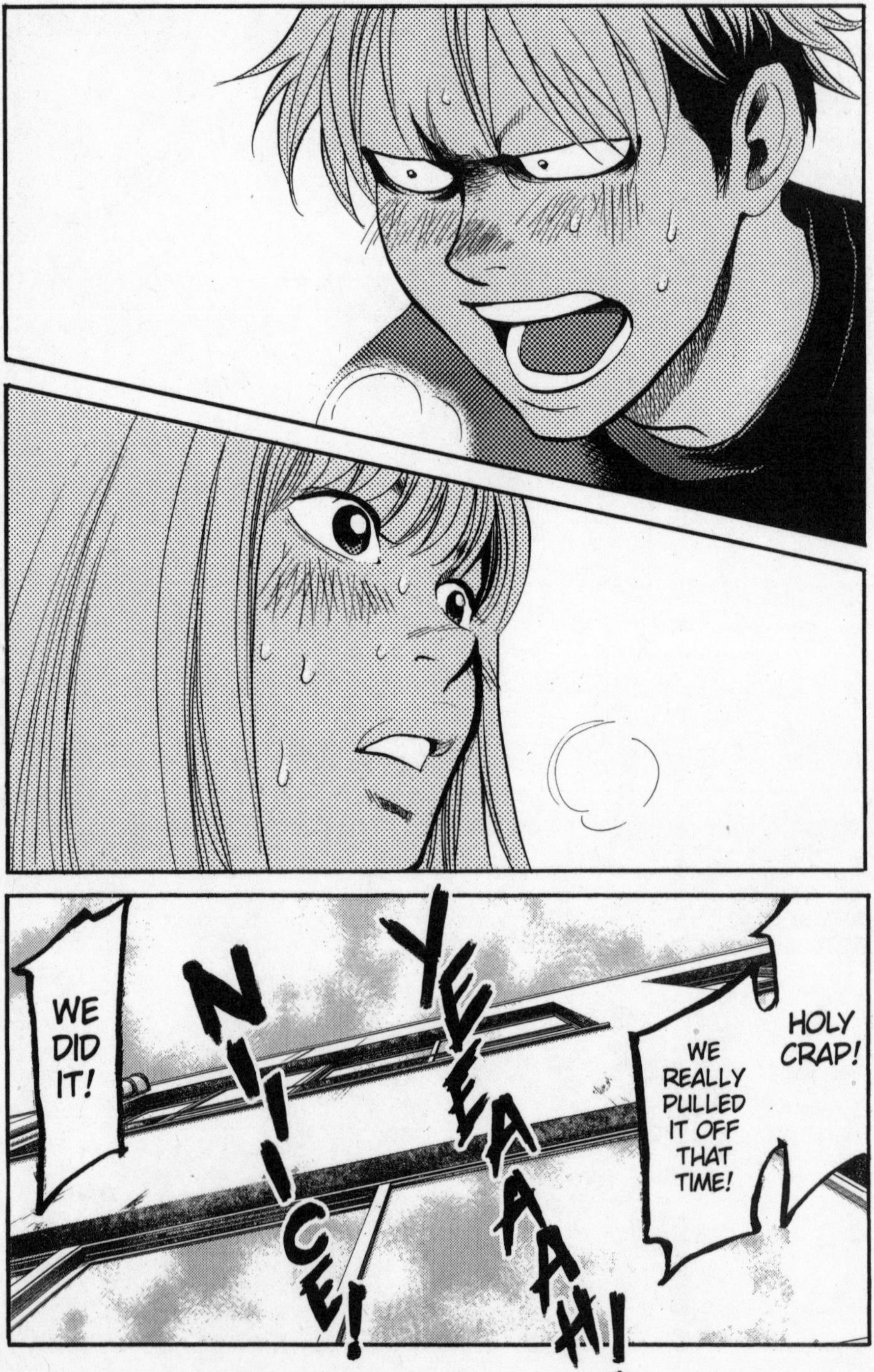
HOLY CRAP!
WE REALLY PULLED IT OFF THAT TIME!
YEEAAAH!
NIIICE!
WE DID IT!

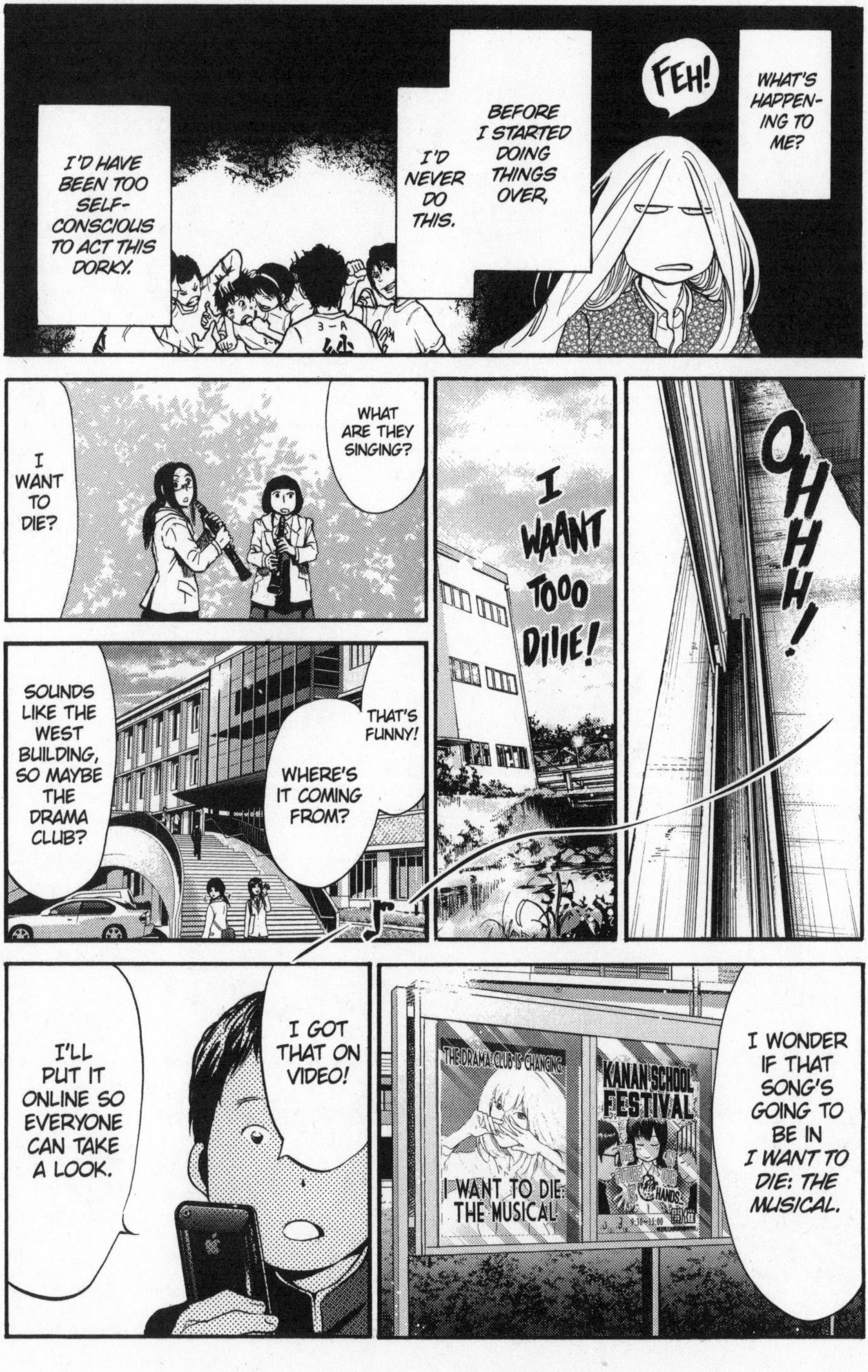
WHAT'S HAPPENING TO ME?
FEH!
BEFORE I STARTED DOING THINGS OVER,
I'D NEVER DO THIS.
I'D HAVE BEEN TOO SELF-CONSCIOUS TO ACT THIS DORKY.
3-A
OHHH!
I WAANT TOOO DIIIE!
WHAT ARE THEY SINGING?
I WANT TO DIE?
THAT'S FUNNY!
WHERE'S IT COMING FROM?
SOUNDS LIKE THE WEST BUILDING, SO MAYBE THE DRAMA CLUB?
THE DRAMA CLUB IS CHANGING
I WANT TO DIE: THE MUSICAL
KANAN SCHOOL FESTIVAL
I WONDER IF THAT SONG'S GOING TO BE IN *I WANT TO DIE: THE MUSICAL*.
I GOT THAT ON VIDEO!
I'LL PUT IT ONLINE SO EVERYONE CAN TAKE A LOOK.

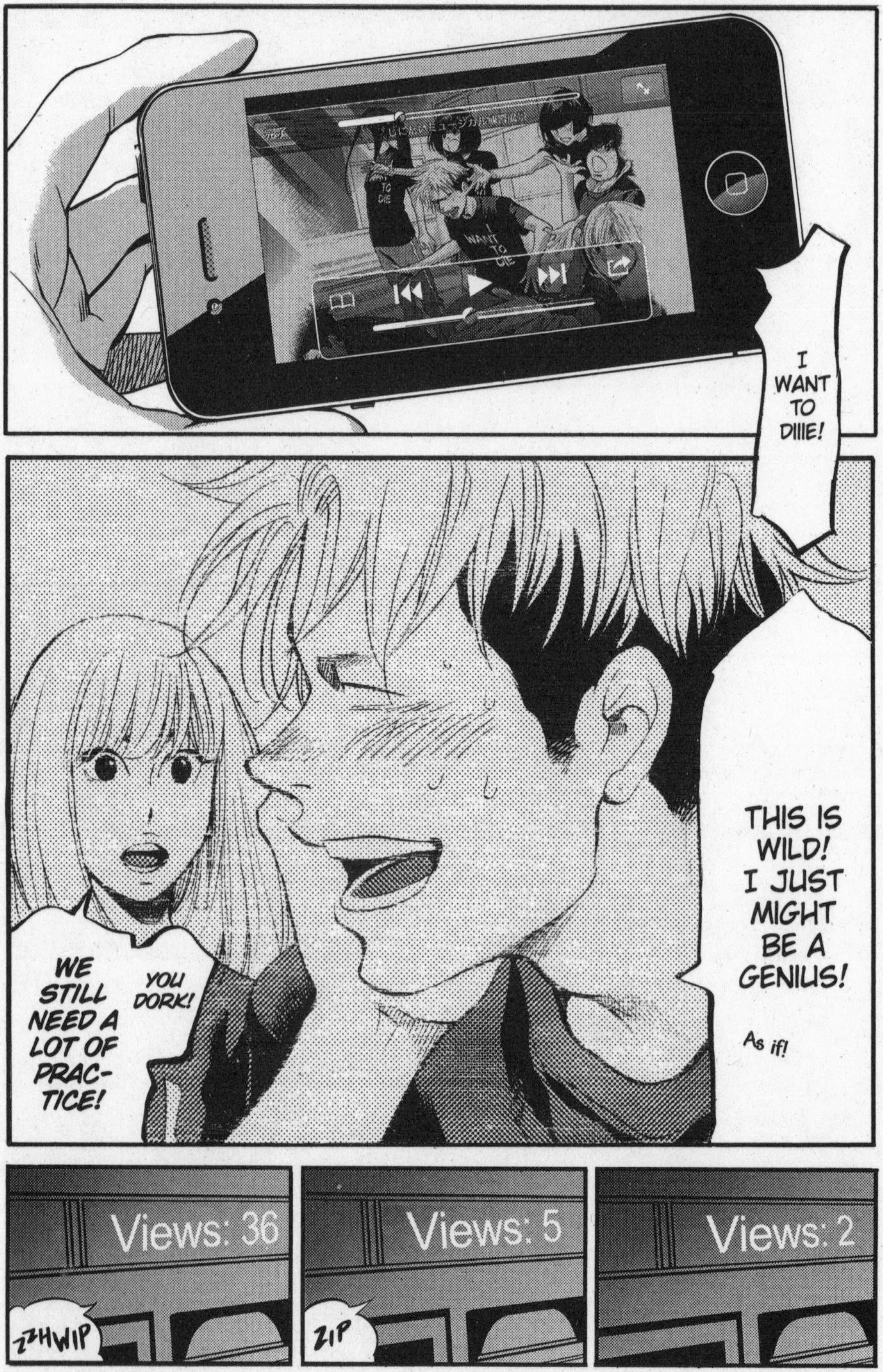
TO DIE
I WANT TO DIE
I WANT TO DIIIE!
THIS IS WILD! I JUST MIGHT BE A GENIUS!
As if!
YOU DORK!
WE STILL NEED A LOT OF PRAC-TICE!
Views: 2
Views: 5
ZIP
Views: 36
ZZHWIP

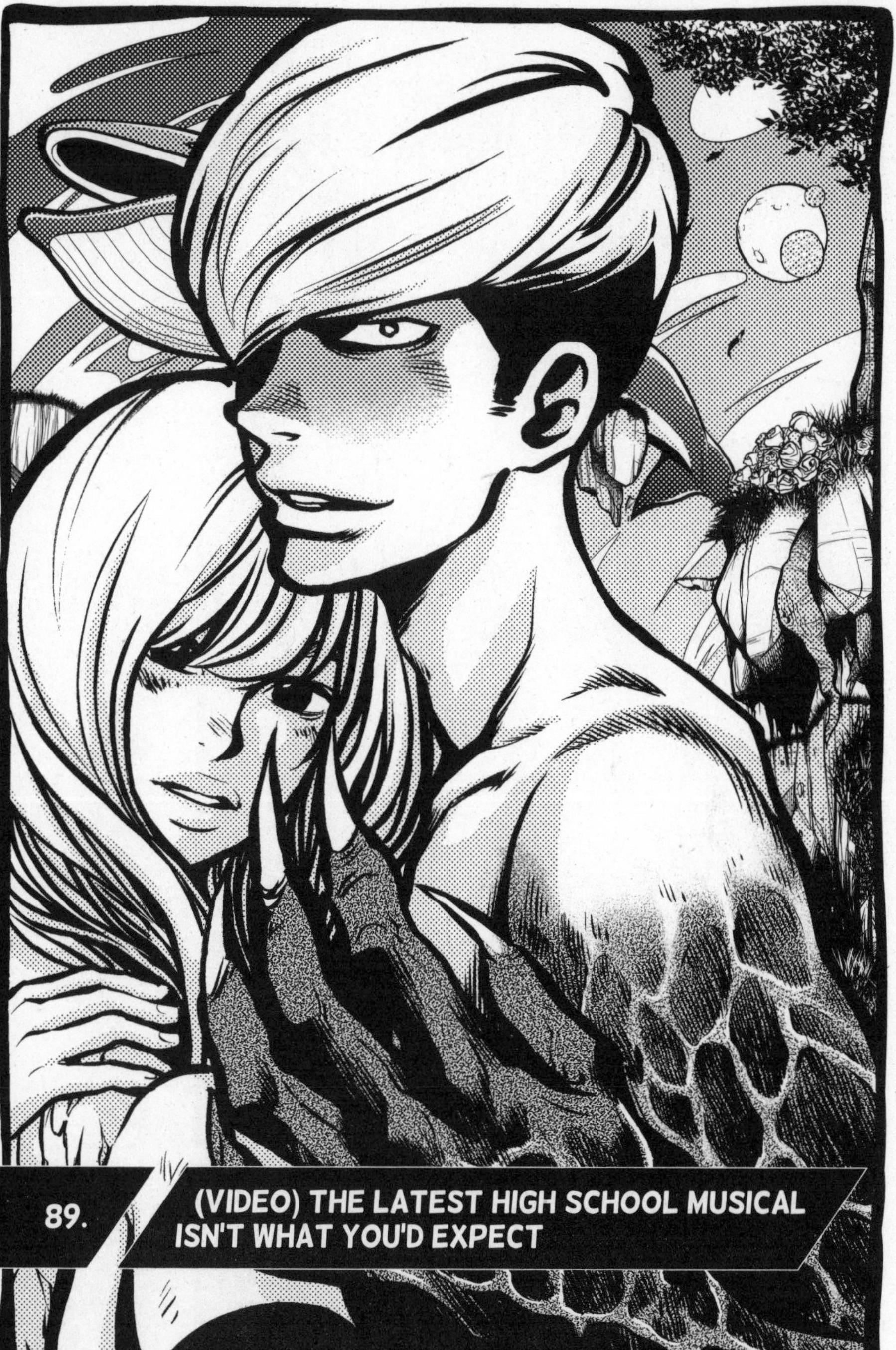

89. (VIDEO) THE LATEST HIGH SCHOOL MUSICAL ISN'T WHAT YOU'D EXPECT

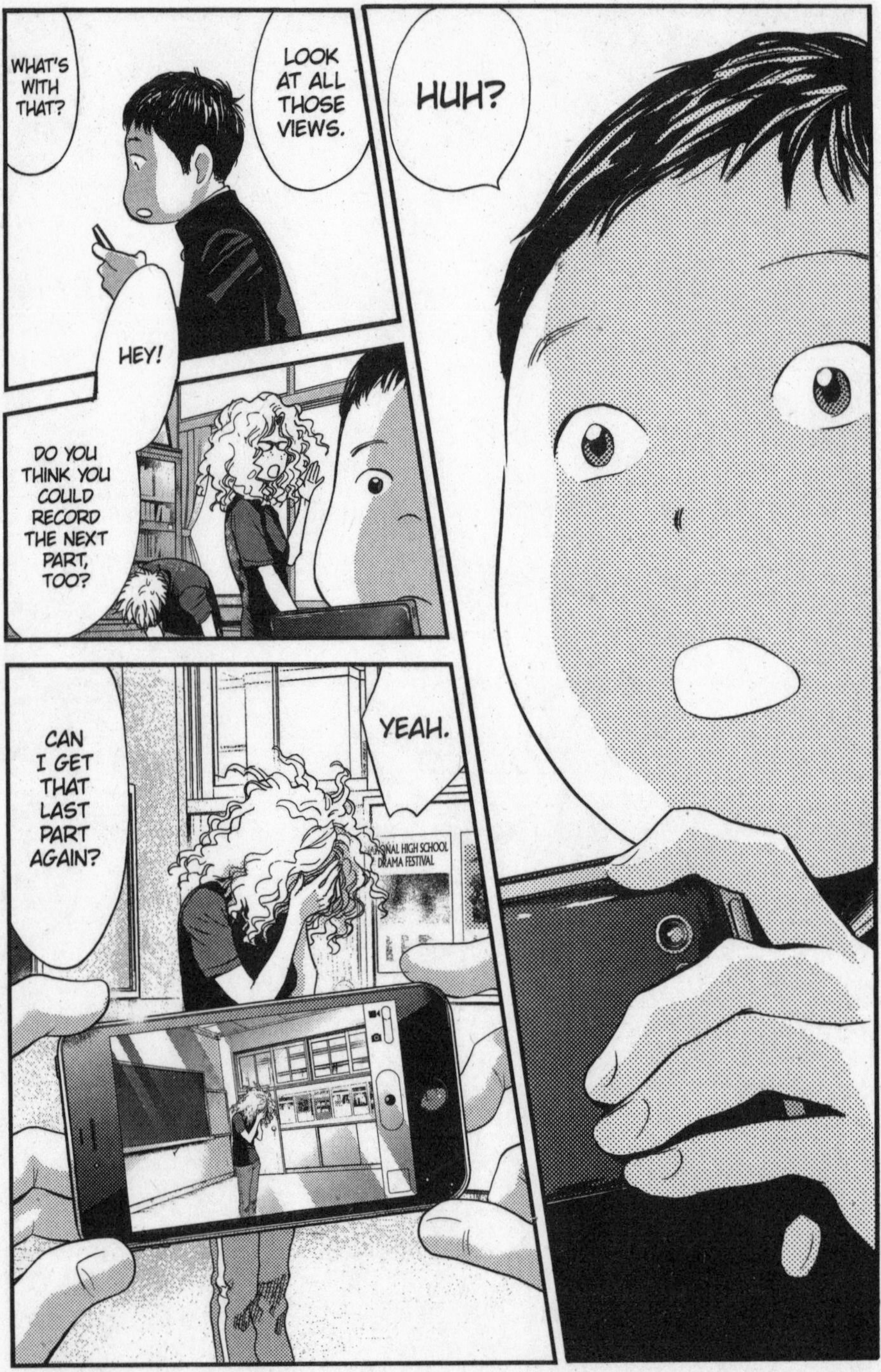
HUH?
LOOK AT ALL THOSE VIEWS.
WHAT'S WITH THAT?
HEY!
DO YOU THINK YOU COULD RECORD THE NEXT PART, TOO?
YEAH.
CAN I GET THAT LAST PART AGAIN?
HIGH SCHOOL DRAMA FESTIVAL

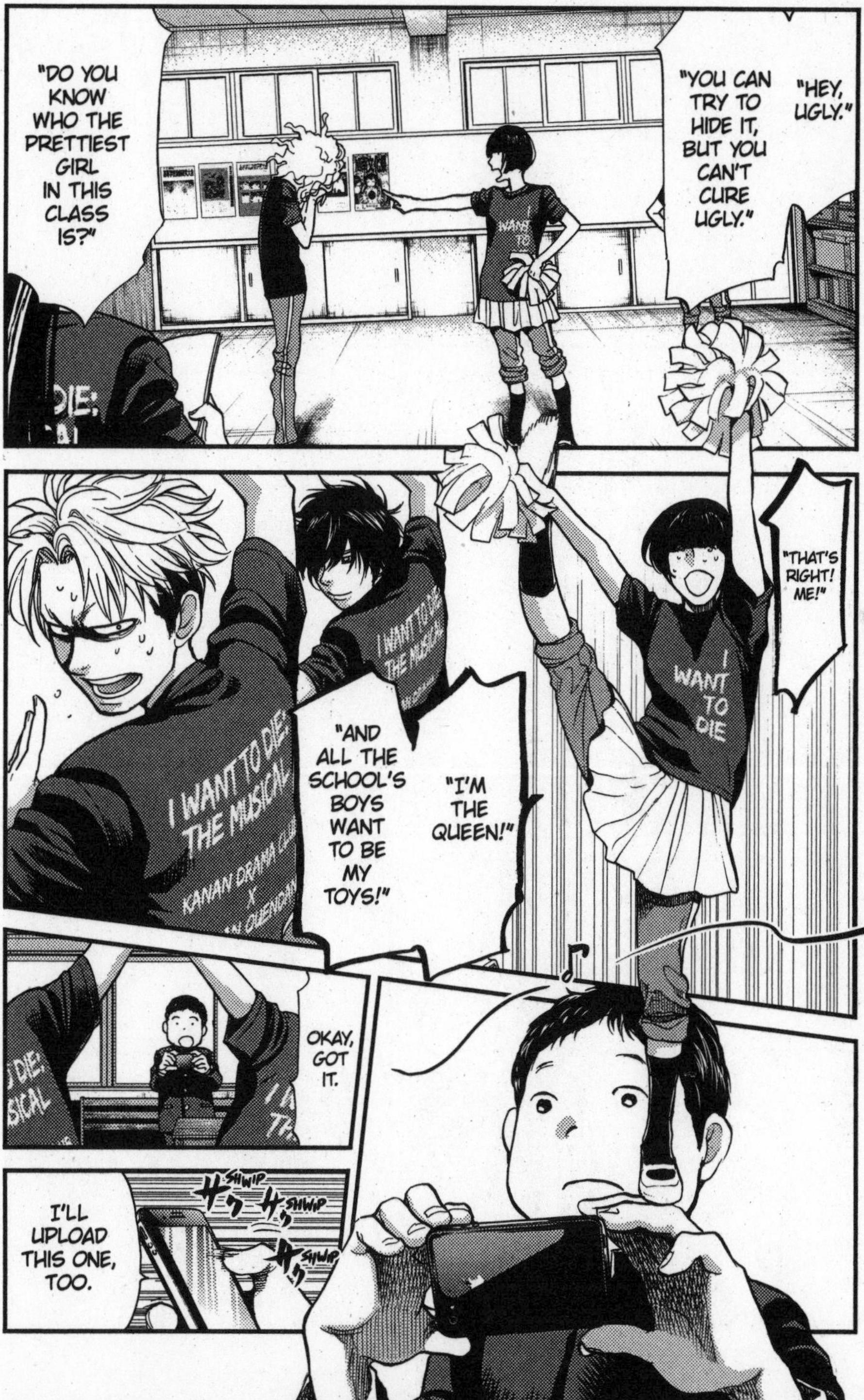
"HEY, UGLY."
"YOU CAN TRY TO HIDE IT, BUT YOU CAN'T CURE UGLY."
"DO YOU KNOW WHO THE PRETTIEST GIRL IN THIS CLASS IS?"
"THAT'S RIGHT! ME!"
I WANT TO DIE
"I'M THE QUEEN!"
"AND ALL THE SCHOOL'S BOYS WANT TO BE MY TOYS!"
I WANT TO DIE: THE MUSICAL
KANAN DRAMA CLUB X
OKAY, GOT IT.
SHWIP
SHWIP
SHWIP
I'LL UPLOAD THIS ONE, TOO.

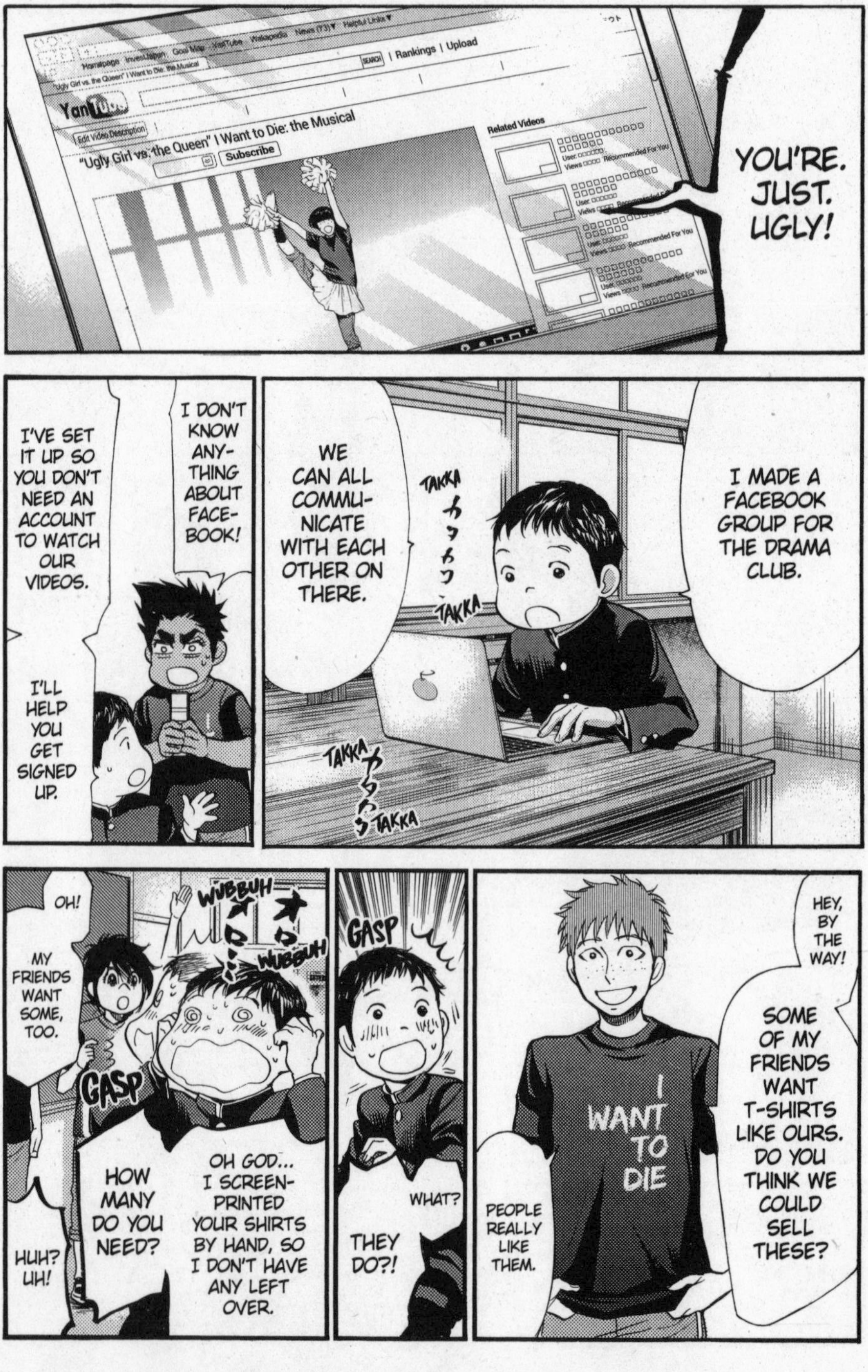

Rankings | Upload
YanTube
"Ugly Girl vs. the Queen" I Want to Die: the Musical
Edit Video Description
Subscribe
Related Videos
YOU'RE. JUST. UGLY!
I MADE A FACEBOOK GROUP FOR THE DRAMA CLUB.
TAKKA TAKKA
WE CAN ALL COMMUNICATE WITH EACH OTHER ON THERE.
TAKKA TAKKA
I DON'T KNOW ANYTHING ABOUT FACEBOOK!
I'VE SET IT UP SO YOU DON'T NEED AN ACCOUNT TO WATCH OUR VIDEOS.
I'LL HELP YOU GET SIGNED UP.
HEY, BY THE WAY!
SOME OF MY FRIENDS WANT T-SHIRTS LIKE OURS. DO YOU THINK WE COULD SELL THESE?
I WANT TO DIE
PEOPLE REALLY LIKE THEM.
GASP
WHAT?
THEY DO?!
OH!
MY FRIENDS WANT SOME, TOO.
WUBBUH WUBBUH
OH GOD... I SCREEN-PRINTED YOUR SHIRTS BY HAND, SO I DON'T HAVE ANY LEFT OVER.
HOW MANY DO YOU NEED?
GASP
HUH? UH!

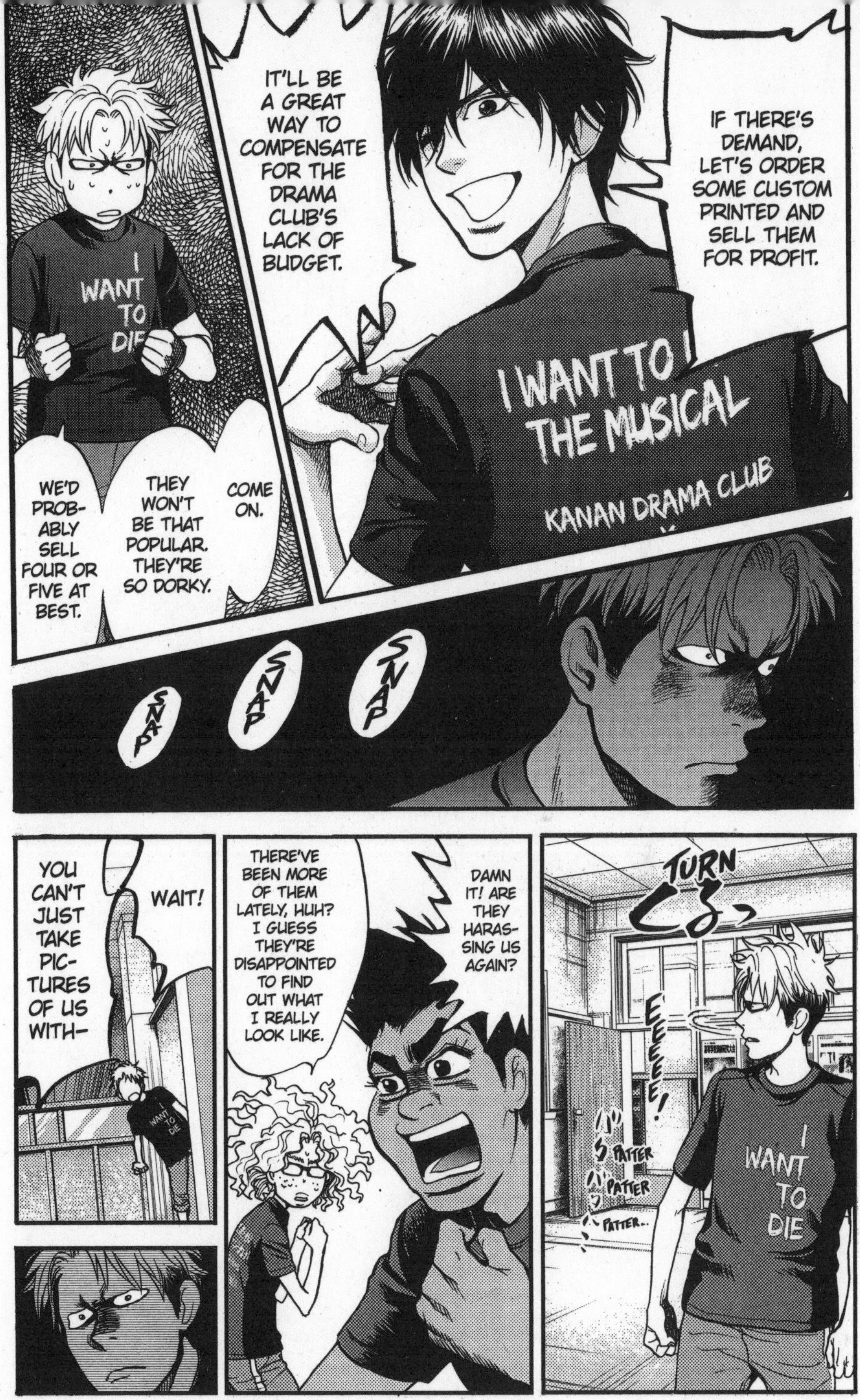

IF THERE'S DEMAND, LET'S ORDER SOME CUSTOM PRINTED AND SELL THEM FOR PROFIT.
IT'LL BE A GREAT WAY TO COMPENSATE FOR THE DRAMA CLUB'S LACK OF BUDGET.
I WANT TO
THE MUSICAL
KANAN DRAMA CLUB
I WANT TO DIE
COME ON.
THEY WON'T BE THAT POPULAR. THEY'RE SO DORKY.
WE'D PROB-ABLY SELL FOUR OR FIVE AT BEST.
SNAP
SNAP
SNAP
TURN くるっ
DAMN IT! ARE THEY HARAS-SING US AGAIN?
EEEEE!
PATTER
PATTER
PATTER...
I WANT TO DIE
THERE'VE BEEN MORE OF THEM LATELY, HUH? I GUESS THEY'RE DISAPPOINTED TO FIND OUT WHAT I REALLY LOOK LIKE.
WAIT!
YOU CAN'T JUST TAKE PIC-TURES OF US WITH-
I WANT TO DIE

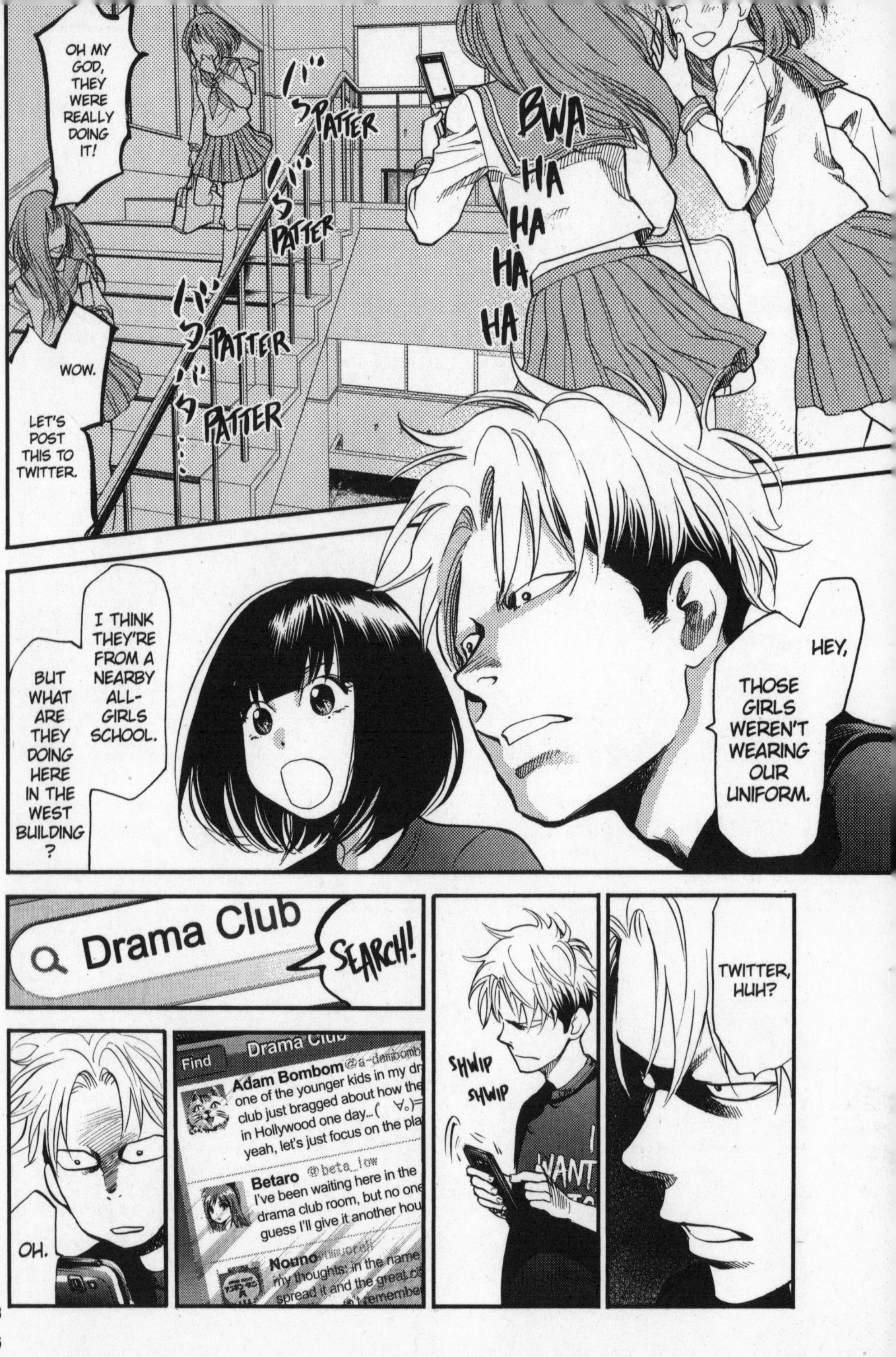
BWA HA HA HA HA
PATTER
PATTER
PATTER
PATTER
OH MY GOD, THEY WERE REALLY DOING IT!
WOW.
LET'S POST THIS TO TWITTER.
HEY, THOSE GIRLS WEREN'T WEARING OUR UNIFORM.
I THINK THEY'RE FROM A NEARBY ALL-GIRLS SCHOOL.
BUT WHAT ARE THEY DOING HERE IN THE WEST BUILDING?
TWITTER, HUH?
SHWIP SHWIP
Drama Club
SEARCH!
Find
Drama Club
Adam Bombom
one of the younger kids in my dr
club just bragged about how the
in Hollywood one day...
yeah, let's just focus on the pla
Betaro @beta_low
I've been waiting here in the
drama club room, but no one
guess I'll give it another hou
OH.

@obuk_ni...
I busted into their school and the drama club really was doing that musical lmao bit.ly/ad1>

5秒

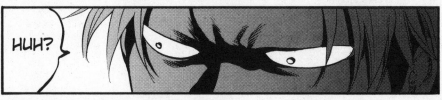

@obuk_...
they posted a new video too. "Ugly Girl vs. the Queen" I Want t...
be/0ab17t~1>@yan

HUH?

OUR REHEARSAL VIDEOS ARE GETTING SHARED AROUND?!

どDUUU ン

HEY!

TA-WARA!

Y-YES ?!

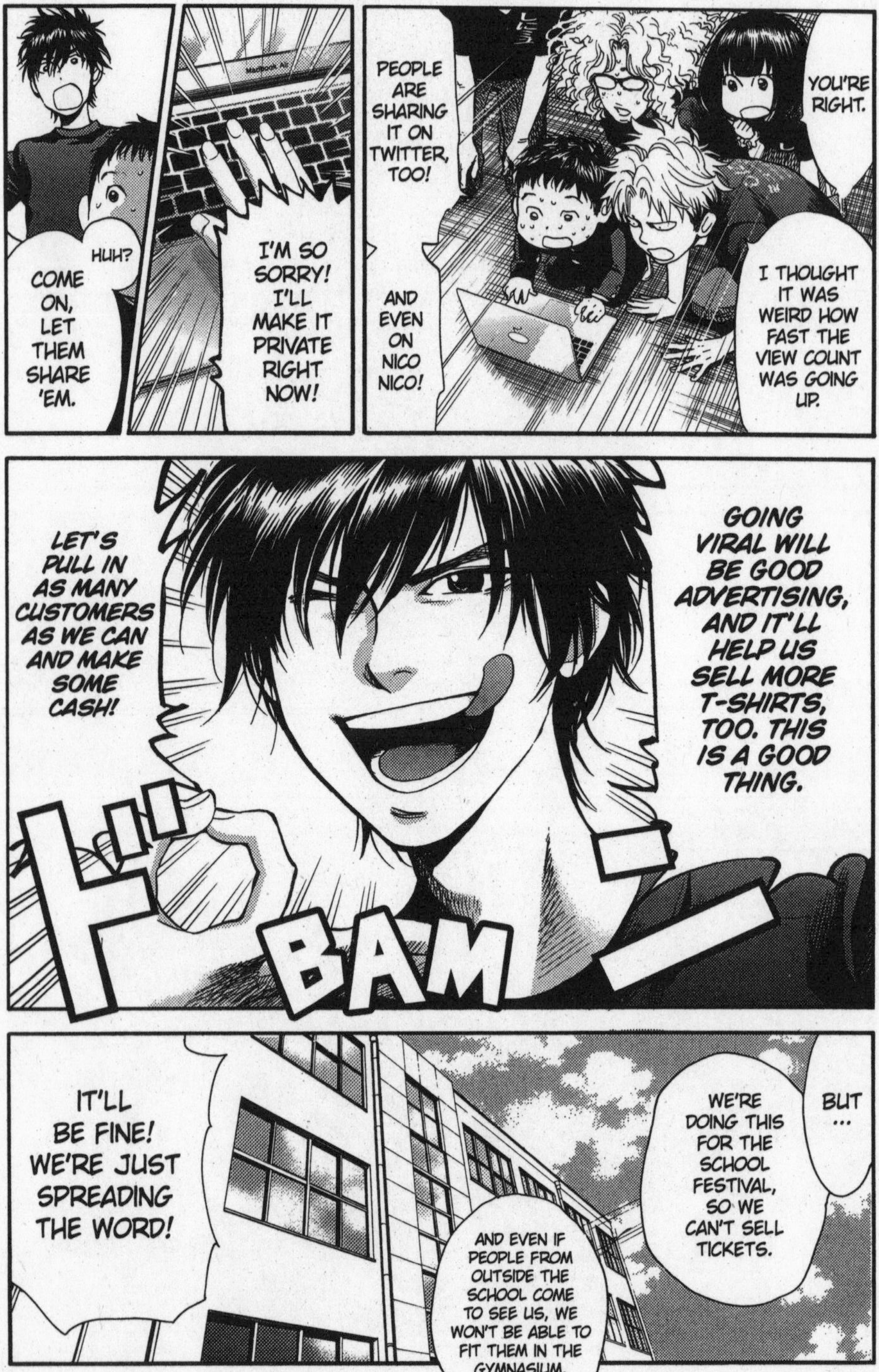
YOU'RE RIGHT.
I THOUGHT IT WAS WEIRD HOW FAST THE VIEW COUNT WAS GOING UP.
PEOPLE ARE SHARING IT ON TWITTER, TOO!
AND EVEN ON NICO NICO!
I'M SO SORRY! I'LL MAKE IT PRIVATE RIGHT NOW!
HUH?
COME ON, LET THEM SHARE 'EM.
GOING VIRAL WILL BE GOOD ADVERTISING, AND IT'LL HELP US SELL MORE T-SHIRTS, TOO. THIS IS A GOOD THING.
LET'S PULL IN AS MANY CUSTOMERS AS WE CAN AND MAKE SOME CASH!
BAM
BUT ...
WE'RE DOING THIS FOR THE SCHOOL FESTIVAL, SO WE CAN'T SELL TICKETS.
AND EVEN IF PEOPLE FROM OUTSIDE THE SCHOOL COME TO SEE US, WE WON'T BE ABLE TO FIT THEM IN THE GYMNASIUM.
IT'LL BE FINE! WE'RE JUST SPREADING THE WORD!

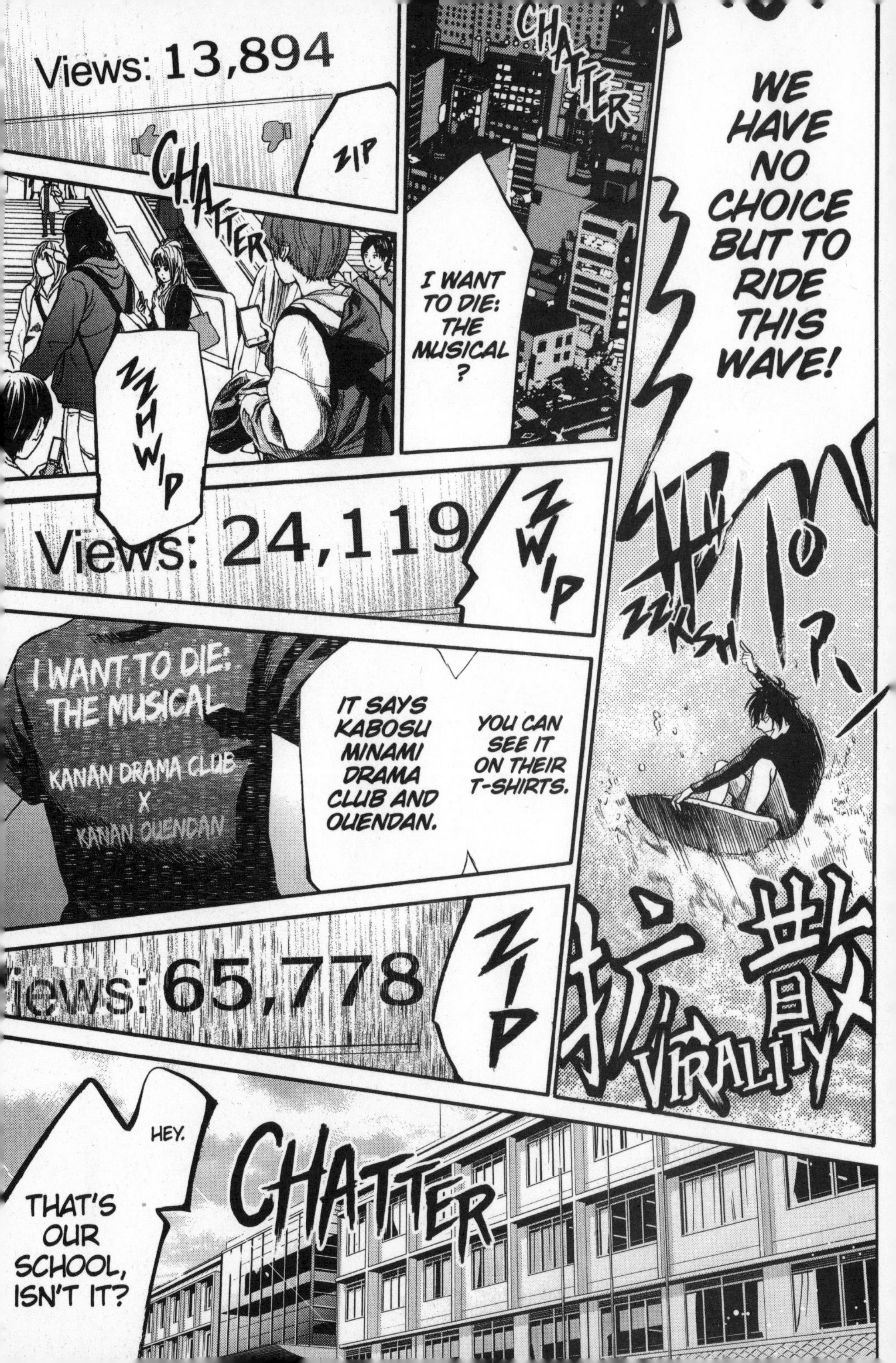
WE HAVE NO CHOICE BUT TO RIDE THIS WAVE!
ZZZKSH
拡散
VIRALITY
CHATTER
I WANT TO DIE: THE MUSICAL?
Views: 13,894
ZIP
CHATTER
ZZHWIP
ZWIP
Views: 24,119
YOU CAN SEE IT ON THEIR T-SHIRTS.
IT SAYS KABOSU MINAMI DRAMA CLUB AND OUENDAN.
I WANT TO DIE: THE MUSICAL
KANAN DRAMA CLUB
X
KANAN OUENDAN
ZIP
iews: 65,778
CHATTER
HEY.
THAT'S OUR SCHOOL, ISN'T IT?

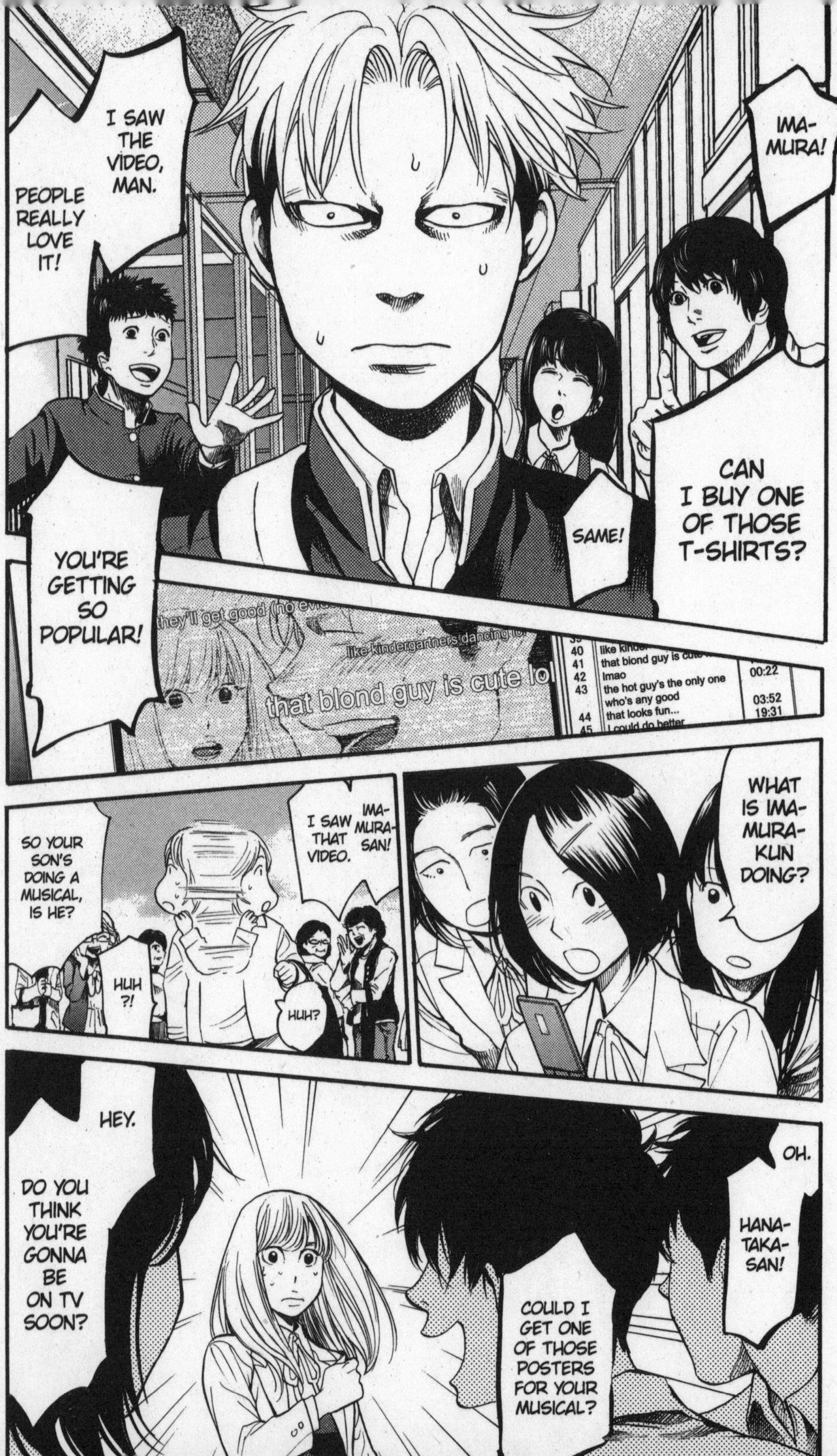

IMA-MURA!
CAN I BUY ONE OF THOSE T-SHIRTS?
SAME!
I SAW THE VIDEO, MAN.
PEOPLE REALLY LOVE IT!
YOU'RE GETTING SO POPULAR!
that blond guy is cute
41 that blond guy is cute
42 lmao 00:22
43 the hot guy's the only one who's any good 03:52
44 that looks fun... 19:31
I could do better
WHAT IS IMA-MURA-KUN DOING?
IMA-MURA-SAN!
I SAW THAT VIDEO.
SO YOUR SON'S DOING A MUSICAL, IS HE?
HUH?
HUH?!
OH.
HANA-TAKA-SAN!
COULD I GET ONE OF THOSE POSTERS FOR YOUR MUSICAL?
HEY.
DO YOU THINK YOU'RE GONNA BE ON TV SOON?

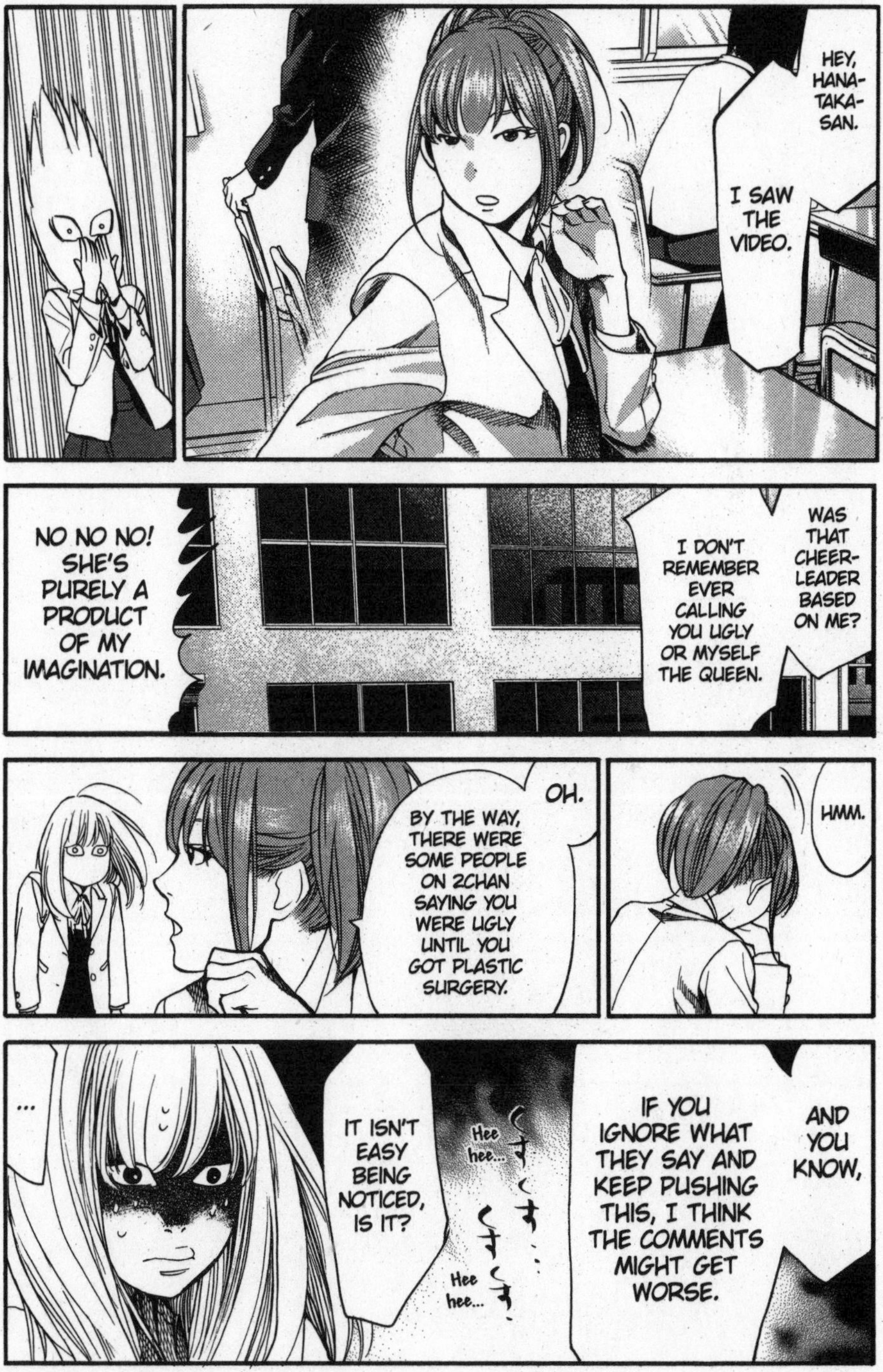
HEY, HANA-TAKA-SAN.
I SAW THE VIDEO.
WAS THAT CHEER-LEADER BASED ON ME?
I DON'T REMEMBER EVER CALLING YOU UGLY OR MYSELF THE QUEEN.
NO NO NO! SHE'S PURELY A PRODUCT OF MY IMAGINATION.
HMM.
OH.
BY THE WAY, THERE WERE SOME PEOPLE ON 2CHAN SAYING YOU WERE UGLY UNTIL YOU GOT PLASTIC SURGERY.
AND YOU KNOW,
IF YOU IGNORE WHAT THEY SAY AND KEEP PUSHING THIS, I THINK THE COMMENTS MIGHT GET WORSE.
くすくす Hee hee...
くすくす Hee hee...
IT ISN'T EASY BEING NOTICED, IS IT?
...

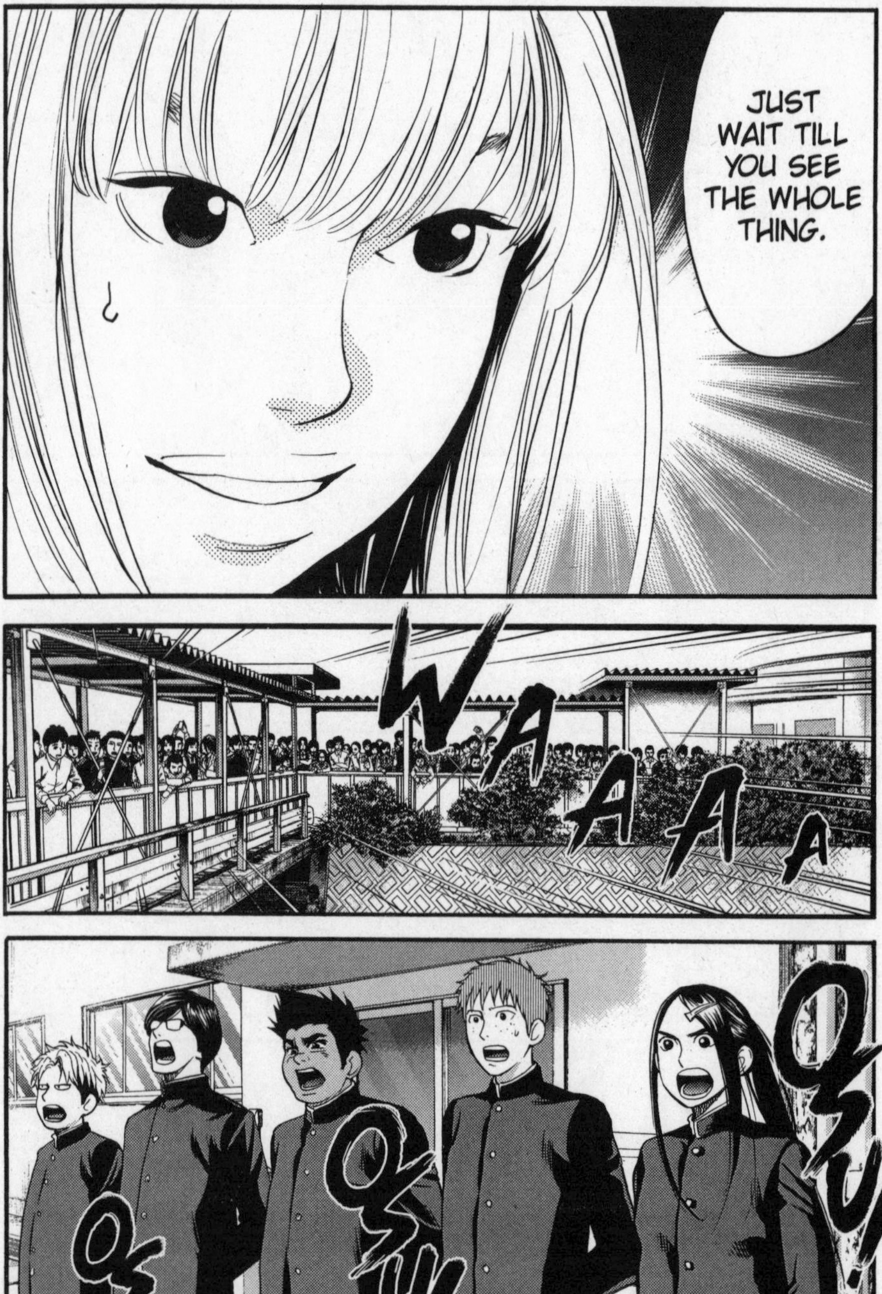
JUST WAIT TILL YOU SEE THE WHOLE THING.
WAAAAA
OSU!
OSU!
OSU!

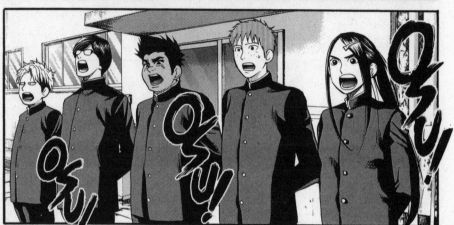

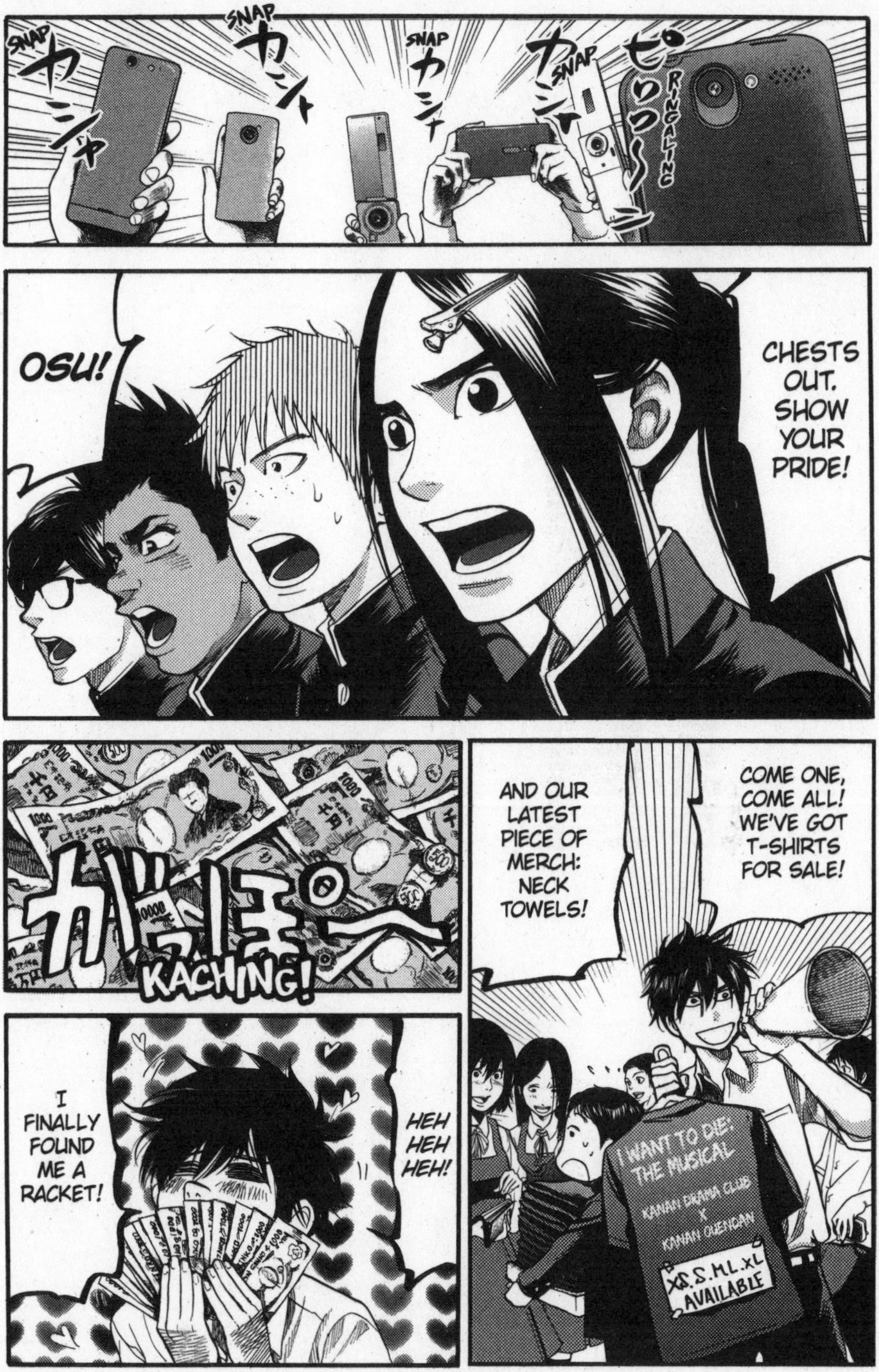
RINGALING
SNAP
SNAP
SNAP
SNAP
CHESTS OUT. SHOW YOUR PRIDE!
OSU!
COME ONE, COME ALL! WE'VE GOT T-SHIRTS FOR SALE!
AND OUR LATEST PIECE OF MERCH: NECK TOWELS!
I WANT TO DIE: THE MUSICAL
KANAN DRAMA CLUB
X
KANAN OUENDAN
XS.S.M.L.XL AVAILABLE
KACHING!
HEH HEH HEH!
I FINALLY FOUND ME A RACKET!

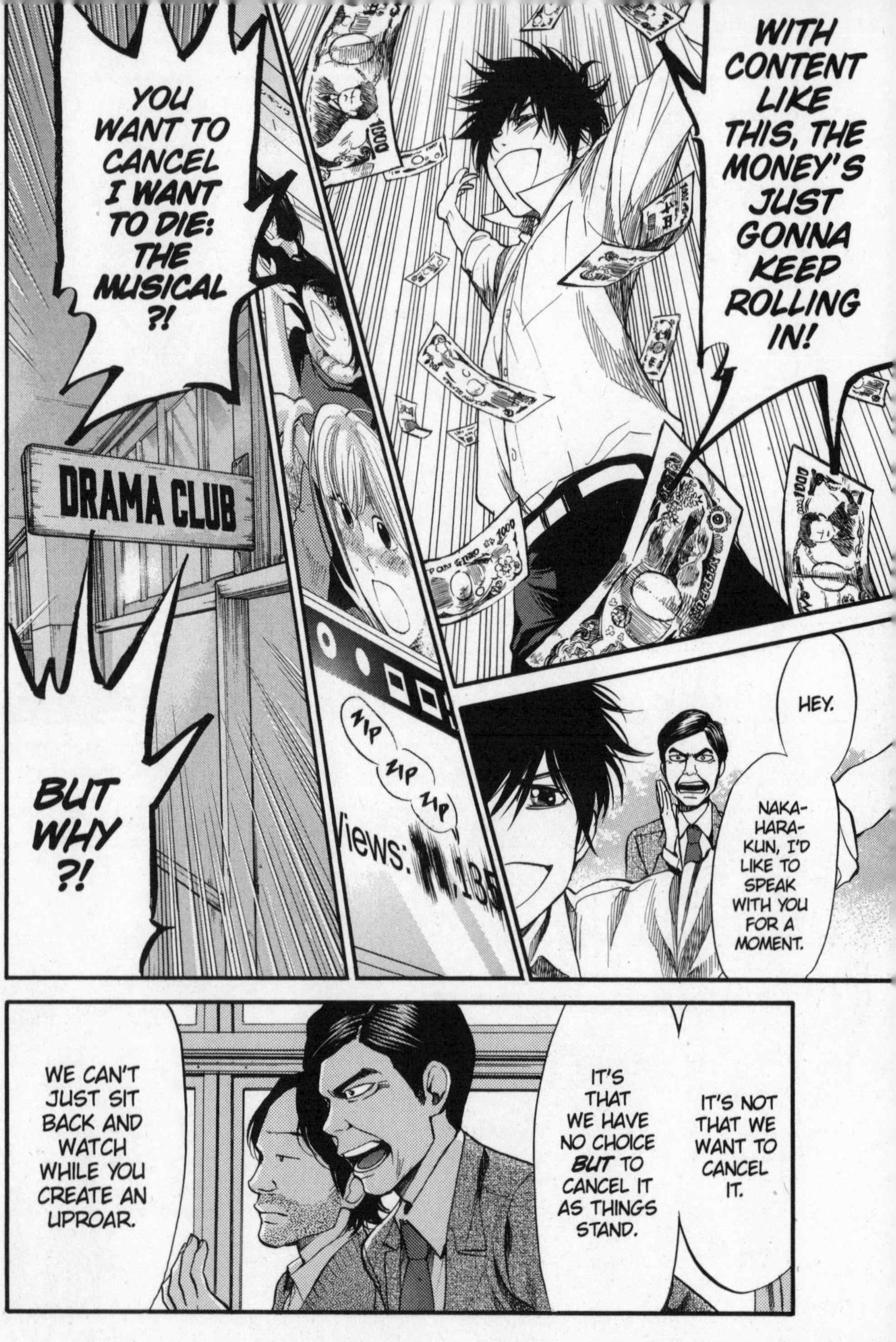
WITH CONTENT LIKE THIS, THE MONEY'S JUST GONNA KEEP ROLLING IN!
HEY.
NAKA-HARA-KUN, I'D LIKE TO SPEAK WITH YOU FOR A MOMENT.
ZIP ZIP ZIP
Views:
DRAMA CLUB
YOU WANT TO CANCEL I WANT TO DIE: THE MUSICAL?!
BUT WHY?!
IT'S NOT THAT WE WANT TO CANCEL IT.
IT'S THAT WE HAVE NO CHOICE *BUT* TO CANCEL IT AS THINGS STAND.
WE CAN'T JUST SIT BACK AND WATCH WHILE YOU CREATE AN UPROAR.

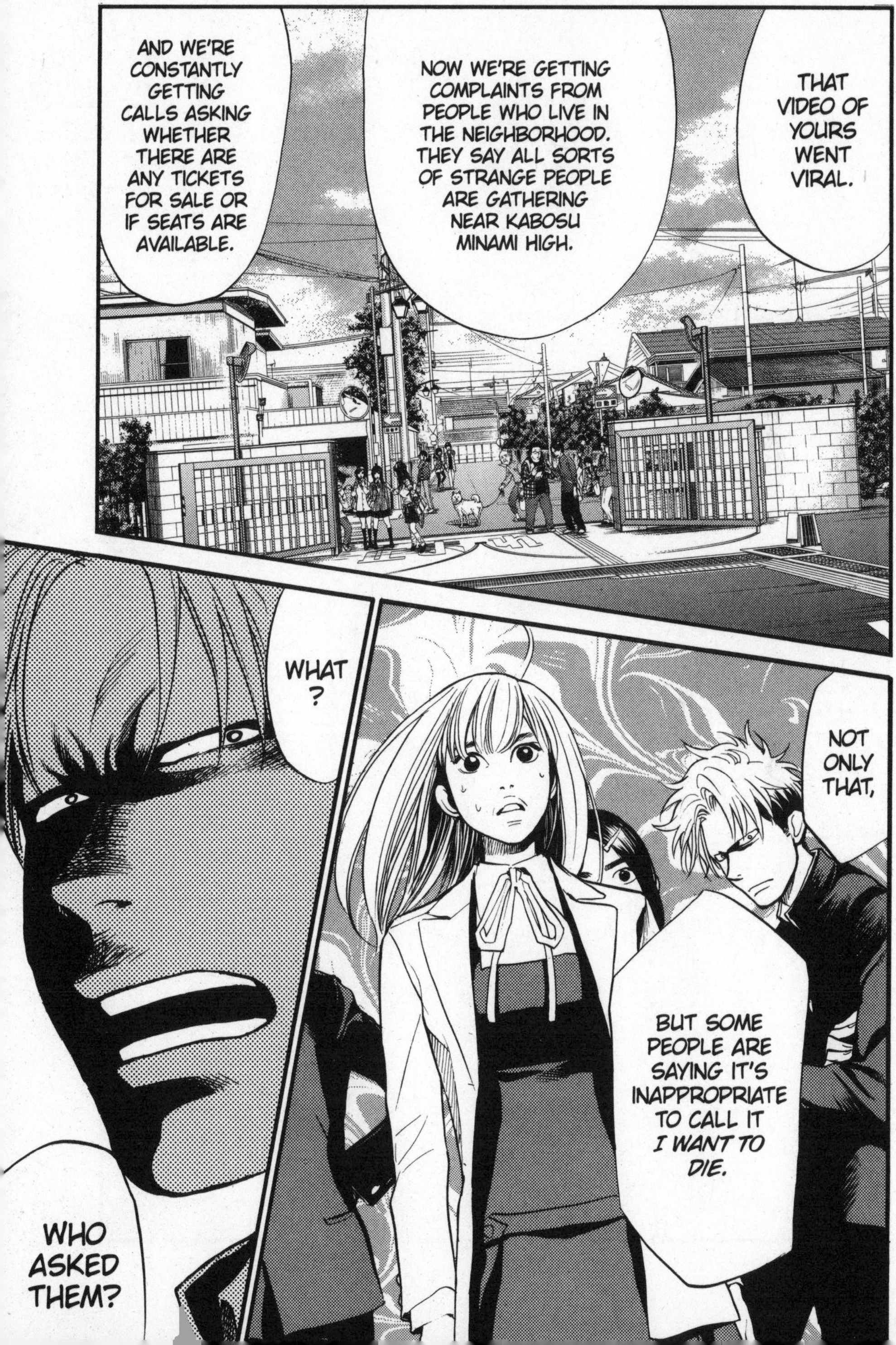
THAT VIDEO OF YOURS WENT VIRAL.
NOW WE'RE GETTING COMPLAINTS FROM PEOPLE WHO LIVE IN THE NEIGHBORHOOD. THEY SAY ALL SORTS OF STRANGE PEOPLE ARE GATHERING NEAR KABOSU MINAMI HIGH.
AND WE'RE CONSTANTLY GETTING CALLS ASKING WHETHER THERE ARE ANY TICKETS FOR SALE OR IF SEATS ARE AVAILABLE.
NOT ONLY THAT,
BUT SOME PEOPLE ARE SAYING IT'S INAPPROPRIATE TO CALL IT *I WANT TO DIE*.
WHAT?
WHO ASKED THEM?

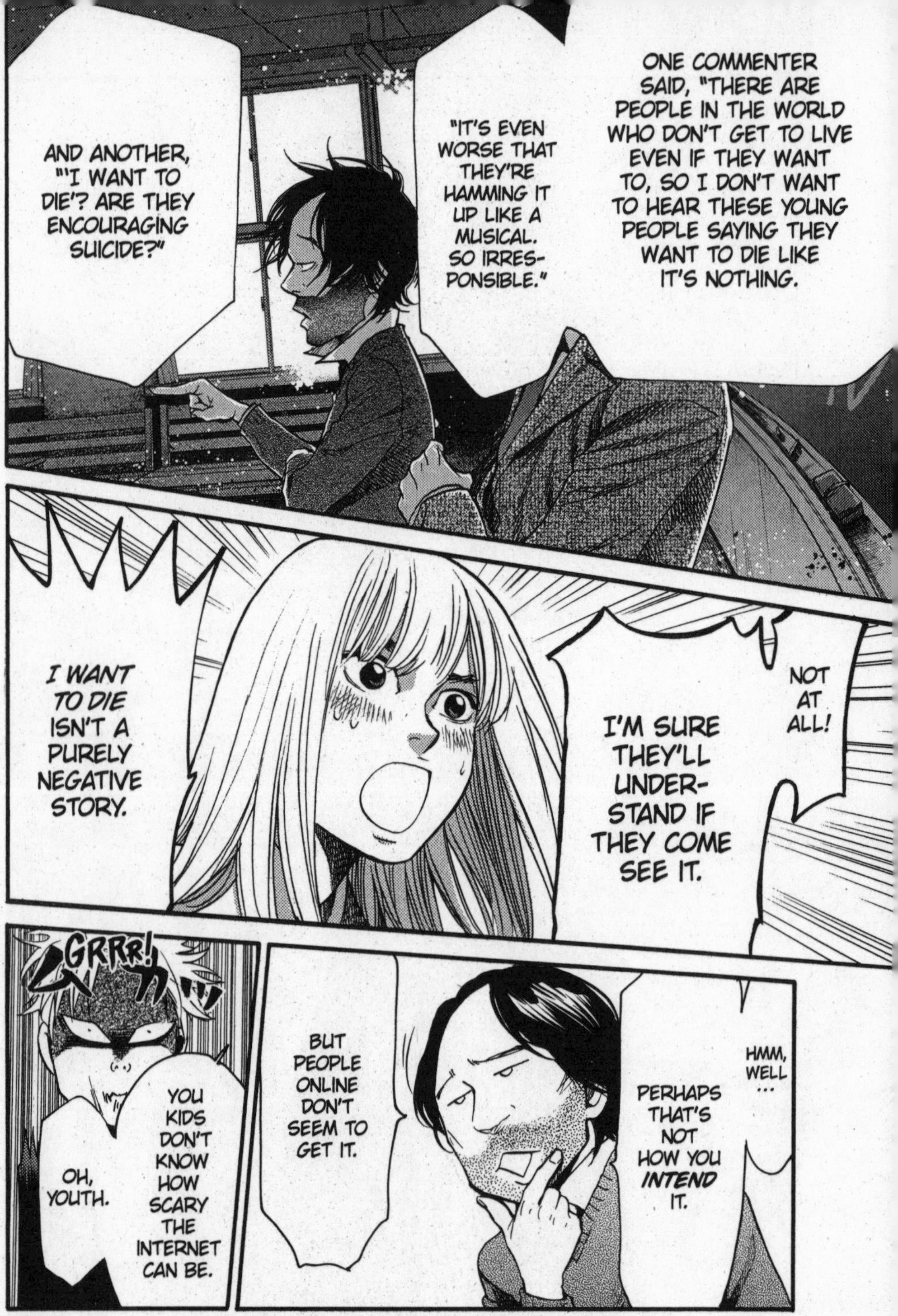
ONE COMMENTER SAID, "THERE ARE PEOPLE IN THE WORLD WHO DON'T GET TO LIVE EVEN IF THEY WANT TO, SO I DON'T WANT TO HEAR THESE YOUNG PEOPLE SAYING THEY WANT TO DIE LIKE IT'S NOTHING.
"IT'S EVEN WORSE THAT THEY'RE HAMMING IT UP LIKE A MUSICAL. SO IRRES-PONSIBLE."
AND ANOTHER, "'I WANT TO DIE'? ARE THEY ENCOURAGING SUICIDE?"
NOT AT ALL!
I'M SURE THEY'LL UNDER-STAND IF THEY COME SEE IT.
I WANT TO DIE ISN'T A PURELY NEGATIVE STORY.
HMM, WELL...
PERHAPS THAT'S NOT HOW YOU *INTEND* IT.
BUT PEOPLE ONLINE DON'T SEEM TO GET IT.
GRRR!
YOU KIDS DON'T KNOW HOW SCARY THE INTERNET CAN BE.
OH, YOUTH.

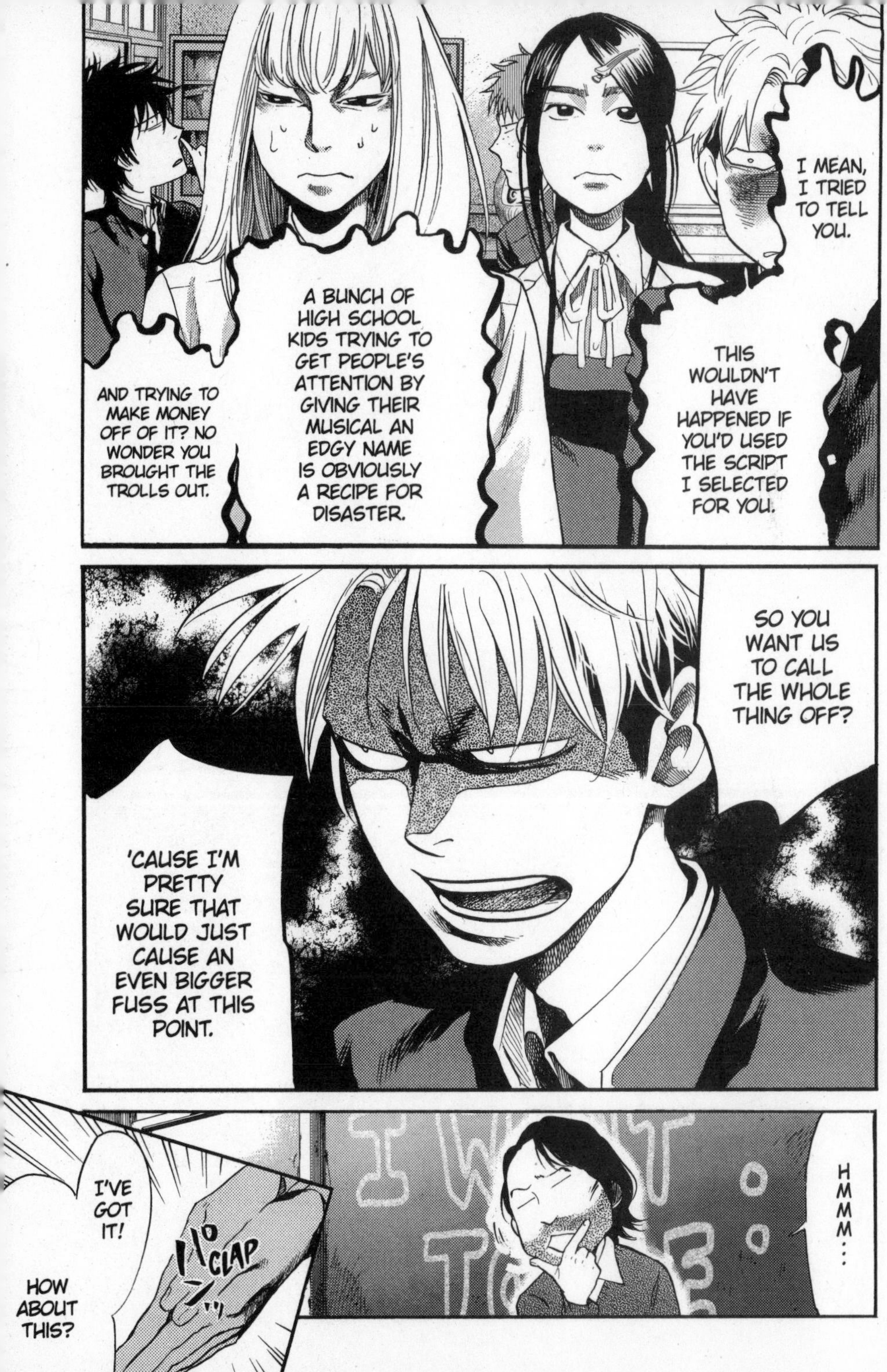
I MEAN, I TRIED TO TELL YOU.
THIS WOULDN'T HAVE HAPPENED IF YOU'D USED THE SCRIPT I SELECTED FOR YOU.
A BUNCH OF HIGH SCHOOL KIDS TRYING TO GET PEOPLE'S ATTENTION BY GIVING THEIR MUSICAL AN EDGY NAME IS OBVIOUSLY A RECIPE FOR DISASTER.
AND TRYING TO MAKE MONEY OFF OF IT? NO WONDER YOU BROUGHT THE TROLLS OUT.
SO YOU WANT US TO CALL THE WHOLE THING OFF?
'CAUSE I'M PRETTY SURE THAT WOULD JUST CAUSE AN EVEN BIGGER FUSS AT THIS POINT.
HMMM...
I'VE GOT IT!
CLAP
HOW ABOUT THIS?

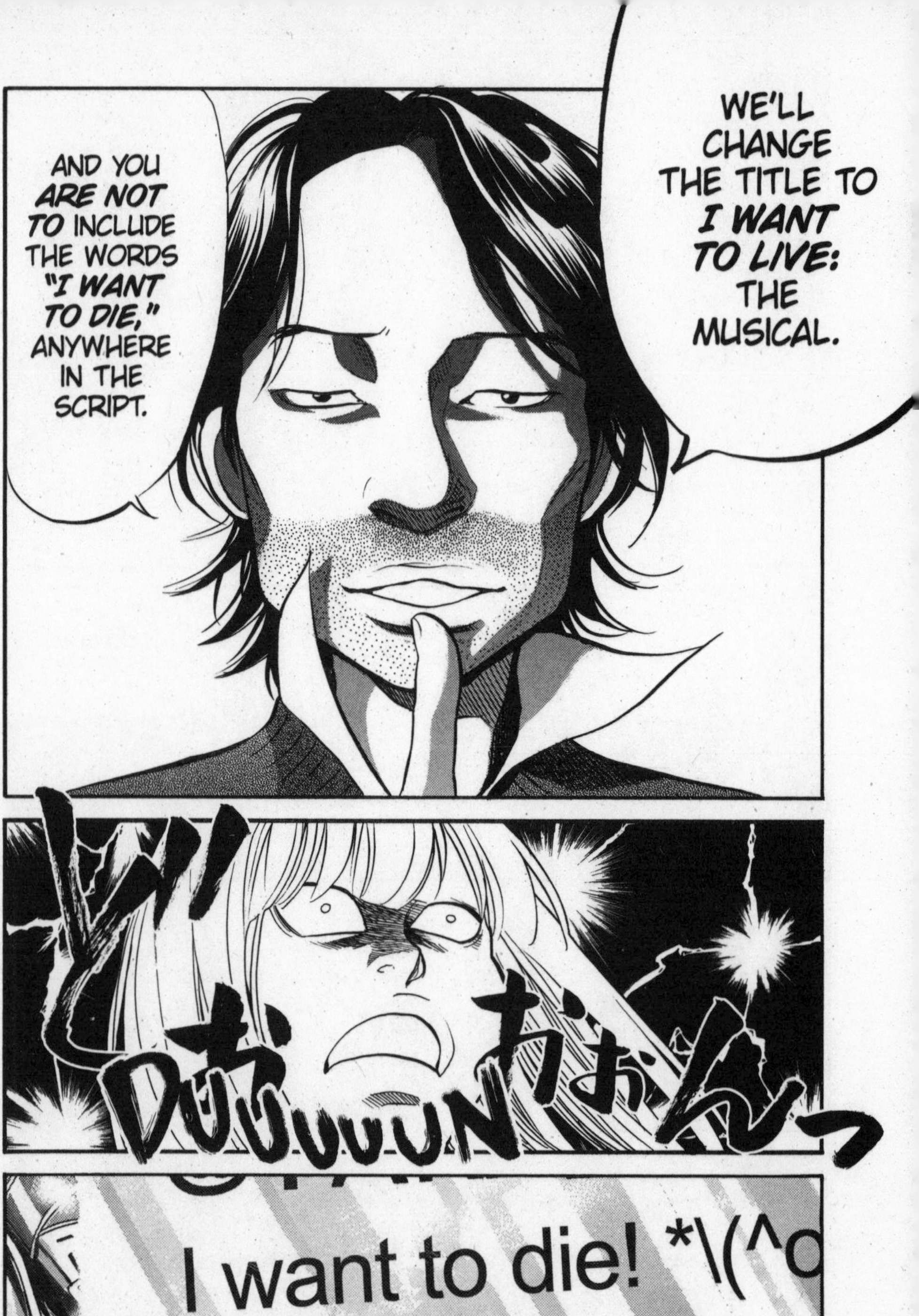
WE'LL CHANGE THE TITLE TO *I WANT TO LIVE:* THE MUSICAL.
AND YOU ***ARE NOT TO*** INCLUDE THE WORDS ***"I WANT TO DIE,"*** ANYWHERE IN THE SCRIPT.
DUUUUUUN
I want to die! *\(^

90. PLEASE STOP, MR. TEACHER

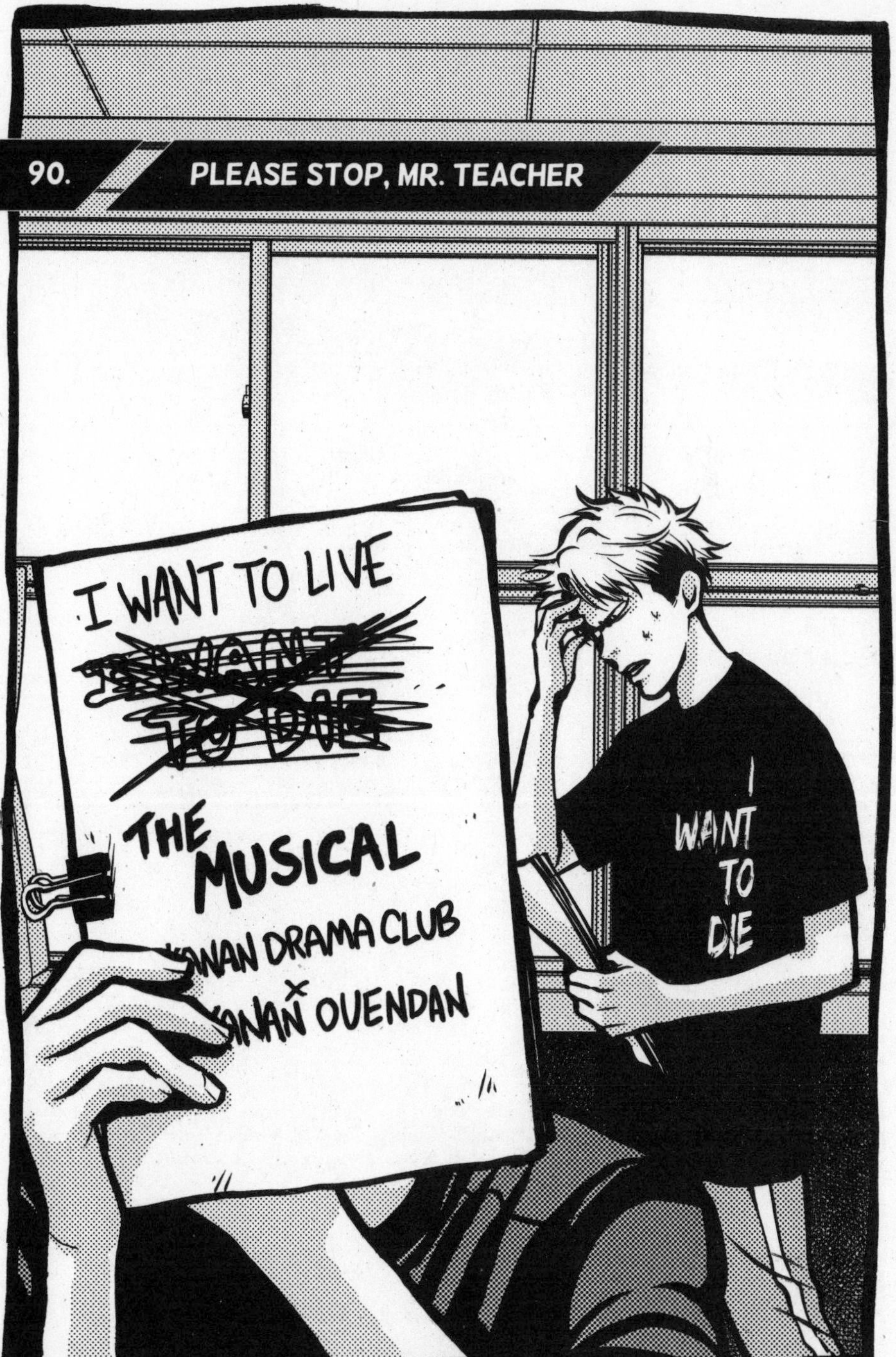

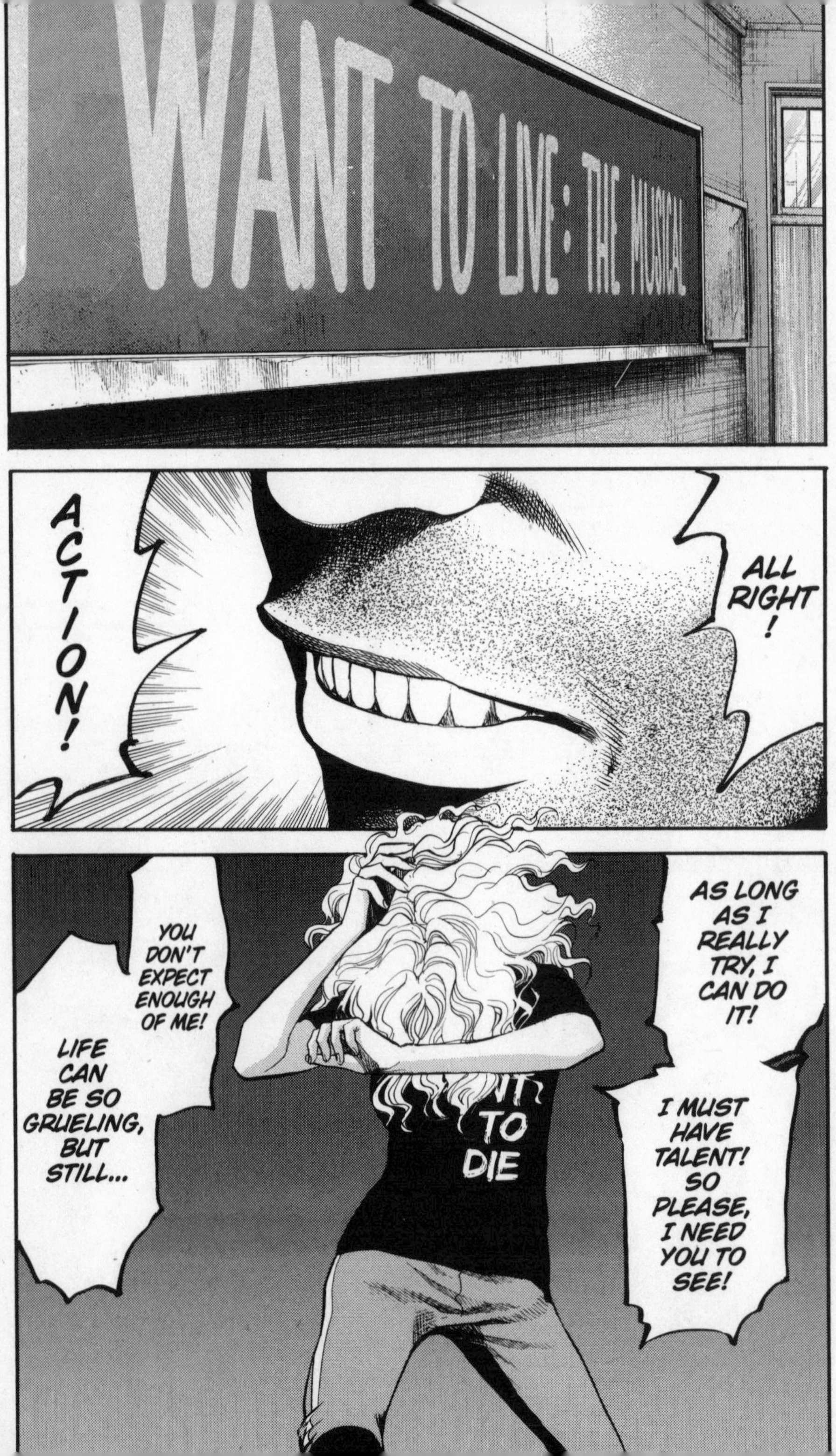
WANT TO LIVE : THE MUSICAL
ALL RIGHT!
ACTION!
AS LONG AS I REALLY TRY, I CAN DO IT!
I MUST HAVE TALENT! SO PLEASE, I NEED YOU TO SEE!
YOU DON'T EXPECT ENOUGH OF ME!
LIFE CAN BE SO GRUELING, BUT STILL...
TO DIE

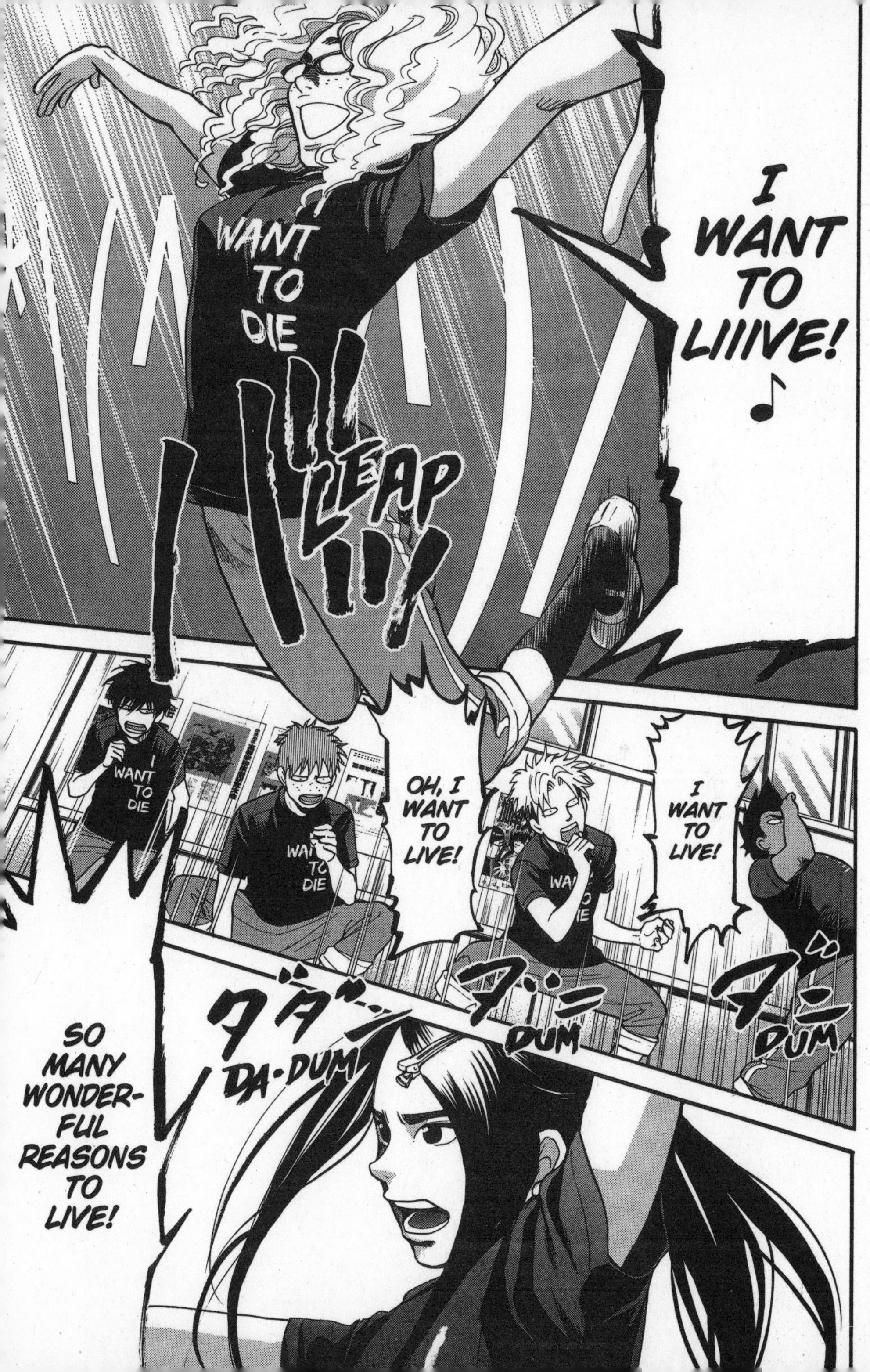
I WANT TO LIIIVE! ♪
I WANT TO DIE
LEAP!!!
I WANT TO LIVE!
DUM
OH, I WANT TO LIVE!
DUM
I WANT TO DIE
DA-DUM
SO MANY WONDERFUL REASONS TO LIVE!

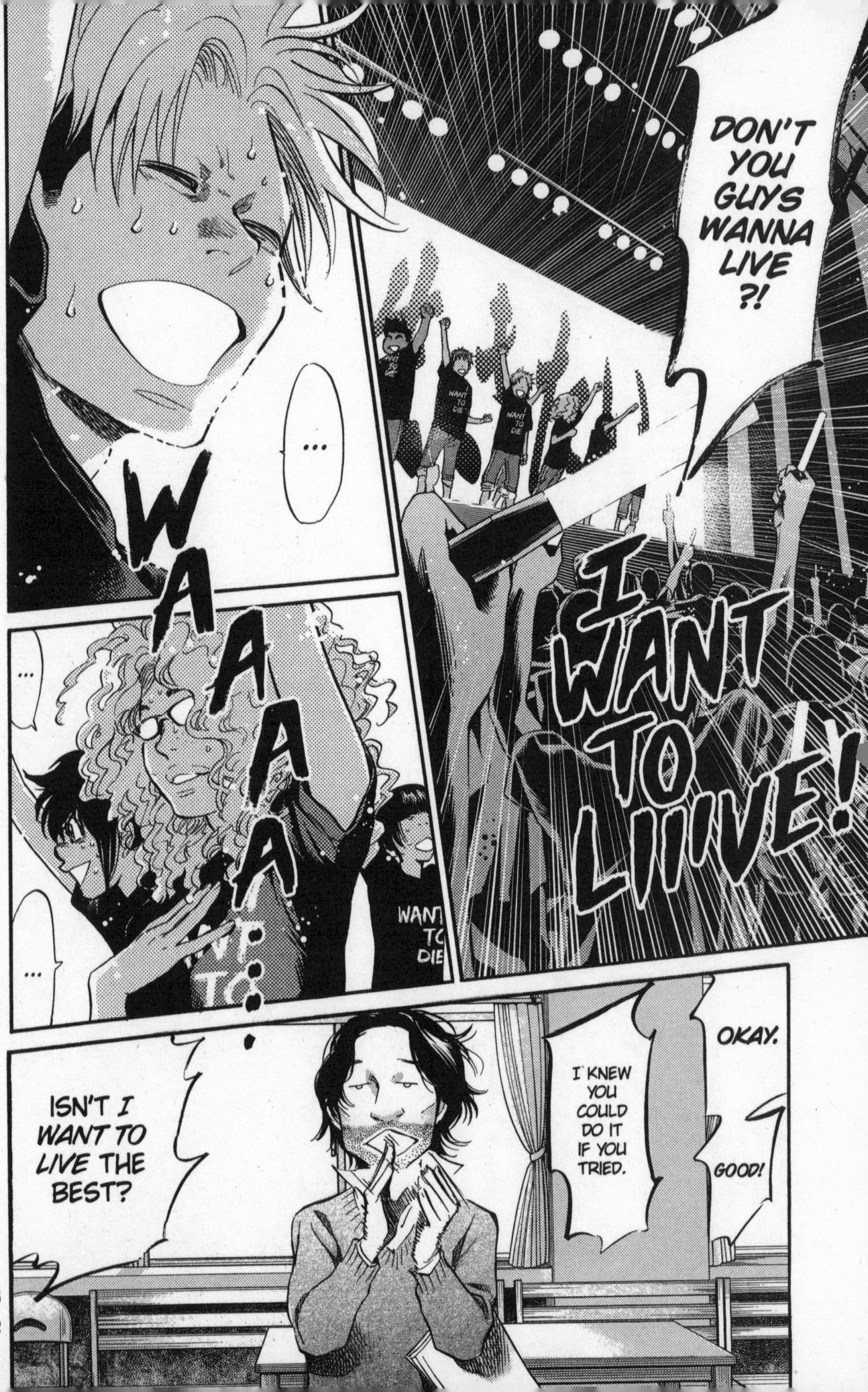
DON'T YOU GUYS WANNA LIVE?!
I WANT TO LIIIVE!
...
WAAAA...
...
...
OKAY.
GOOD!
I KNEW YOU COULD DO IT IF YOU TRIED.
ISN'T *I WANT TO LIVE* THE BEST?

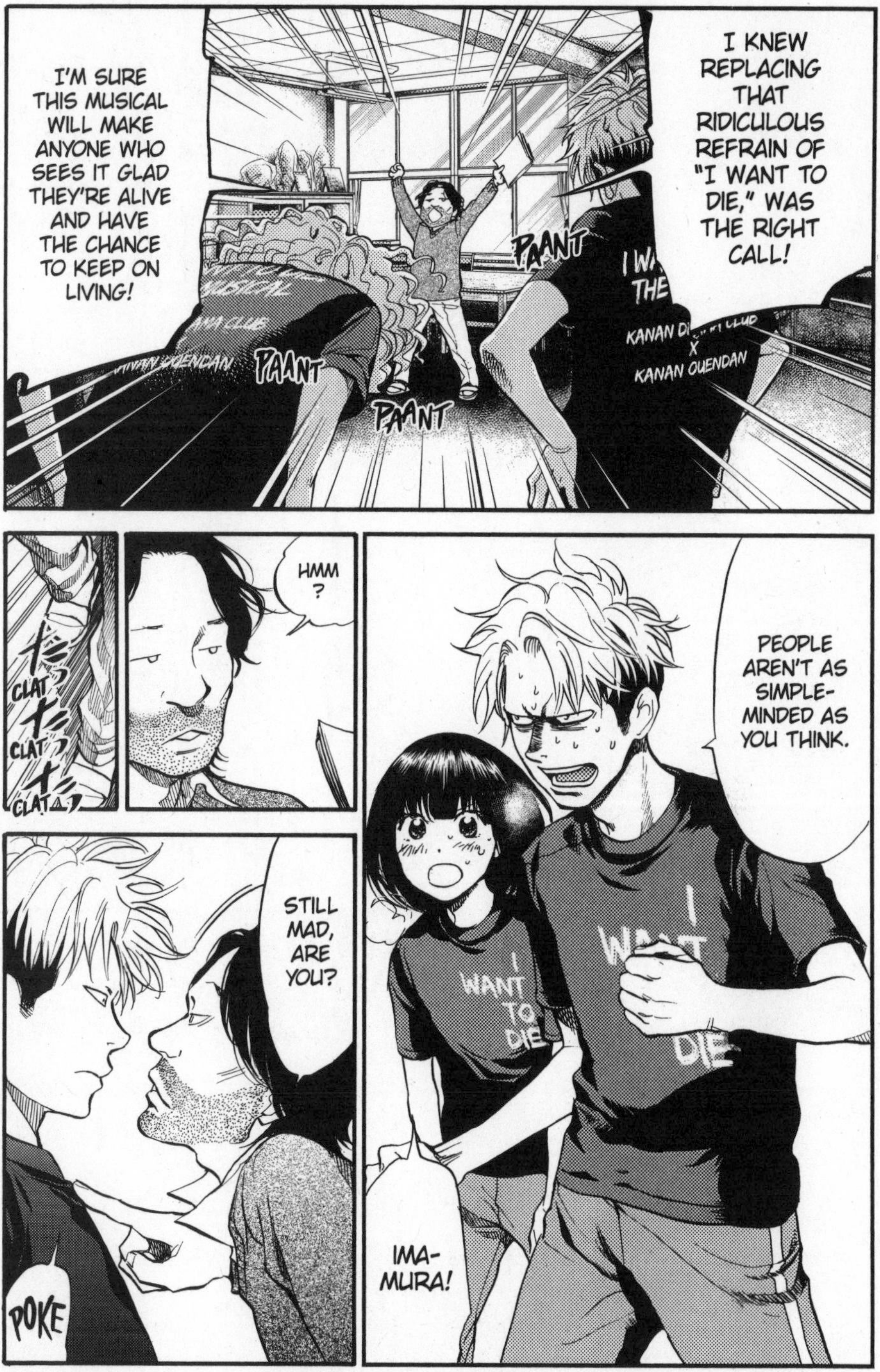
I KNEW REPLACING THAT RIDICULOUS REFRAIN OF "I WANT TO DIE," WAS THE RIGHT CALL!
PAANT
KANAN OUENDAN
I'M SURE THIS MUSICAL WILL MAKE ANYONE WHO SEES IT GLAD THEY'RE ALIVE AND HAVE THE CHANCE TO KEEP ON LIVING!
PAANT
PAANT
PEOPLE AREN'T AS SIMPLE-MINDED AS YOU THINK.
I WANT TO DIE
IMA-MURA!
HMM ?
CLAT
CLAT
CLAT
STILL MAD, ARE YOU?
POKE

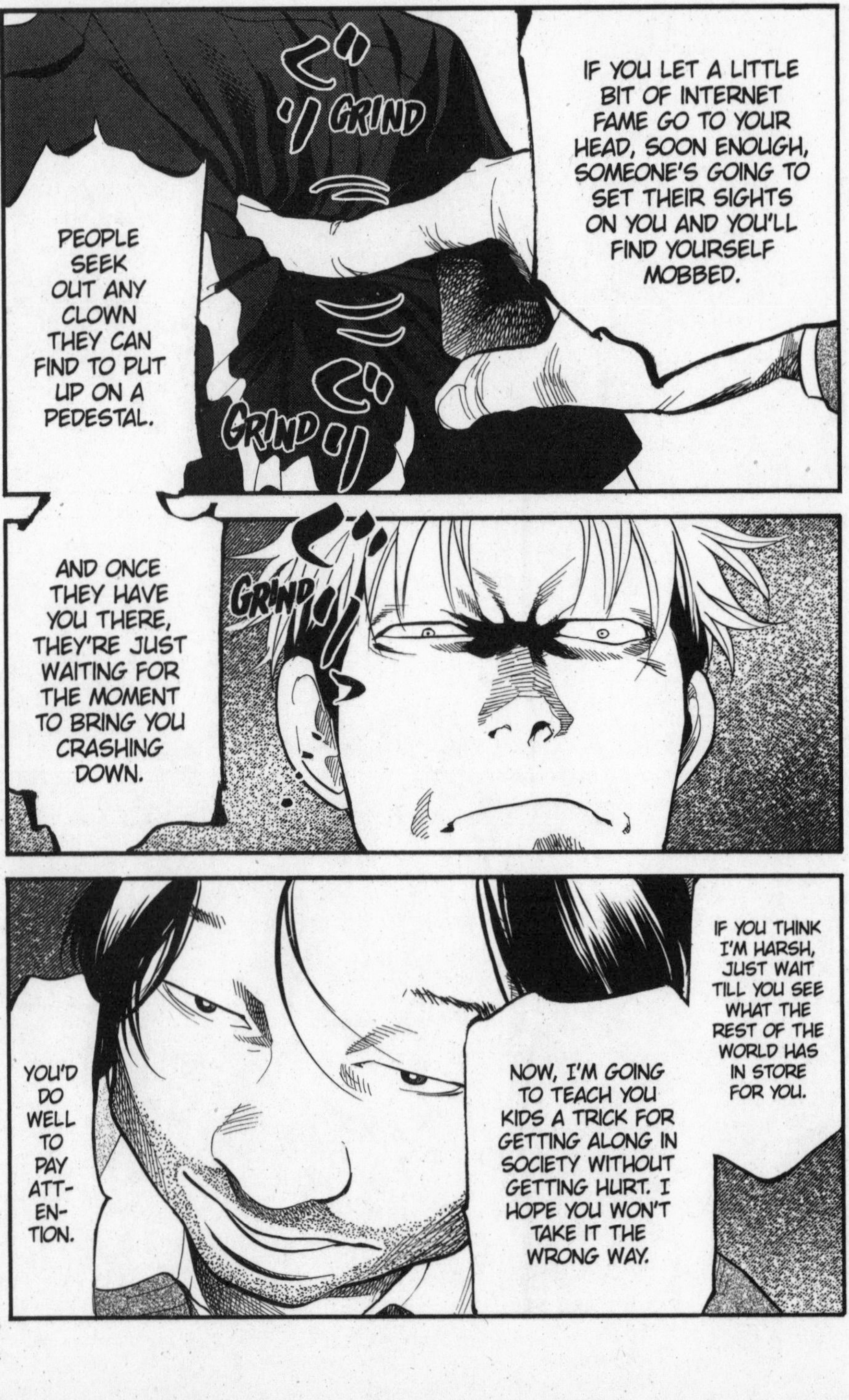
IF YOU LET A LITTLE BIT OF INTERNET FAME GO TO YOUR HEAD, SOON ENOUGH, SOMEONE'S GOING TO SET THEIR SIGHTS ON YOU AND YOU'LL FIND YOURSELF MOBBED.
GRIND
GRIND
PEOPLE SEEK OUT ANY CLOWN THEY CAN FIND TO PUT UP ON A PEDESTAL.
GRIND
AND ONCE THEY HAVE YOU THERE, THEY'RE JUST WAITING FOR THE MOMENT TO BRING YOU CRASHING DOWN.
IF YOU THINK I'M HARSH, JUST WAIT TILL YOU SEE WHAT THE REST OF THE WORLD HAS IN STORE FOR YOU.
NOW, I'M GOING TO TEACH YOU KIDS A TRICK FOR GETTING ALONG IN SOCIETY WITHOUT GETTING HURT. I HOPE YOU WON'T TAKE IT THE WRONG WAY.
YOU'D DO WELL TO PAY ATT-EN-TION.

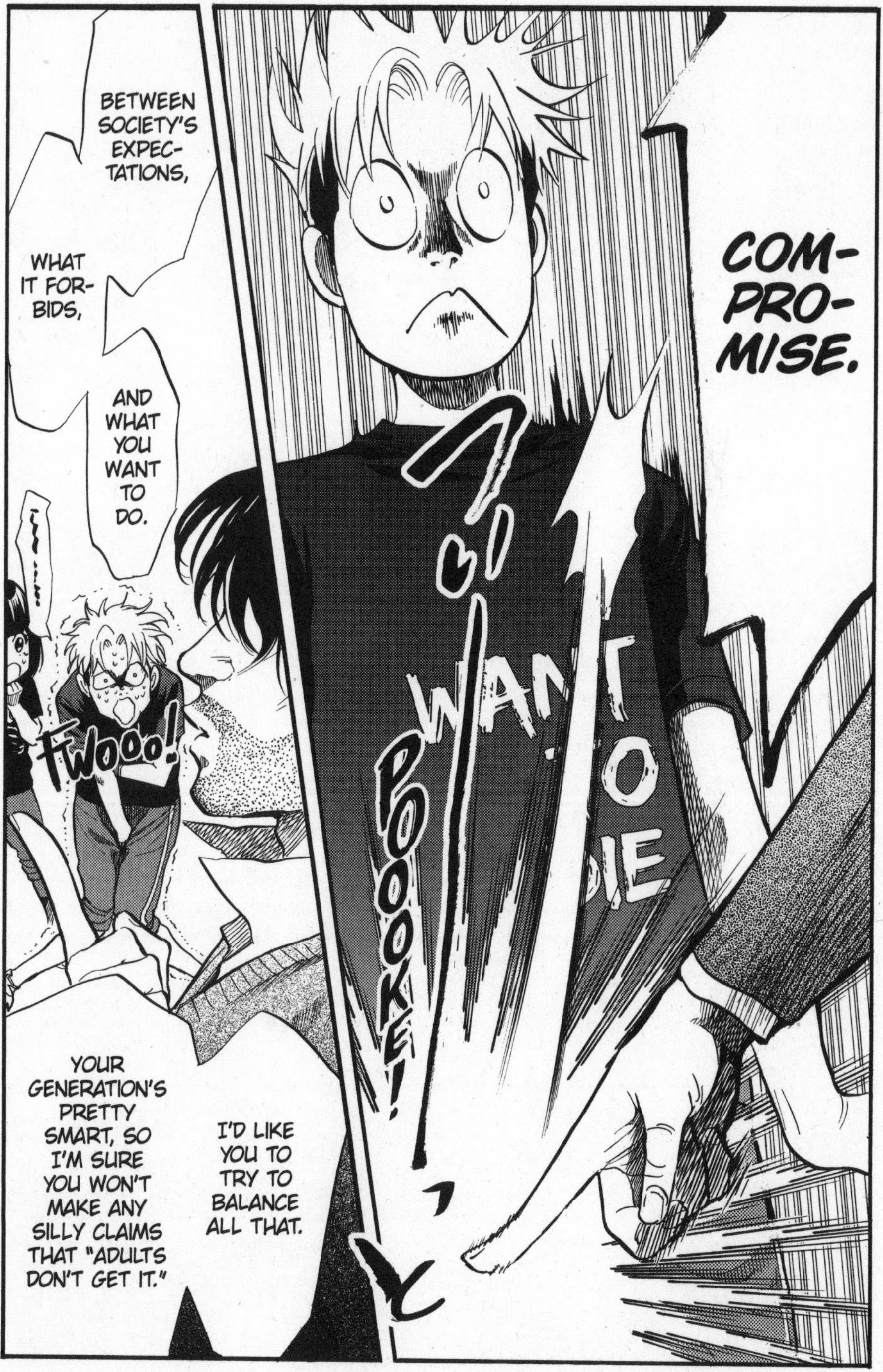
COM-PRO-MISE.
POOOKE!
BETWEEN SOCIETY'S EXPEC-TATIONS,
WHAT IT FOR-BIDS,
AND WHAT YOU WANT TO DO.
FWOOO!
I'D LIKE YOU TO TRY TO BALANCE ALL THAT.
YOUR GENERATION'S PRETTY SMART, SO I'M SURE YOU WON'T MAKE ANY SILLY CLAIMS THAT "ADULTS DON'T GET IT."

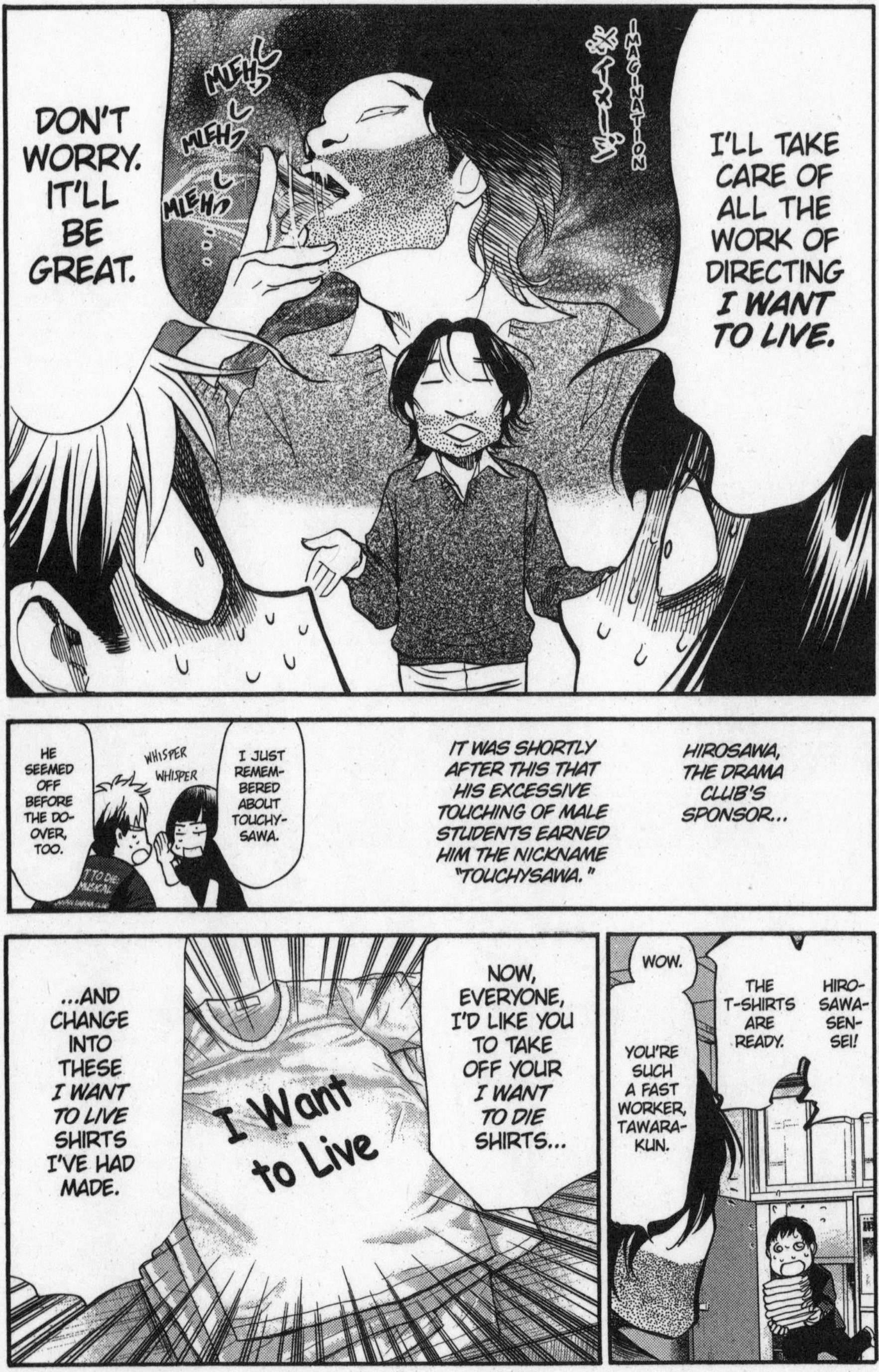
I'LL TAKE CARE OF ALL THE WORK OF DIRECTING *I WANT TO LIVE.*
IMAGINATION ※イメージ
MLEH MLEH MLEH...
DON'T WORRY. IT'LL BE GREAT.
HIROSAWA, THE DRAMA CLUB'S SPONSOR...
IT WAS SHORTLY AFTER THIS THAT HIS EXCESSIVE TOUCHING OF MALE STUDENTS EARNED HIM THE NICKNAME "TOUCHYSAWA."
I JUST REMEMBERED ABOUT TOUCHY-SAWA.
WHISPER WHISPER
HE SEEMED OFF BEFORE THE DO-OVER, TOO.
HIRO-SAWA-SENSEI!
THE T-SHIRTS ARE READY.
WOW.
YOU'RE SUCH A FAST WORKER, TAWARA-KUN.
NOW, EVERYONE, I'D LIKE YOU TO TAKE OFF YOUR *I WANT TO DIE* SHIRTS...
...AND CHANGE INTO THESE *I WANT TO LIVE* SHIRTS I'VE HAD MADE.
I Want to Live

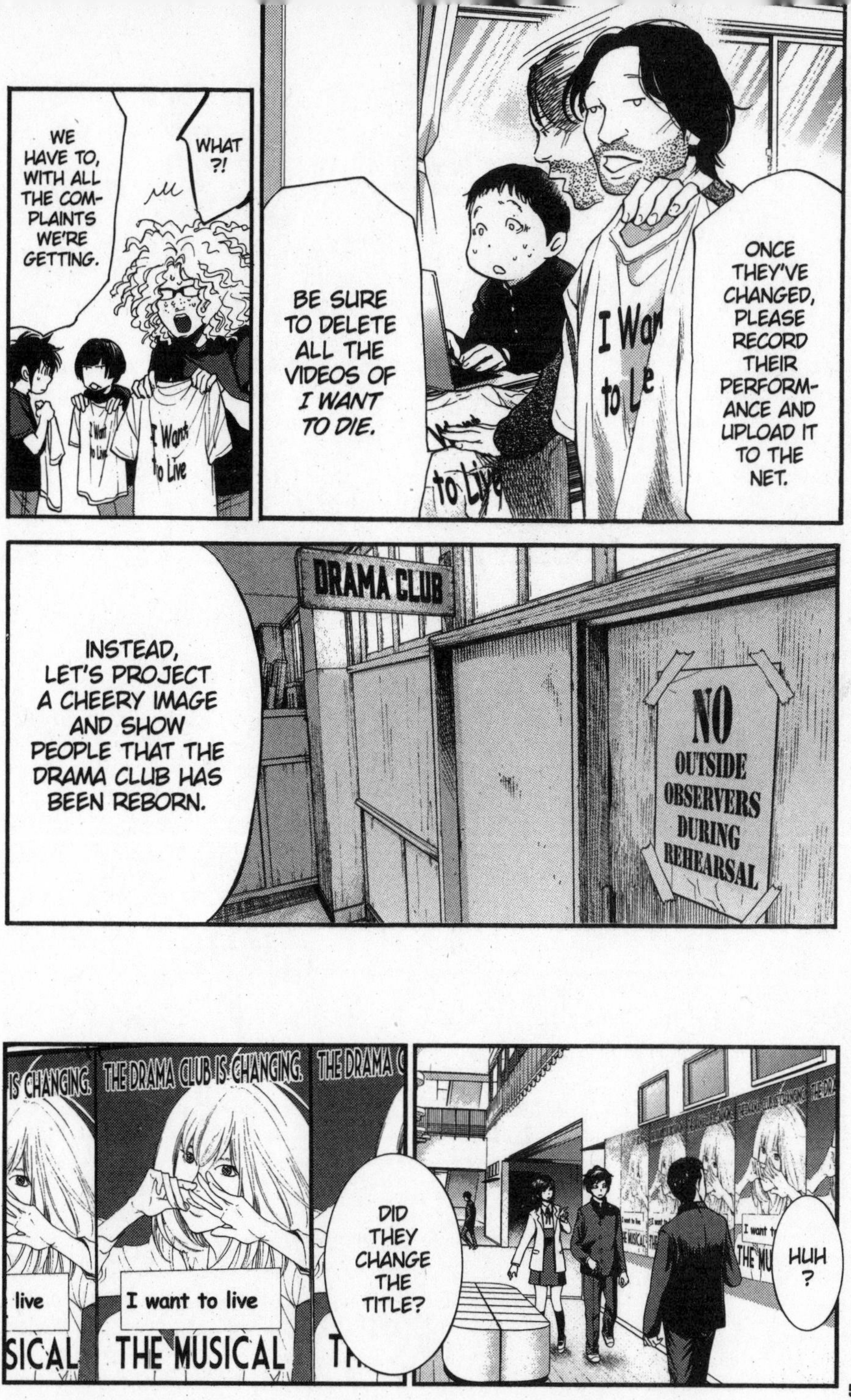
ONCE THEY'VE CHANGED, PLEASE RECORD THEIR PERFORMANCE AND UPLOAD IT TO THE NET.
BE SURE TO DELETE ALL THE VIDEOS OF *I WANT TO DIE.*
I Want to Live
to Live
WHAT ?!
WE HAVE TO, WITH ALL THE COMPLAINTS WE'RE GETTING.
I Want to Live
I Want to Live
NO OUTSIDE OBSERVERS DURING REHEARSAL
DRAMA CLUB
INSTEAD, LET'S PROJECT A CHEERY IMAGE AND SHOW PEOPLE THAT THE DRAMA CLUB HAS BEEN REBORN.
HUH ?
DID THEY CHANGE THE TITLE?
THE DRAMA CLUB IS CHANGING.
I want to live
THE MUSICAL
IS CHANGING.
live
SICAL

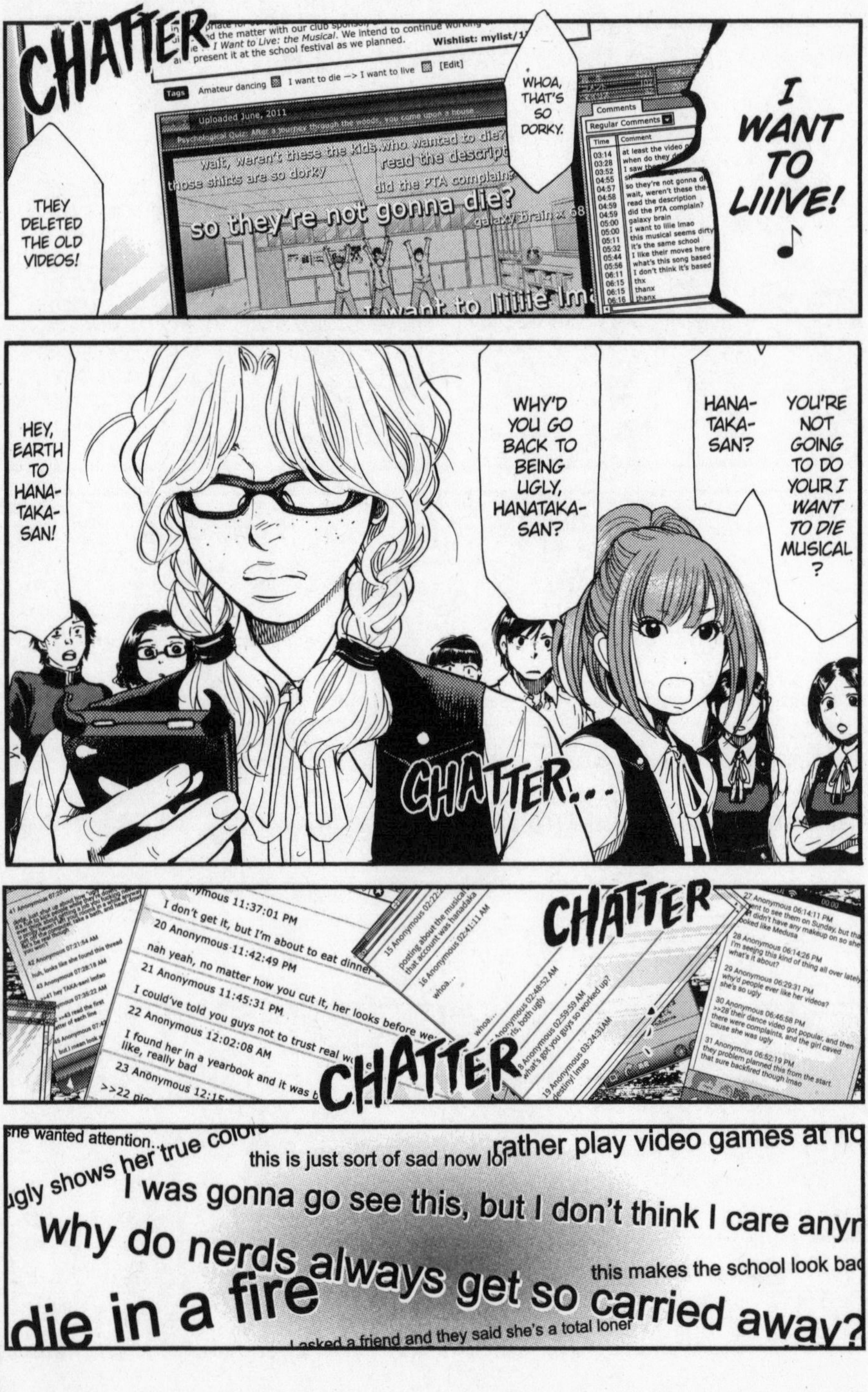
I WANT TO LIIIVE! ♪
WHOA, THAT'S SO DORKY.
CHATTER
d the matter with our club sponsor
I Want to Live: the Musical. We intend to continue working
present it at the school festival as we planned.
Wishlist: mylist/1
Tags Amateur dancing I want to die —> I want to live [Edit]
Uploaded June, 2011
Comments
Regular Comments
Time Comment
03:14 at least the video
03:28 when do they
03:52 I saw the
04:57 so they're not gonna di
04:58 wait, weren't these the
04:59 read the description
04:59 did the PTA complain?
05:00 galaxy brain
05:00 I want to liiie lmao
05:11 this musical seems dirty
05:32 it's the same school
05:46 I like their moves here
05:56 what's this song based
06:11 I don't think it's based
06:15 thx
06:16 thanx
wait, weren't these the kids who wanted to die?
read the descript
those shirts are so dorky
did the PTA complain?
so they're not gonna die?
galaxy brain
I want to liiiie lmao
THEY DELETED THE OLD VIDEOS!
YOU'RE NOT GOING TO DO YOUR I WANT TO DIE MUSICAL?
HANA-TAKA-SAN?
WHY'D YOU GO BACK TO BEING UGLY, HANATAKA-SAN?
HEY, EARTH TO HANA-TAKA-SAN!
CHATTER...
CHATTER
27 Anonymous 06:14:11 PM
went to see them on Sunday, but tha
didn't have any makeup on so she
looked like Medusa
28 Anonymous 06:14:26 PM
I'm seeing this kind of thing all over lately
what's it about?
29 Anonymous 06:29:31 PM
why'd people ever like her videos?
she's so ugly
30 Anonymous 06:46:58 PM
>>28 their dance video got popular, and then
there were complaints, and the girl caved
'cause she was ugly
31 Anonymous 06:52:19 PM
they problem planned this from the start
that sure backfired though lmao
15 Anonymous 02:22
posting about the musical
that account was hanadaka
16 Anonymous 02:41:11 AM
whoa...
Anonymous 02:48:52 AM
whoa...
8 Anonymous 02:59:59 AM
what's got you guys so worked up?
19 Anonymous 03:24:31 AM
destiny! lmao
Anonymous 11:37:01 PM
I don't get it, but I'm about to eat dinner
20 Anonymous 11:42:49 PM
nah yeah, no matter how you cut it, her looks before we
21 Anonymous 11:45:31 PM
I could've told you guys not to trust real wo
22 Anonymous 12:02:08 AM
I found her in a yearbook and it was b
like, really bad
23 Anonymous 12:15
>>22
42 Anonymous 07:21:54 AM
huh, looks like she found this thread
43 Anonymous 07:28:18 AM
CHATTER
she wanted attention...
ugly shows her true colors
this is just sort of sad now lol
rather play video games at ho
I was gonna go see this, but I don't think I care anyr
why do nerds always get so carried away?
this makes the school look ba
die in a fire
I asked a friend and they said she's a total loner

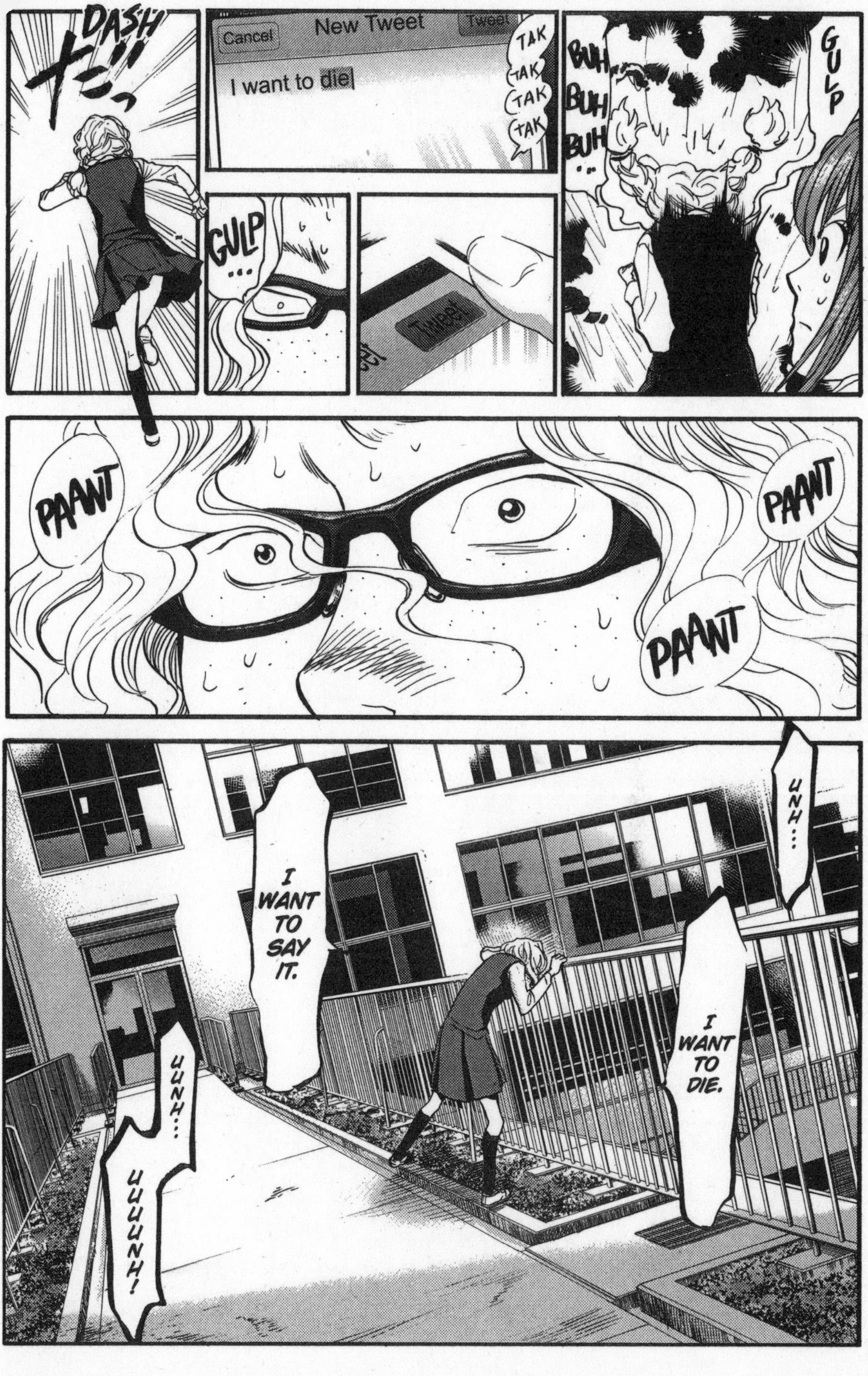
BUH
BUH
BUH
...
GULP
Cancel
New Tweet
Tweet
I want to die
TAK
TAK
TAK
TAK
Tweet
GULP
...
DASH
ダッ
PAANT
PAANT
PAANT
UNH...
I WANT TO DIE.
I WANT TO SAY IT.
UUNH...
UUUUNH!

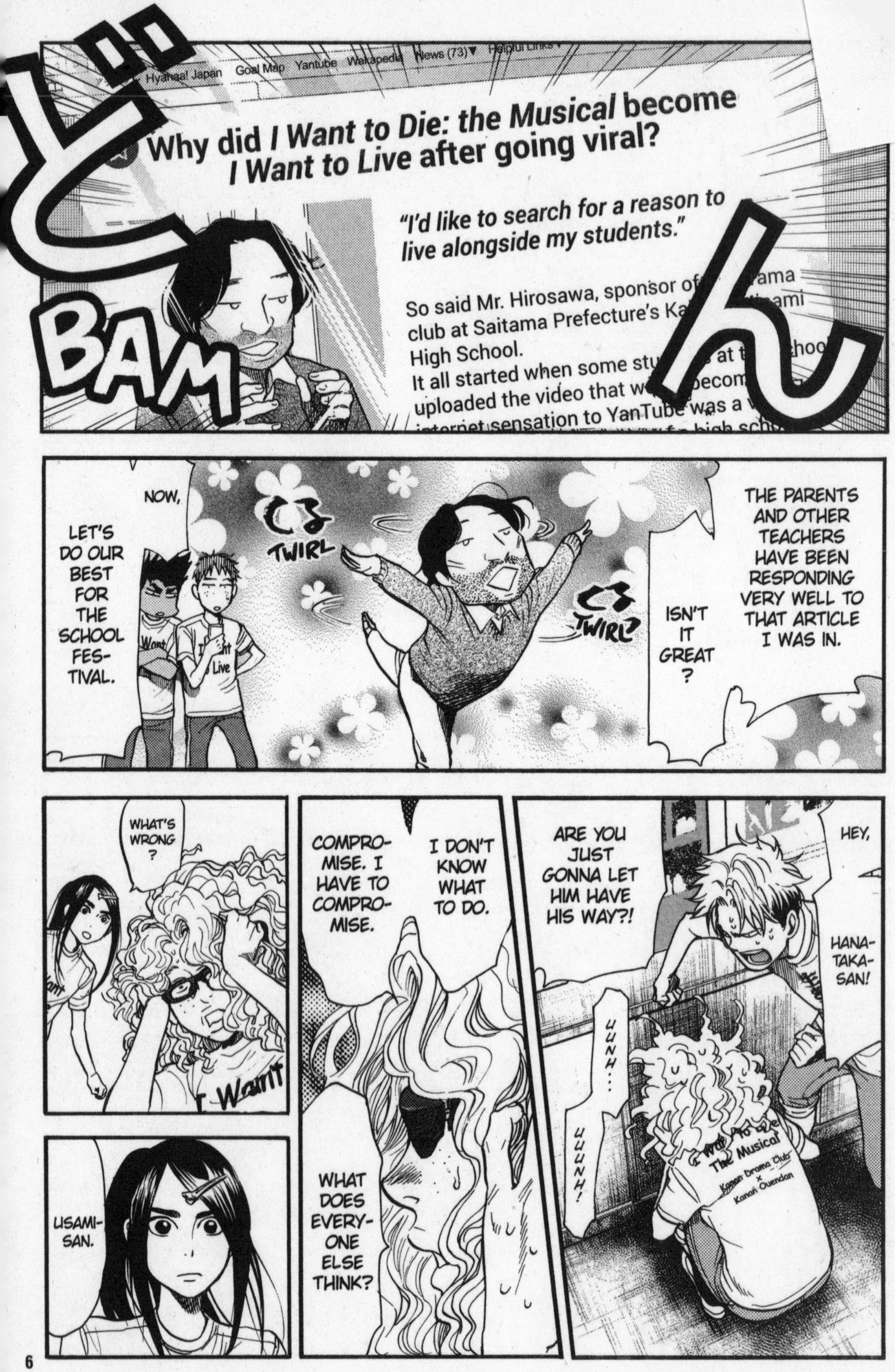
Hyahaa! Japan Goal Map Yantube Wakapedia News (73)▼
Why did I Want to Die: the Musical become I Want to Live after going viral?
"I'd like to search for a reason to live alongside my students."
So said Mr. Hirosawa, sponsor of
club at Saitama Prefecture's
High School.
It all started when some stu
uploaded the video that w
sensation to YanTube was a
ん
BAM
ど
THE PARENTS AND OTHER TEACHERS HAVE BEEN RESPONDING VERY WELL TO THAT ARTICLE I WAS IN.
ISN'T IT GREAT?
TWIRL
TWIRL
NOW,
LET'S DO OUR BEST FOR THE SCHOOL FESTIVAL.
HEY,
HANATAKA-SAN!
ARE YOU JUST GONNA LET HIM HAVE HIS WAY?!
UUNH...
UUUNH!
The Musical
Kanan Drama Club × Kanan Ouendan
I DON'T KNOW WHAT TO DO.
COMPROMISE. I HAVE TO COMPROMISE.
WHAT DOES EVERYONE ELSE THINK?
WHAT'S WRONG?
USAMI-SAN.

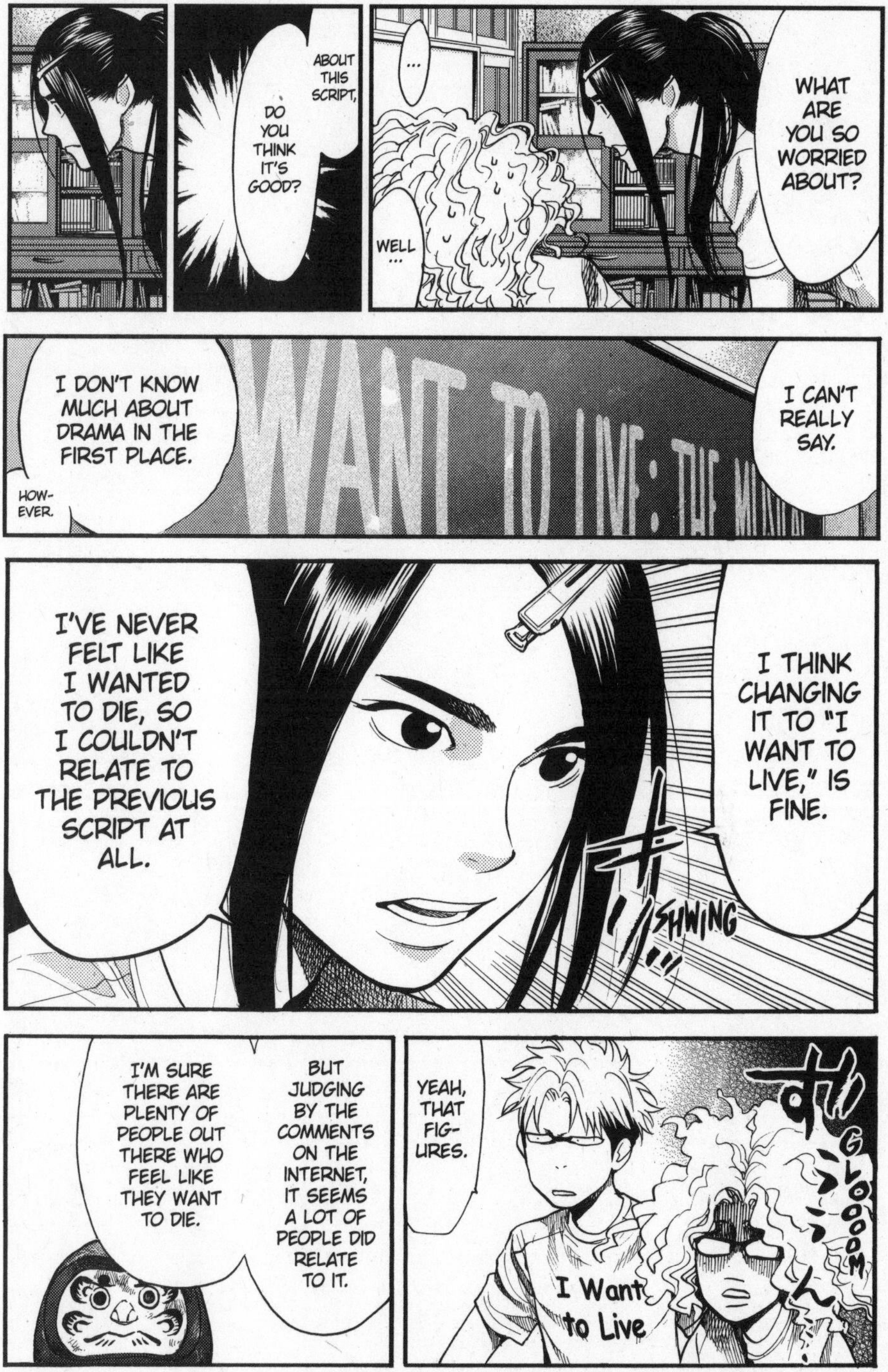
WHAT ARE YOU SO WORRIED ABOUT?
...
WELL...
ABOUT THIS SCRIPT,
DO YOU THINK IT'S GOOD?
I CAN'T REALLY SAY.
WANT TO LIVE: THE
I DON'T KNOW MUCH ABOUT DRAMA IN THE FIRST PLACE.
HOW-EVER.
I THINK CHANGING IT TO "I WANT TO LIVE," IS FINE.
SHWING
I'VE NEVER FELT LIKE I WANTED TO DIE, SO I COULDN'T RELATE TO THE PREVIOUS SCRIPT AT ALL.
GLOOOOOM
YEAH, THAT FIG-URES.
I Want to Live
BUT JUDGING BY THE COMMENTS ON THE INTERNET, IT SEEMS A LOT OF PEOPLE DID RELATE TO IT.
I'M SURE THERE ARE PLENTY OF PEOPLE OUT THERE WHO FEEL LIKE THEY WANT TO DIE.

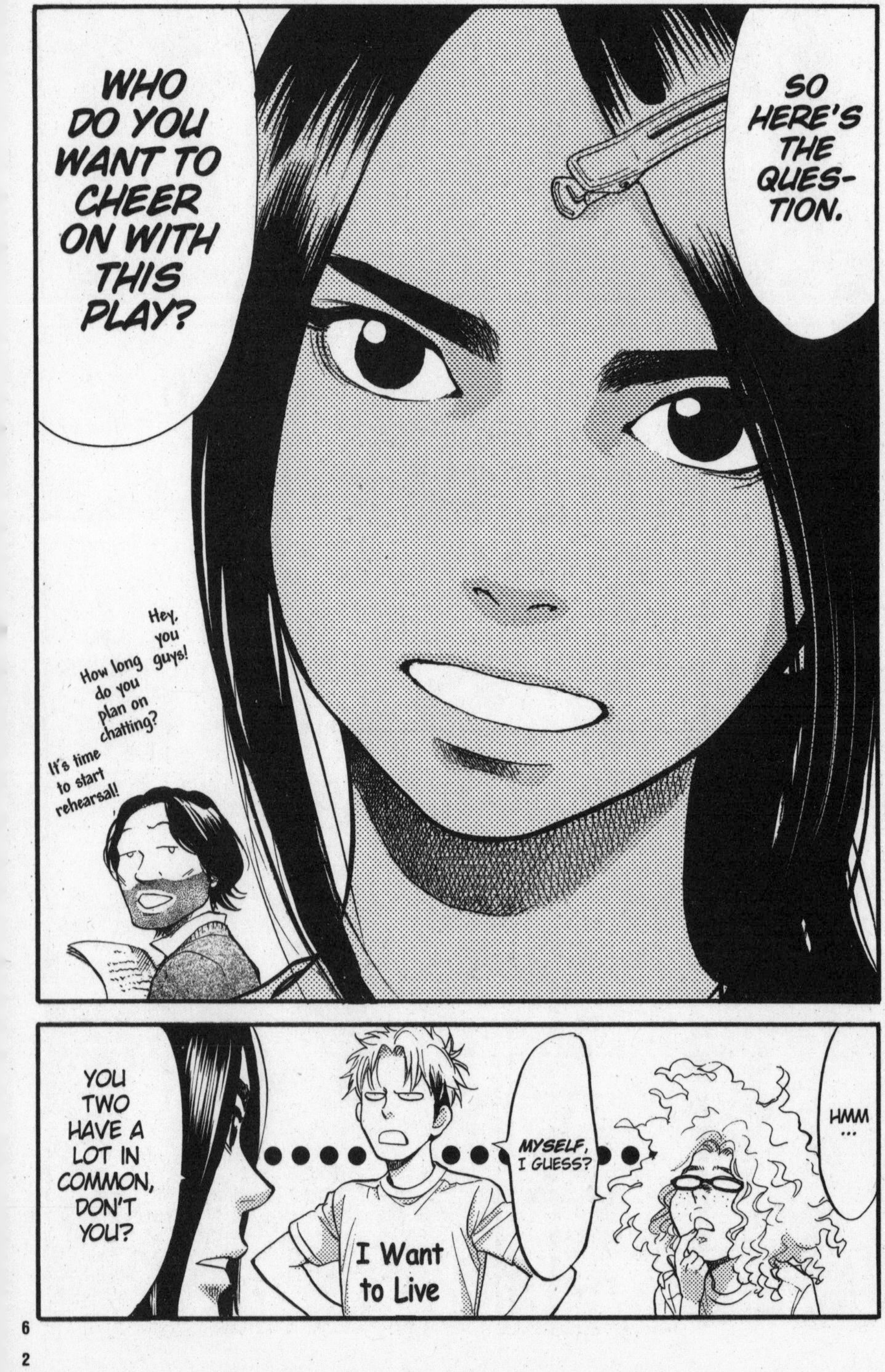
SO HERE'S THE QUES-TION.
WHO DO YOU WANT TO CHEER ON WITH THIS PLAY?
Hey, you guys!
How long do you plan on chatting?
It's time to start rehearsal!
HMM ...
MYSELF, I GUESS?
I Want to Live
YOU TWO HAVE A LOT IN COMMON, DON'T YOU?

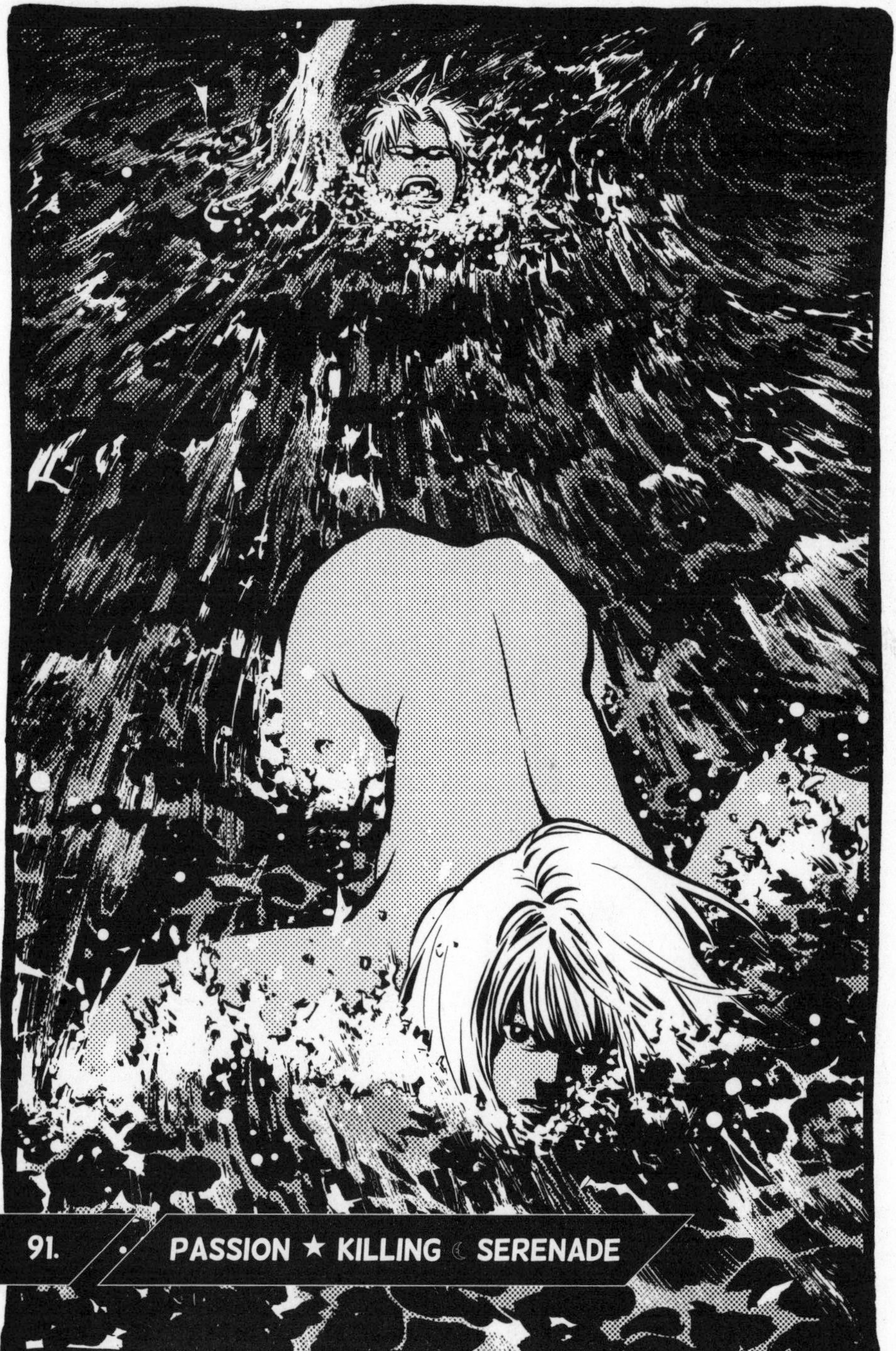

91. PASSION ★ KILLING ☾ SERENADE

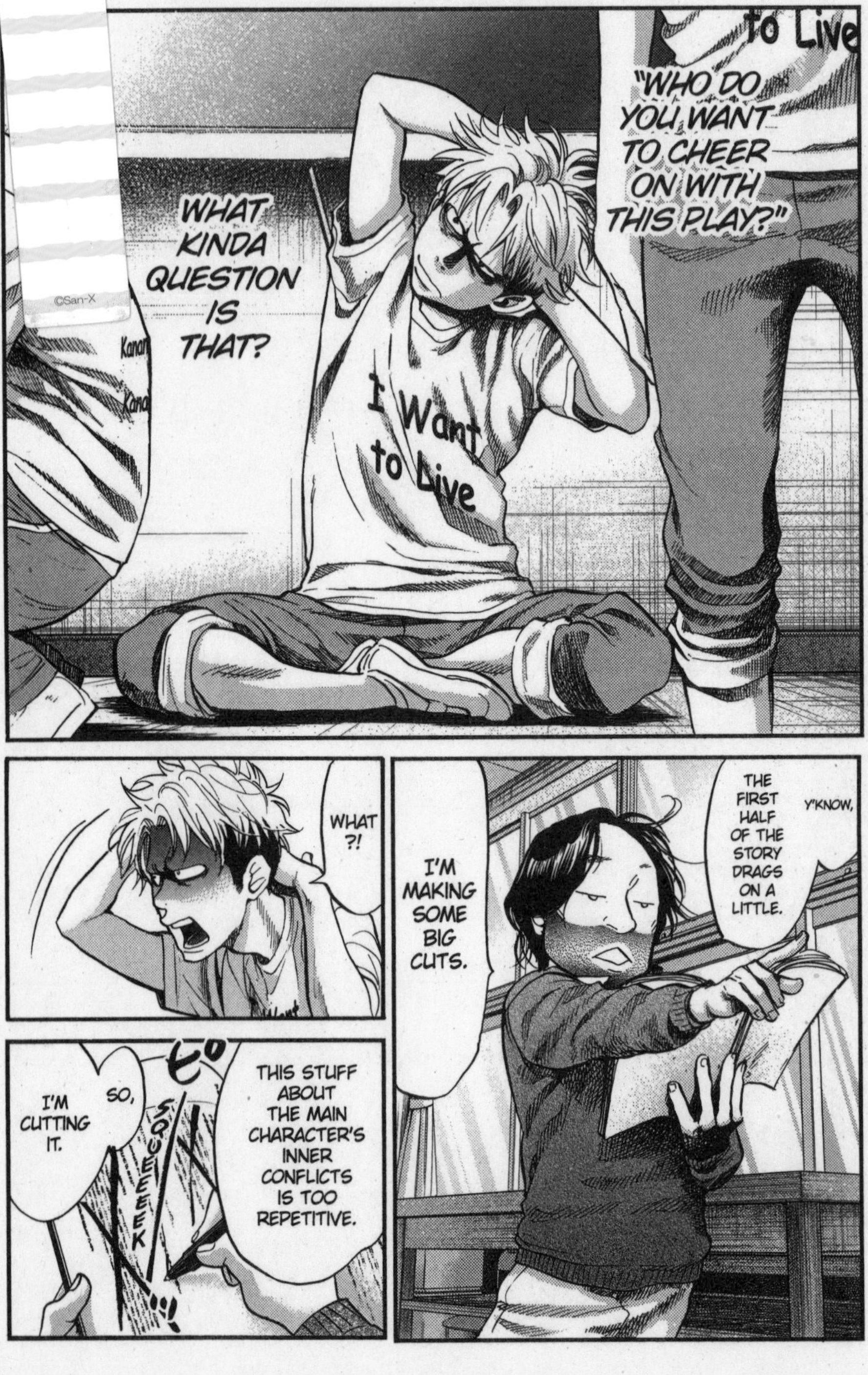

to Live
"WHO DO YOU WANT TO CHEER ON WITH THIS PLAY?"
WHAT KINDA QUESTION IS THAT?
I Want to Live
Y'KNOW,
THE FIRST HALF OF THE STORY DRAGS ON A LITTLE.
I'M MAKING SOME BIG CUTS.
WHAT?!
THIS STUFF ABOUT THE MAIN CHARACTER'S INNER CONFLICTS IS TOO REPETITIVE.
SO,
I'M CUTTING IT.
SQUEEEEK

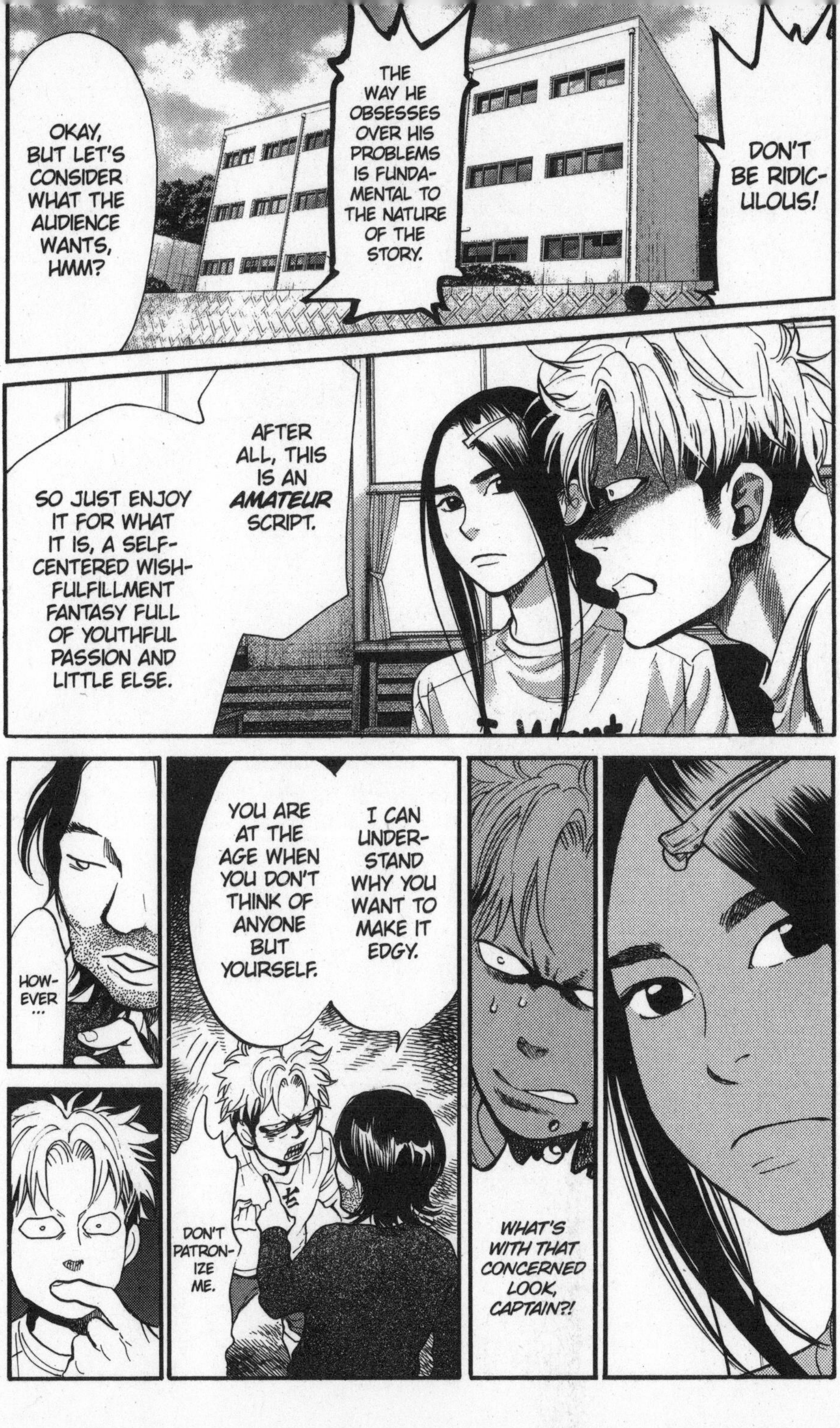
DON'T BE RIDICULOUS!
THE WAY HE OBSESSES OVER HIS PROBLEMS IS FUNDAMENTAL TO THE NATURE OF THE STORY.
OKAY, BUT LET'S CONSIDER WHAT THE AUDIENCE WANTS, HMM?
AFTER ALL, THIS IS AN *AMATEUR* SCRIPT.
SO JUST ENJOY IT FOR WHAT IT IS, A SELF-CENTERED WISH-FULFILLMENT FANTASY FULL OF YOUTHFUL PASSION AND LITTLE ELSE.
WHAT'S WITH THAT CONCERNED LOOK, CAPTAIN?!
I CAN UNDERSTAND WHY YOU WANT TO MAKE IT EDGY.
YOU ARE AT THE AGE WHEN YOU DON'T THINK OF ANYONE BUT YOURSELF.
DON'T PATRONIZE ME.
HOWEVER...

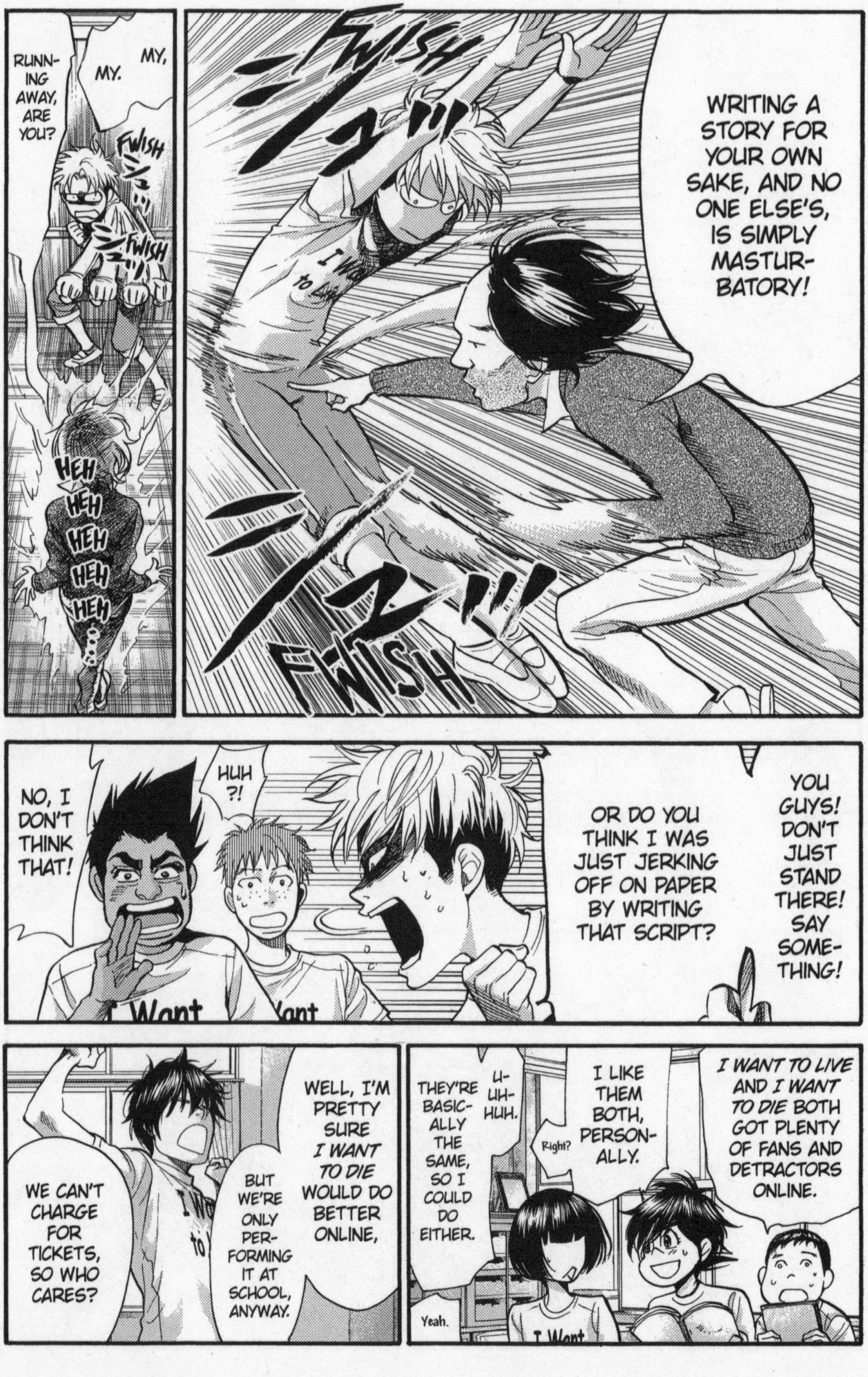
FWISH
WRITING A STORY FOR YOUR OWN SAKE, AND NO ONE ELSE'S, IS SIMPLY MASTURBATORY!
FWISH
MY, MY.
RUNNING AWAY, ARE YOU?
FWISH
FWISH
HEH HEH HEH HEH HEH...
YOU GUYS! DON'T JUST STAND THERE! SAY SOMETHING!
OR DO YOU THINK I WAS JUST JERKING OFF ON PAPER BY WRITING THAT SCRIPT?
HUH?!
NO, I DON'T THINK THAT!
I WANT TO LIVE AND *I WANT TO DIE* BOTH GOT PLENTY OF FANS AND DETRACTORS ONLINE.
I LIKE THEM BOTH, PERSONALLY.
Right?
UH-HUH.
THEY'RE BASICALLY THE SAME, SO I COULD DO EITHER.
Yeah.
WELL, I'M PRETTY SURE *I WANT TO DIE* WOULD DO BETTER ONLINE,
BUT WE'RE ONLY PERFORMING IT AT SCHOOL, ANYWAY.
WE CAN'T CHARGE FOR TICKETS, SO WHO CARES?

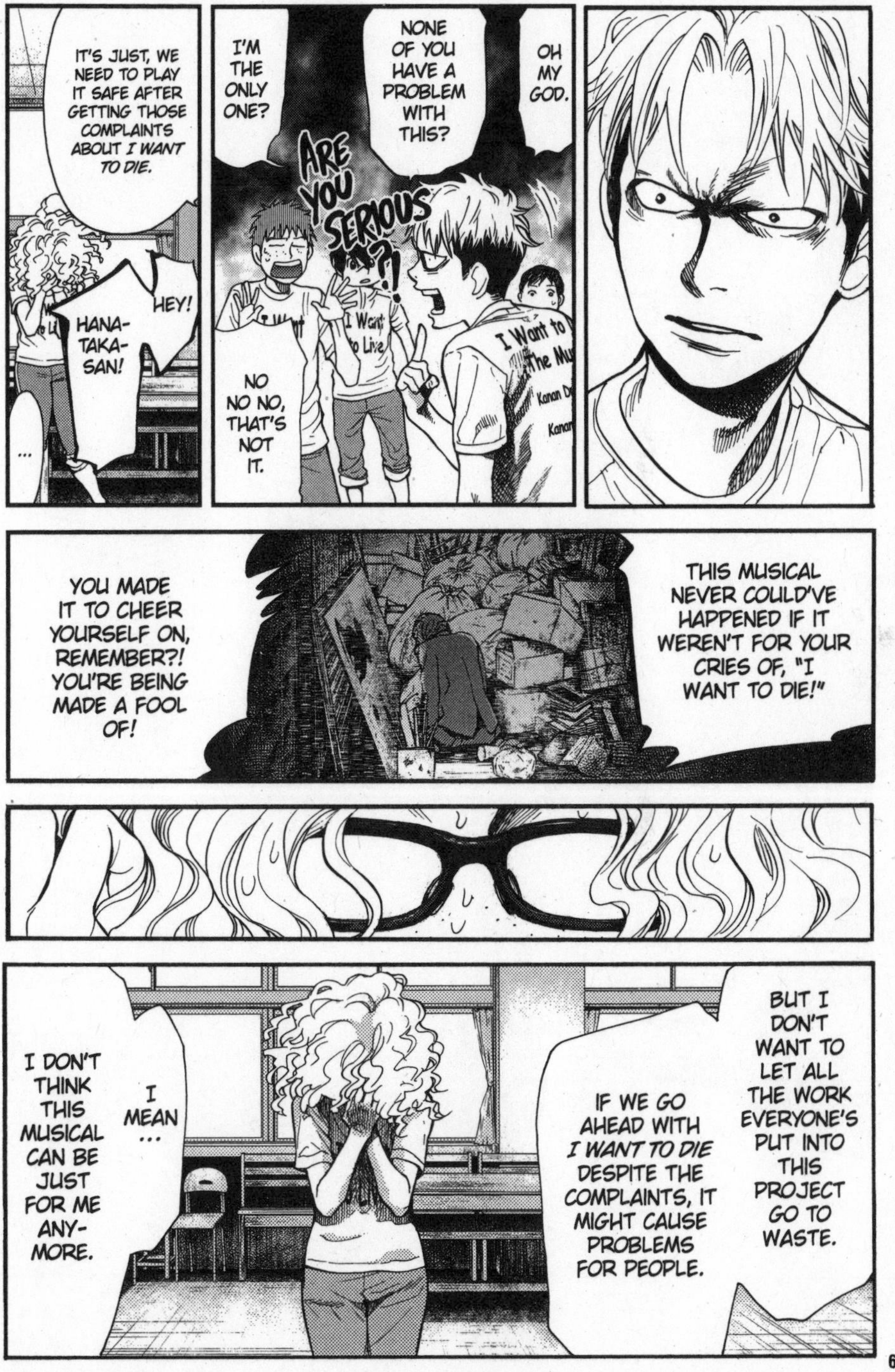
OH MY GOD.
NONE OF YOU HAVE A PROBLEM WITH THIS?
I'M THE ONLY ONE?
ARE YOU SERIOUS?!
NO NO NO, THAT'S NOT IT.
IT'S JUST, WE NEED TO PLAY IT SAFE AFTER GETTING THOSE COMPLAINTS ABOUT *I WANT TO DIE*.
HEY! HANA-TAKA-SAN!
...
THIS MUSICAL NEVER COULD'VE HAPPENED IF IT WEREN'T FOR YOUR CRIES OF, "I WANT TO DIE!"
YOU MADE IT TO CHEER YOURSELF ON, REMEMBER?! YOU'RE BEING MADE A FOOL OF!
BUT I DON'T WANT TO LET ALL THE WORK EVERYONE'S PUT INTO THIS PROJECT GO TO WASTE.
IF WE GO AHEAD WITH *I WANT TO DIE* DESPITE THE COMPLAINTS, IT MIGHT CAUSE PROBLEMS FOR PEOPLE.
I MEAN...
I DON'T THINK THIS MUSICAL CAN BE JUST FOR ME ANY-MORE.

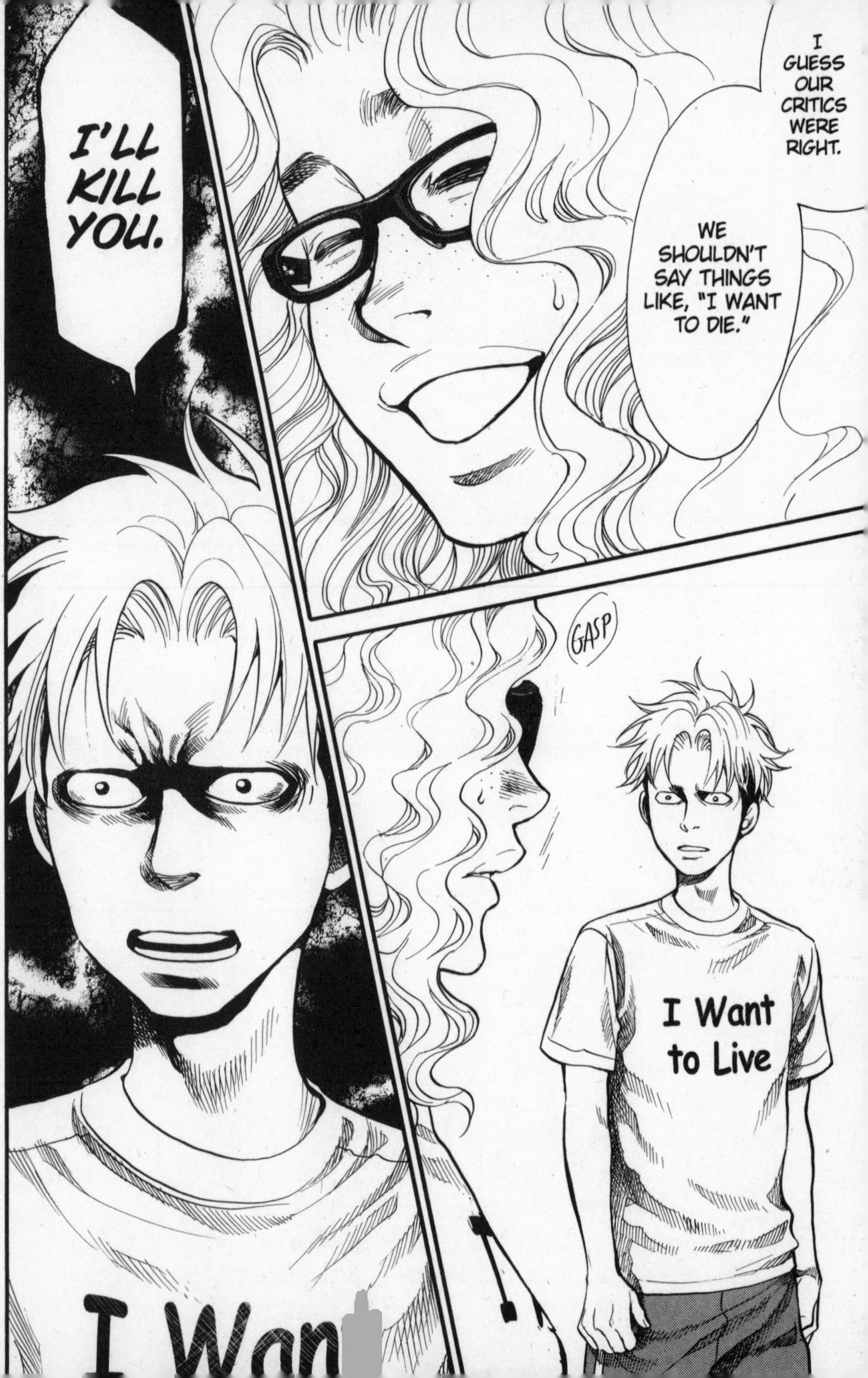
I GUESS OUR CRITICS WERE RIGHT.
WE SHOULDN'T SAY THINGS LIKE, "I WANT TO DIE."
GASP
I Want to Live
I'LL KILL YOU.
I Wan

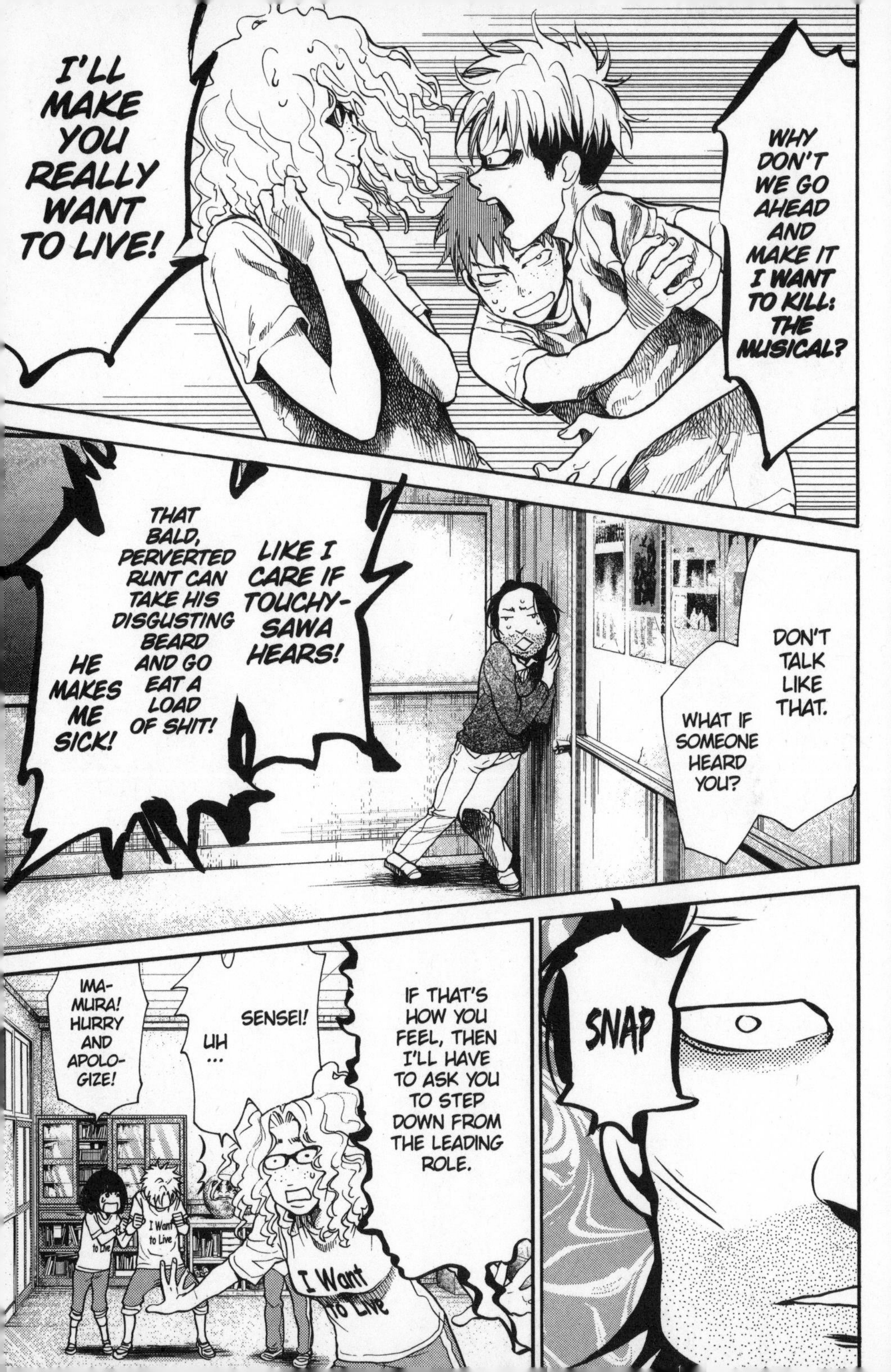
WHY DON'T WE GO AHEAD AND MAKE IT I WANT TO KILL: THE MUSICAL?
I'LL MAKE YOU REALLY WANT TO LIVE!
DON'T TALK LIKE THAT.
WHAT IF SOMEONE HEARD YOU?
LIKE I CARE IF TOUCHY-SAWA HEARS!
THAT BALD, PERVERTED RUNT CAN TAKE HIS DISGUSTING BEARD AND GO EAT A LOAD OF SHIT!
HE MAKES ME SICK!
SNAP
IF THAT'S HOW YOU FEEL, THEN I'LL HAVE TO ASK YOU TO STEP DOWN FROM THE LEADING ROLE.
SENSEI!
UH ...
IMA-MURA! HURRY AND APOLO-GIZE!

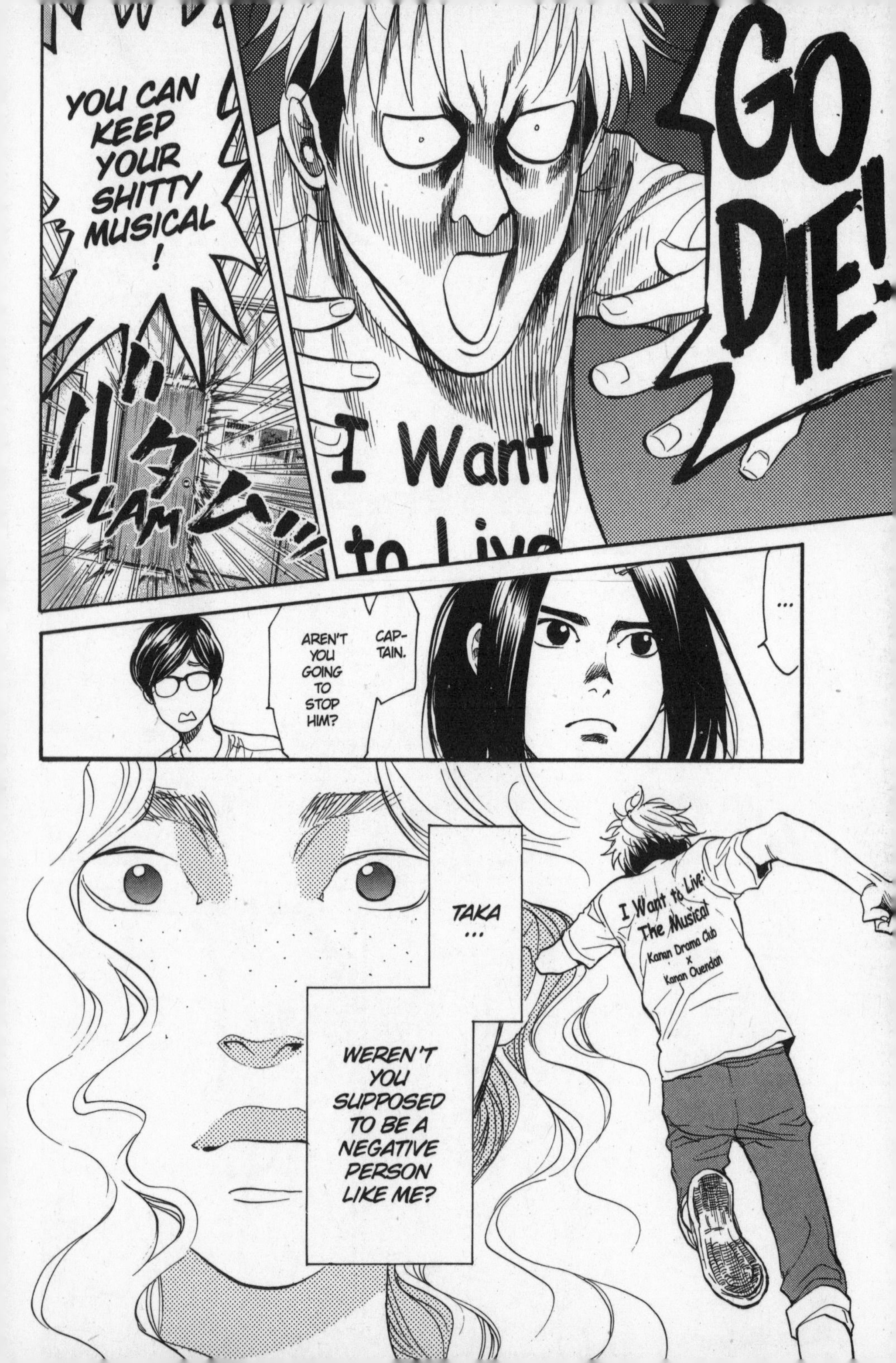
GO DIE!
I Want to Live
YOU CAN KEEP YOUR SHITTY MUSICAL!
SLAM
...
CAPTAIN.
AREN'T YOU GOING TO STOP HIM?
TAKA ...
WEREN'T YOU SUPPOSED TO BE A NEGATIVE PERSON LIKE ME?
I Want to Live: The Musical
Kanan Drama Club x Kanan Ouendan

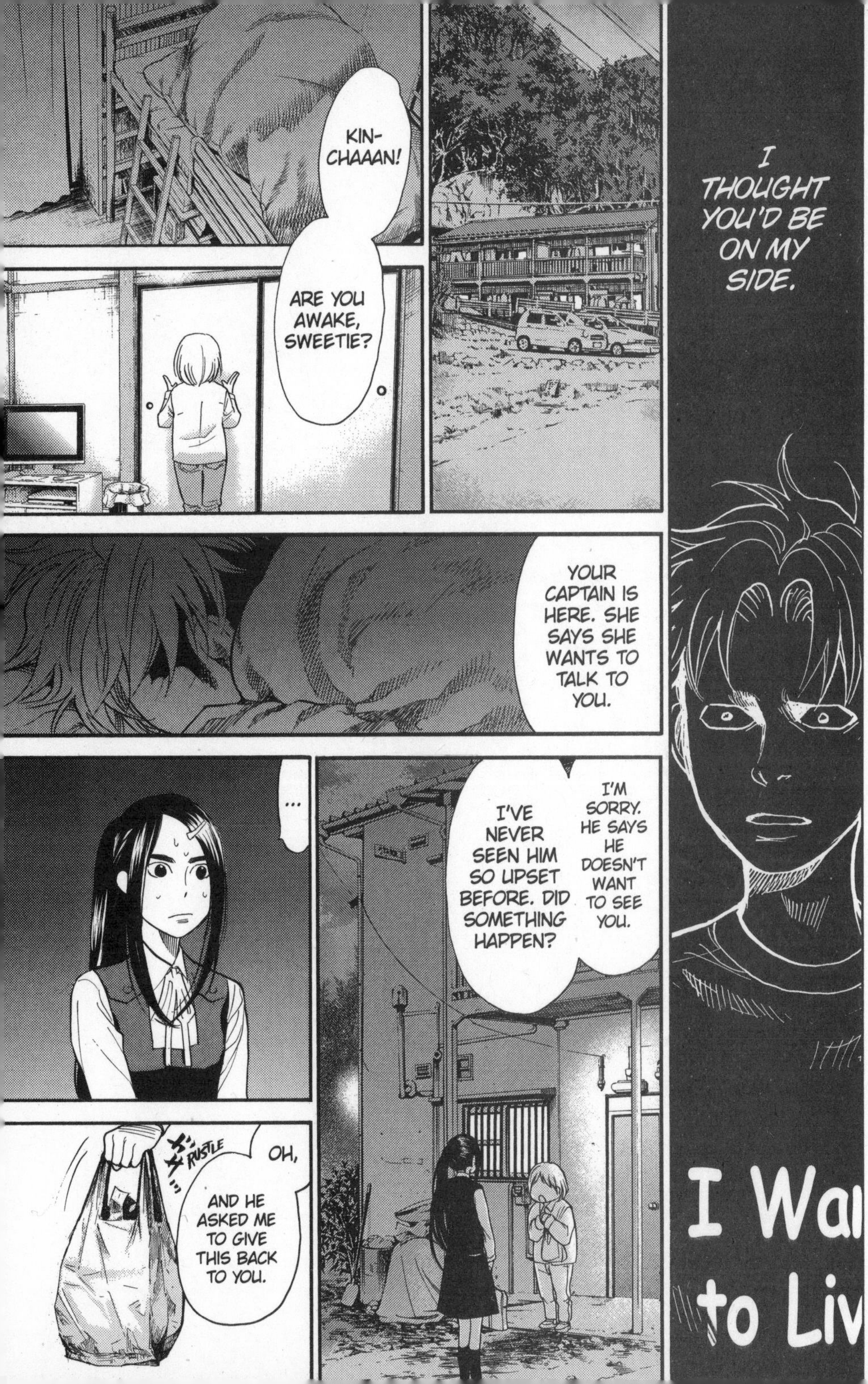
I THOUGHT YOU'D BE ON MY SIDE.
I Wan
to Liv
KIN-CHAAAN!
ARE YOU AWAKE, SWEETIE?
YOUR CAPTAIN IS HERE. SHE SAYS SHE WANTS TO TALK TO YOU.
I'M SORRY. HE SAYS HE DOESN'T WANT TO SEE YOU.
I'VE NEVER SEEN HIM SO UPSET BEFORE. DID SOMETHING HAPPEN?
OH,
AND HE ASKED ME TO GIVE THIS BACK TO YOU.
...
RUSTLE

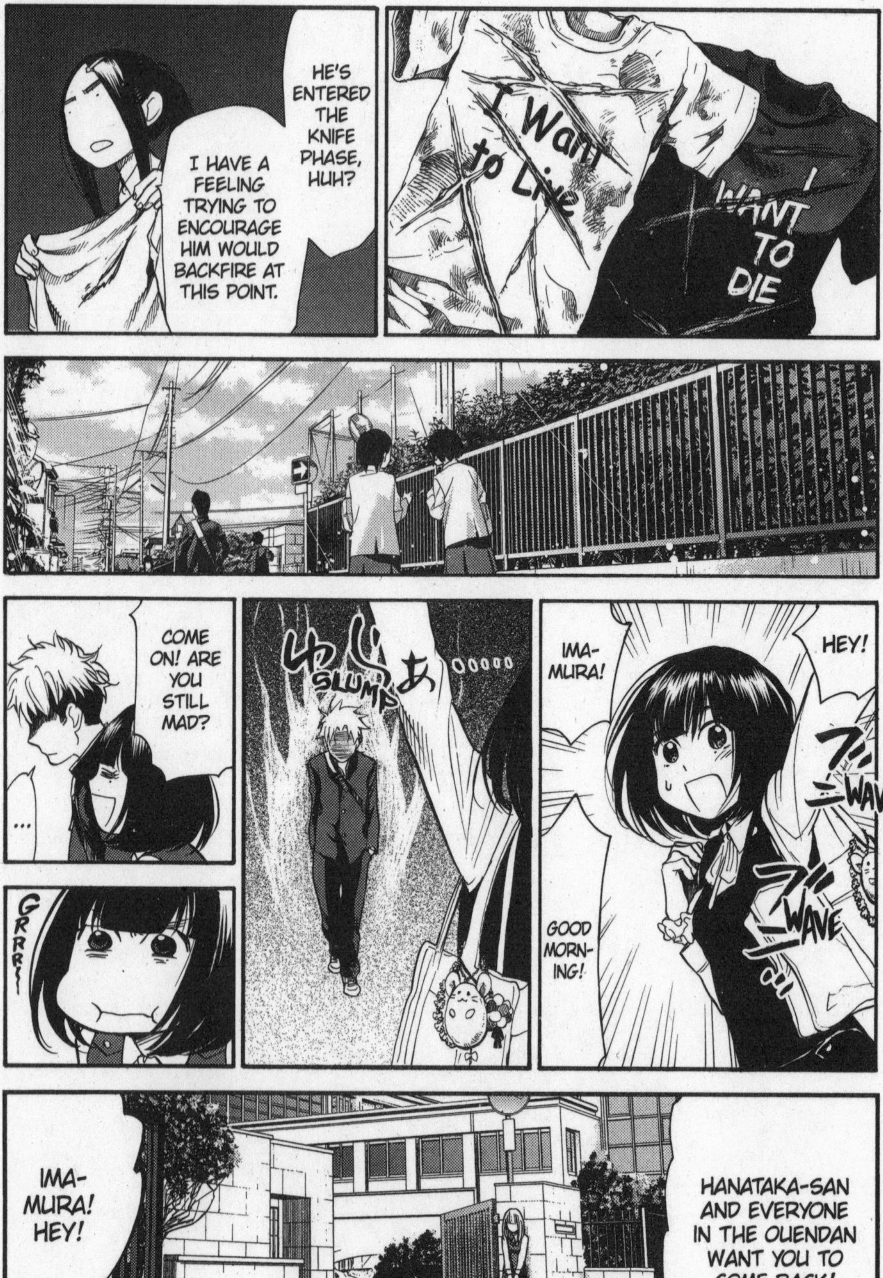
I Want to Die
I WANT TO DIE
HE'S ENTERED THE KNIFE PHASE, HUH?
I HAVE A FEELING TRYING TO ENCOURAGE HIM WOULD BACKFIRE AT THIS POINT.
HEY!
IMA-MURA!
WAVE
WAVE
GOOD MORN-ING!
SLUMP
ooooo
COME ON! ARE YOU STILL MAD?
...
GRRR~
HANATAKA-SAN AND EVERYONE IN THE OUENDAN WANT YOU TO COME BACK!
IMA-MURA! HEY!

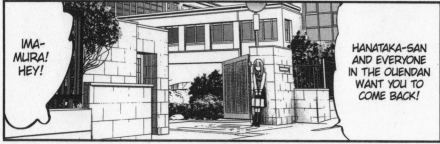

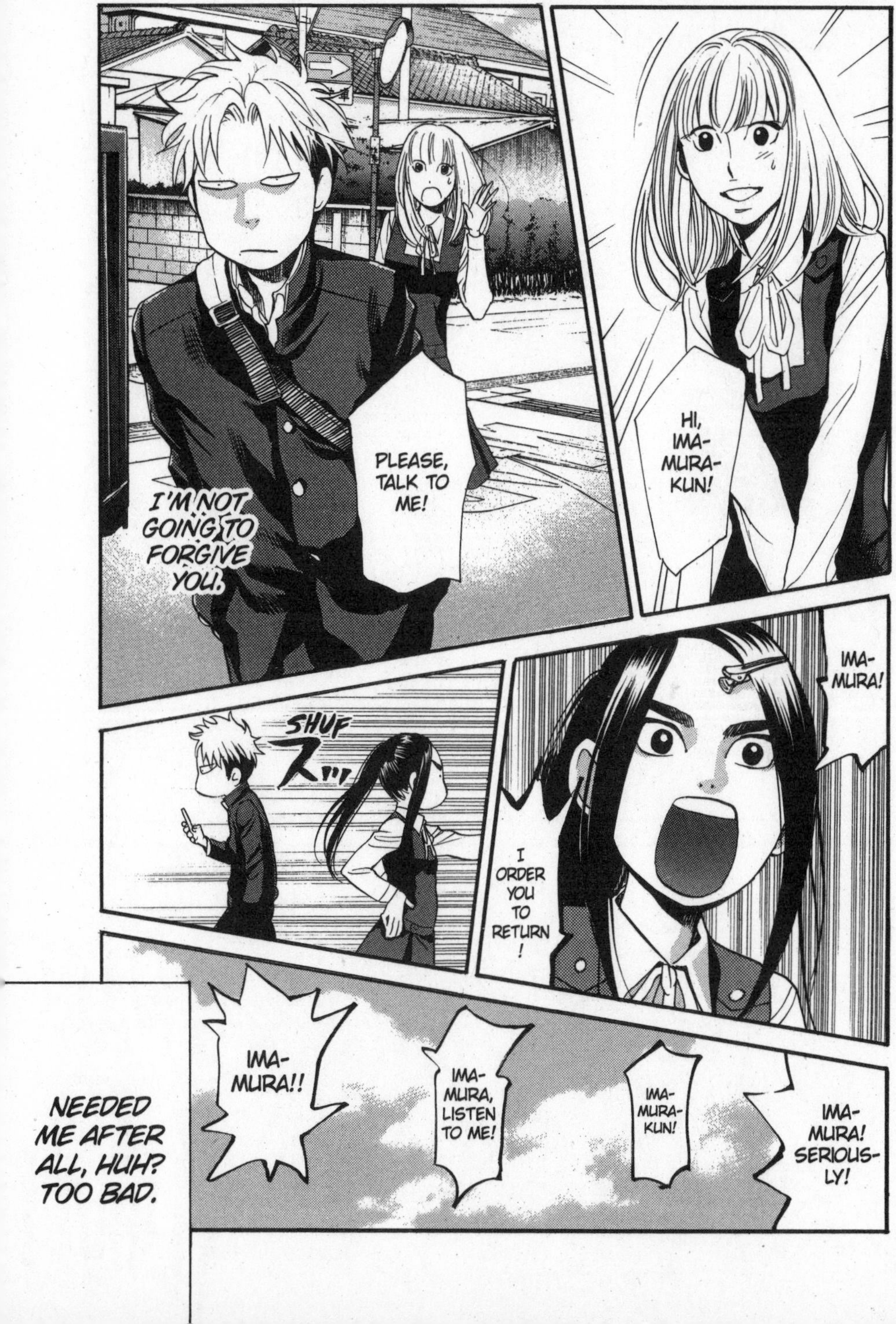
HI, IMA-MURA-KUN!
PLEASE, TALK TO ME!
I'M NOT GOING TO FORGIVE YOU.
IMA-MURA!
I ORDER YOU TO RETURN!
SHUF
ス
IMA-MURA! SERIOUS-LY!
IMA-MURA-KUN!
IMA-MURA, LISTEN TO ME!
IMA-MURA!!
NEEDED ME AFTER ALL, HUH? TOO BAD.

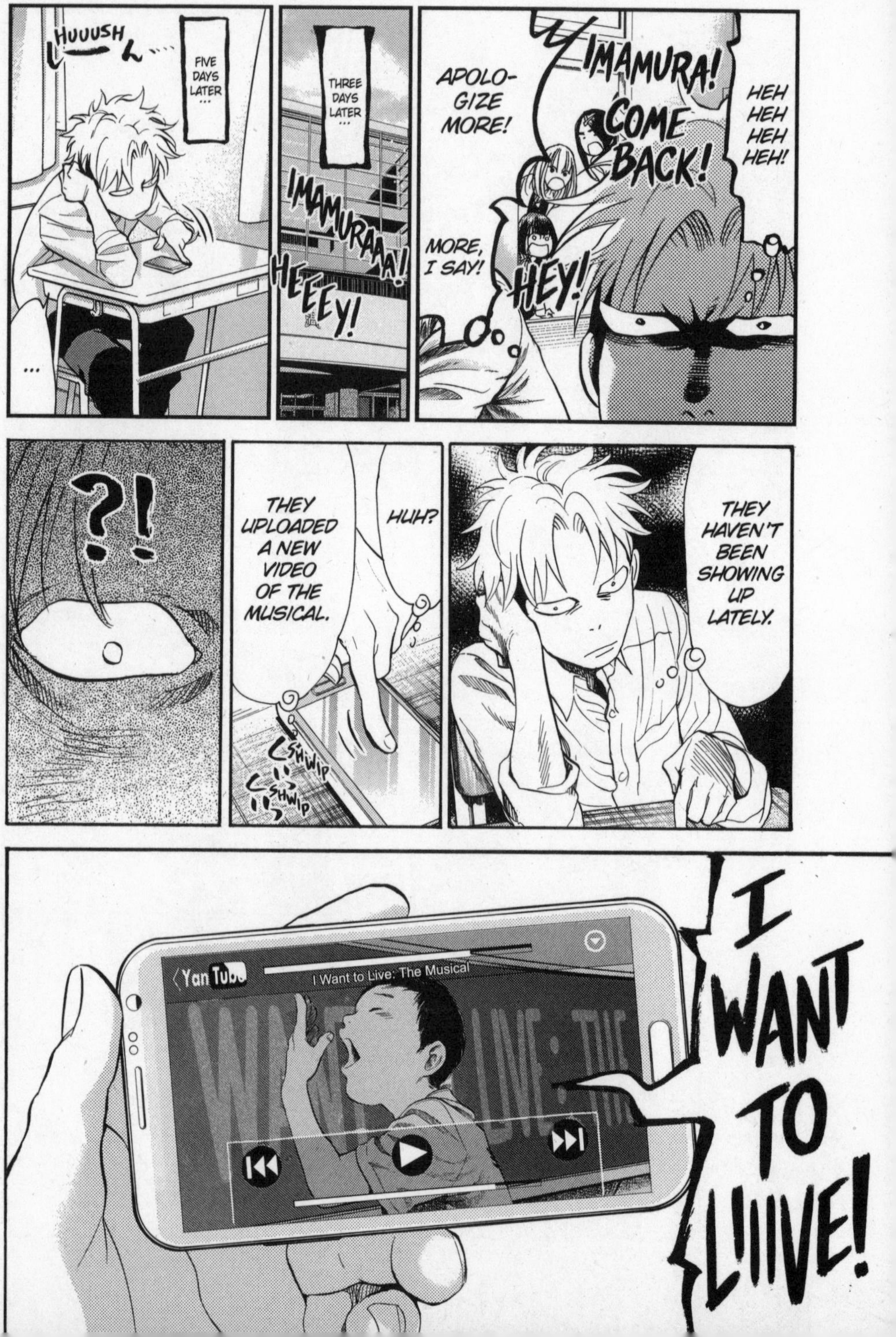
HEH HEH HEH HEH!
IMAMURA! COME BACK!
APOLO-GIZE MORE!
HEY!
MORE, I SAY!
THREE DAYS LATER...
IMAMURAAAA! HEEEEY!
FIVE DAYS LATER...
HUUUSH
...
THEY HAVEN'T BEEN SHOWING UP LATELY.
HUH?
THEY UPLOADED A NEW VIDEO OF THE MUSICAL.
SHWIP
SHWIP
?!
I WANT TO LIIIVE!
YanTube
I Want to Live: The Musical

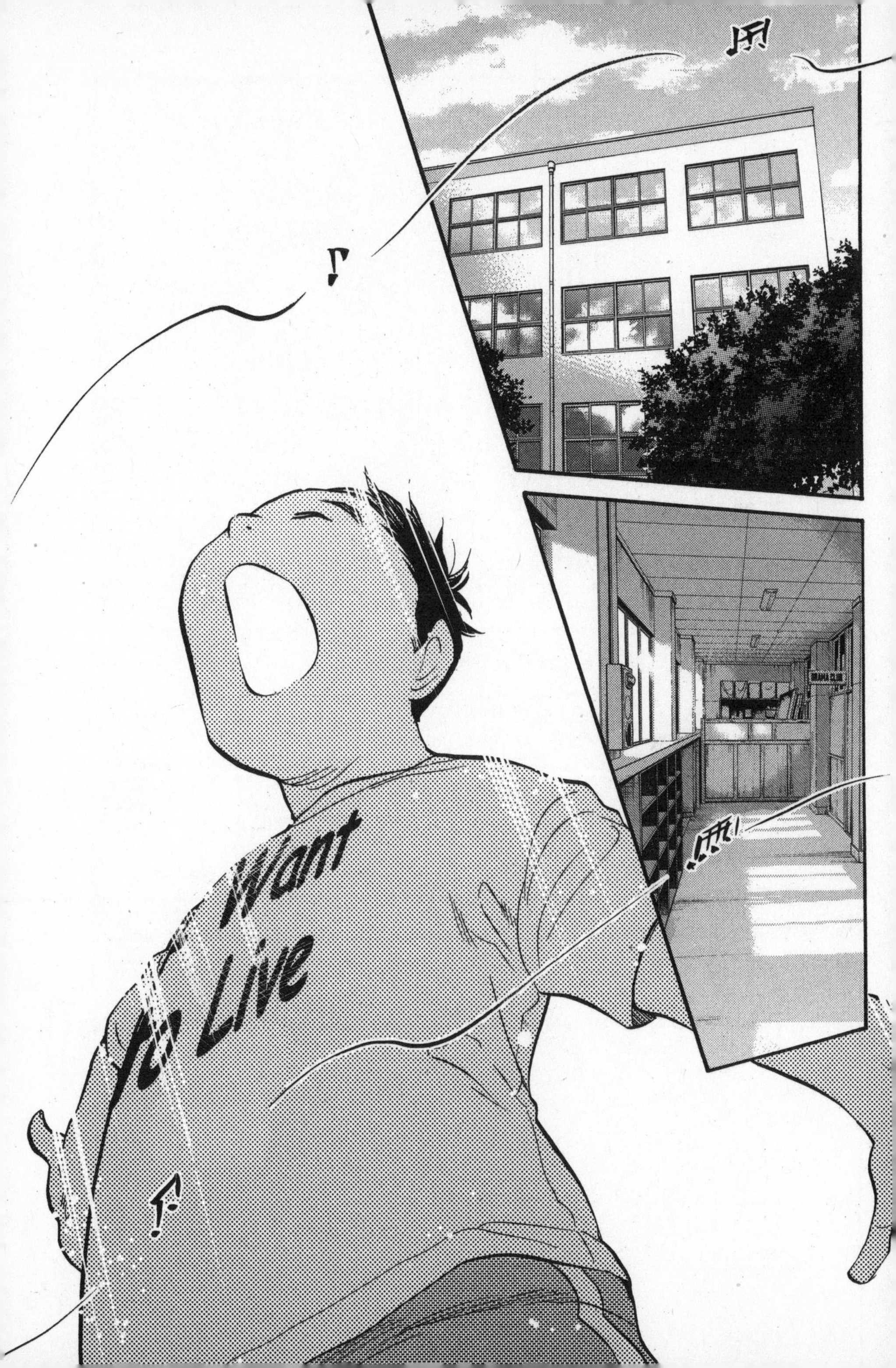
DRAMA CLUB
Want
Live

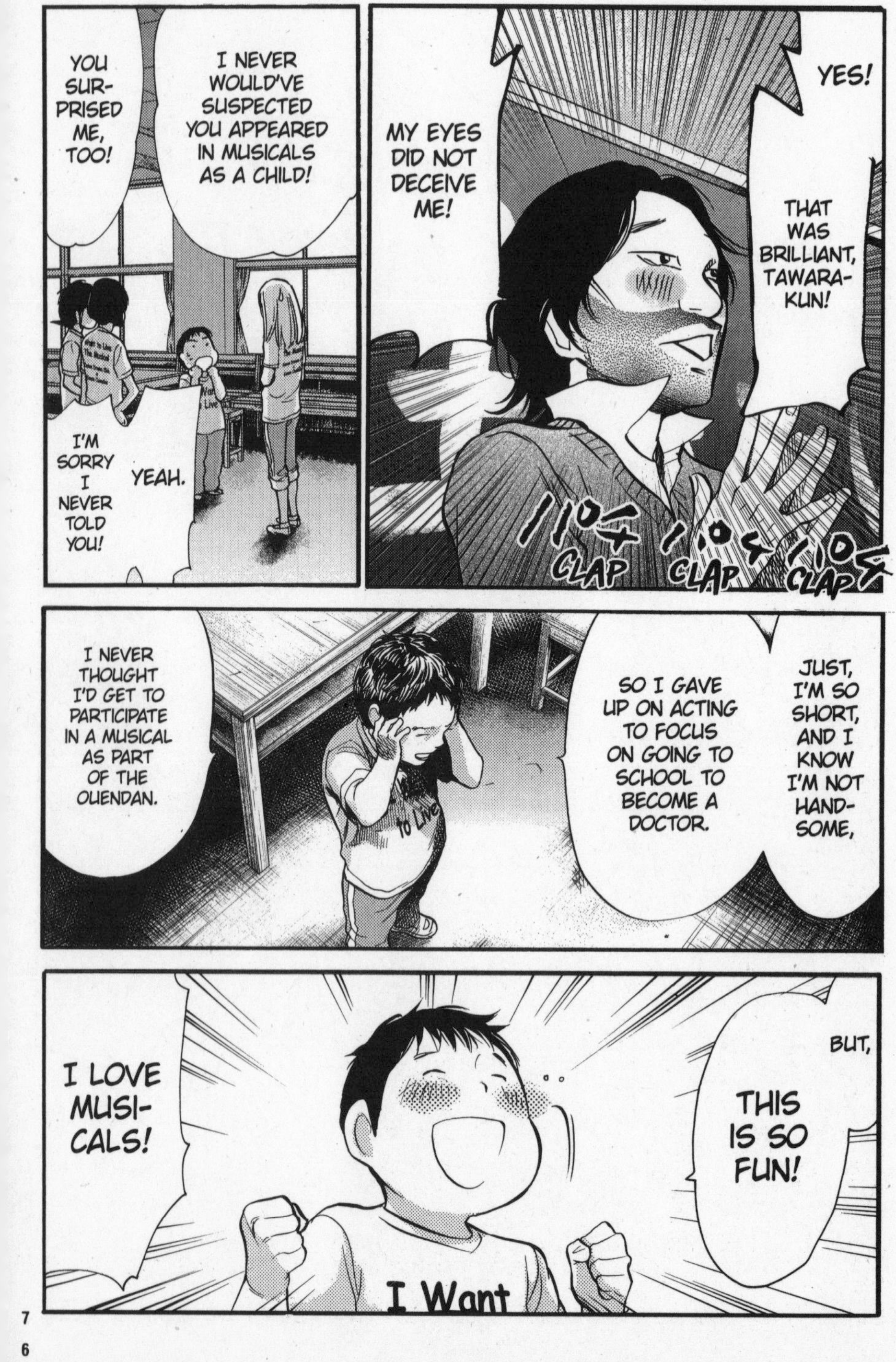
YES!
MY EYES DID NOT DECEIVE ME!
THAT WAS BRILLIANT, TAWARA-KUN!
CLAP CLAP CLAP
I NEVER WOULD'VE SUSPECTED YOU APPEARED IN MUSICALS AS A CHILD!
YOU SURPRISED ME, TOO!
YEAH.
I'M SORRY I NEVER TOLD YOU!
JUST, I'M SO SHORT, AND I KNOW I'M NOT HANDSOME,
SO I GAVE UP ON ACTING TO FOCUS ON GOING TO SCHOOL TO BECOME A DOCTOR.
I NEVER THOUGHT I'D GET TO PARTICIPATE IN A MUSICAL AS PART OF THE OUENDAN.
BUT,
THIS IS SO FUN!
I LOVE MUSICALS!
I Want

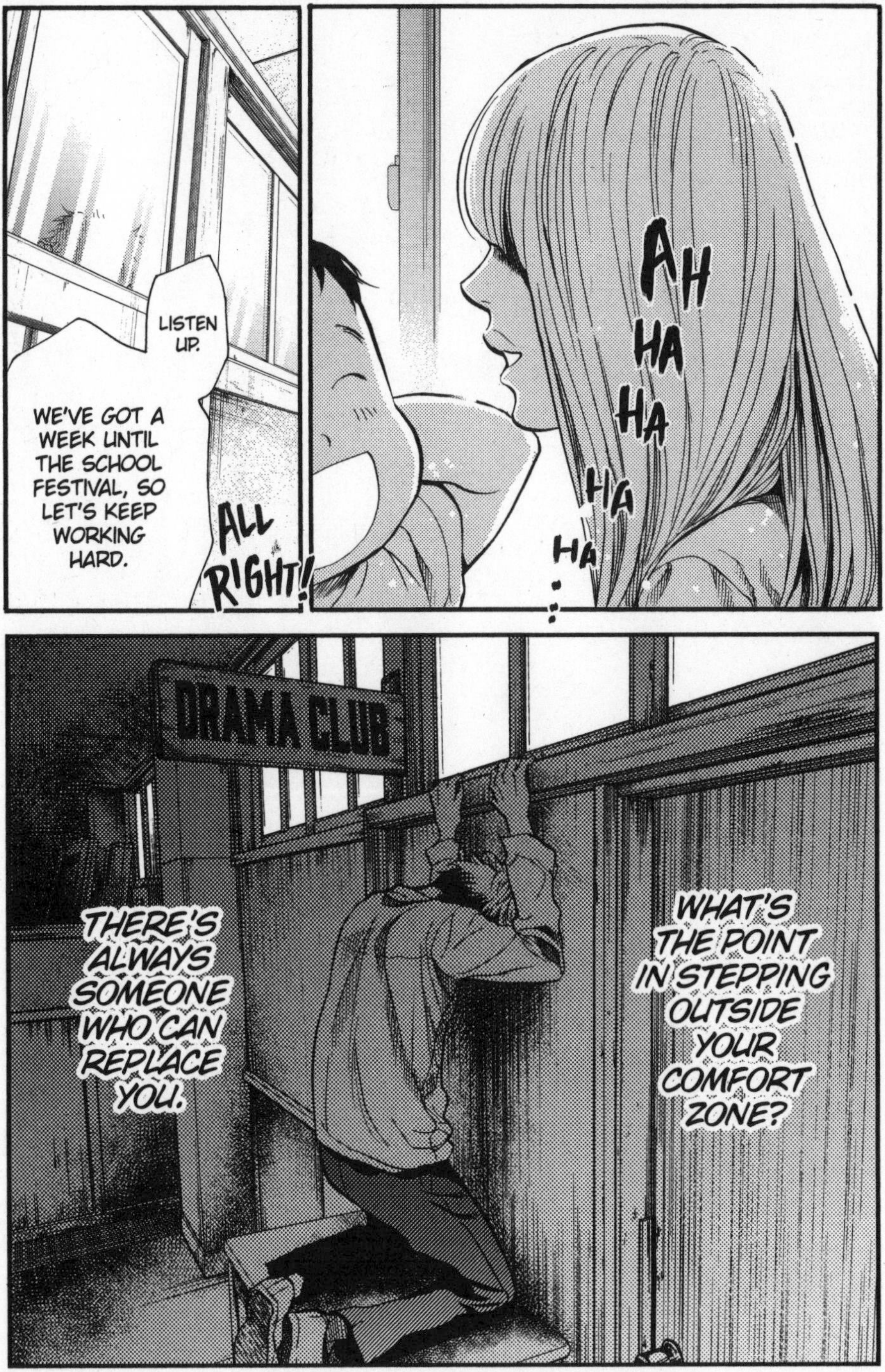
AH HA HA HA HA...
LISTEN UP.
WE'VE GOT A WEEK UNTIL THE SCHOOL FESTIVAL, SO LET'S KEEP WORKING HARD.
ALL RIGHT!
DRAMA CLUB
WHAT'S THE POINT IN STEPPING OUTSIDE YOUR COMFORT ZONE?
THERE'S ALWAYS SOMEONE WHO CAN REPLACE YOU.

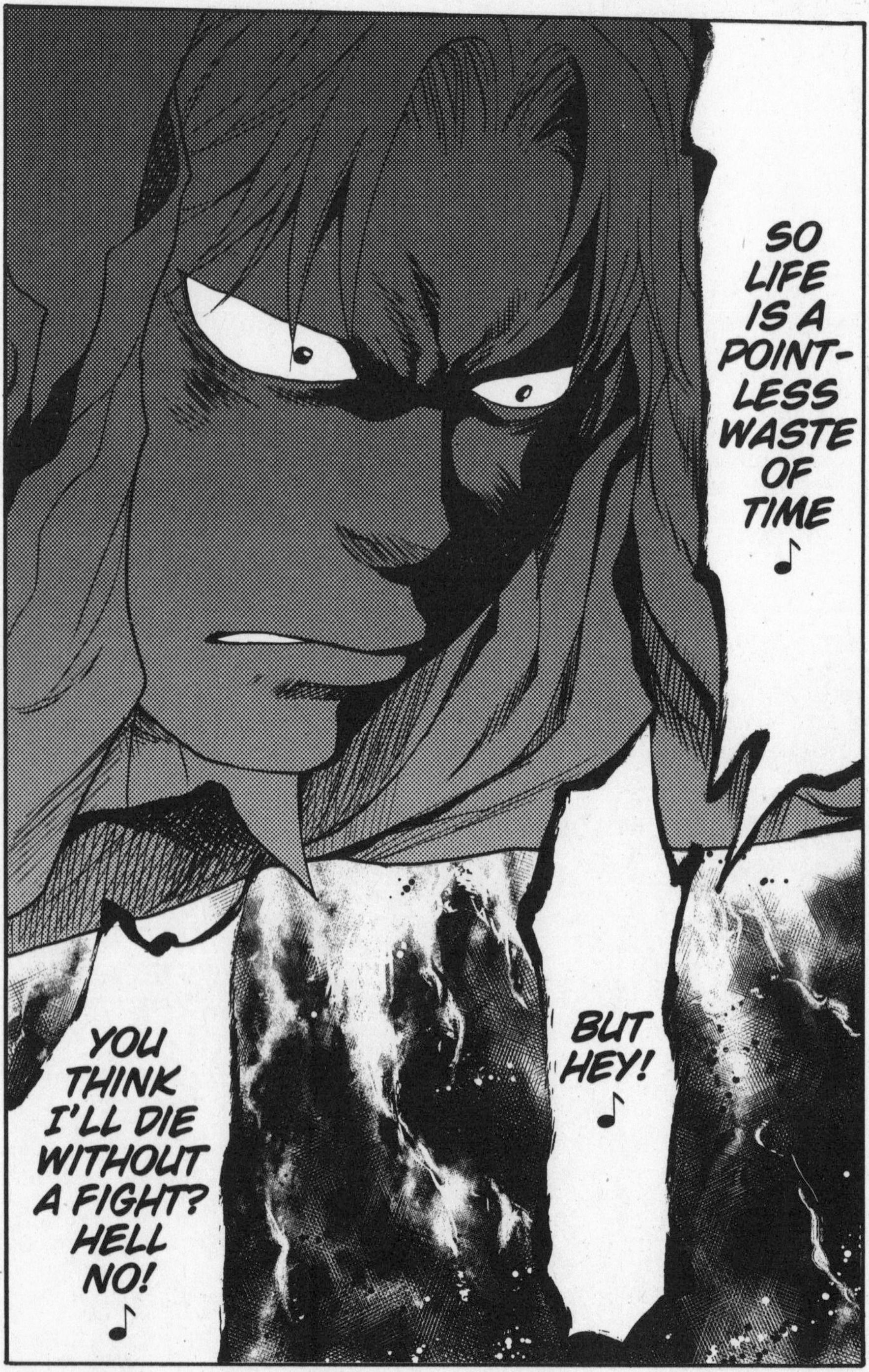
SO LIFE IS A POINTLESS WASTE OF TIME ♪
BUT HEY! ♪
YOU THINK I'LL DIE WITHOUT A FIGHT? HELL NO! ♪

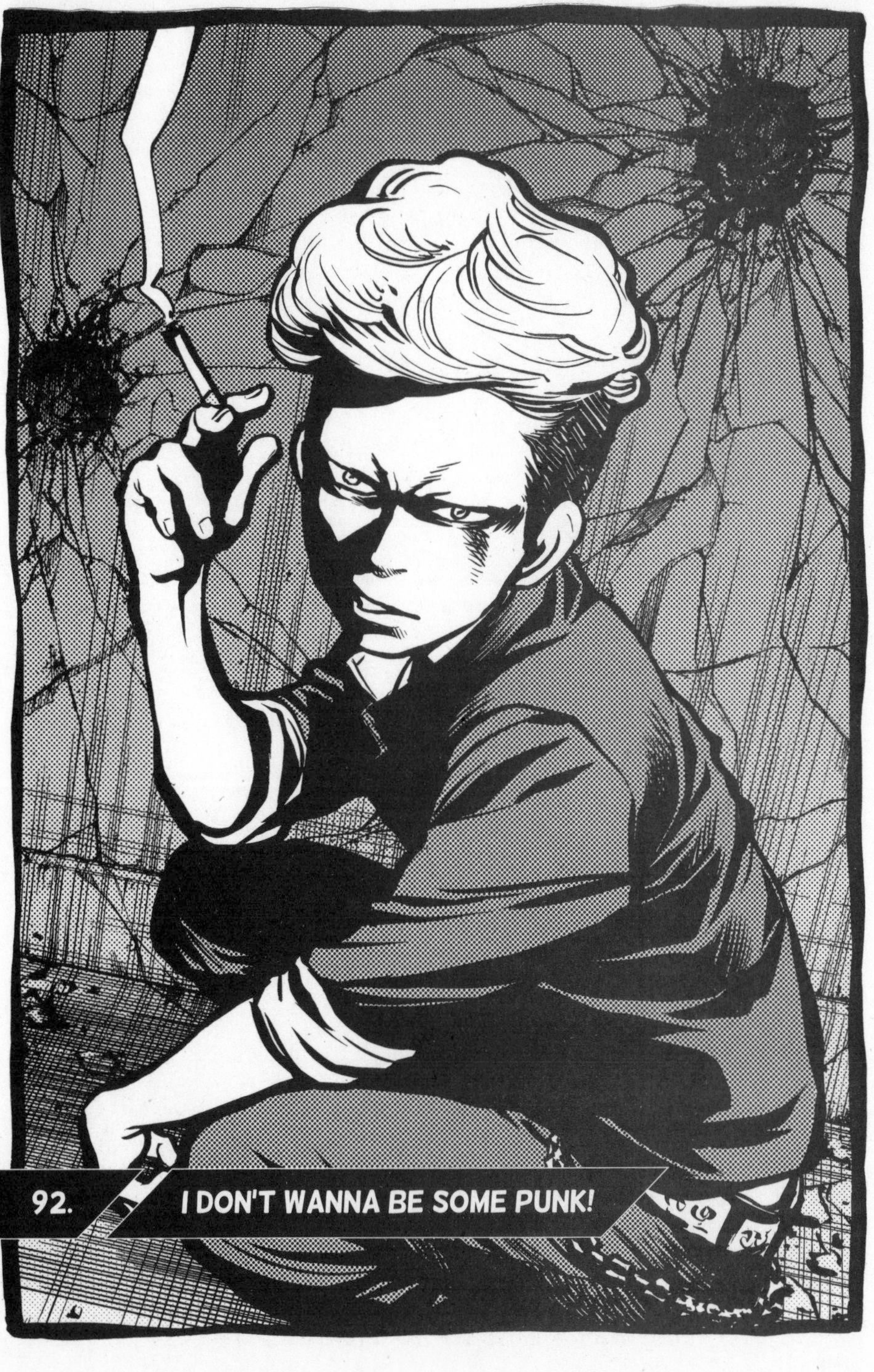

92. I DON'T WANNA BE SOME PUNK!

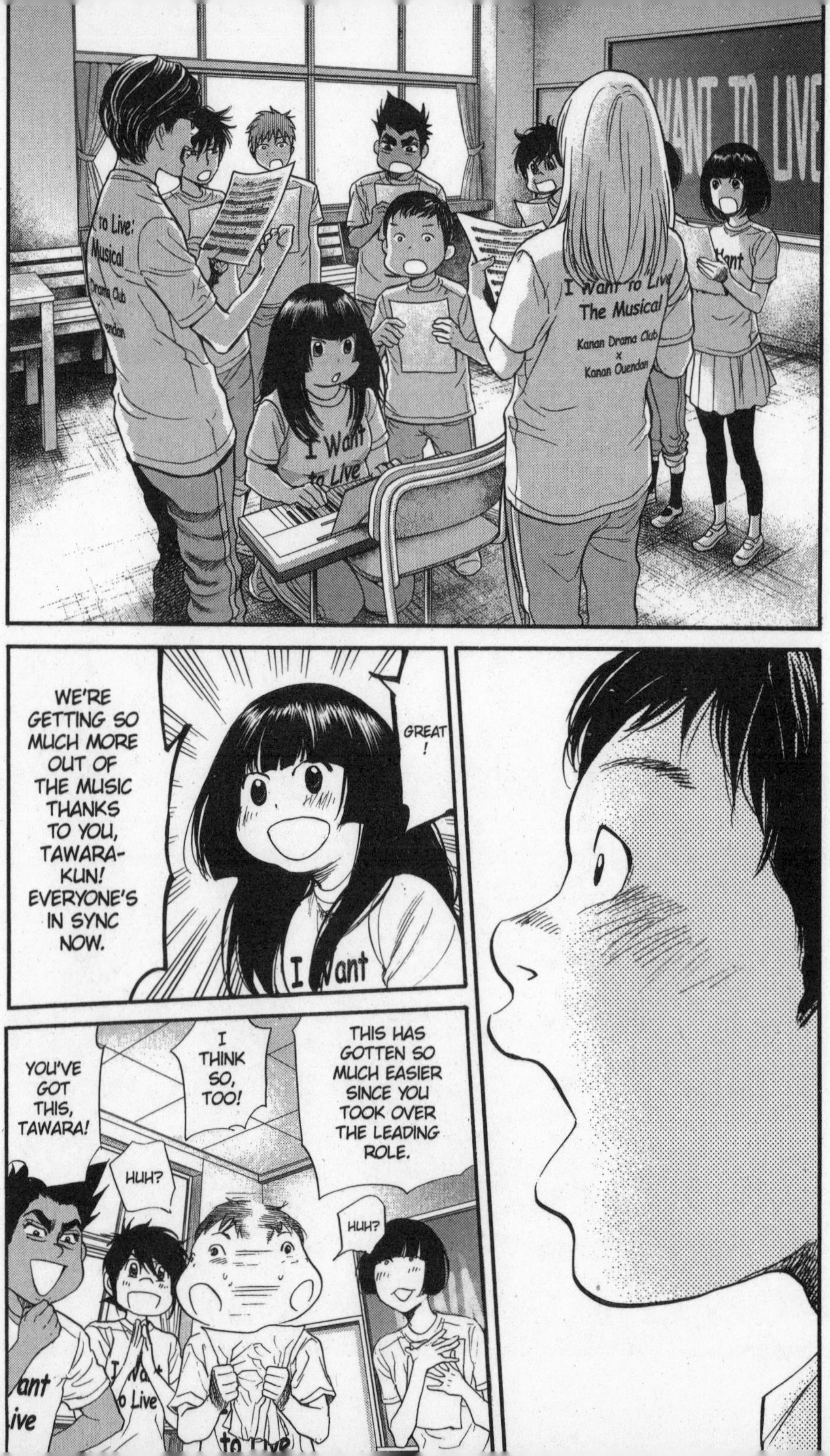
WANT TO LIVE
I Want to Live
The Musical
Kanan Drama Club
x
Kanan Ouendan
GREAT!
WE'RE GETTING SO MUCH MORE OUT OF THE MUSIC THANKS TO YOU, TAWARA-KUN! EVERYONE'S IN SYNC NOW.
THIS HAS GOTTEN SO MUCH EASIER SINCE YOU TOOK OVER THE LEADING ROLE.
I THINK SO, TOO!
YOU'VE GOT THIS, TAWARA!
HUH?
HUH?

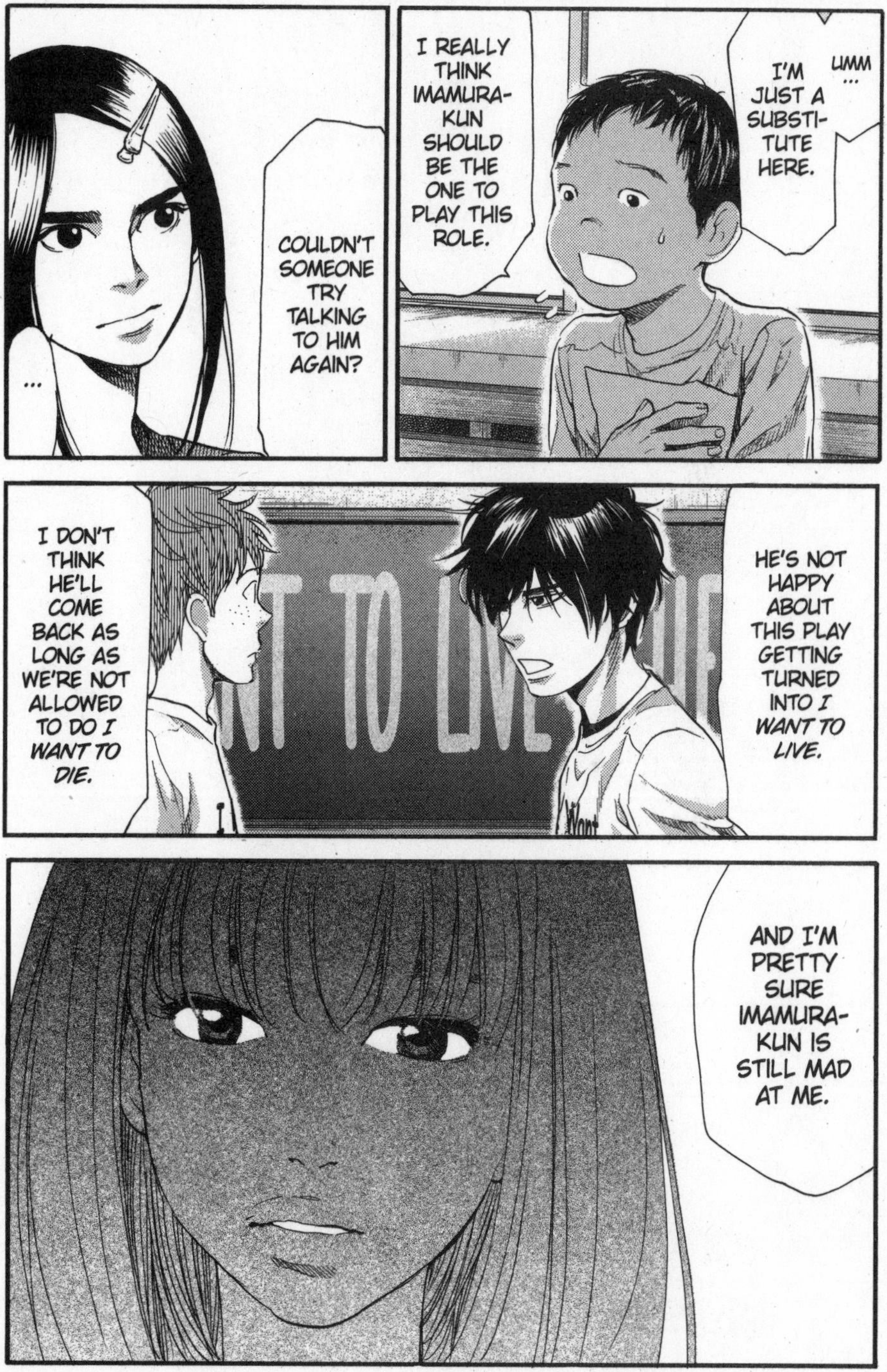
UMM...
I'M JUST A SUBSTI-TUTE HERE.
I REALLY THINK IMAMURA-KUN SHOULD BE THE ONE TO PLAY THIS ROLE.
COULDN'T SOMEONE TRY TALKING TO HIM AGAIN?
...
HE'S NOT HAPPY ABOUT THIS PLAY GETTING TURNED INTO *I WANT TO LIVE*.
I DON'T THINK HE'LL COME BACK AS LONG AS WE'RE NOT ALLOWED TO DO *I WANT TO DIE*.
AND I'M PRETTY SURE IMAMURA-KUN IS STILL MAD AT ME.

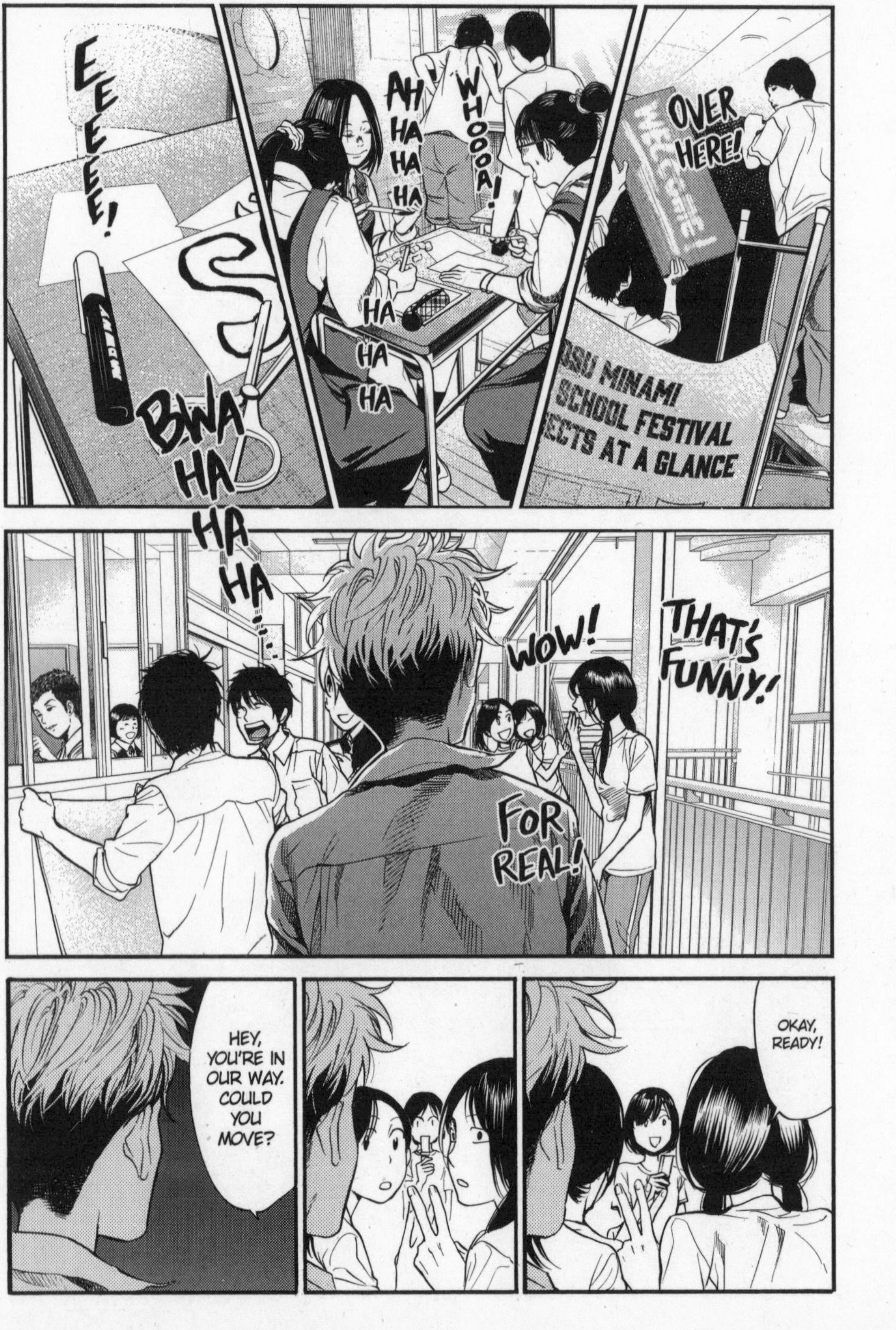
OVER HERE!
OSU MINAMI
SCHOOL FESTIVAL
ECTS AT A GLANCE
WHOOOA!
AH HA HA HA HA
HA HA HA HA
EEEEEE!
BWA HA HA HA...!
THAT'S FUNNY!
WOW!
FOR REAL!
OKAY, READY!
HEY, YOU'RE IN OUR WAY. COULD YOU MOVE?

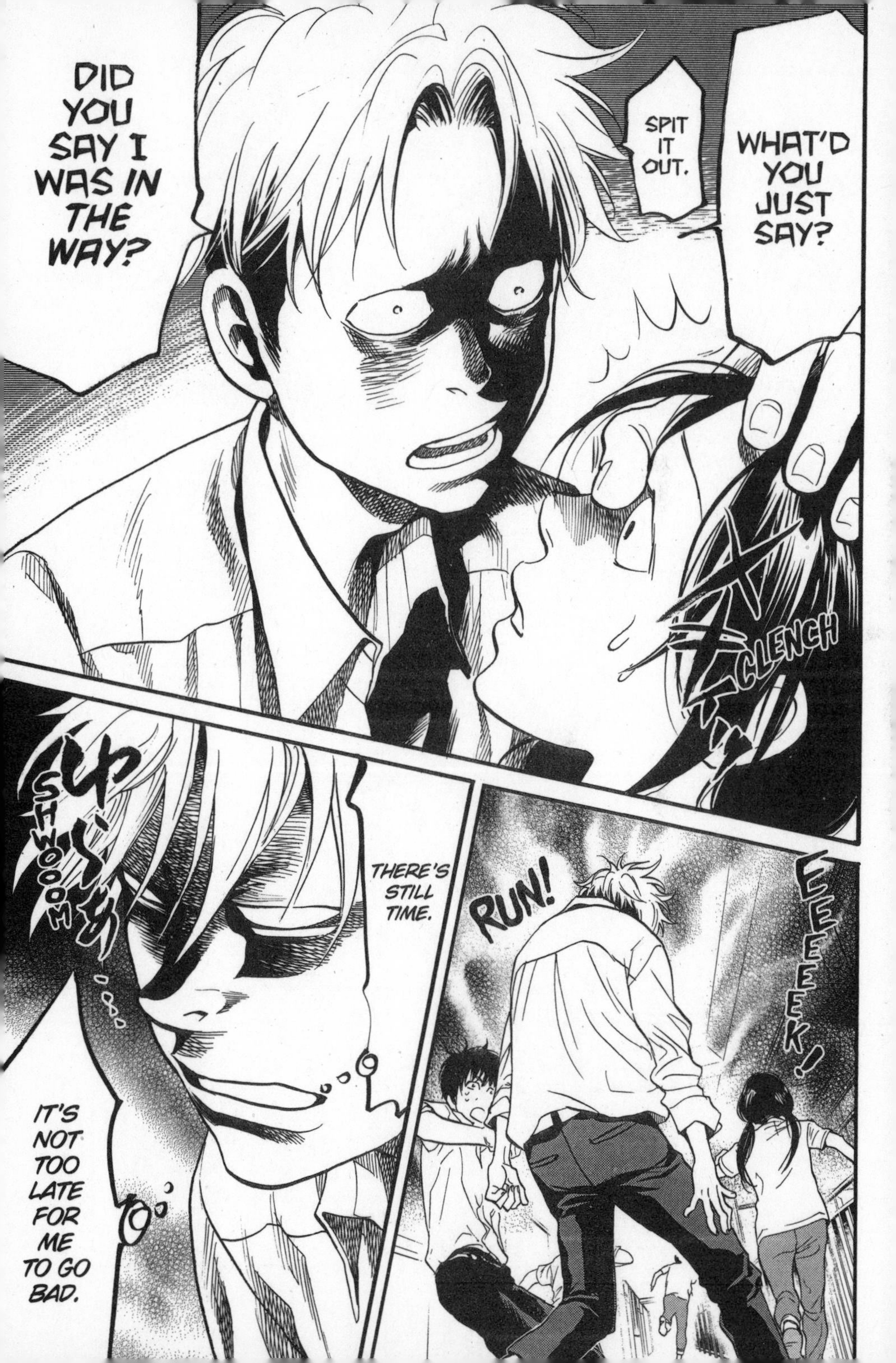
WHAT'D YOU JUST SAY?
SPIT IT OUT.
DID YOU SAY I WAS IN THE WAY?
CLENCH
EEEEEK!
RUN!
THERE'S STILL TIME.
IT'S NOT TOO LATE FOR ME TO GO BAD.
SHWOOOM

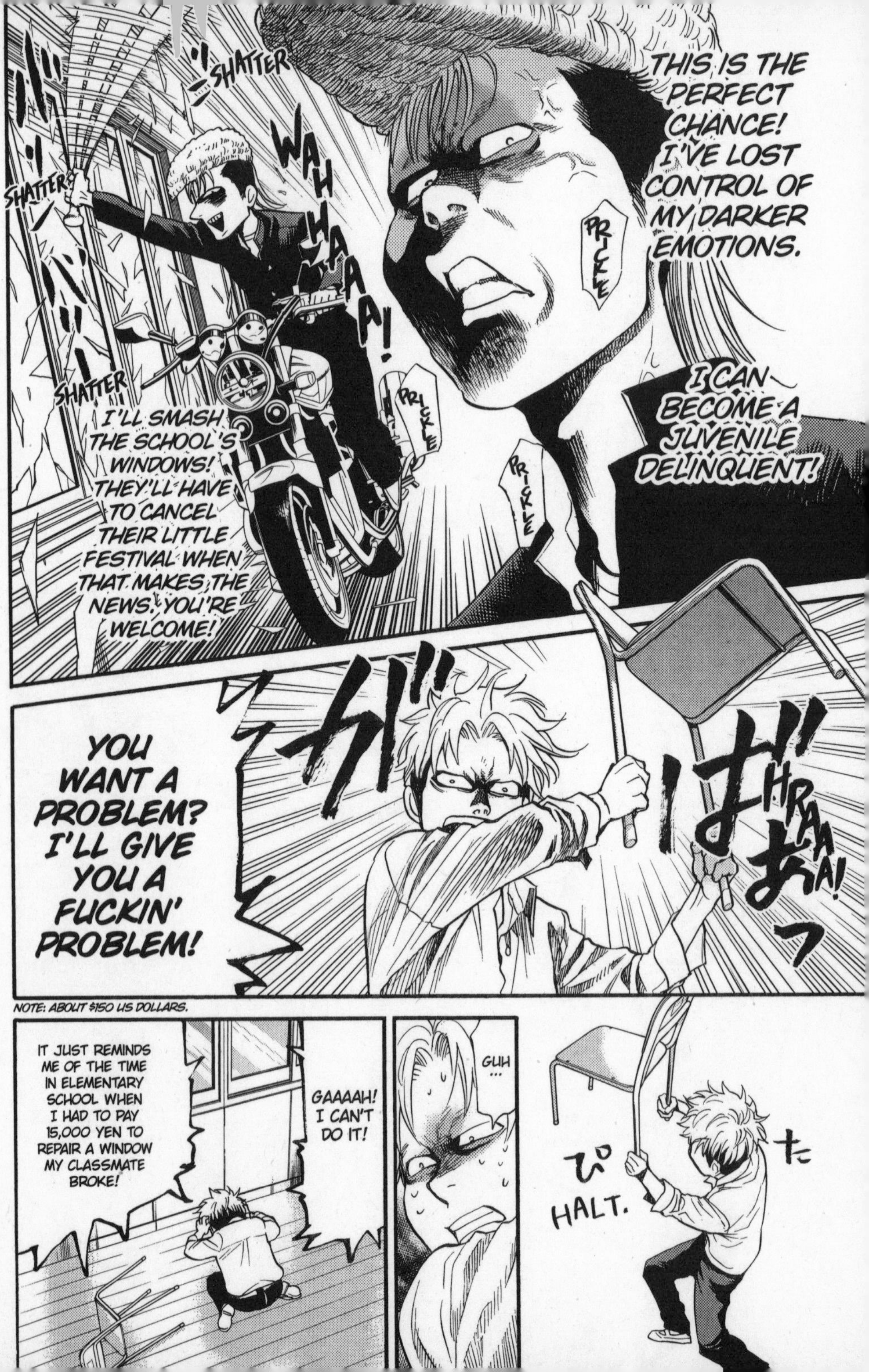
THIS IS THE PERFECT CHANCE! I'VE LOST CONTROL OF MY DARKER EMOTIONS.
PRICKLE
I CAN BECOME A JUVENILE DELINQUENT!
PRICKLE
PRICKLE
WAHAHAAA!
SHATTER
SHATTER
SHATTER
I'LL SMASH THE SCHOOL'S WINDOWS! THEY'LL HAVE TO CANCEL THEIR LITTLE FESTIVAL WHEN THAT MAKES THE NEWS. YOU'RE WELCOME!
HRAAAA!
YOU WANT A PROBLEM? I'LL GIVE YOU A FUCKIN' PROBLEM!
HALT.
GUH...
GAAAAH! I CAN'T DO IT!
IT JUST REMINDS ME OF THE TIME IN ELEMENTARY SCHOOL WHEN I HAD TO PAY 15,000 YEN TO REPAIR A WINDOW MY CLASSMATE BROKE!

NOTE: ABOUT $150 US DOLLARS.

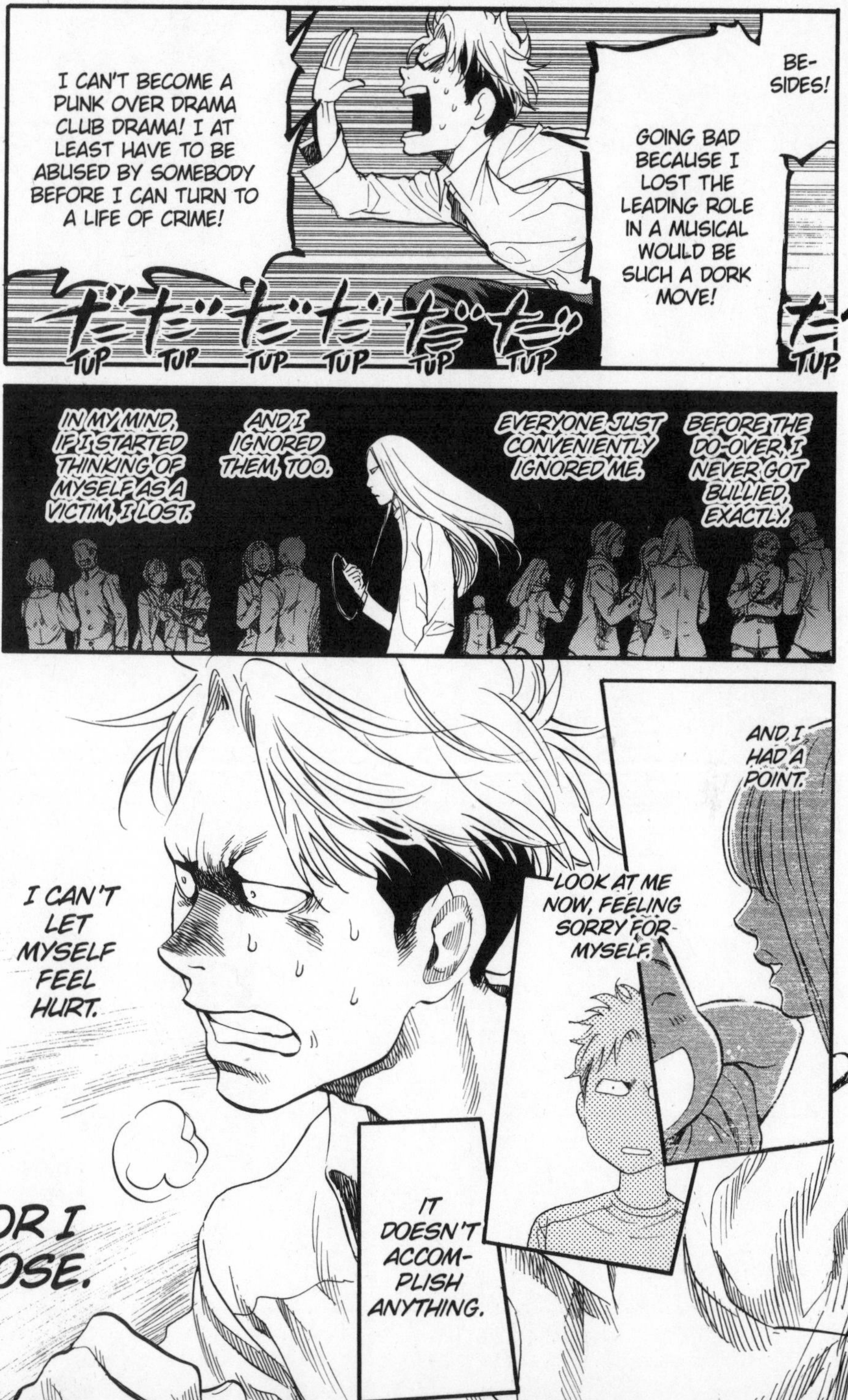
BE-SIDES!
GOING BAD BECAUSE I LOST THE LEADING ROLE IN A MUSICAL WOULD BE SUCH A DORK MOVE!
I CAN'T BECOME A PUNK OVER DRAMA CLUB DRAMA! I AT LEAST HAVE TO BE ABUSED BY SOMEBODY BEFORE I CAN TURN TO A LIFE OF CRIME!
TUP
TUP TUP TUP TUP TUP TUP
BEFORE THE DO-OVER, I NEVER GOT BULLIED, EXACTLY.
EVERYONE JUST CONVENIENTLY IGNORED ME.
AND I IGNORED THEM, TOO.
IN MY MIND, IF I STARTED THINKING OF MYSELF AS A VICTIM, I LOST.
AND I HAD A POINT.
LOOK AT ME NOW, FEELING SORRY FOR MYSELF.
IT DOESN'T ACCOMPLISH ANYTHING.
I CAN'T LET MYSELF FEEL HURT.
OR I LOSE.

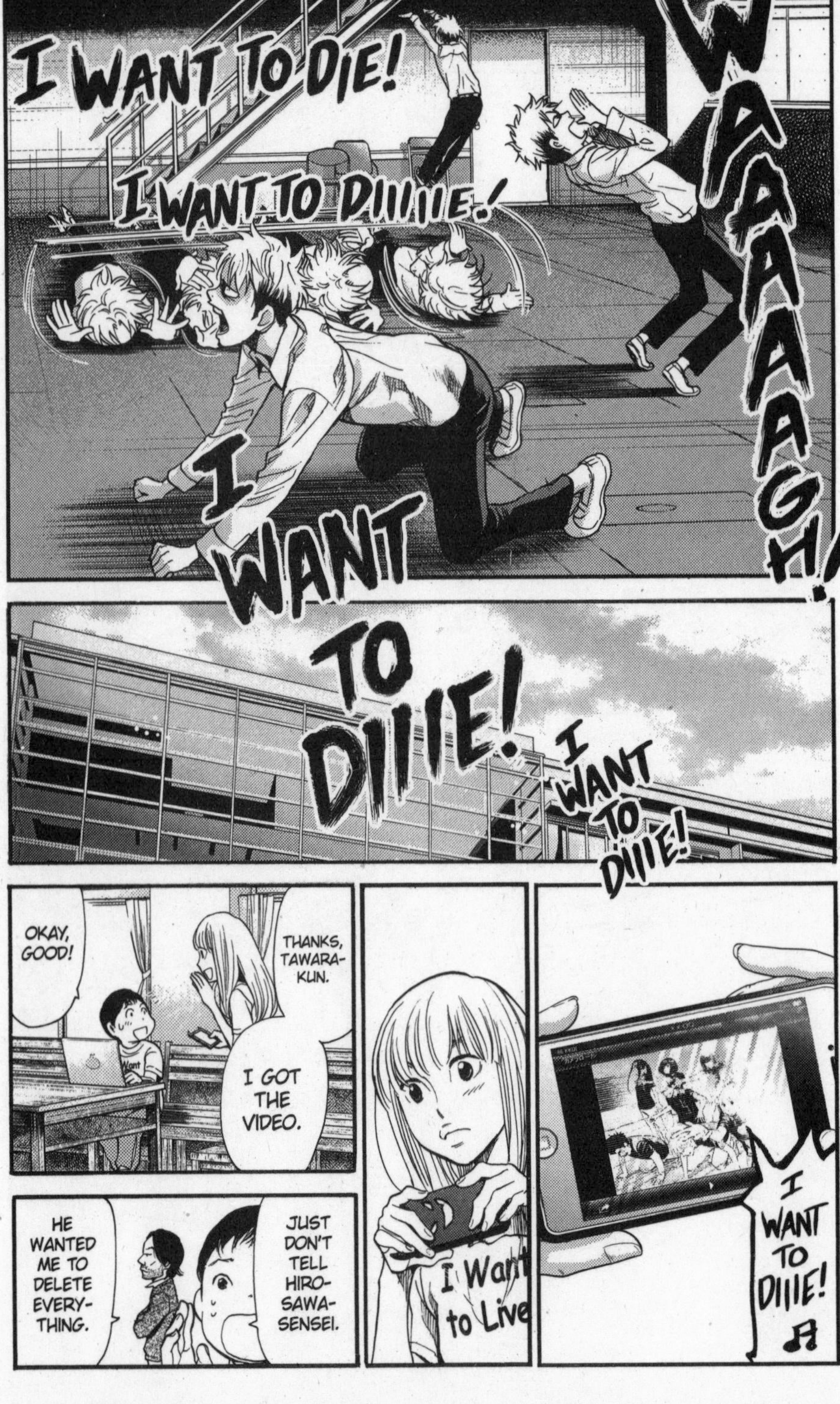
WAAAAAAGH!
I WANT TO DIE!
I WANT TO DIIIIIE!
I WANT TO DIIIE!
I WANT TO DIIIE!
I WANT TO DIIIE!
I Want to Live
THANKS, TAWARA-KUN.
I GOT THE VIDEO.
OKAY, GOOD!
JUST DON'T TELL HIRO-SAWA-SENSEI.
HE WANTED ME TO DELETE EVERY-THING.

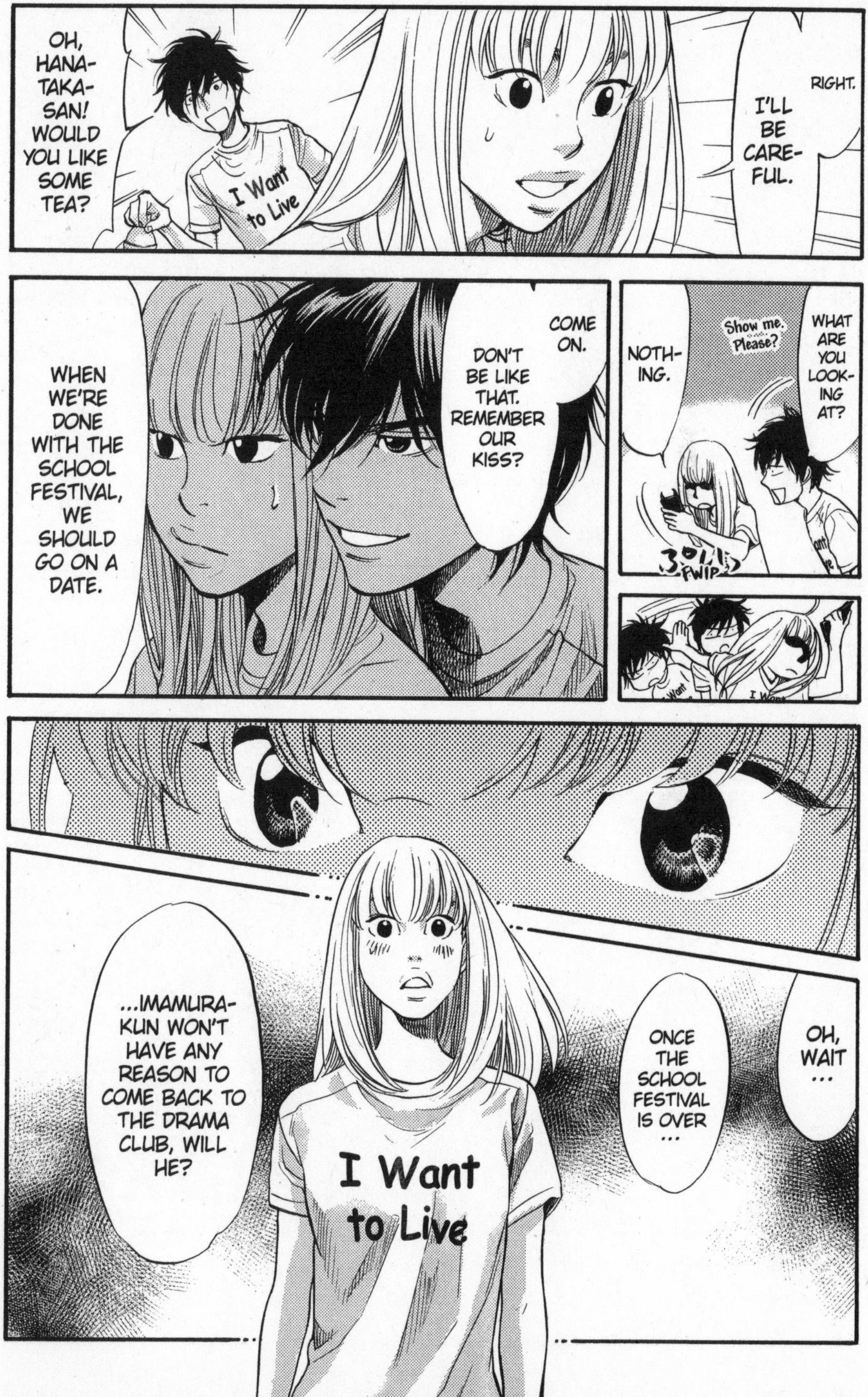
RIGHT.
I'LL BE CAREFUL.
OH, HANA-TAKA-SAN! WOULD YOU LIKE SOME TEA?
I Want to Live
WHAT ARE YOU LOOKING AT?
Show me. Please?
NOTHING.
FWIP
COME ON.
DON'T BE LIKE THAT. REMEMBER OUR KISS?
WHEN WE'RE DONE WITH THE SCHOOL FESTIVAL, WE SHOULD GO ON A DATE.
OH, WAIT ...
ONCE THE SCHOOL FESTIVAL IS OVER ...
...IMAMURA-KUN WON'T HAVE ANY REASON TO COME BACK TO THE DRAMA CLUB, WILL HE?
I Want to Live

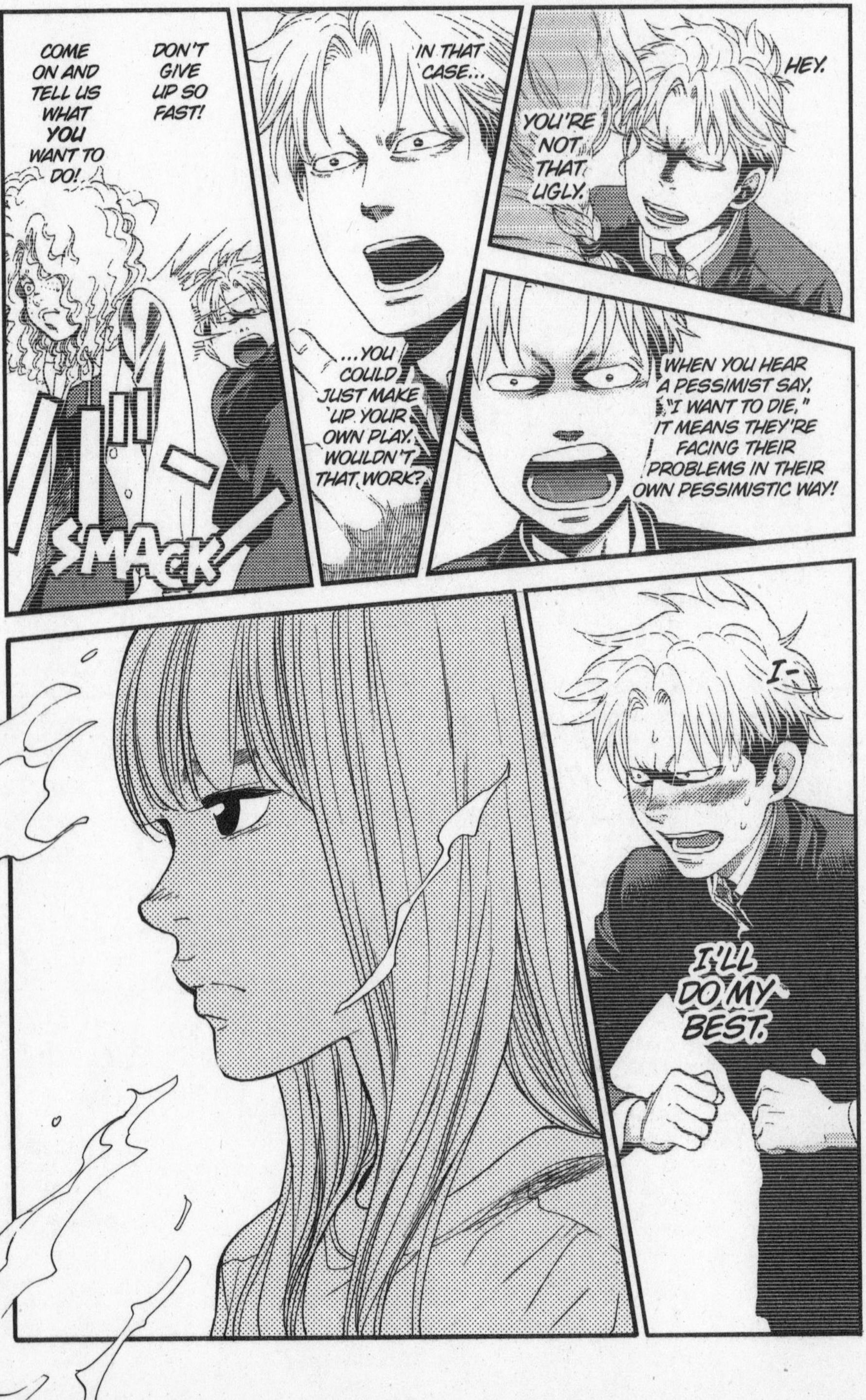
HEY.
YOU'RE NOT THAT UGLY.
WHEN YOU HEAR A PESSIMIST SAY, "I WANT TO DIE," IT MEANS THEY'RE FACING THEIR PROBLEMS IN THEIR OWN PESSIMISTIC WAY!
IN THAT CASE...
...YOU COULD JUST MAKE UP YOUR OWN PLAY. WOULDN'T THAT WORK?
DON'T GIVE UP SO FAST!
COME ON AND TELL US WHAT YOU WANT TO DO!
SMACK!
I-
I'LL DO MY BEST.

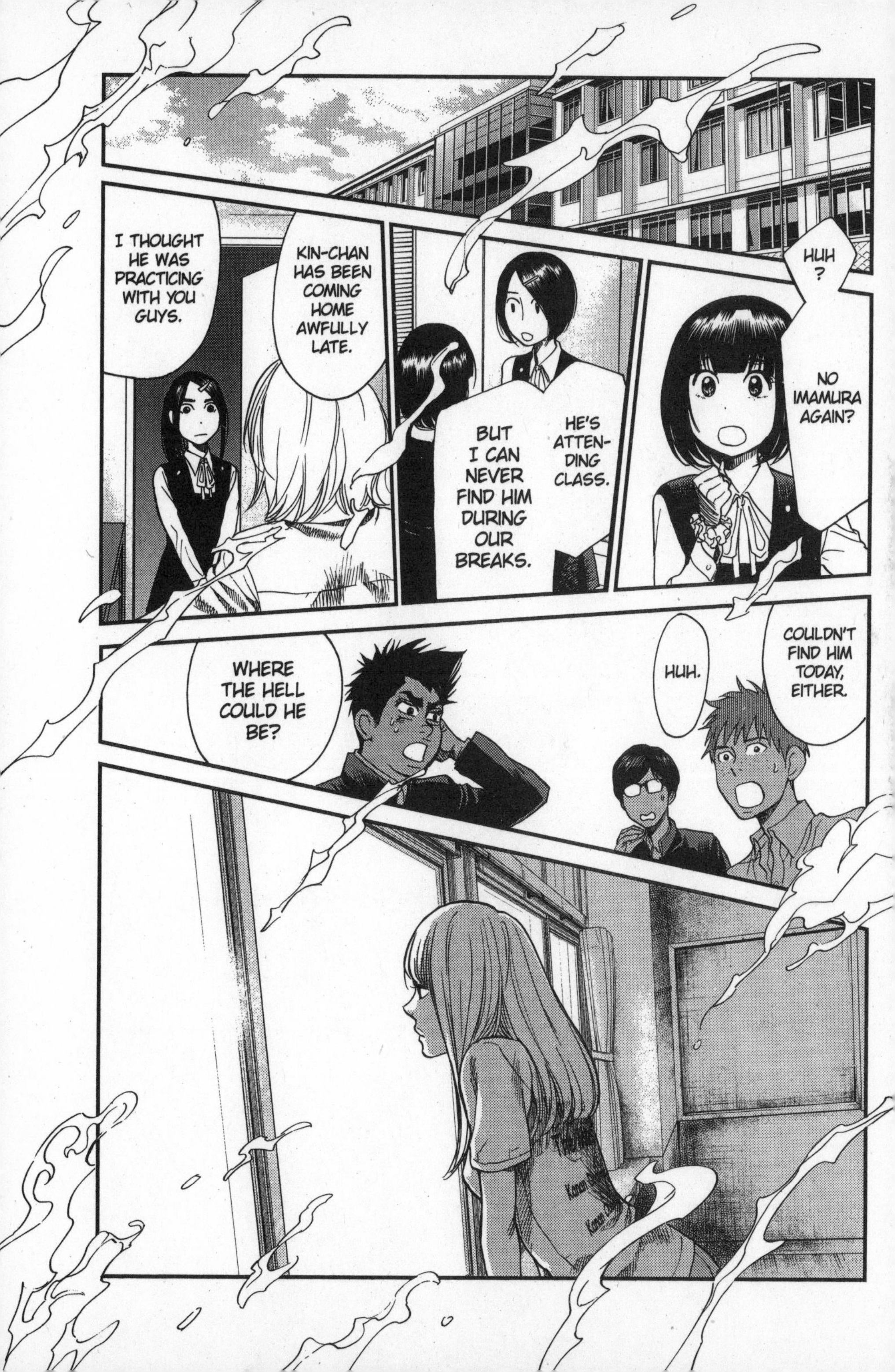
HUH?
NO IMAMURA AGAIN?
HE'S ATTENDING CLASS.
BUT I CAN NEVER FIND HIM DURING OUR BREAKS.
KIN-CHAN HAS BEEN COMING HOME AWFULLY LATE.
I THOUGHT HE WAS PRACTICING WITH YOU GUYS.
COULDN'T FIND HIM TODAY, EITHER.
HUH.
WHERE THE HELL COULD HE BE?

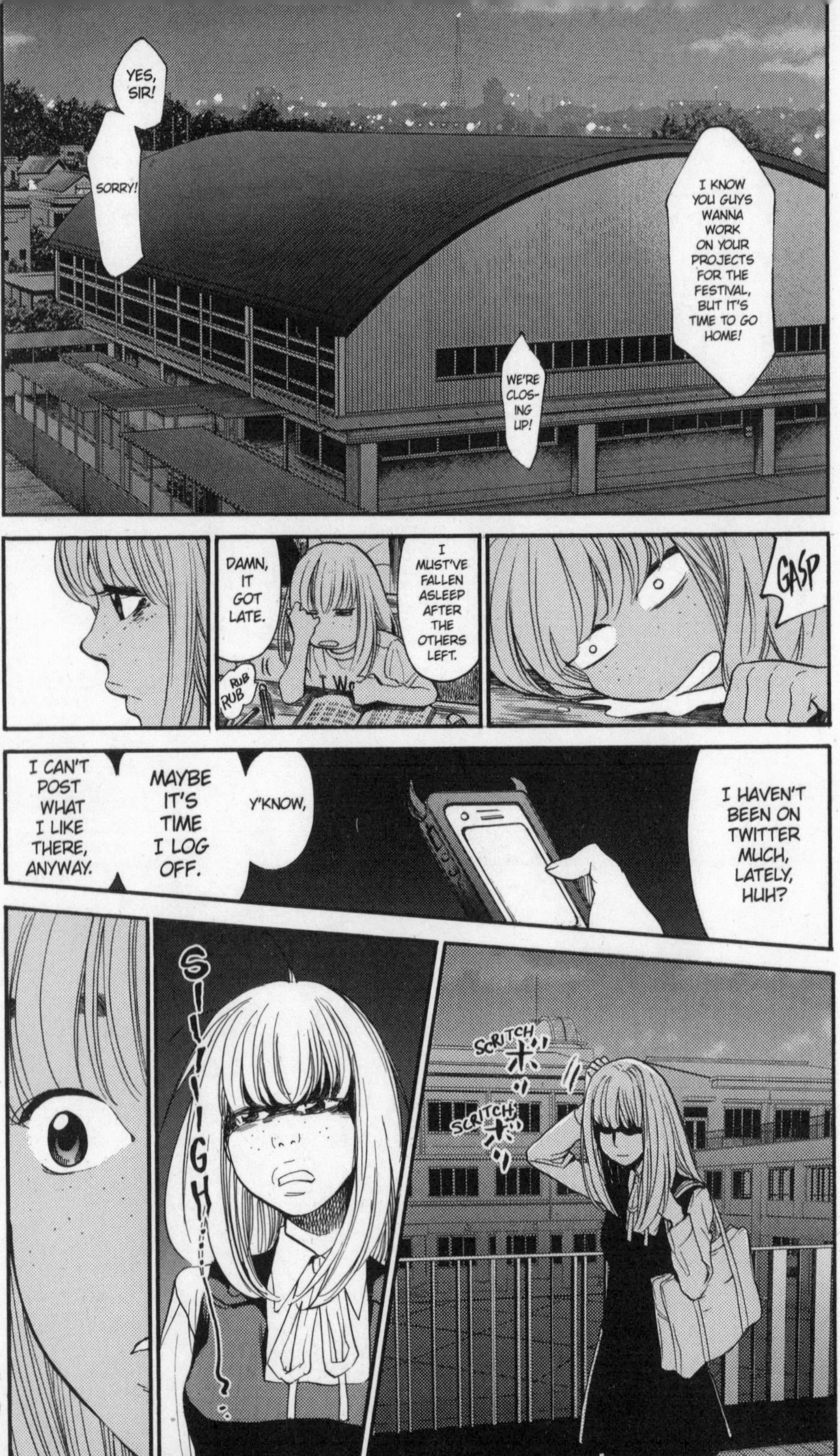
I KNOW YOU GUYS WANNA WORK ON YOUR PROJECTS FOR THE FESTIVAL, BUT IT'S TIME TO GO HOME!
WE'RE CLOSING UP!
YES, SIR!
SORRY!
GASP
I MUST'VE FALLEN ASLEEP AFTER THE OTHERS LEFT.
DAMN, IT GOT LATE.
RUB RUB
I HAVEN'T BEEN ON TWITTER MUCH, LATELY, HUH?
Y'KNOW,
MAYBE IT'S TIME I LOG OFF.
I CAN'T POST WHAT I LIKE THERE, ANYWAY.
SCRITCH
SCRITCH
SIIIIIGH...

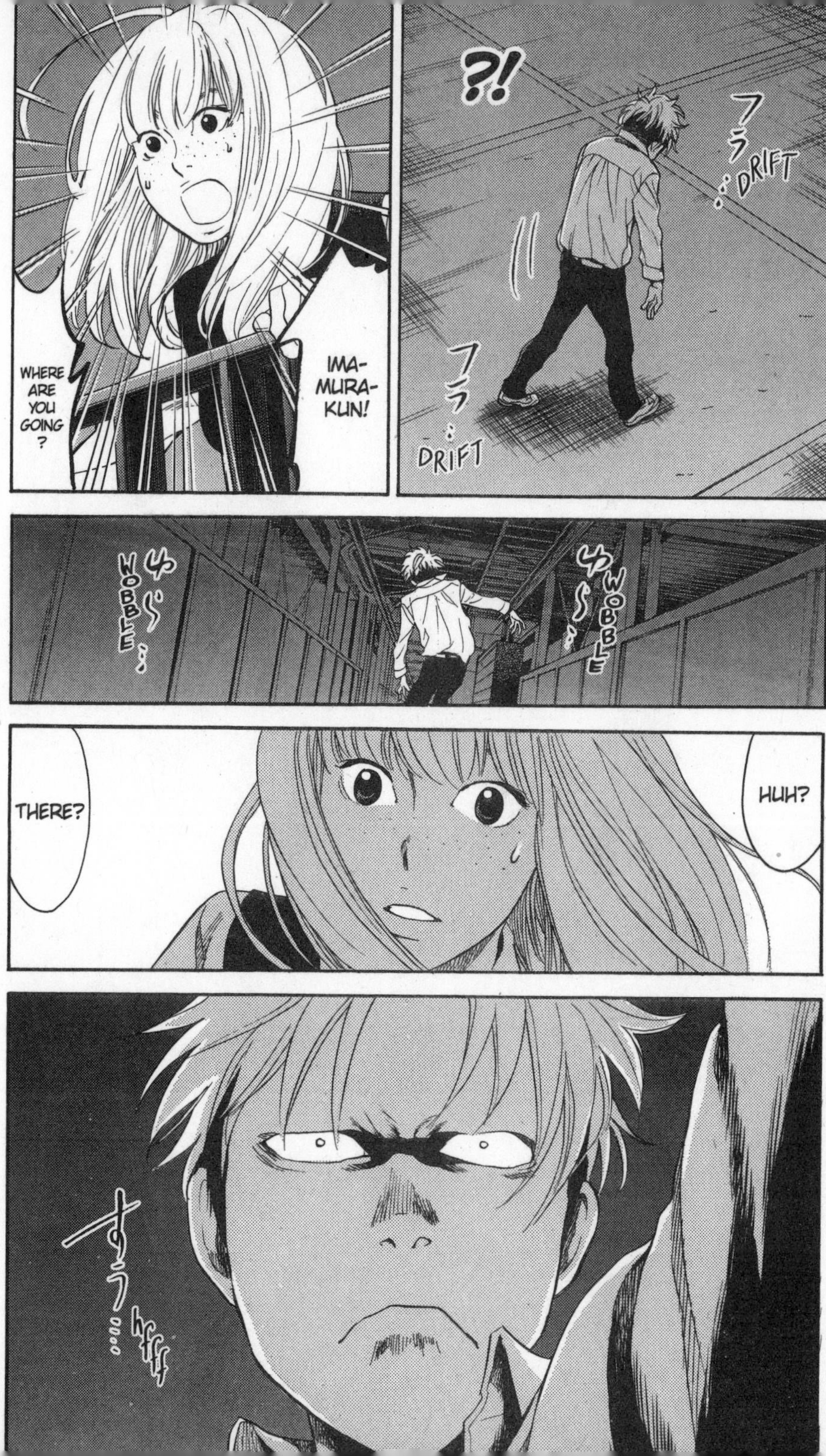
?!
フラ… DRIFT
フラ… DRIFT
IMA-MURA-KUN!
WHERE ARE YOU GOING?
ゆら… WOBBLE
ゆら… WOBBLE
HUH?
THERE?
すう… hfff

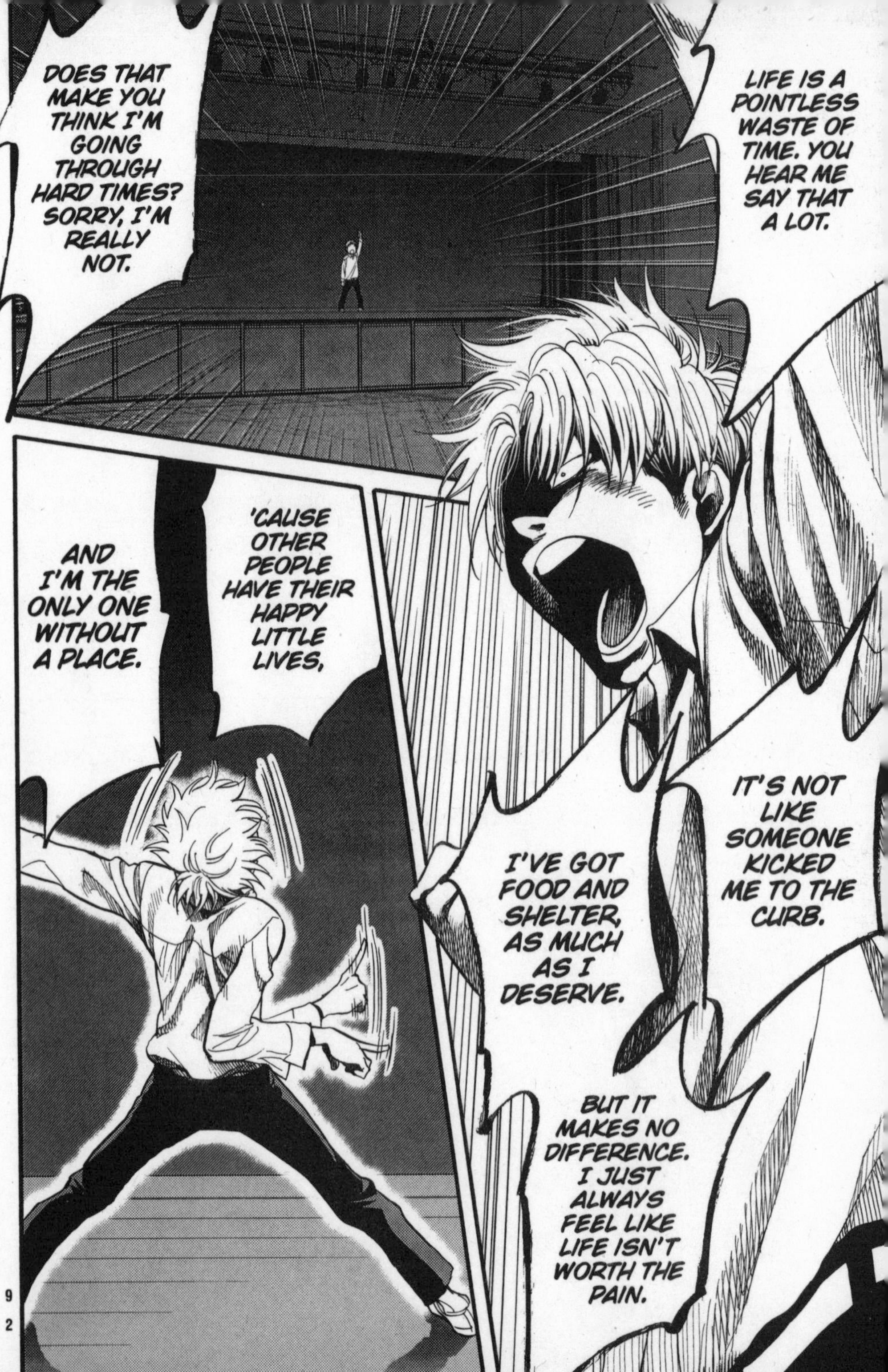
LIFE IS A POINTLESS WASTE OF TIME. YOU HEAR ME SAY THAT A LOT.
DOES THAT MAKE YOU THINK I'M GOING THROUGH HARD TIMES? SORRY, I'M REALLY NOT.
IT'S NOT LIKE SOMEONE KICKED ME TO THE CURB.
I'VE GOT FOOD AND SHELTER, AS MUCH AS I DESERVE.
BUT IT MAKES NO DIFFERENCE. I JUST ALWAYS FEEL LIKE LIFE ISN'T WORTH THE PAIN.
'CAUSE OTHER PEOPLE HAVE THEIR HAPPY LITTLE LIVES,
AND I'M THE ONLY ONE WITHOUT A PLACE.

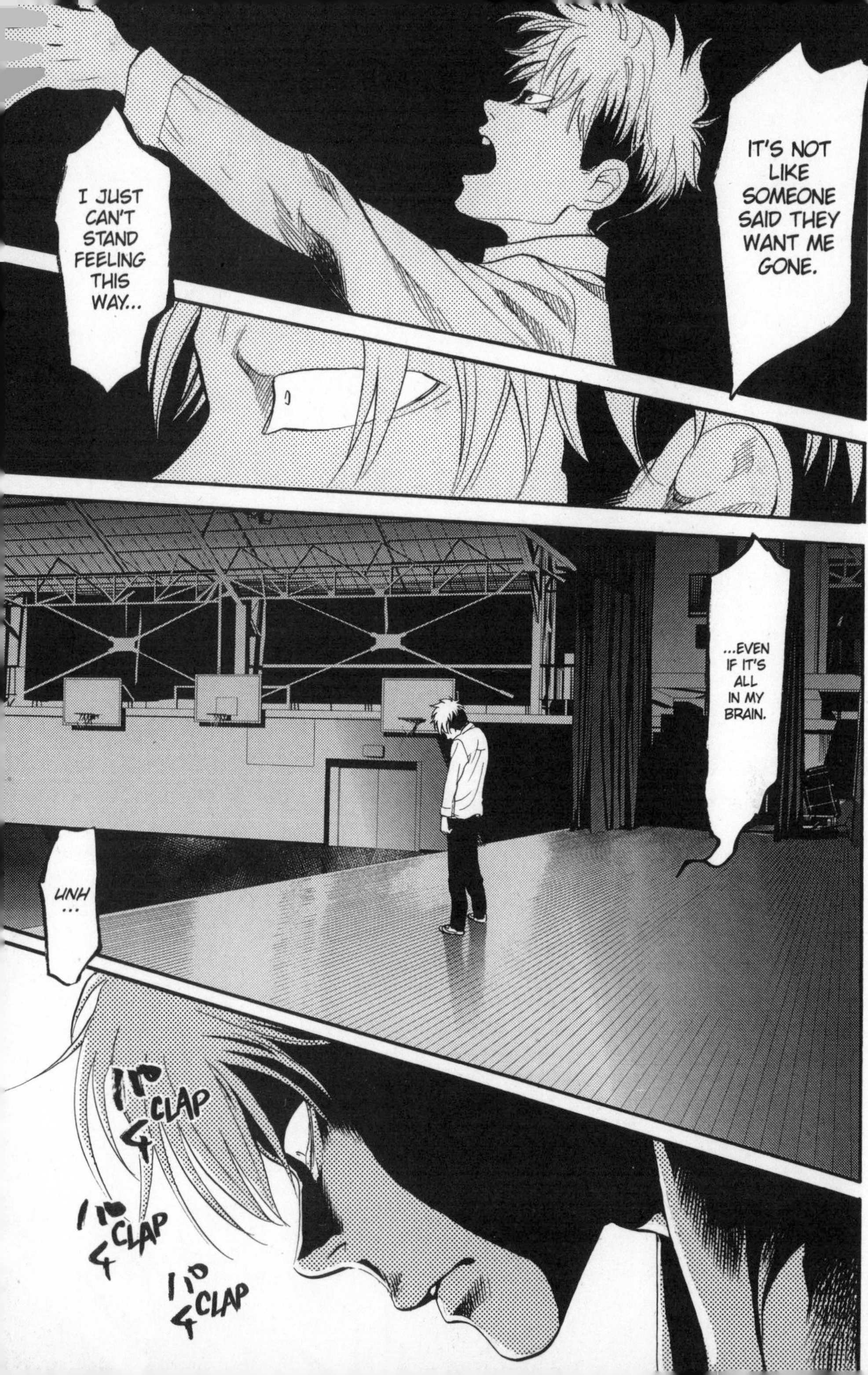
IT'S NOT LIKE SOMEONE SAID THEY WANT ME GONE.
I JUST CAN'T STAND FEELING THIS WAY...
...EVEN IF IT'S ALL IN MY BRAIN.
UNH...
CLAP
CLAP
CLAP

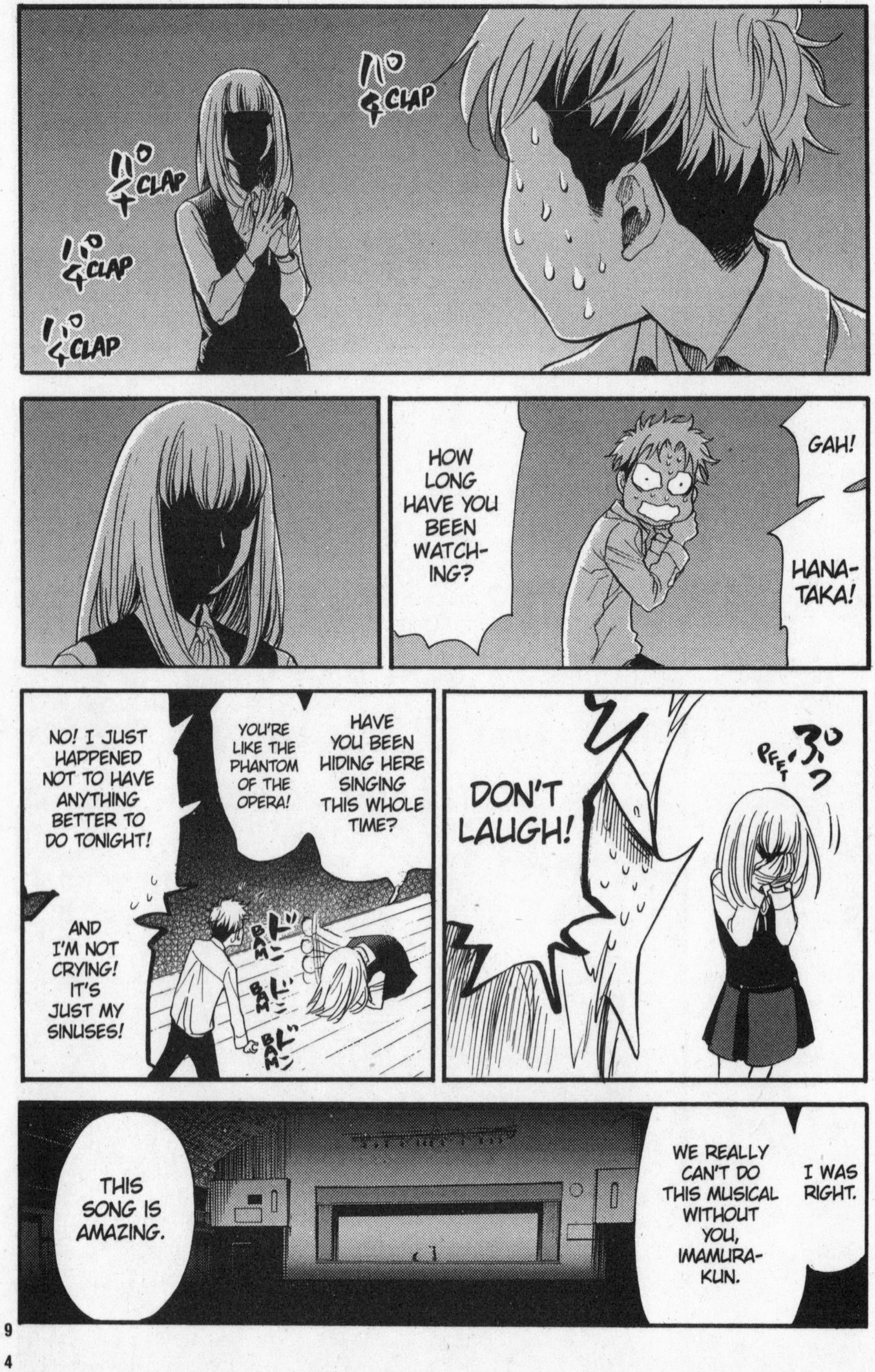
パチ CLAP
パチ CLAP
パチ CLAP
パチ CLAP
GAH!
HANA-TAKA!
HOW LONG HAVE YOU BEEN WATCH-ING?
PFFT ぷっ
DON'T LAUGH!
HAVE YOU BEEN HIDING HERE SINGING THIS WHOLE TIME?
YOU'RE LIKE THE PHANTOM OF THE OPERA!
NO! I JUST HAPPENED NOT TO HAVE ANYTHING BETTER TO DO TONIGHT!
AND I'M NOT CRYING! IT'S JUST MY SINUSES!
BAM
BAM
BAM
I WAS RIGHT.
WE REALLY CAN'T DO THIS MUSICAL WITHOUT YOU, IMAMURA-KUN.
THIS SONG IS AMAZING.

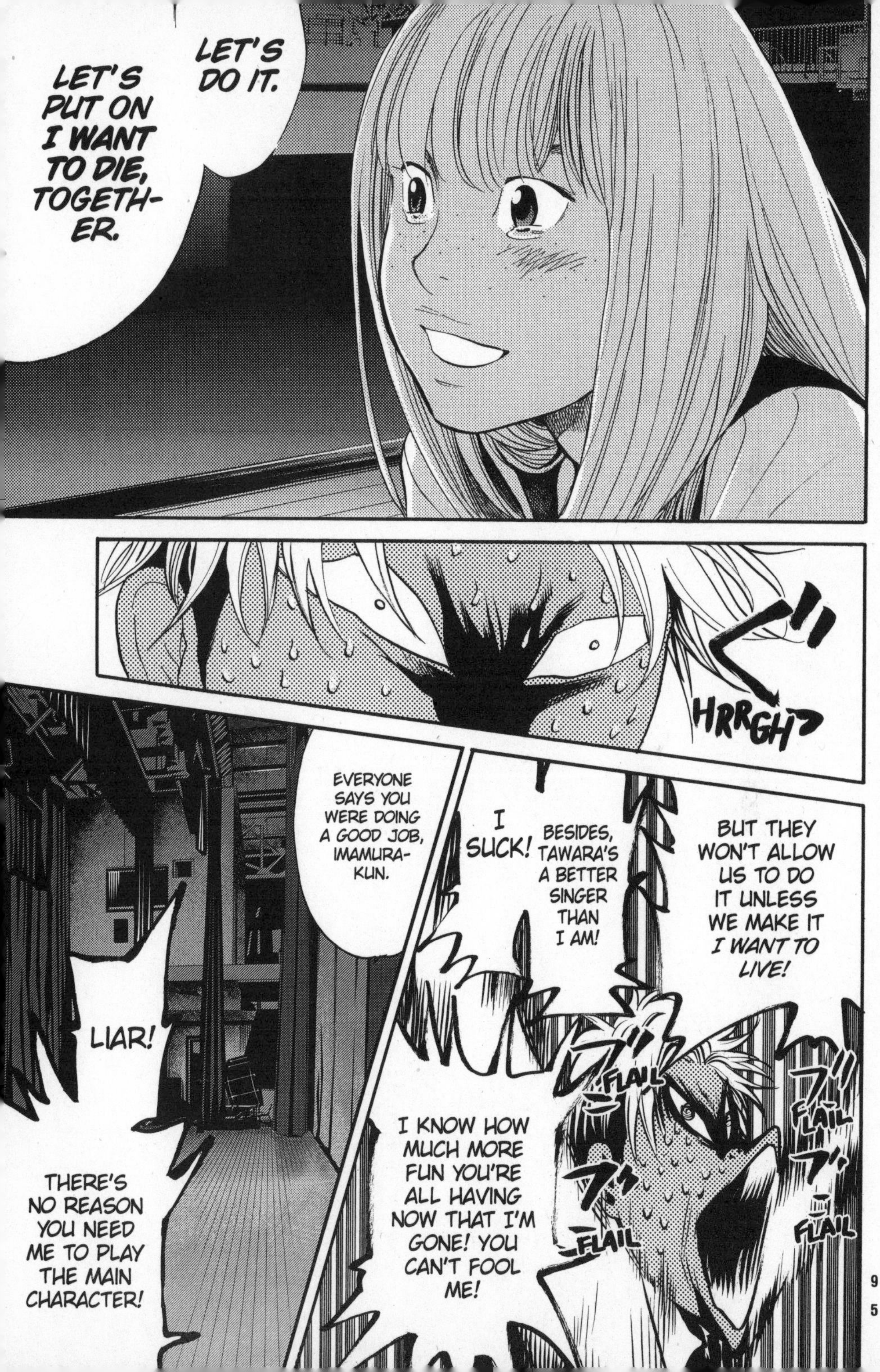
LET'S DO IT.
LET'S PUT ON I WANT TO DIE, TOGETH-ER.
HRRGH
BUT THEY WON'T ALLOW US TO DO IT UNLESS WE MAKE IT I WANT TO LIVE!
BESIDES, TAWARA'S A BETTER SINGER THAN I AM!
I SUCK!
FLAIL
FLAIL
I KNOW HOW MUCH MORE FUN YOU'RE ALL HAVING NOW THAT I'M GONE! YOU CAN'T FOOL ME!
FLAIL
FLAIL
EVERYONE SAYS YOU WERE DOING A GOOD JOB, IMAMURA-KUN.
LIAR!
THERE'S NO REASON YOU NEED ME TO PLAY THE MAIN CHARACTER!

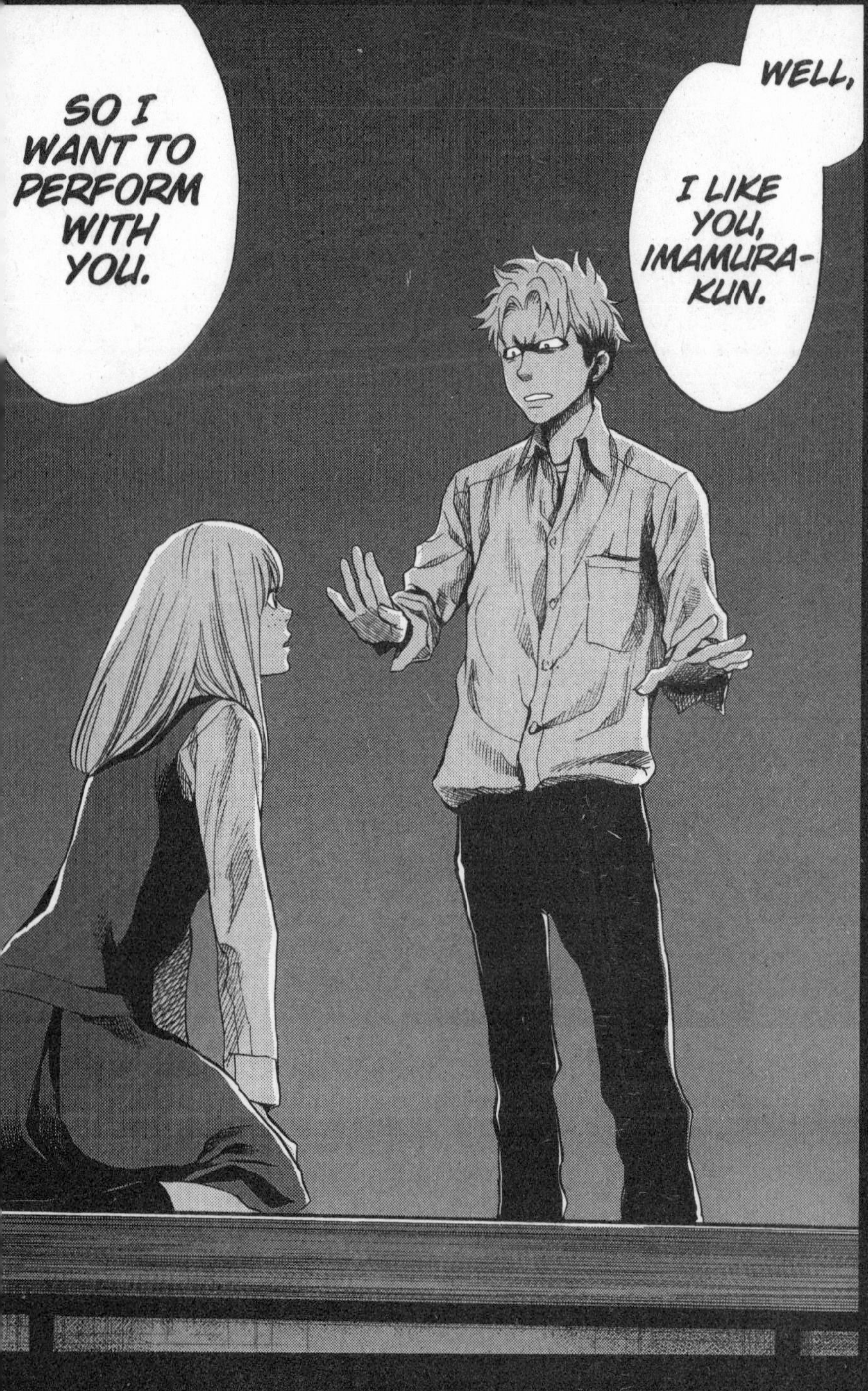
WELL,
I LIKE YOU, IMAMURA-KUN.
SO I WANT TO PERFORM WITH YOU.

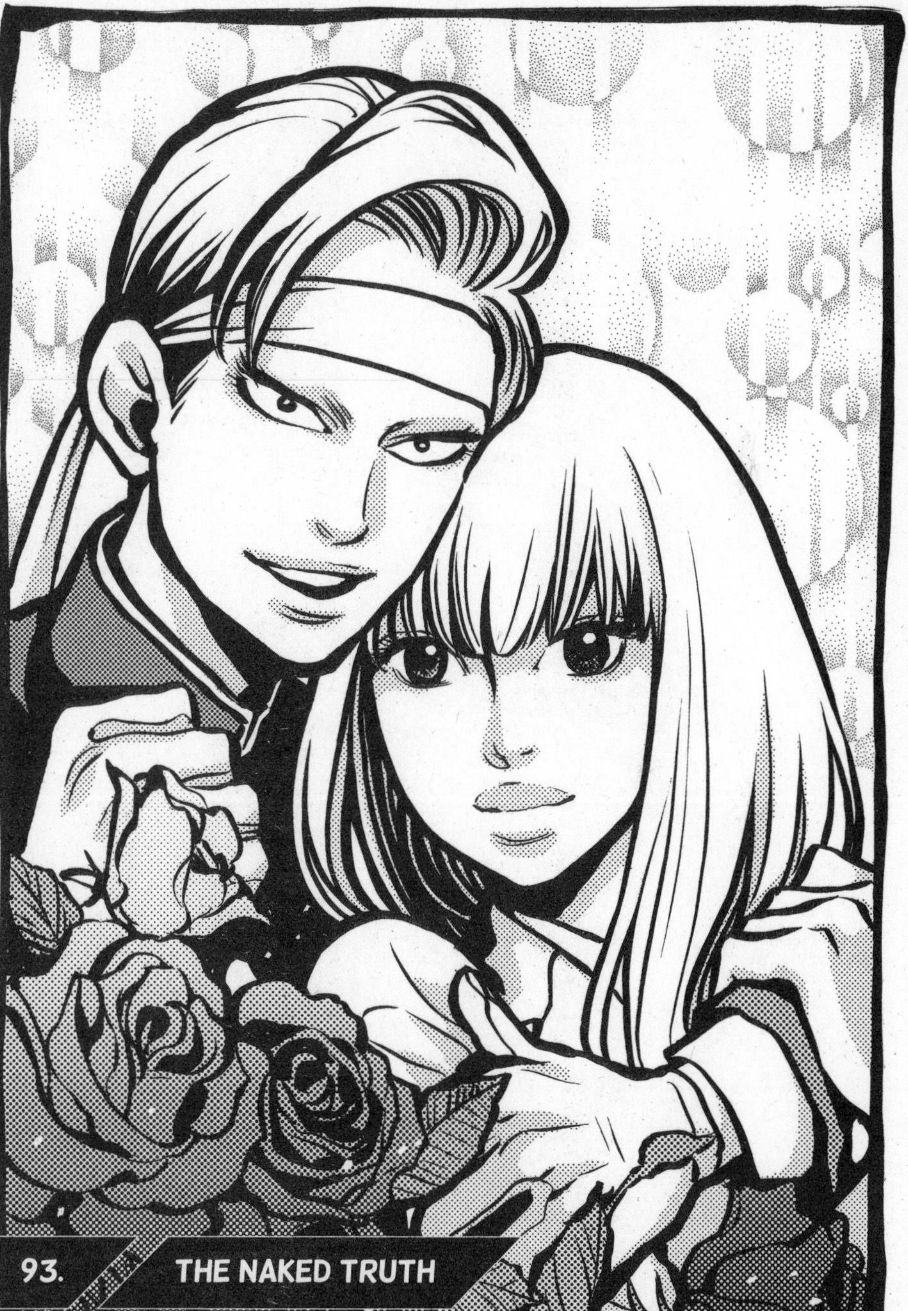

93. THE NAKED TRUTH

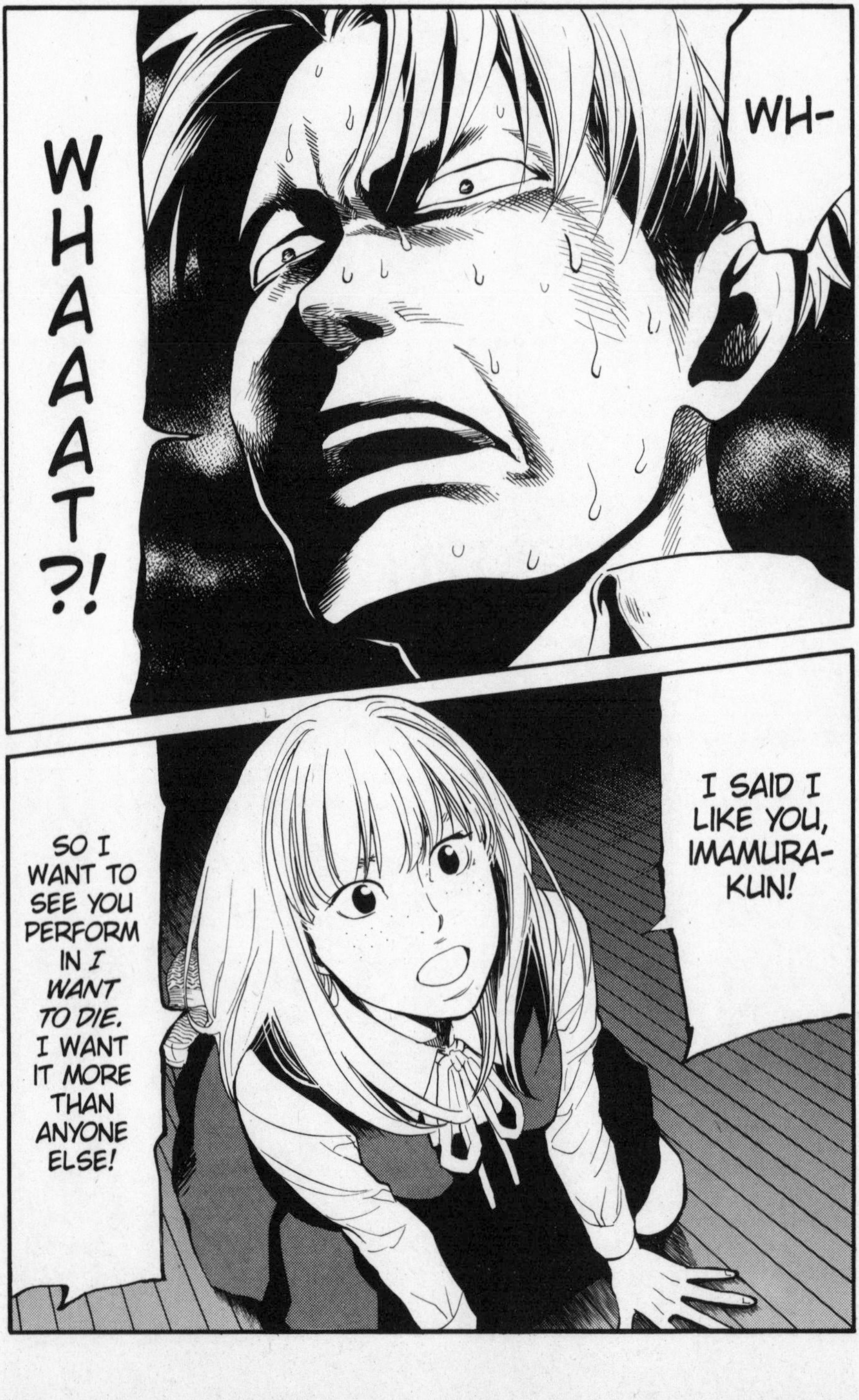
WH-
WHAAAT?!
I SAID I LIKE YOU, IMAMURA-KUN!
SO I WANT TO SEE YOU PERFORM IN *I WANT TO DIE.* I WANT IT MORE THAN ANYONE ELSE!

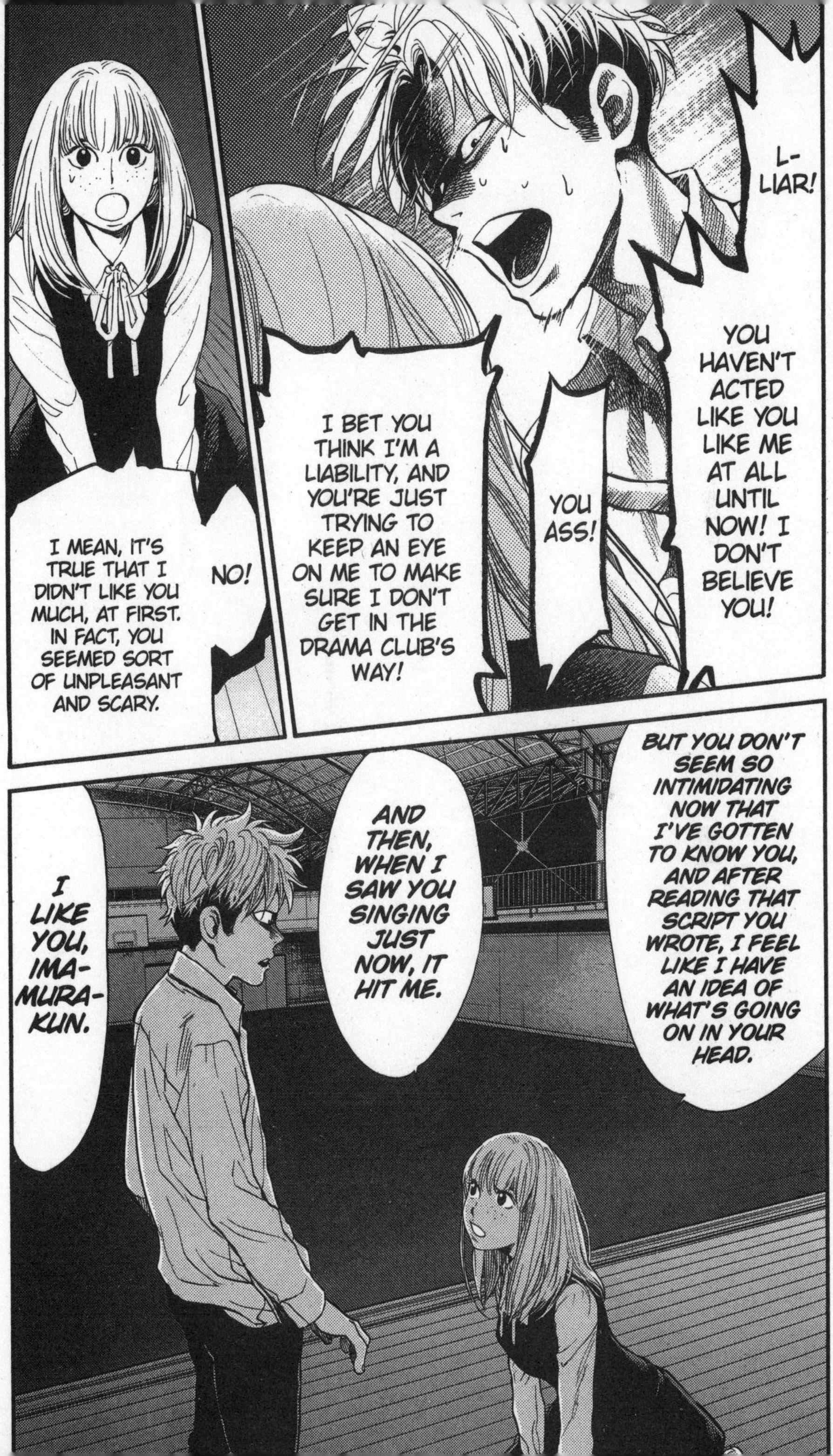
L-LIAR!
YOU HAVEN'T ACTED LIKE YOU LIKE ME AT ALL UNTIL NOW! I DON'T BELIEVE YOU!
YOU ASS!
I BET YOU THINK I'M A LIABILITY, AND YOU'RE JUST TRYING TO KEEP AN EYE ON ME TO MAKE SURE I DON'T GET IN THE DRAMA CLUB'S WAY!
NO!
I MEAN, IT'S TRUE THAT I DIDN'T LIKE YOU MUCH, AT FIRST. IN FACT, YOU SEEMED SORT OF UNPLEASANT AND SCARY.
BUT YOU DON'T SEEM SO INTIMIDATING NOW THAT I'VE GOTTEN TO KNOW YOU, AND AFTER READING THAT SCRIPT YOU WROTE, I FEEL LIKE I HAVE AN IDEA OF WHAT'S GOING ON IN YOUR HEAD.
AND THEN, WHEN I SAW YOU SINGING JUST NOW, IT HIT ME.
I LIKE YOU, IMAMURA-KUN.

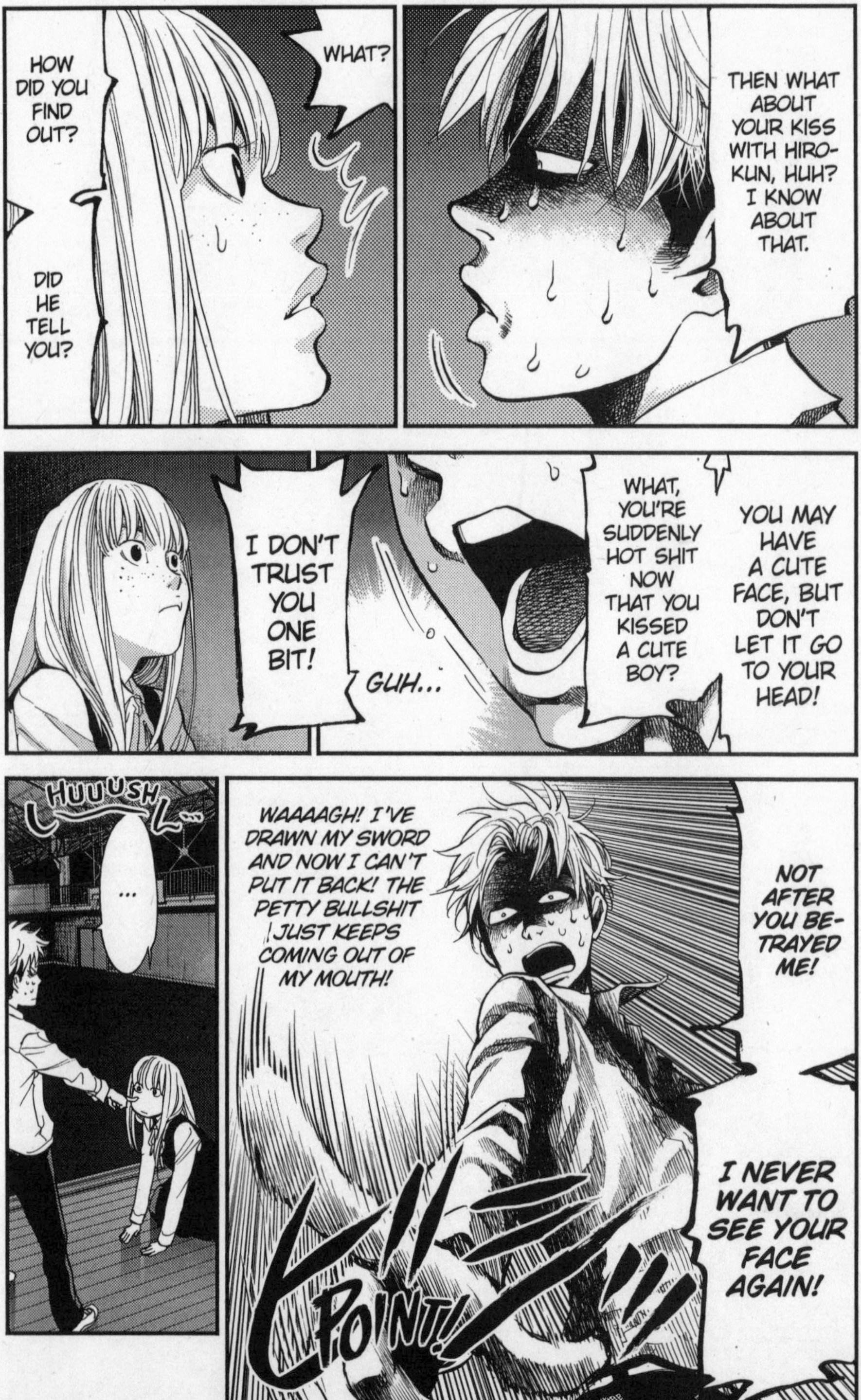
THEN WHAT ABOUT YOUR KISS WITH HIRO-KUN, HUH? I KNOW ABOUT THAT.
WHAT?
HOW DID YOU FIND OUT?
DID HE TELL YOU?
YOU MAY HAVE A CUTE FACE, BUT DON'T LET IT GO TO YOUR HEAD!
WHAT, YOU'RE SUDDENLY HOT SHIT NOW THAT YOU KISSED A CUTE BOY?
GUH...
I DON'T TRUST YOU ONE BIT!
NOT AFTER YOU BE-TRAYED ME!
WAAAAGH! I'VE DRAWN MY SWORD AND NOW I CAN'T PUT IT BACK! THE PETTY BULLSHIT JUST KEEPS COMING OUT OF MY MOUTH!
I NEVER WANT TO SEE YOUR FACE AGAIN!
POINT!
HUUUSH
...

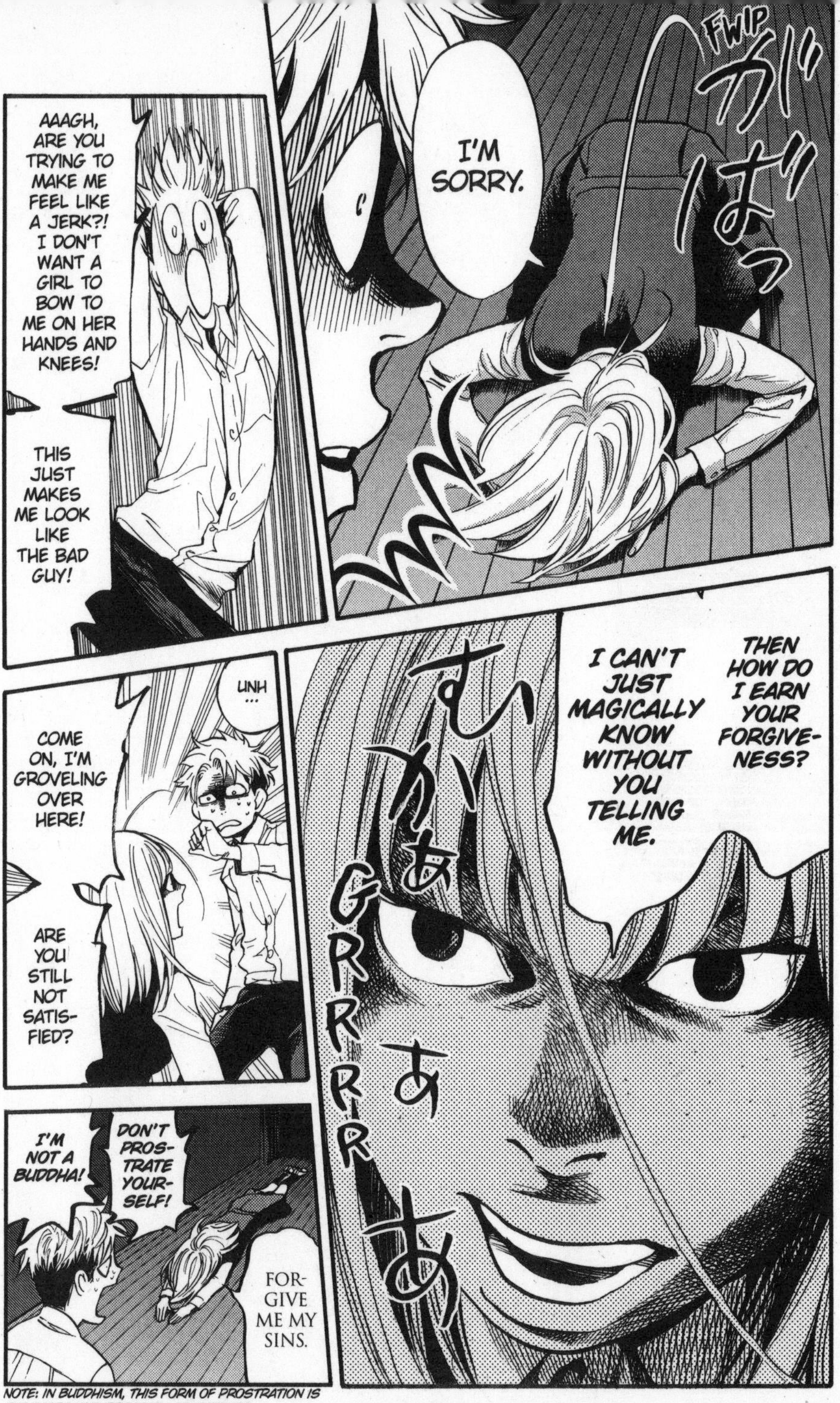
FWIP
I'M SORRY.
AAAGH, ARE YOU TRYING TO MAKE ME FEEL LIKE A JERK?! I DON'T WANT A GIRL TO BOW TO ME ON HER HANDS AND KNEES!
THIS JUST MAKES ME LOOK LIKE THE BAD GUY!
GRRRRR
THEN HOW DO I EARN YOUR FORGIVENESS?
I CAN'T JUST MAGICALLY KNOW WITHOUT YOU TELLING ME.
UNH ...
COME ON, I'M GROVELING OVER HERE!
ARE YOU STILL NOT SATISFIED?
DON'T PROSTRATE YOURSELF!
I'M NOT A BUDDHA!
FORGIVE ME MY SINS.

NOTE: IN BUDDHISM, THIS FORM OF PROSTRATION IS THE DEEPEST EXPRESSION OF HUMILITY.

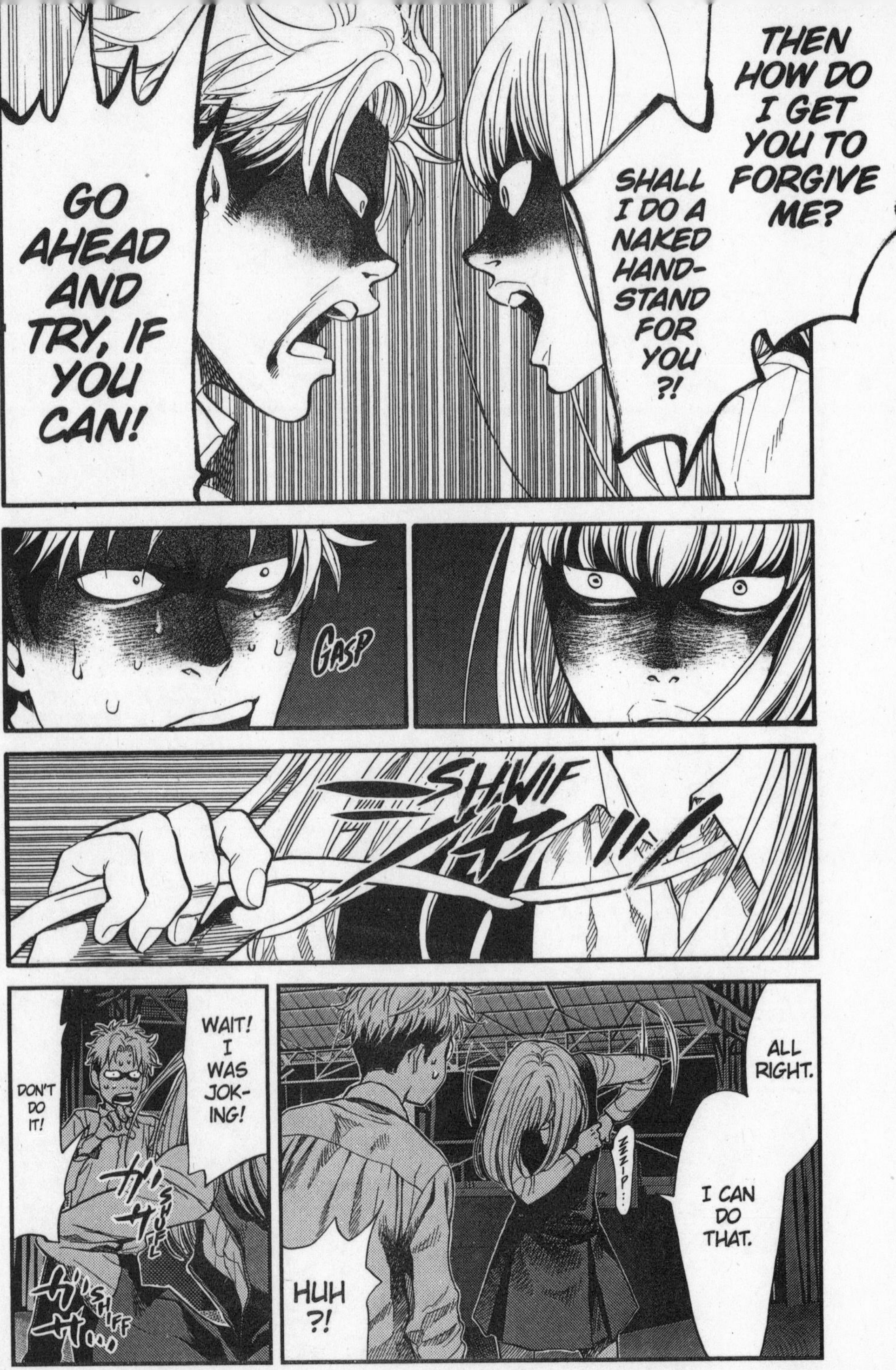
THEN HOW DO I GET YOU TO FORGIVE ME?
SHALL I DO A NAKED HAND-STAND FOR YOU ?!
GO AHEAD AND TRY, IF YOU CAN!
GASP
SHWIF
ALL RIGHT.
I CAN DO THAT.
ZZZIP...
HUH ?!
WAIT! I WAS JOK-ING!
DON'T DO IT!
SHUFFL
SHIFF...

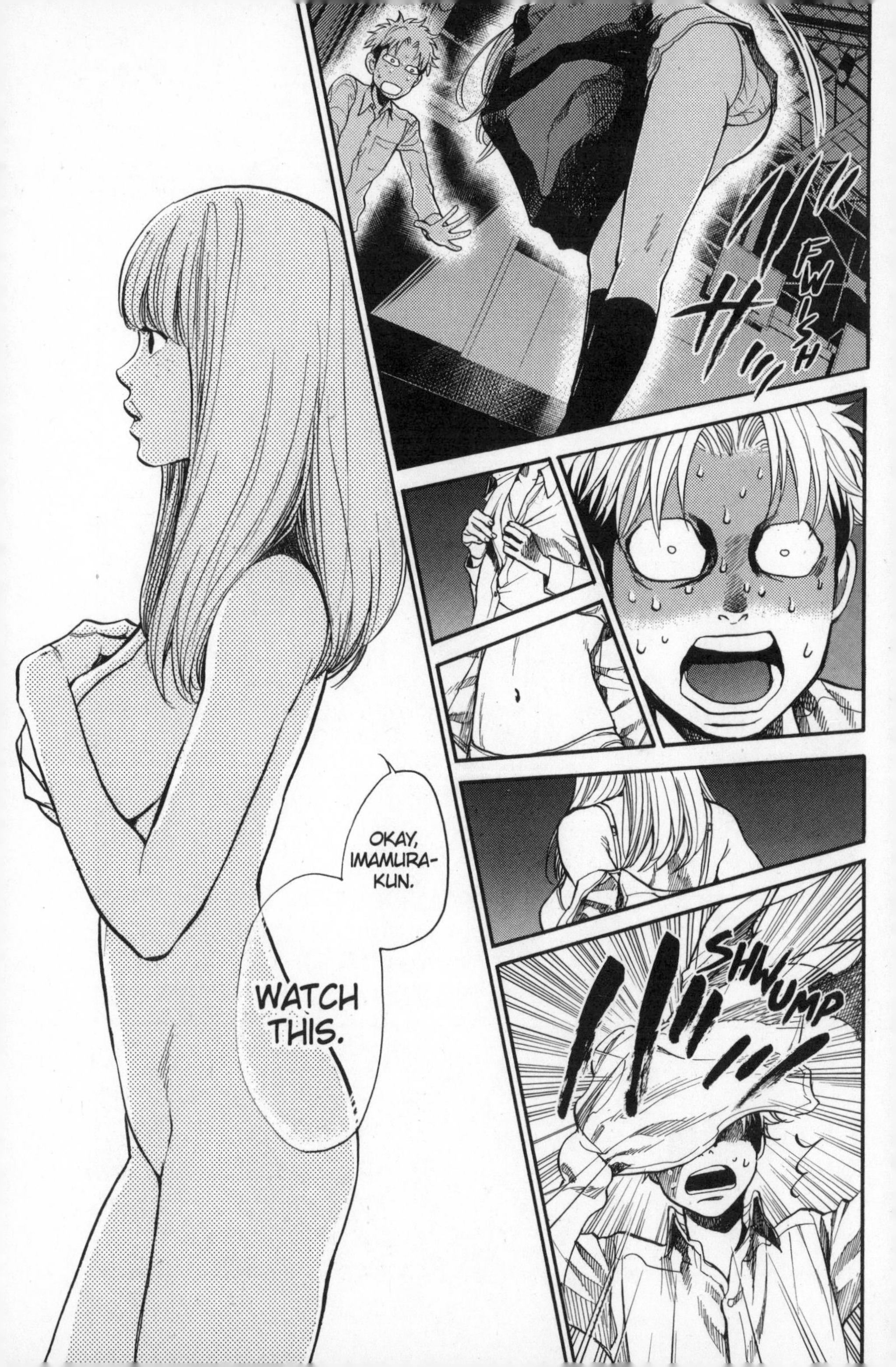
FWISH
SHWUMP
OKAY, IMAMURA-KUN.
WATCH THIS.

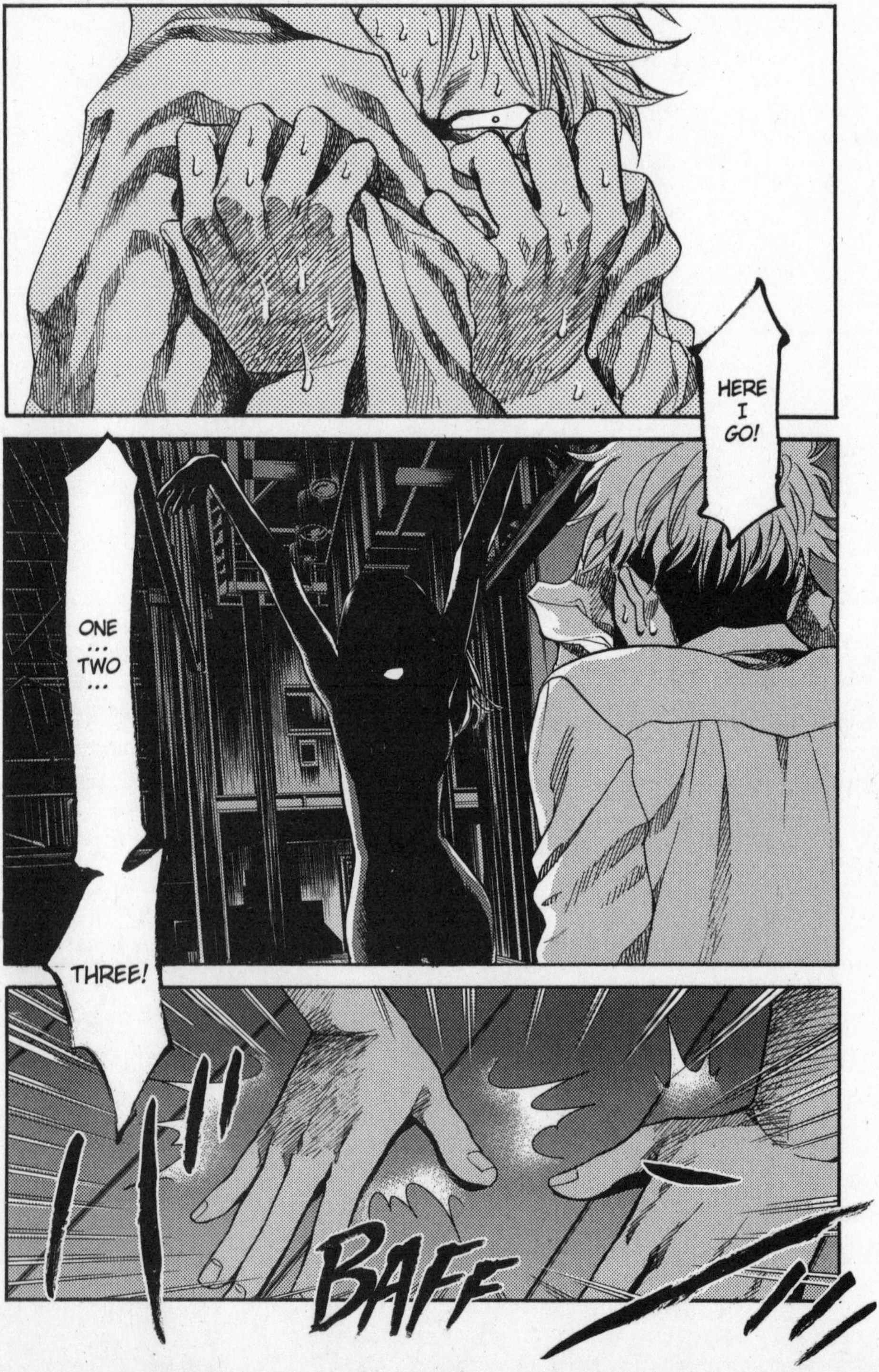
HERE I GO!
ONE... TWO...
THREE!
BAFF

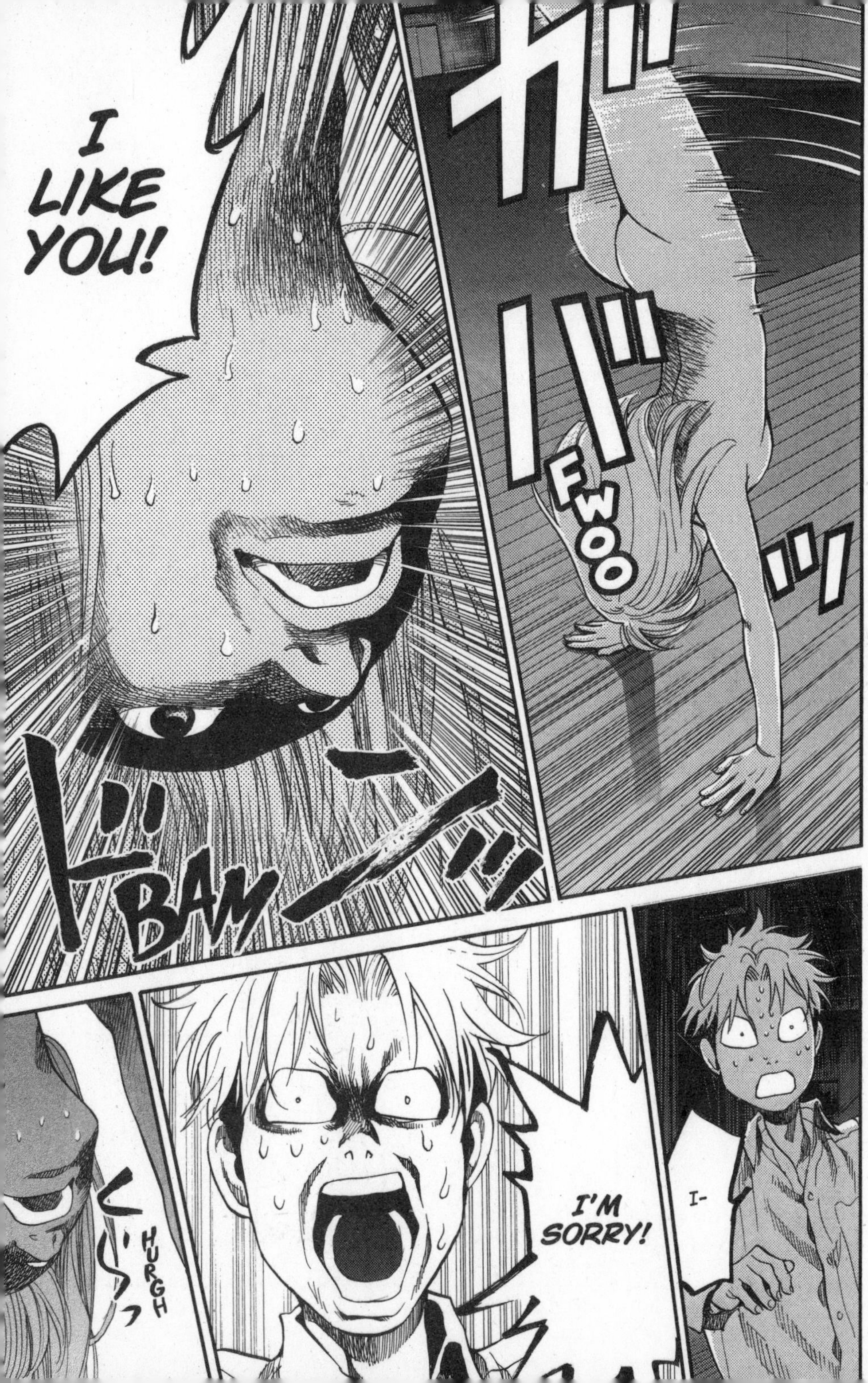
FWOO
I LIKE YOU!
BAM
I-
I'M SORRY!
HURGH

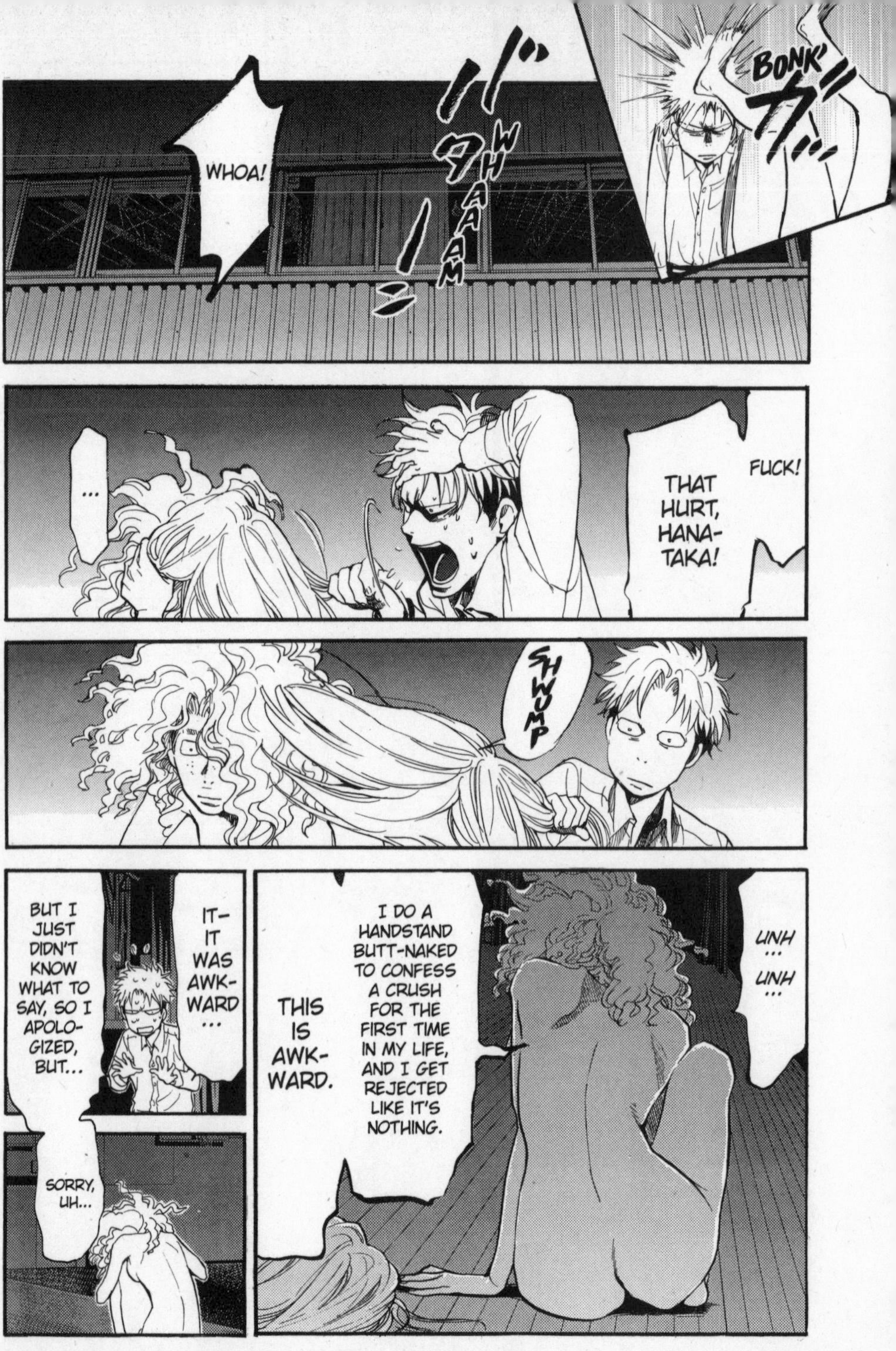

BONK'
WHOA!
WHAAAAM
FUCK!
THAT HURT, HANA-TAKA!
...
SHWUMP
UNH... UNH...
I DO A HANDSTAND BUTT-NAKED TO CONFESS A CRUSH FOR THE FIRST TIME IN MY LIFE, AND I GET REJECTED LIKE IT'S NOTHING.
THIS IS AWK-WARD.
IT-IT WAS AWK-WARD...
BUT I JUST DIDN'T KNOW WHAT TO SAY, SO I APOLO-GIZED, BUT...
SORRY, UH...

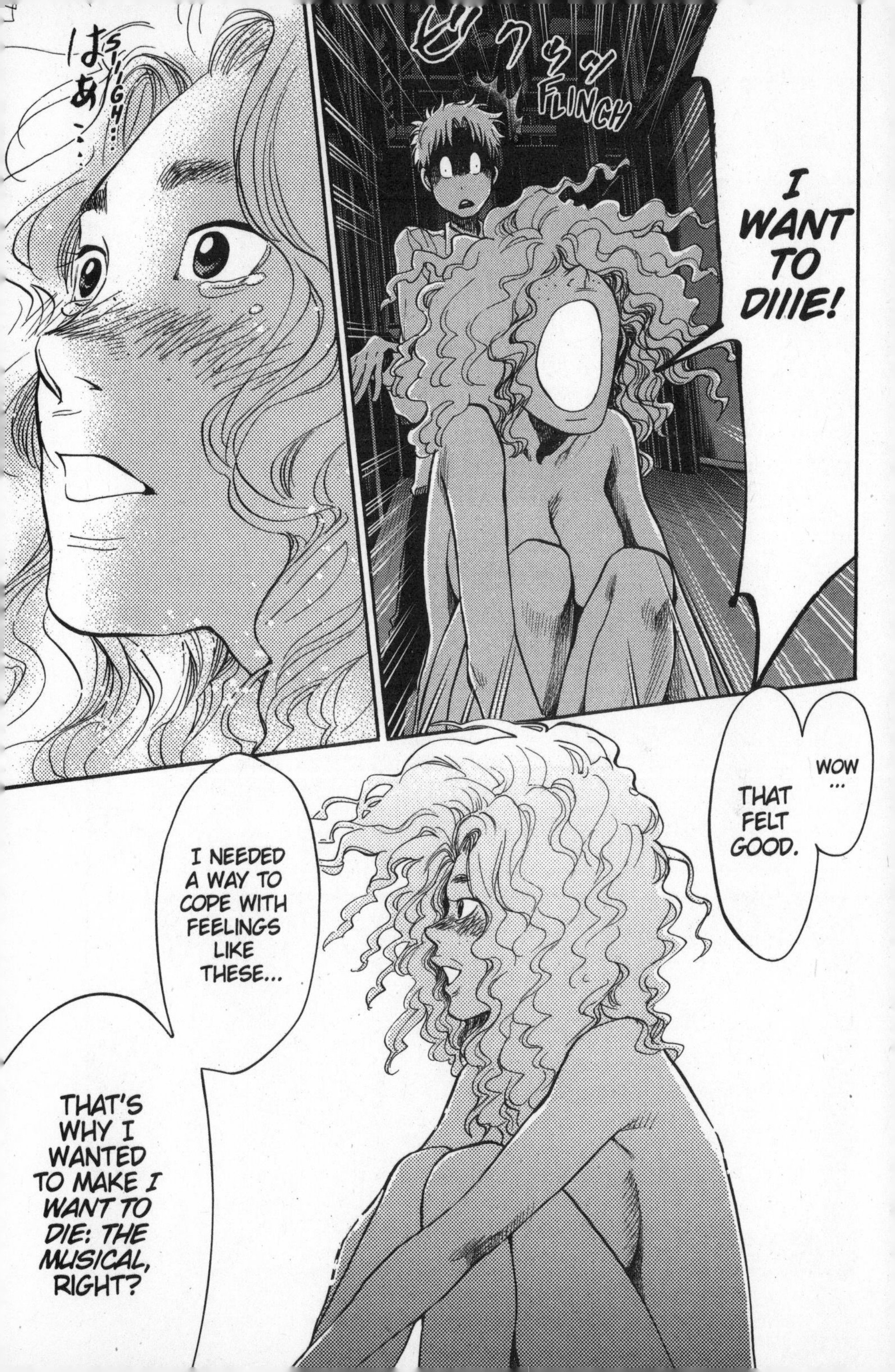
FLINCH
I WANT TO DIIIE!
SIGH...
WOW...
THAT FELT GOOD.
I NEEDED A WAY TO COPE WITH FEELINGS LIKE THESE...
THAT'S WHY I WANTED TO MAKE *I WANT TO DIE: THE MUSICAL*, RIGHT?

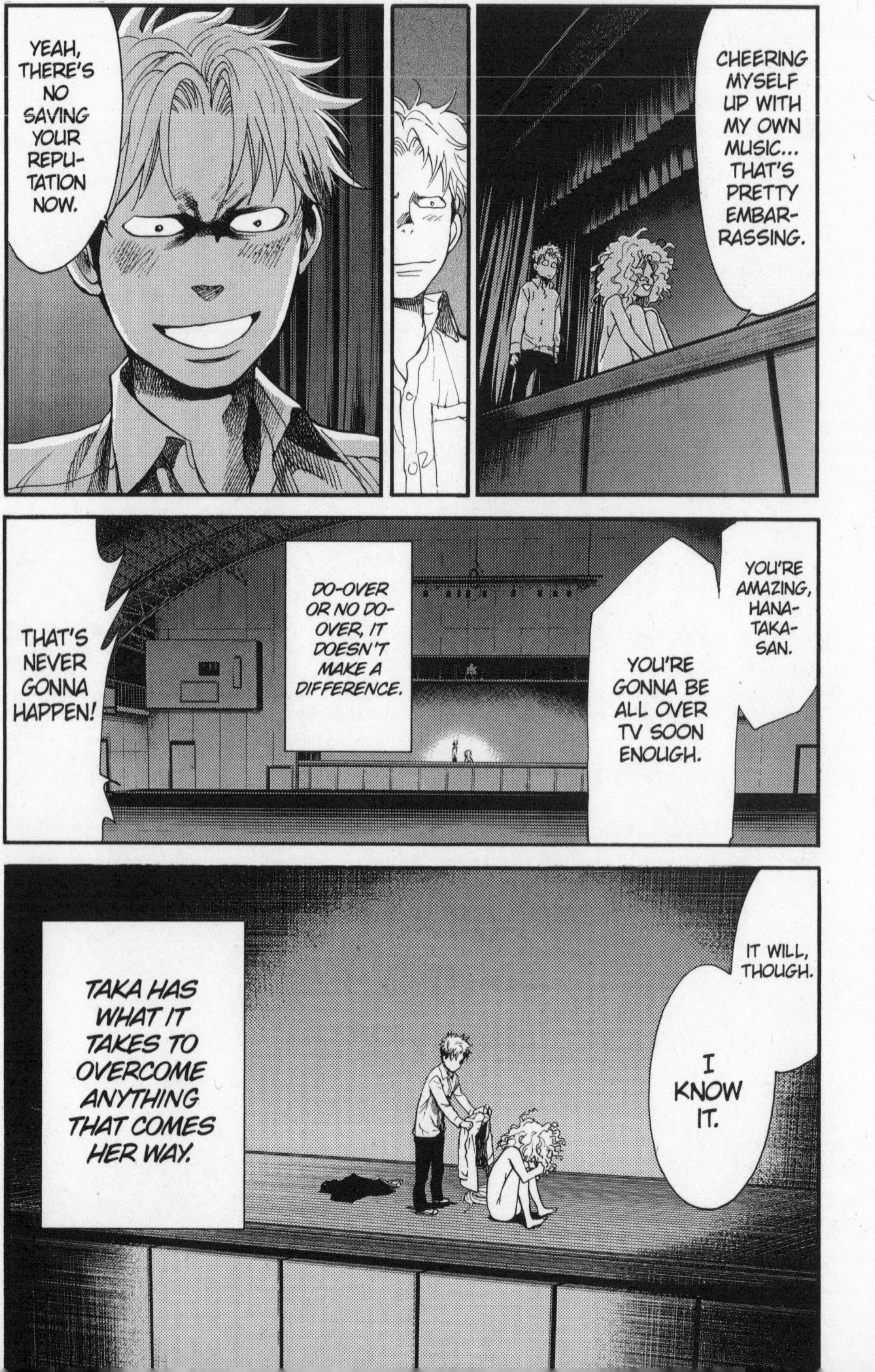
CHEERING MYSELF UP WITH MY OWN MUSIC... THAT'S PRETTY EMBARRASSING.
YEAH, THERE'S NO SAVING YOUR REPUTATION NOW.
YOU'RE AMAZING, HANA-TAKA-SAN.
YOU'RE GONNA BE ALL OVER TV SOON ENOUGH.
DO-OVER OR NO DO-OVER, IT DOESN'T MAKE A DIFFERENCE.
THAT'S NEVER GONNA HAPPEN!
IT WILL, THOUGH.
I KNOW IT.
TAKA HAS WHAT IT TAKES TO OVERCOME ANYTHING THAT COMES HER WAY.

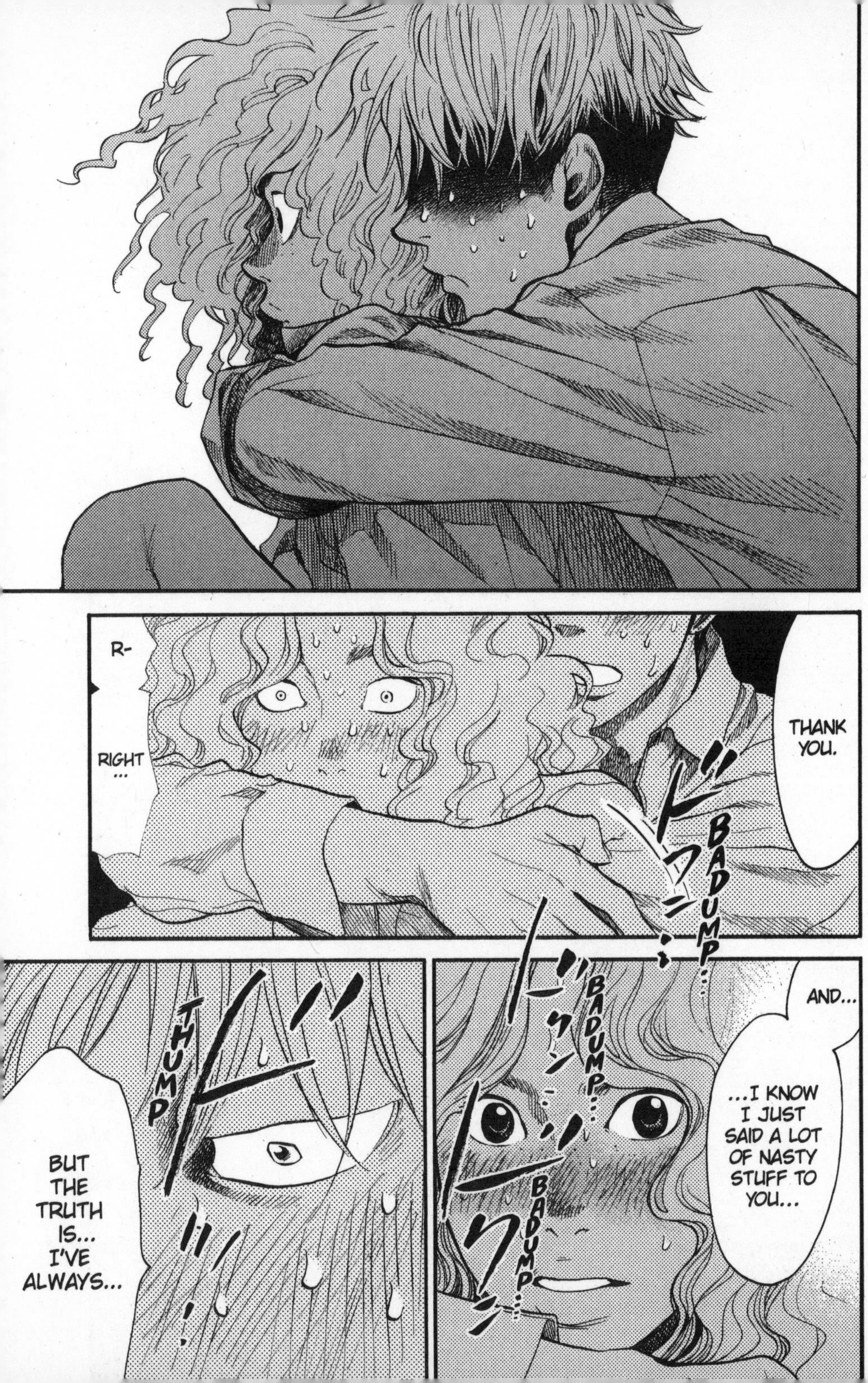
THANK YOU.
BADUMP...
R-
RIGHT...
AND...
BADUMP...
...I KNOW I JUST SAID A LOT OF NASTY STUFF TO YOU...
BADUMP...
THUMP
BUT THE TRUTH IS... I'VE ALWAYS...

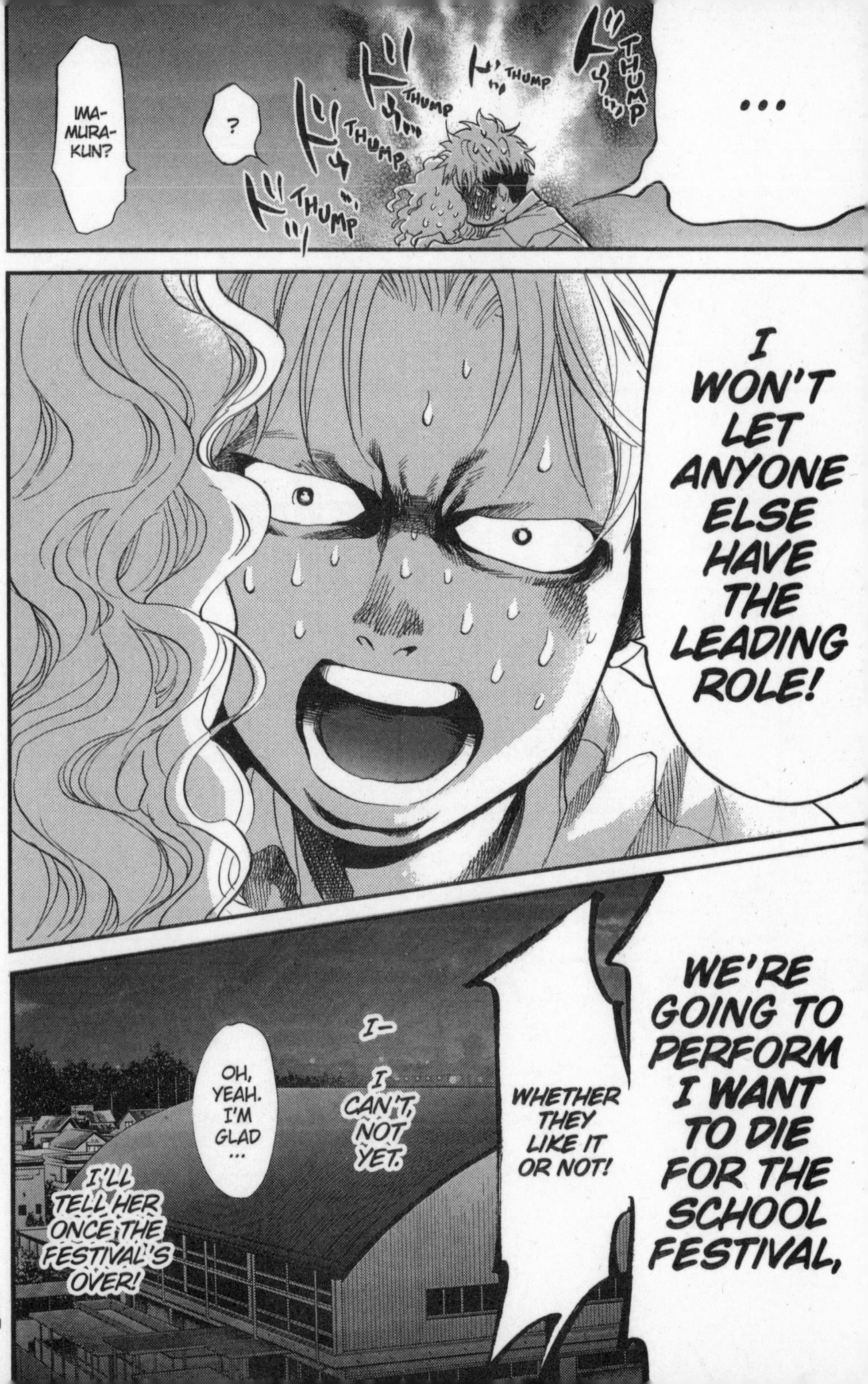
...
THUMP
THUMP
THUMP
THUMP
THUMP
?
IMA-MURA-KUN?
I WON'T LET ANYONE ELSE HAVE THE LEADING ROLE!
WE'RE GOING TO PERFORM I WANT TO DIE FOR THE SCHOOL FESTIVAL,
WHETHER THEY LIKE IT OR NOT!
I—
I CAN'T, NOT YET.
OH, YEAH. I'M GLAD...
I'LL TELL HER ONCE THE FESTIVAL'S OVER!

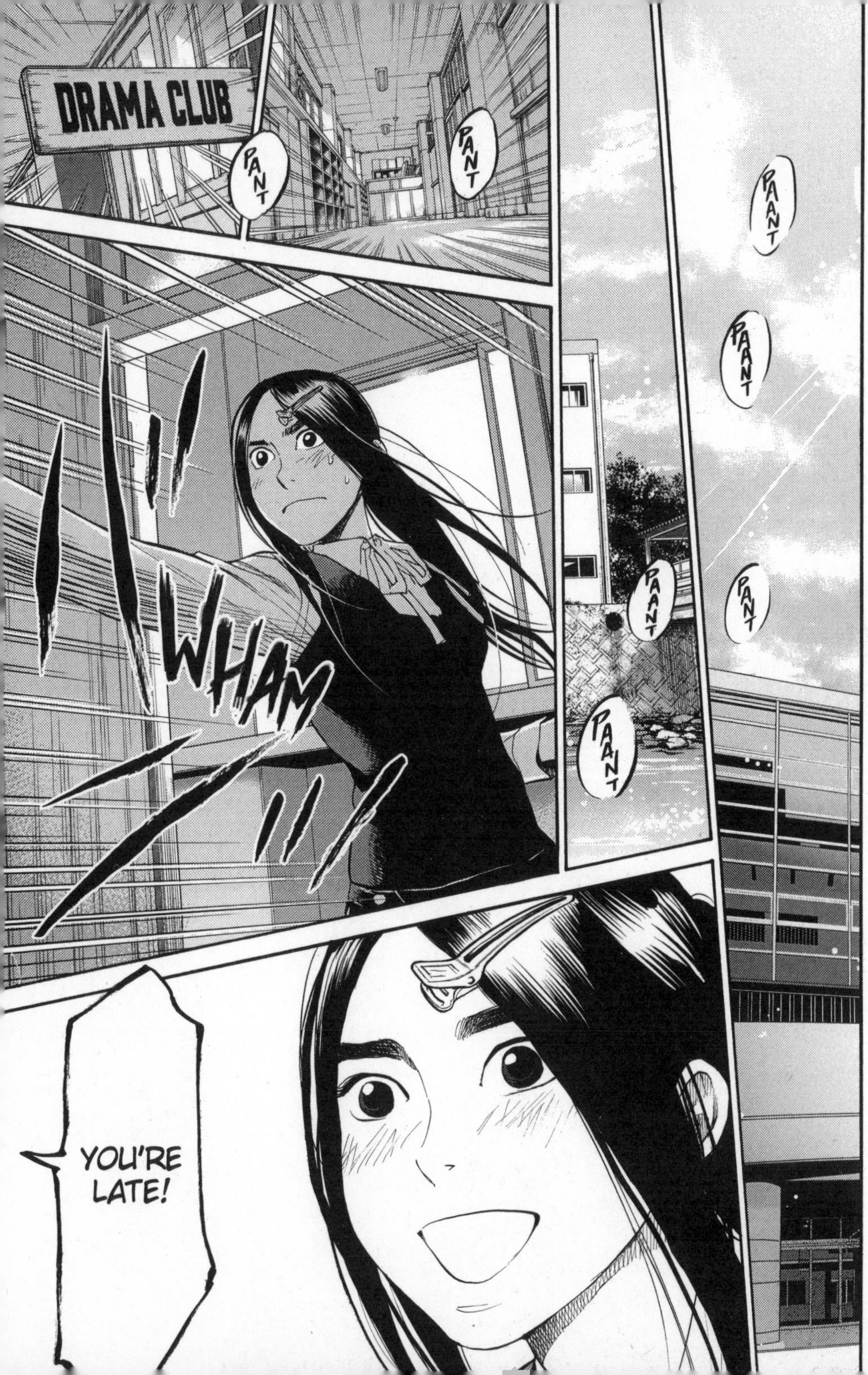
PAAANT
PAAANT
PANT
PAAANT
PAAANT
DRAMA CLUB
PANT
PANT
WHAM
YOU'RE LATE!

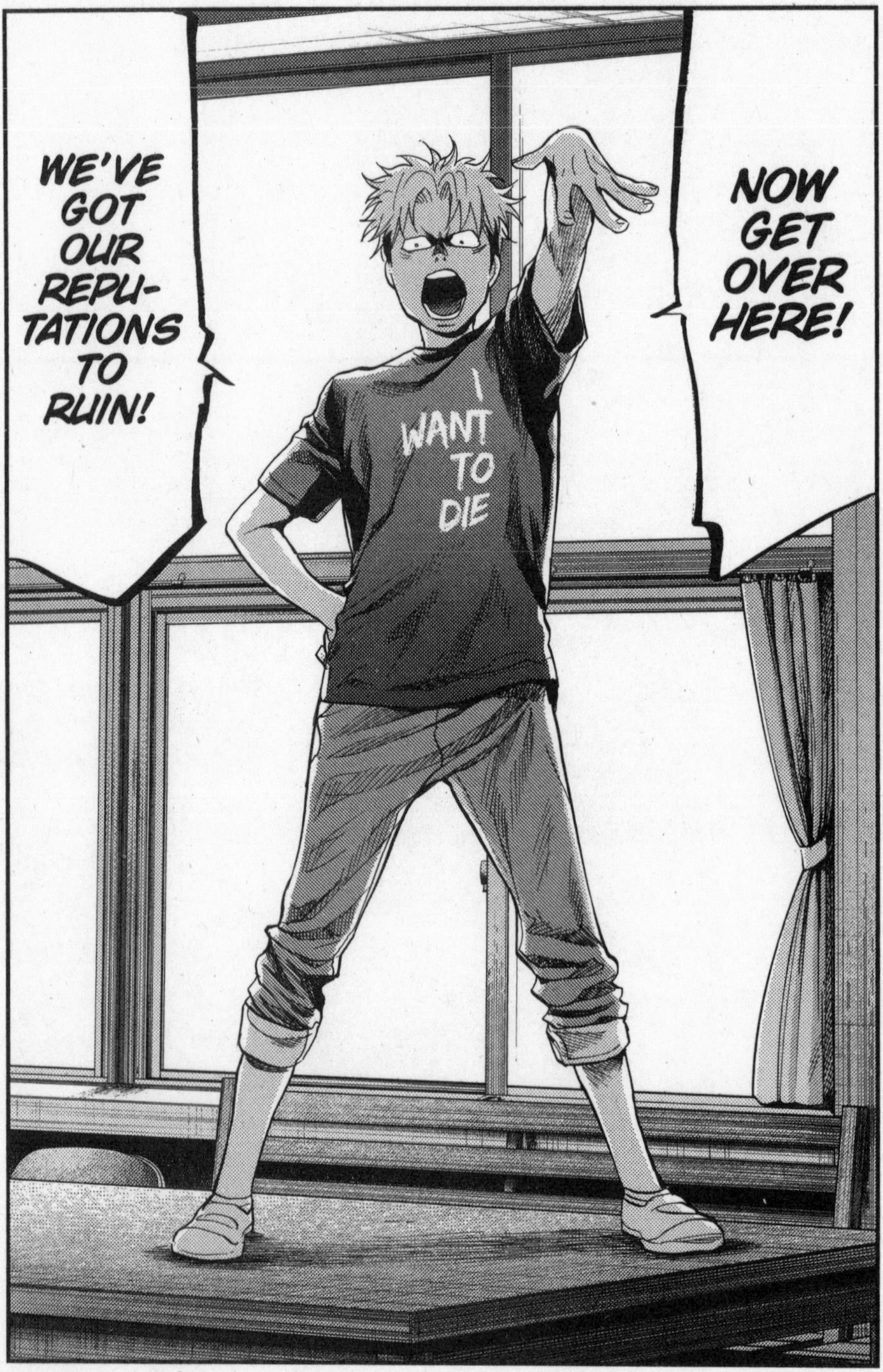
NOW GET OVER HERE!
I WANT TO DIE
WE'VE GOT OUR REPU-TATIONS TO RUIN!

94. THE SECRET DEATH WISH SHOW

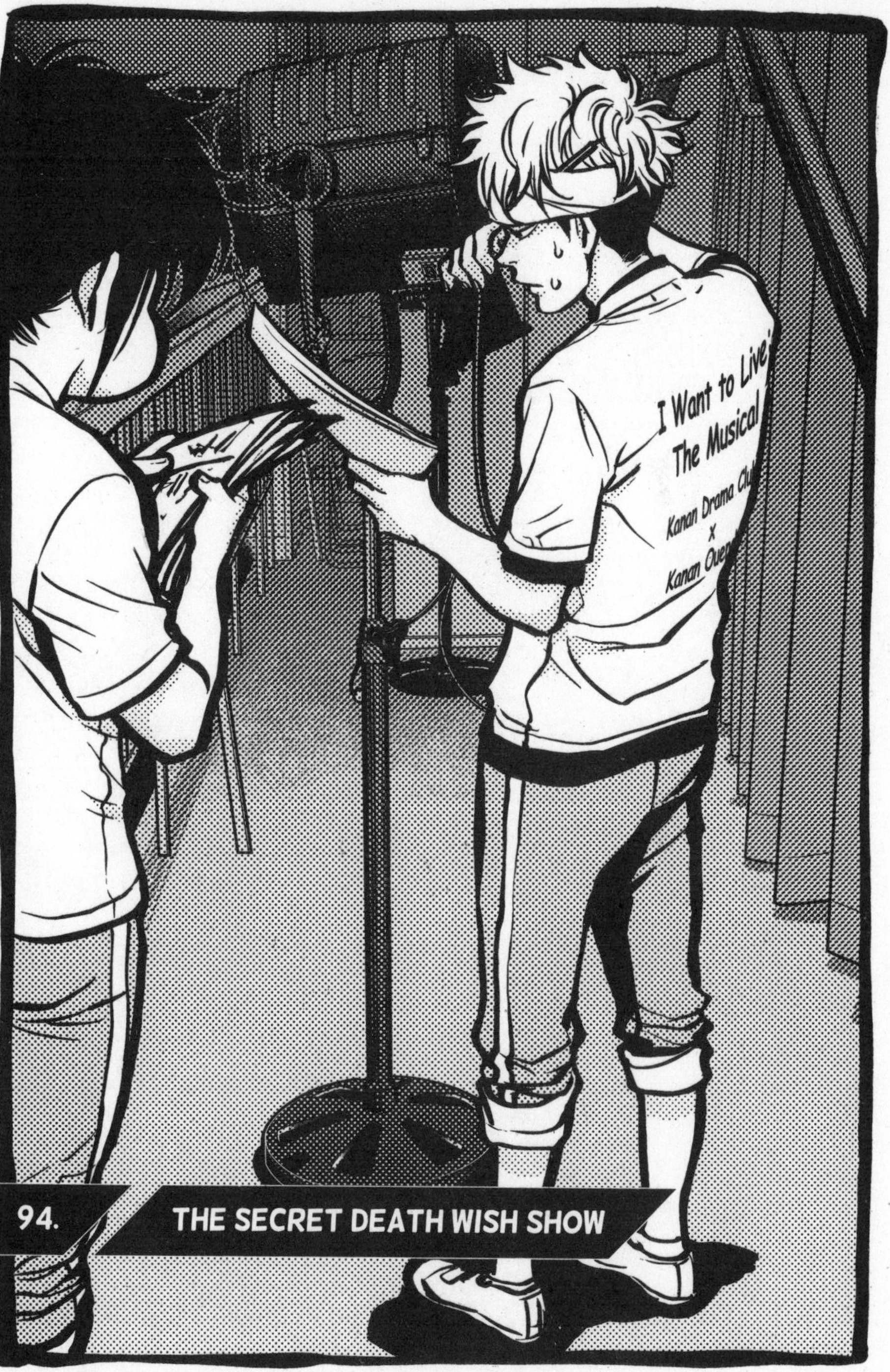
I Want to Live
The Musical
Kanan Drama
x

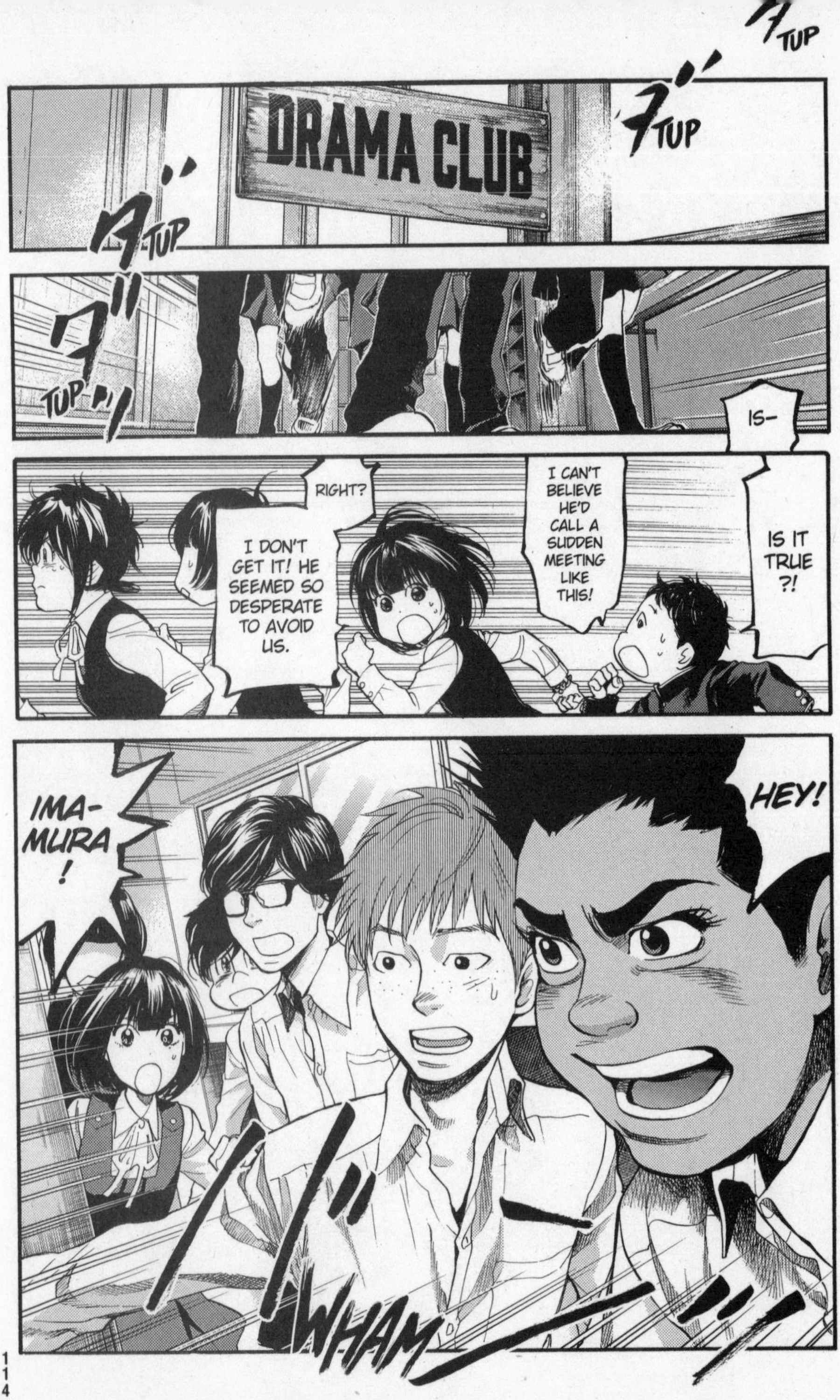
TUP
TUP
DRAMA CLUB
TUP
TUP
IS-
IS IT TRUE?!
I CAN'T BELIEVE HE'D CALL A SUDDEN MEETING LIKE THIS!
RIGHT?
I DON'T GET IT! HE SEEMED SO DESPERATE TO AVOID US.
HEY!
IMAMURA!
WHAM

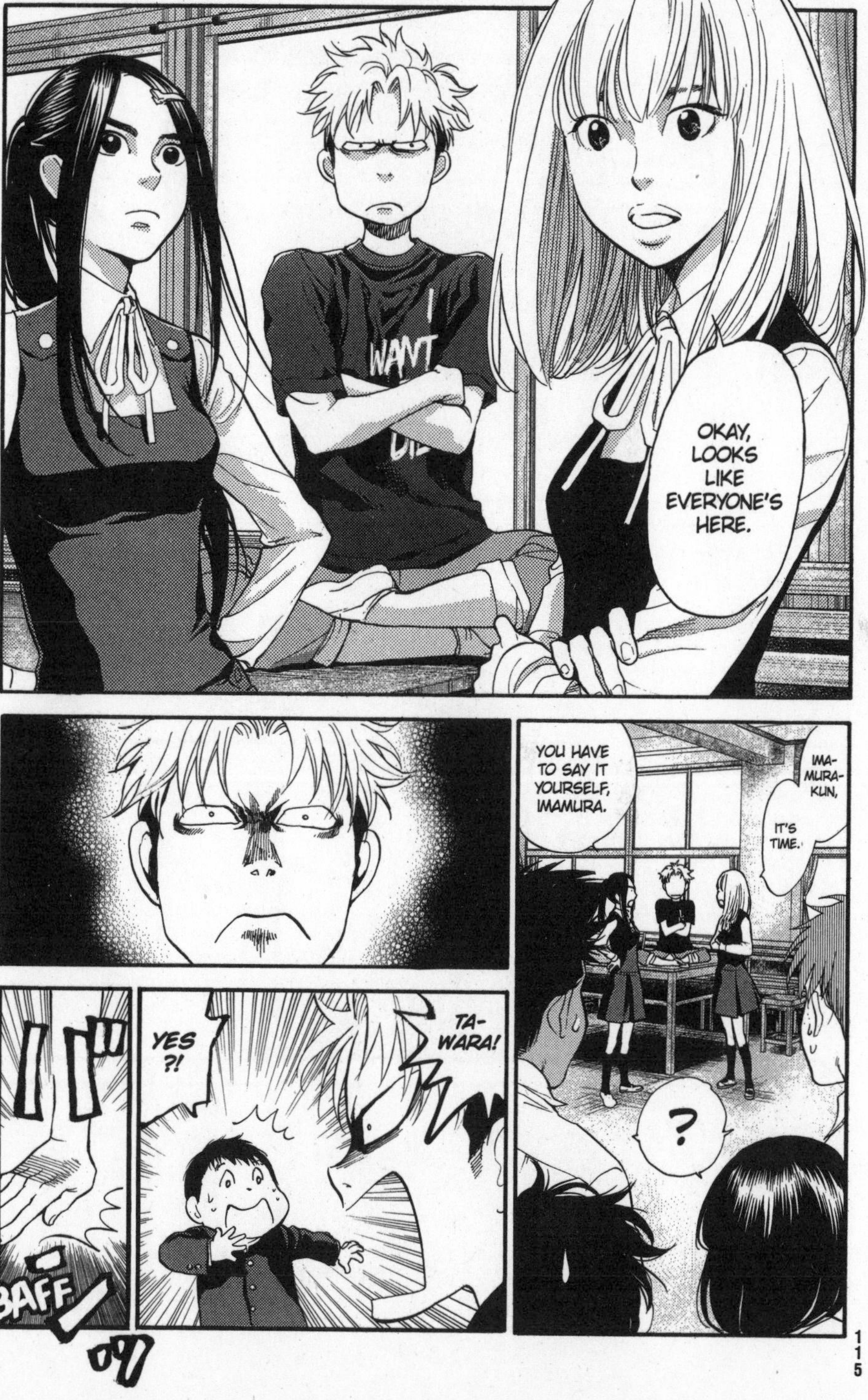
OKAY, LOOKS LIKE EVERYONE'S HERE.
IMAMURA-KUN,
IT'S TIME.
YOU HAVE TO SAY IT YOURSELF, IMAMURA.
?
TA-WARA!
YES ?!
BAFF

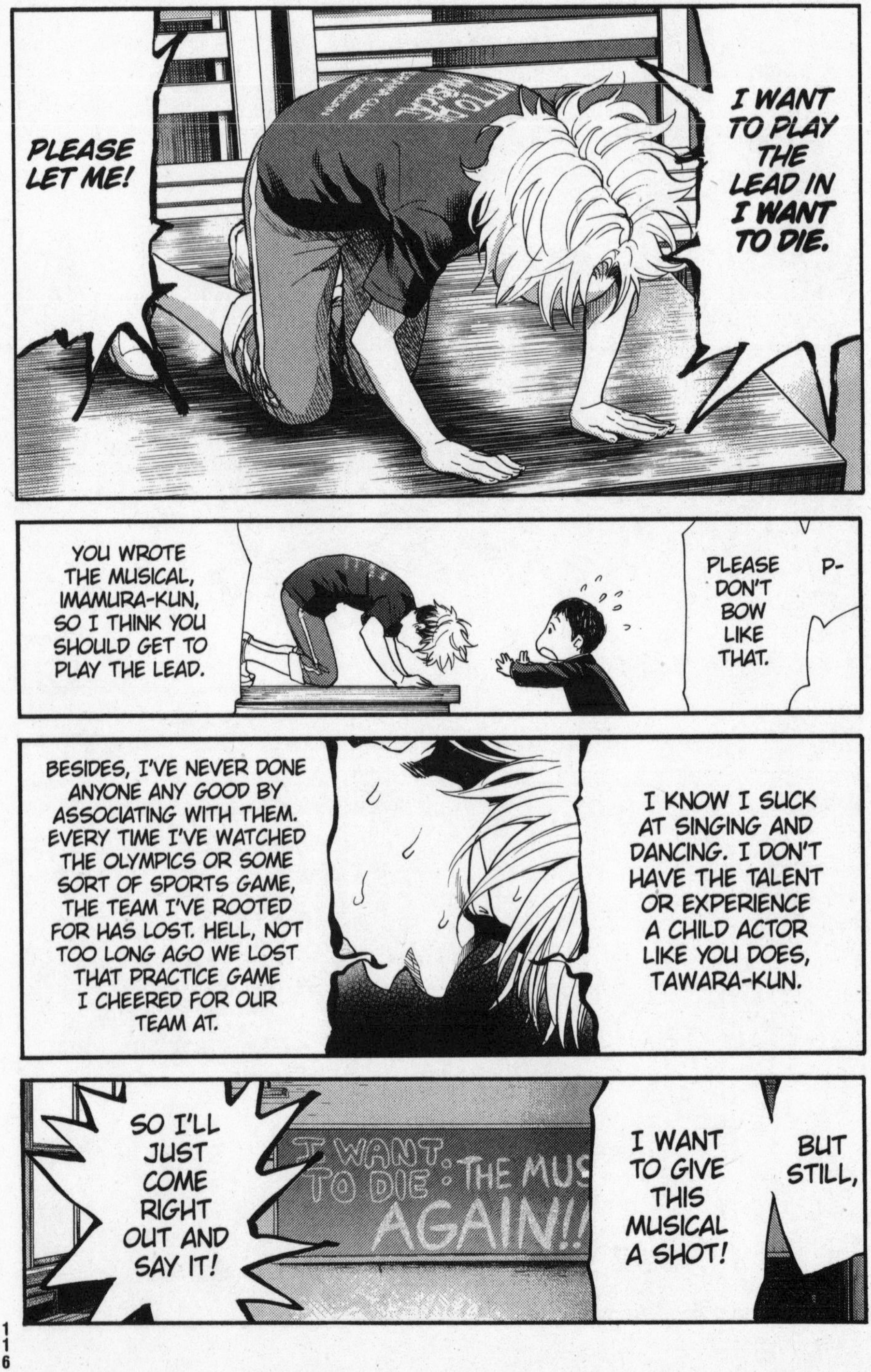

I WANT TO PLAY THE LEAD IN I WANT TO DIE.
PLEASE LET ME!
P-
PLEASE DON'T BOW LIKE THAT.
YOU WROTE THE MUSICAL, IMAMURA-KUN, SO I THINK YOU SHOULD GET TO PLAY THE LEAD.
I KNOW I SUCK AT SINGING AND DANCING. I DON'T HAVE THE TALENT OR EXPERIENCE A CHILD ACTOR LIKE YOU DOES, TAWARA-KUN.
BESIDES, I'VE NEVER DONE ANYONE ANY GOOD BY ASSOCIATING WITH THEM. EVERY TIME I'VE WATCHED THE OLYMPICS OR SOME SORT OF SPORTS GAME, THE TEAM I'VE ROOTED FOR HAS LOST. HELL, NOT TOO LONG AGO WE LOST THAT PRACTICE GAME I CHEERED FOR OUR TEAM AT.
BUT STILL,
I WANT TO GIVE THIS MUSICAL A SHOT!
SO I'LL JUST COME RIGHT OUT AND SAY IT!
I WANT TO DIE : THE MUS
AGAIN!!

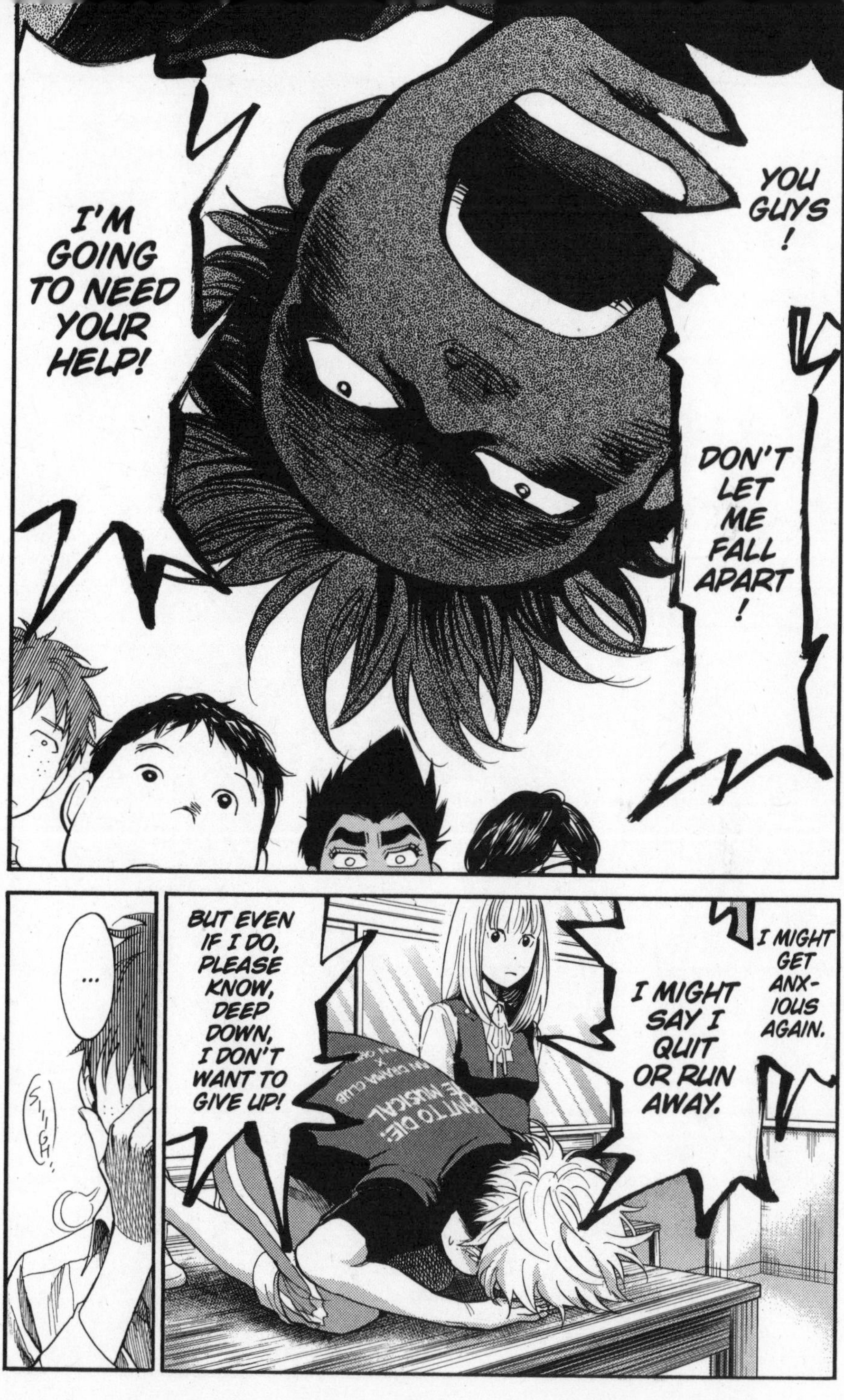
YOU GUYS!
DON'T LET ME FALL APART!
I'M GOING TO NEED YOUR HELP!
I MIGHT GET ANX-IOUS AGAIN.
I MIGHT SAY I QUIT OR RUN AWAY.
BUT EVEN IF I DO, PLEASE KNOW, DEEP DOWN, I DON'T WANT TO GIVE UP!
...
SIIIGH

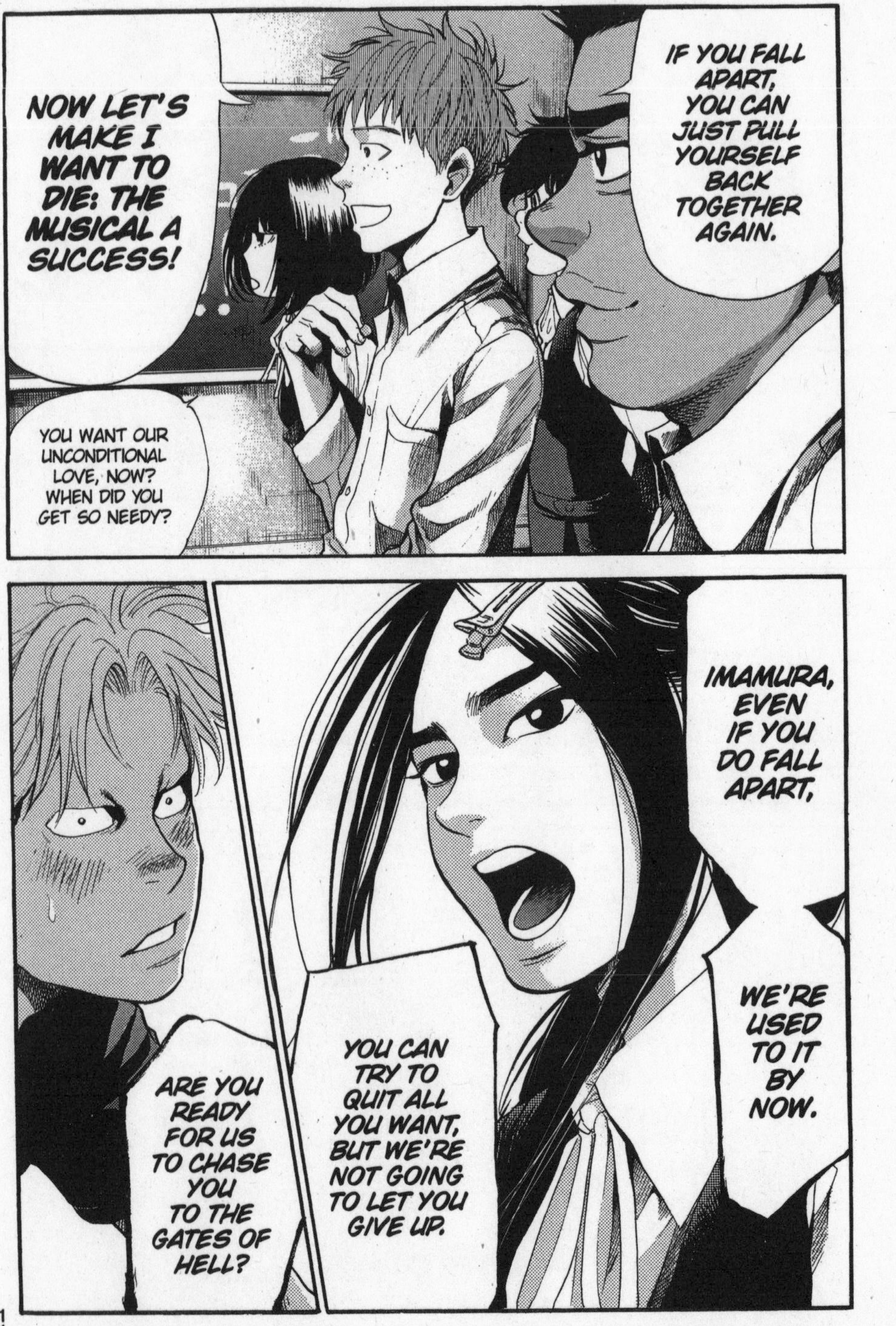
IF YOU FALL APART, YOU CAN JUST PULL YOURSELF BACK TOGETHER AGAIN.
NOW LET'S MAKE I WANT TO DIE: THE MUSICAL A SUCCESS!
YOU WANT OUR UNCONDITIONAL LOVE, NOW? WHEN DID YOU GET SO NEEDY?
IMAMURA, EVEN IF YOU DO FALL APART,
WE'RE USED TO IT BY NOW.
YOU CAN TRY TO QUIT ALL YOU WANT, BUT WE'RE NOT GOING TO LET YOU GIVE UP.
ARE YOU READY FOR US TO CHASE YOU TO THE GATES OF HELL?

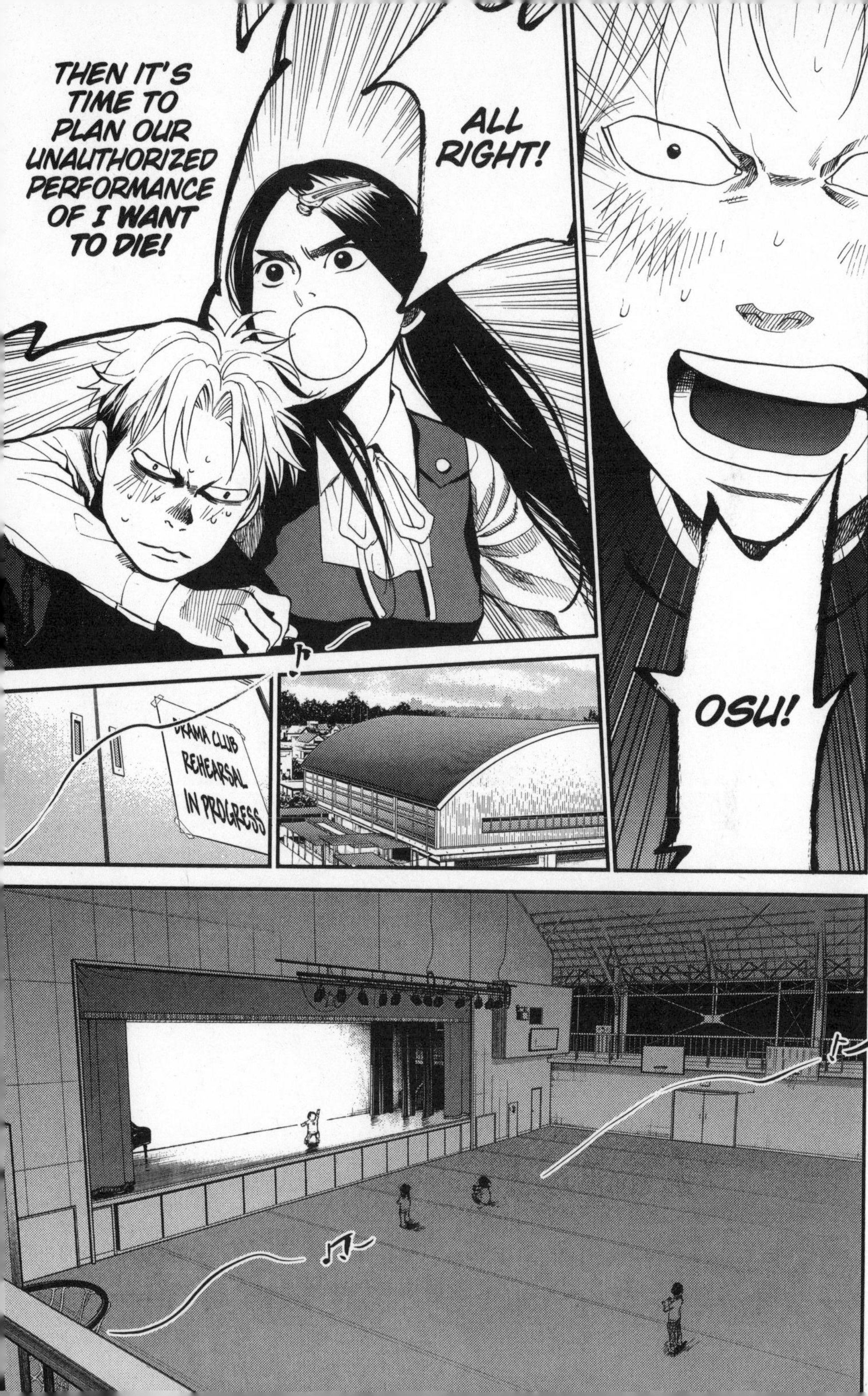
OSU!
ALL RIGHT!
THEN IT'S TIME TO PLAN OUR UNAUTHORIZED PERFORMANCE OF I WANT TO DIE!
DRAMA CLUB REHEARSAL IN PROGRESS

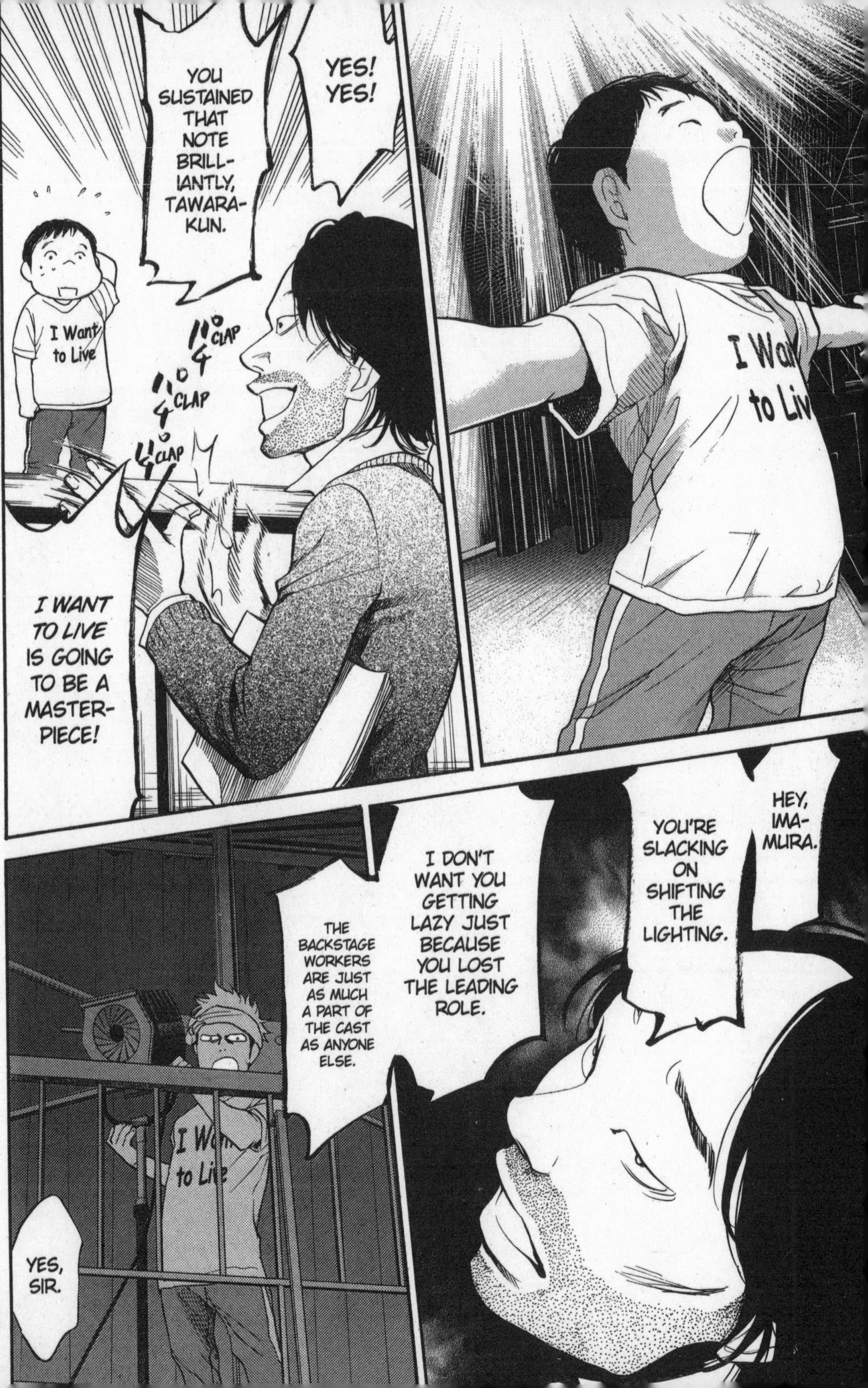
I Want to Live
YES! YES!
YOU SUSTAINED THAT NOTE BRILLIANTLY, TAWARA-KUN.
I Want to Live
CLAP
CLAP
CLAP
I WANT TO LIVE IS GOING TO BE A MASTERPIECE!
HEY, IMAMURA.
YOU'RE SLACKING ON SHIFTING THE LIGHTING.
I DON'T WANT YOU GETTING LAZY JUST BECAUSE YOU LOST THE LEADING ROLE.
THE BACKSTAGE WORKERS ARE JUST AS MUCH A PART OF THE CAST AS ANYONE ELSE.
YES, SIR.

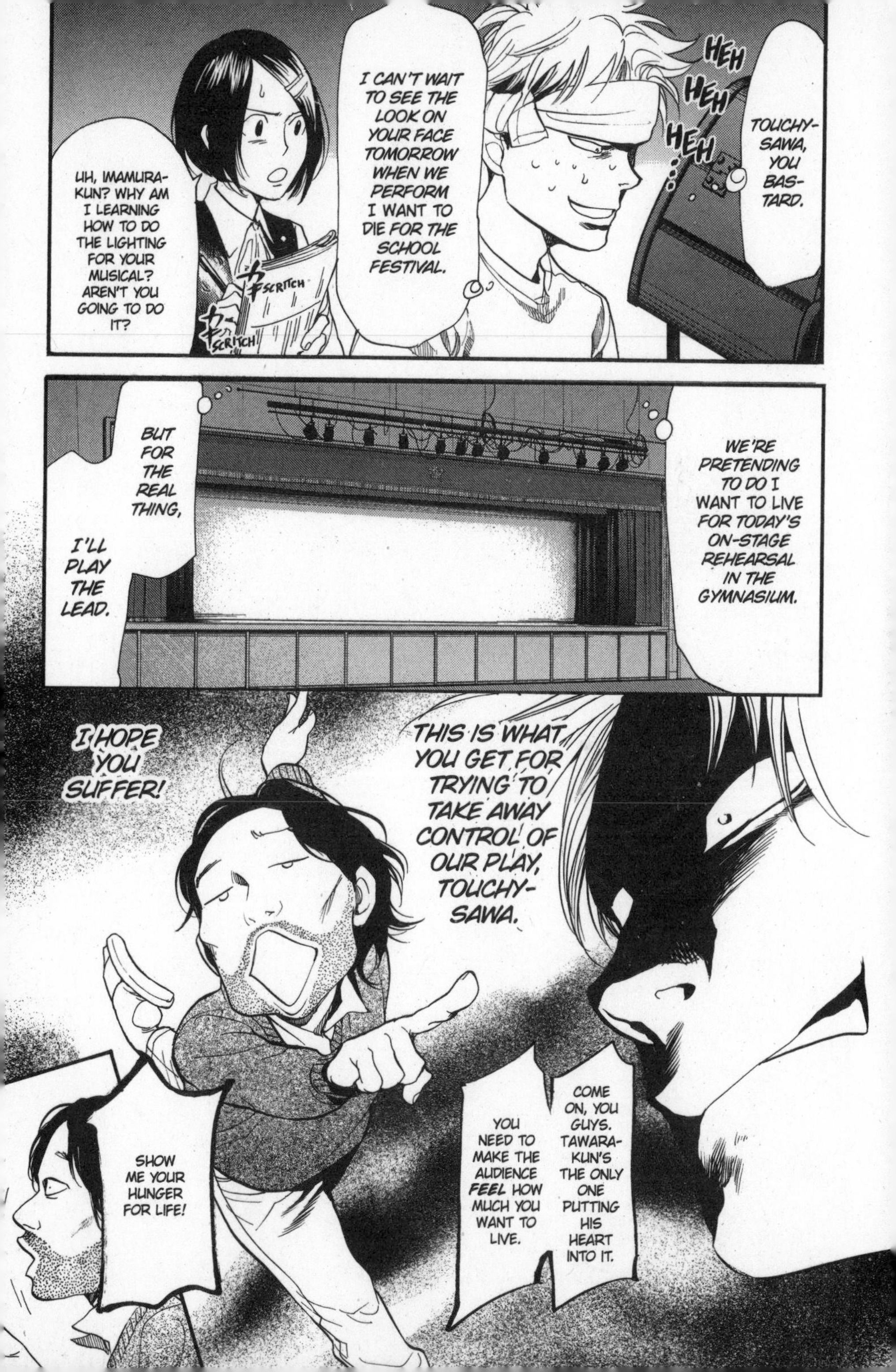
TOUCHY-SAWA, YOU BASTARD.
HEH HEH HEH
I CAN'T WAIT TO SEE THE LOOK ON YOUR FACE TOMORROW WHEN WE PERFORM I WANT TO DIE FOR THE SCHOOL FESTIVAL.
UH, IMAMURA-KUN? WHY AM I LEARNING HOW TO DO THE LIGHTING FOR YOUR MUSICAL? AREN'T YOU GOING TO DO IT?
SCRITCH
SCRITCH
WE'RE PRETENDING TO DO I WANT TO LIVE FOR TODAY'S ON-STAGE REHEARSAL IN THE GYMNASIUM.
BUT FOR THE REAL THING,
I'LL PLAY THE LEAD.
THIS IS WHAT YOU GET FOR TRYING TO TAKE AWAY CONTROL OF OUR PLAY, TOUCHY-SAWA.
I HOPE YOU SUFFER!
COME ON, YOU GUYS. TAWARA-KUN'S THE ONLY ONE PUTTING HIS HEART INTO IT.
YOU NEED TO MAKE THE AUDIENCE FEEL HOW MUCH YOU WANT TO LIVE.
SHOW ME YOUR HUNGER FOR LIFE!

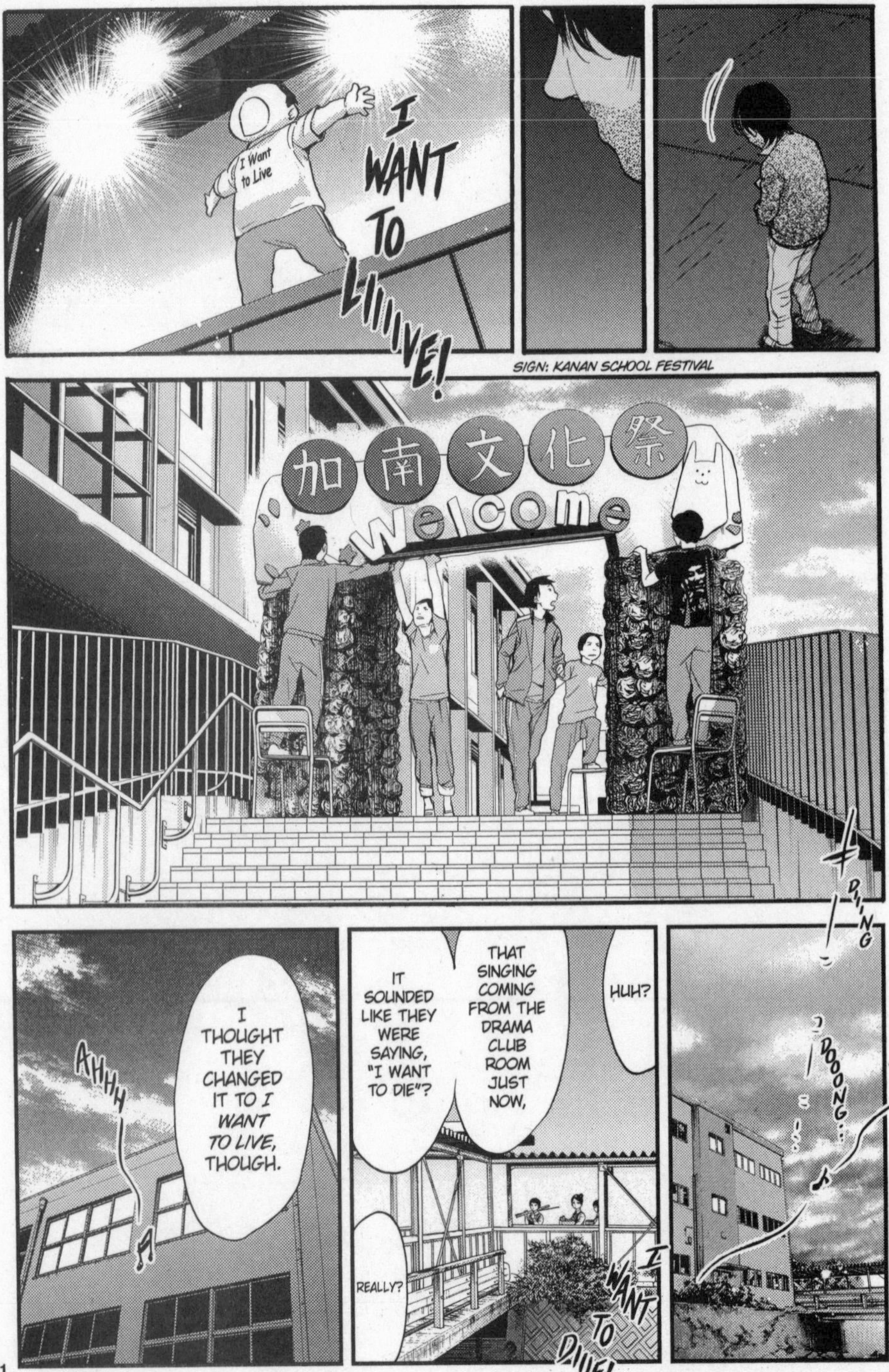
I Want to Live
I WANT TO LIIIIVE!
SIGN: KANAN SCHOOL FESTIVAL
加南文化祭
welcome
DIIING
DOOONG...
I WANT TO DIIIE!
HUH?
THAT SINGING COMING FROM THE DRAMA CLUB ROOM JUST NOW,
IT SOUNDED LIKE THEY WERE SAYING, "I WANT TO DIE"?
REALLY?
I THOUGHT THEY CHANGED IT TO *I WANT TO LIVE*, THOUGH.
AHHH

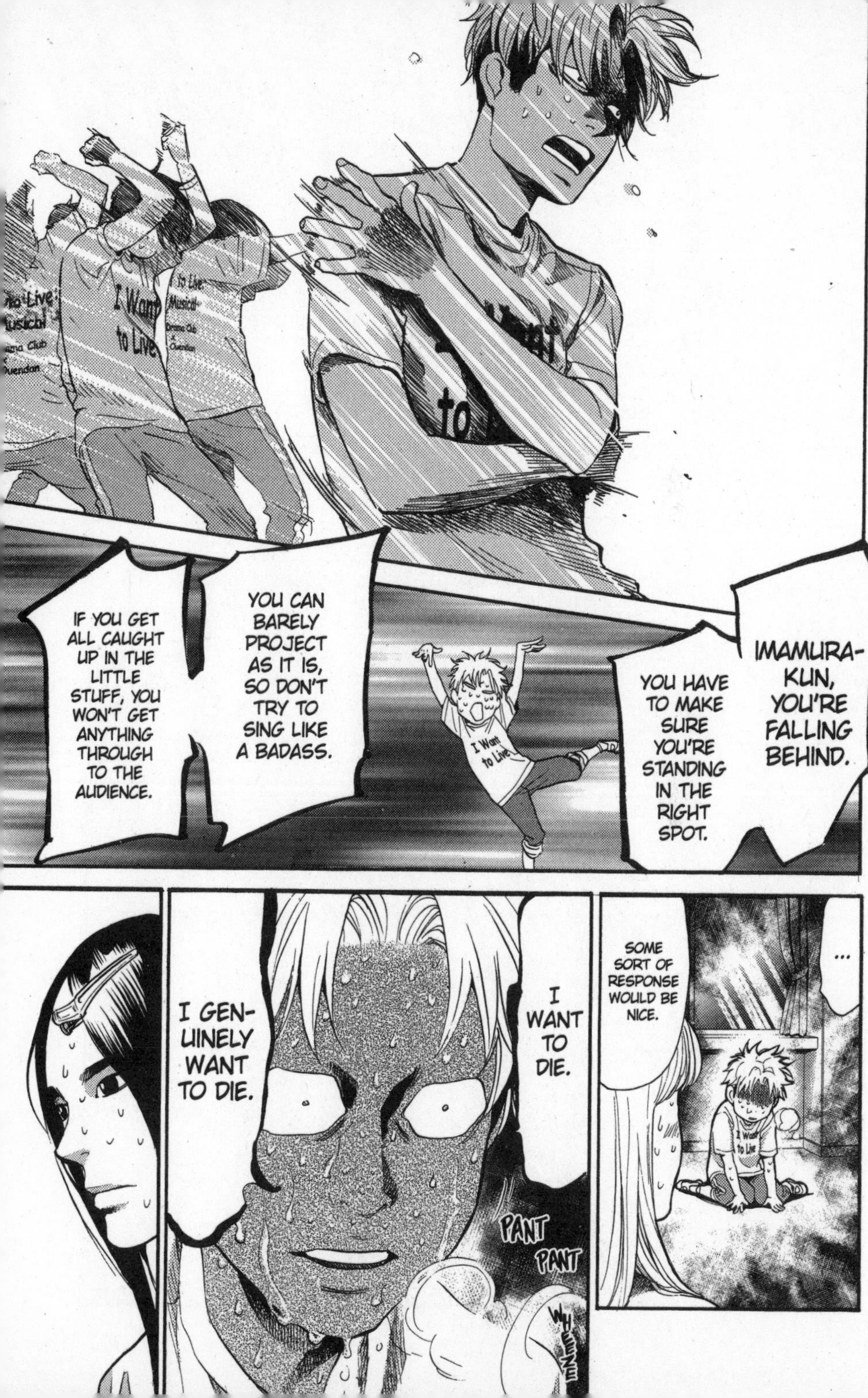
IMAMURA-KUN, YOU'RE FALLING BEHIND.
YOU HAVE TO MAKE SURE YOU'RE STANDING IN THE RIGHT SPOT.
YOU CAN BARELY PROJECT AS IT IS, SO DON'T TRY TO SING LIKE A BADASS.
IF YOU GET ALL CAUGHT UP IN THE LITTLE STUFF, YOU WON'T GET ANYTHING THROUGH TO THE AUDIENCE.
...
SOME SORT OF RESPONSE WOULD BE NICE.
PANT PANT
I WANT TO DIE.
I GEN-UINELY WANT TO DIE.

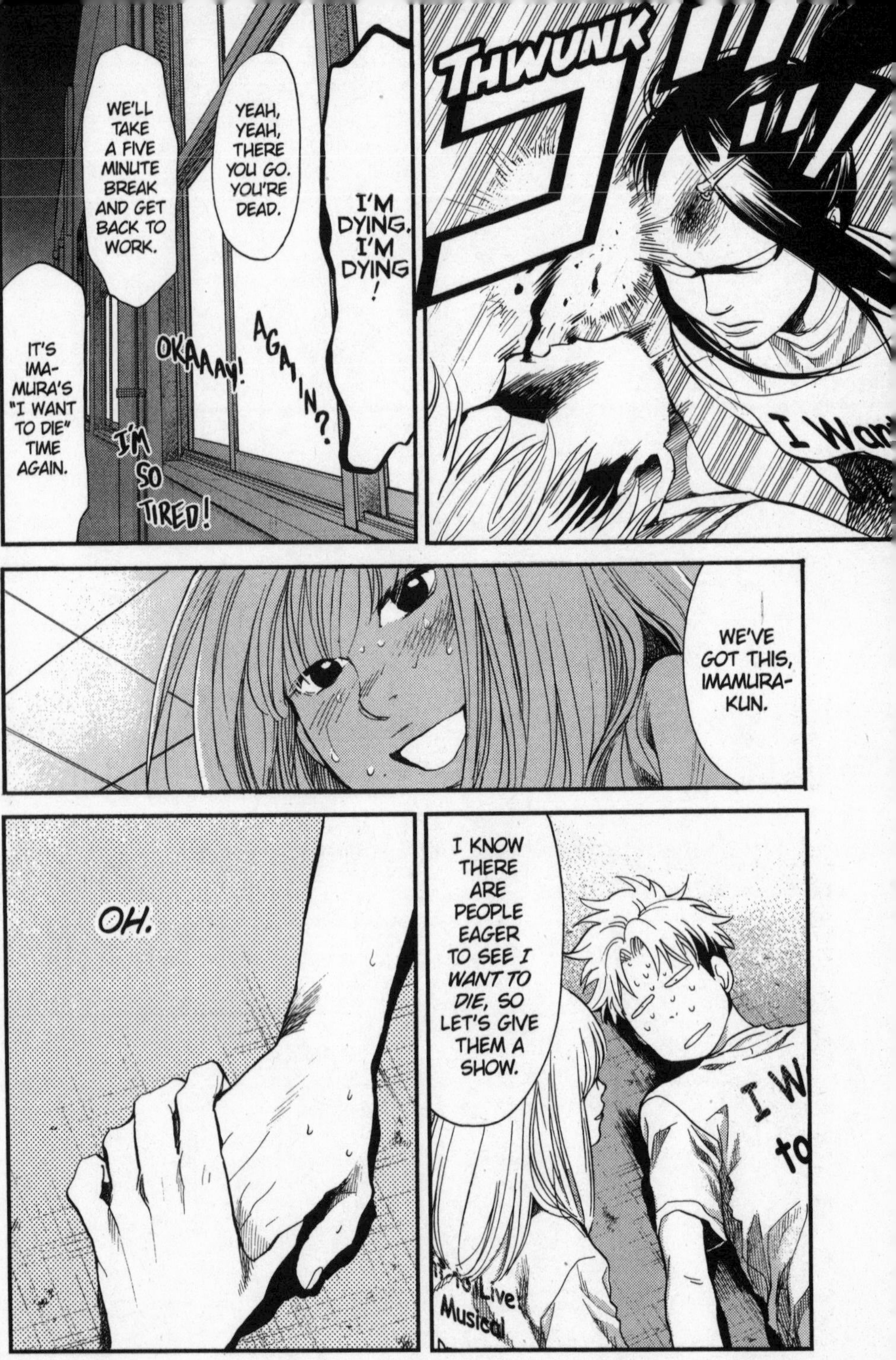
THWUNK
I Want
I'M DYING. I'M DYING!
AGAIN?
YEAH, YEAH, THERE YOU GO. YOU'RE DEAD.
OKAAAAY!
WE'LL TAKE A FIVE MINUTE BREAK AND GET BACK TO WORK.
IT'S IMAMURA'S "I WANT TO DIE" TIME AGAIN.
I'M SO TIRED!
WE'VE GOT THIS, IMAMURA-KUN.
I KNOW THERE ARE PEOPLE EAGER TO SEE *I WANT TO DIE*, SO LET'S GIVE THEM A SHOW.
Musical
OH.

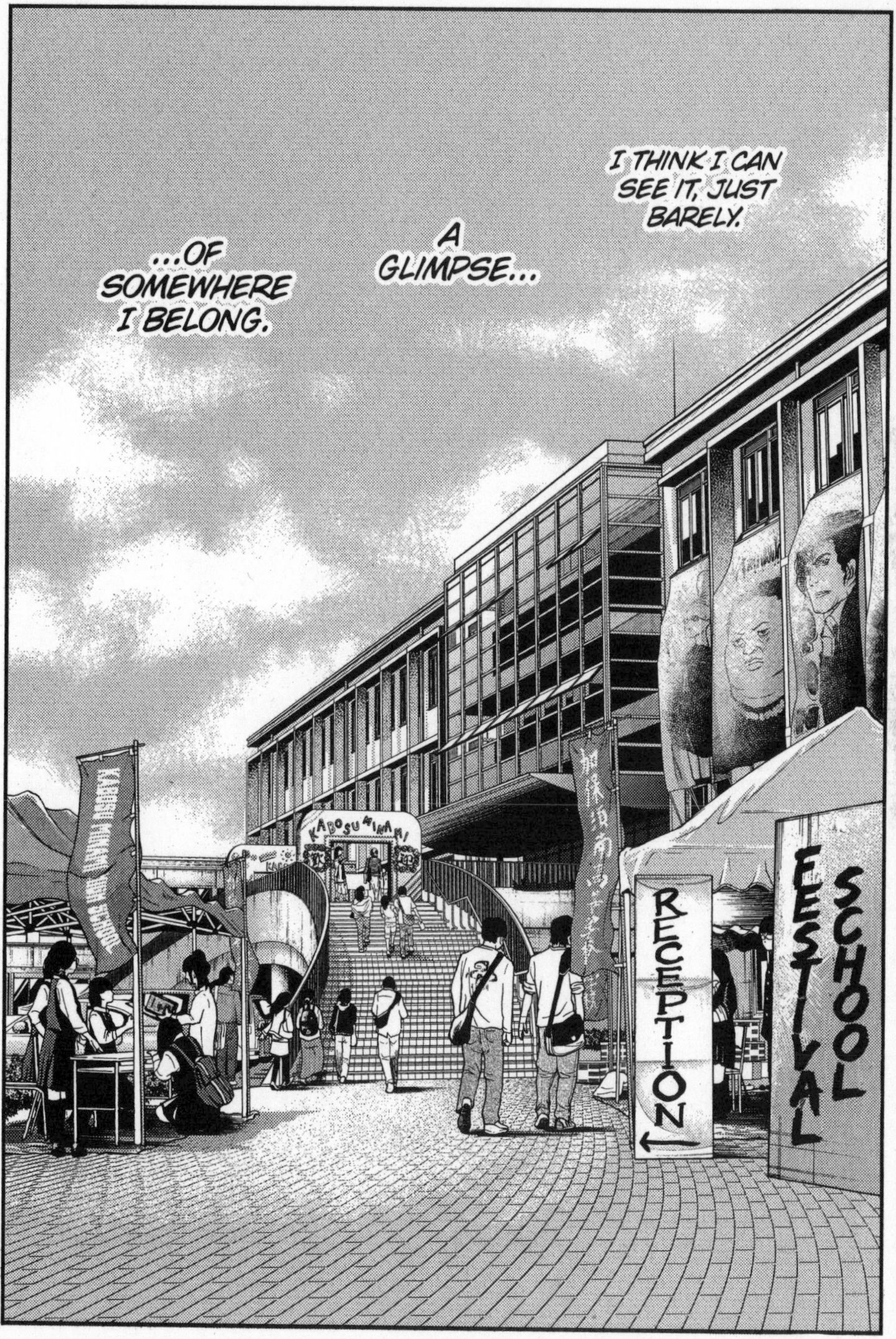
I THINK I CAN SEE IT, JUST BARELY.
A GLIMPSE...
...OF SOMEWHERE I BELONG.
KABOSU MINAMI
SCHOOL FESTIVAL
RECEPTION ←

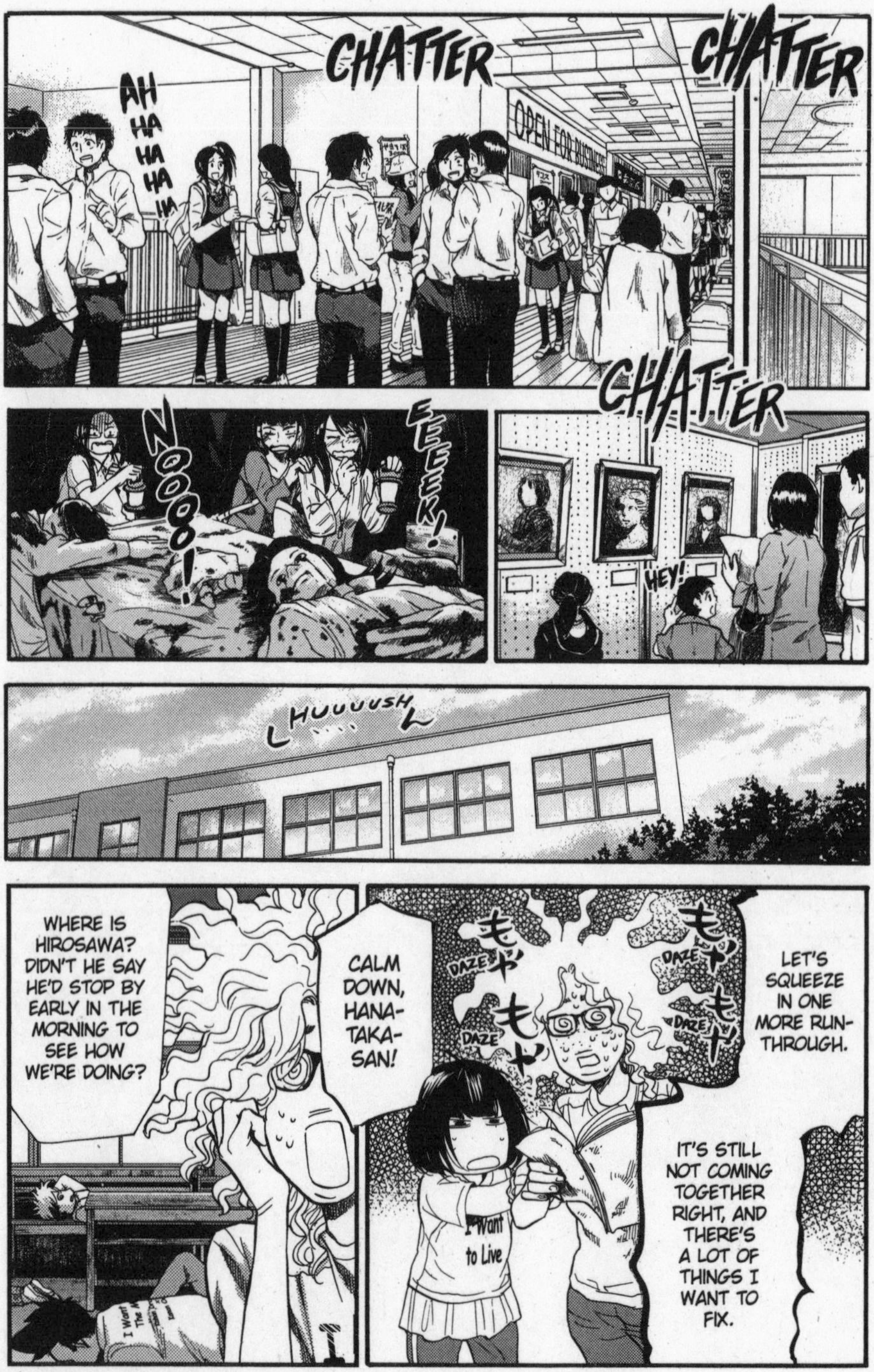
CHATTER
OPEN FOR BUSINESS
CHATTER
AH HA HA HA HA
CHATTER
HEY!
EEEEEK!
NOOOOO!
HUUUUSH
LET'S SQUEEZE IN ONE MORE RUN-THROUGH.
IT'S STILL NOT COMING TOGETHER RIGHT, AND THERE'S A LOT OF THINGS I WANT TO FIX.
DAZE
DAZE
DAZE
DAZE
もや もや
もや もや
I Want to Live
CALM DOWN, HANA-TAKA-SAN!
WHERE IS HIROSAWA? DIDN'T HE SAY HE'D STOP BY EARLY IN THE MORNING TO SEE HOW WE'RE DOING?

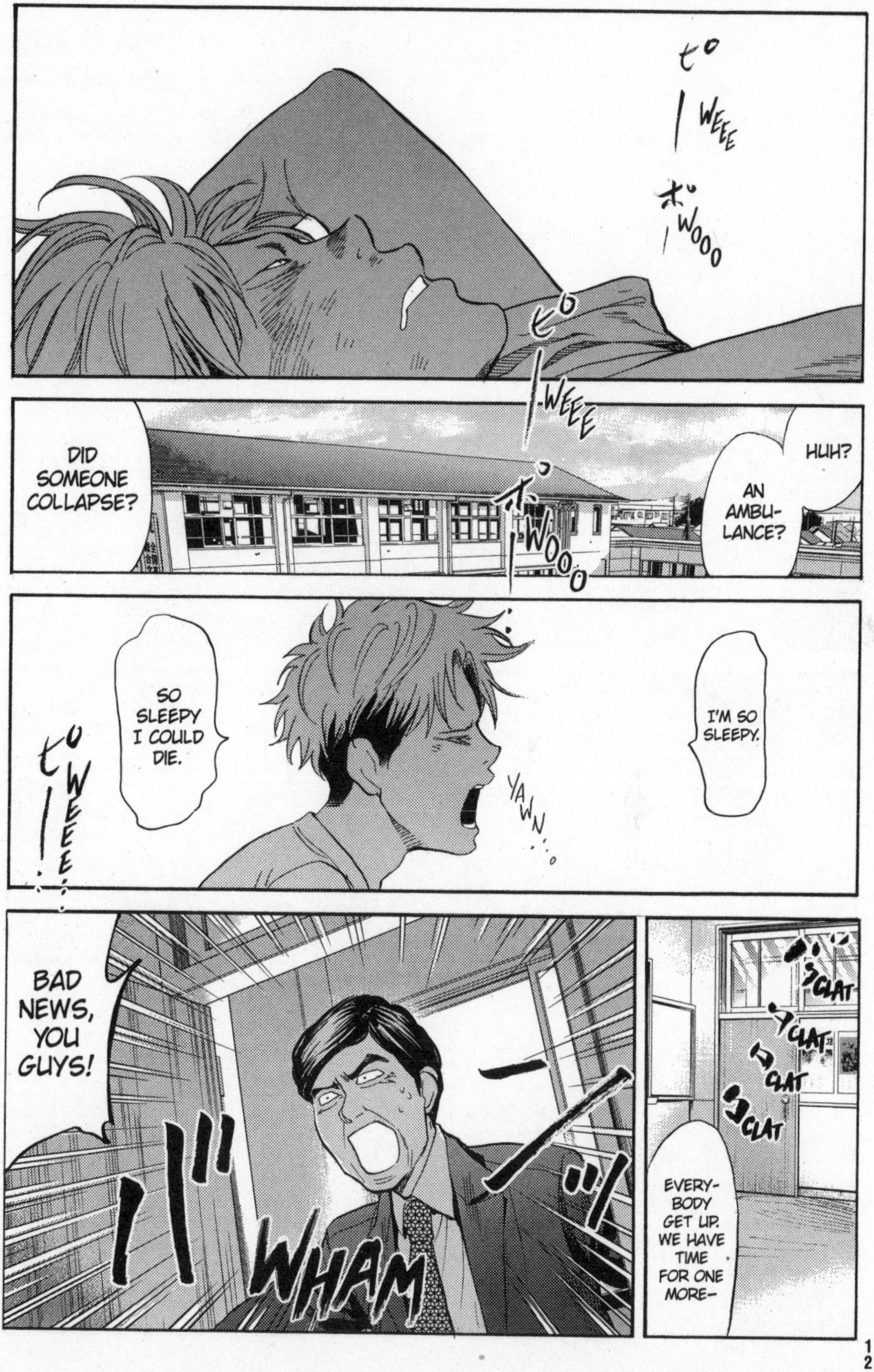
ピー WEEE
ポー WOOO
ピー WEEE
HUH?
AN AMBU-LANCE?
DID SOMEONE COLLAPSE?
ポー WOOO
I'M SO SLEEPY.
YAWN...
SO SLEEPY I COULD DIE.
WEEEE...
CLAT CLAT CLAT CLAT
EVERY-BODY GET UP. WE HAVE TIME FOR ONE MORE-
BAD NEWS, YOU GUYS!
WHAM

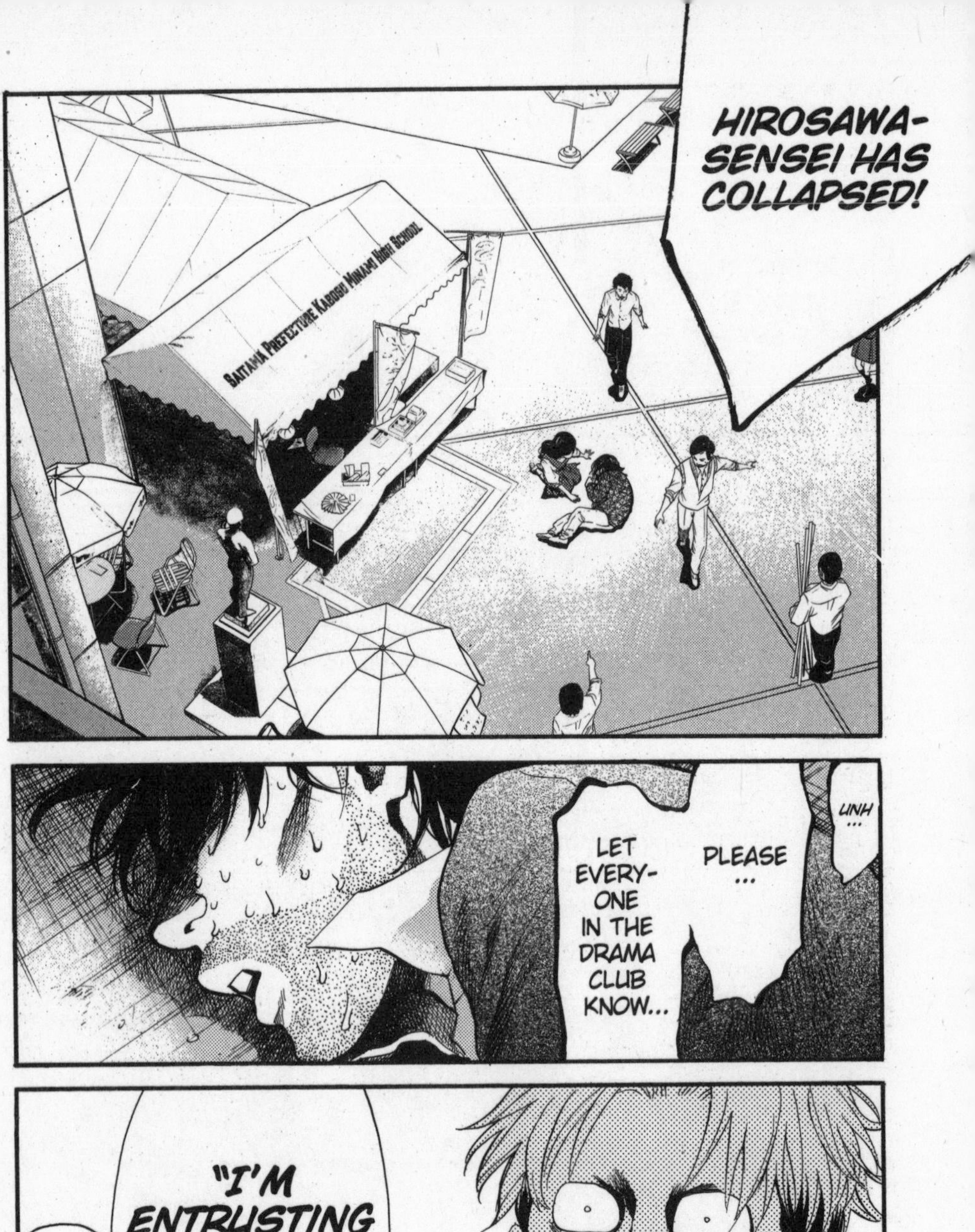
HIROSAWA-SENSEI HAS COLLAPSED!
SAITAMA PREFECTURE KABOSU MINAMI HIGH SCHOOL
UNH ...
PLEASE ...
LET EVERYONE IN THE DRAMA CLUB KNOW...
"I'M ENTRUSTING I WANT TO LIVE TO THEM."
...WAS THE LAST THING HE SAID.

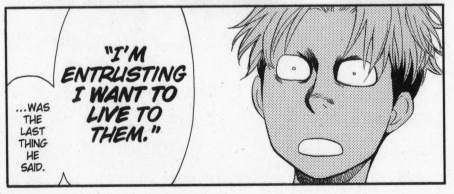

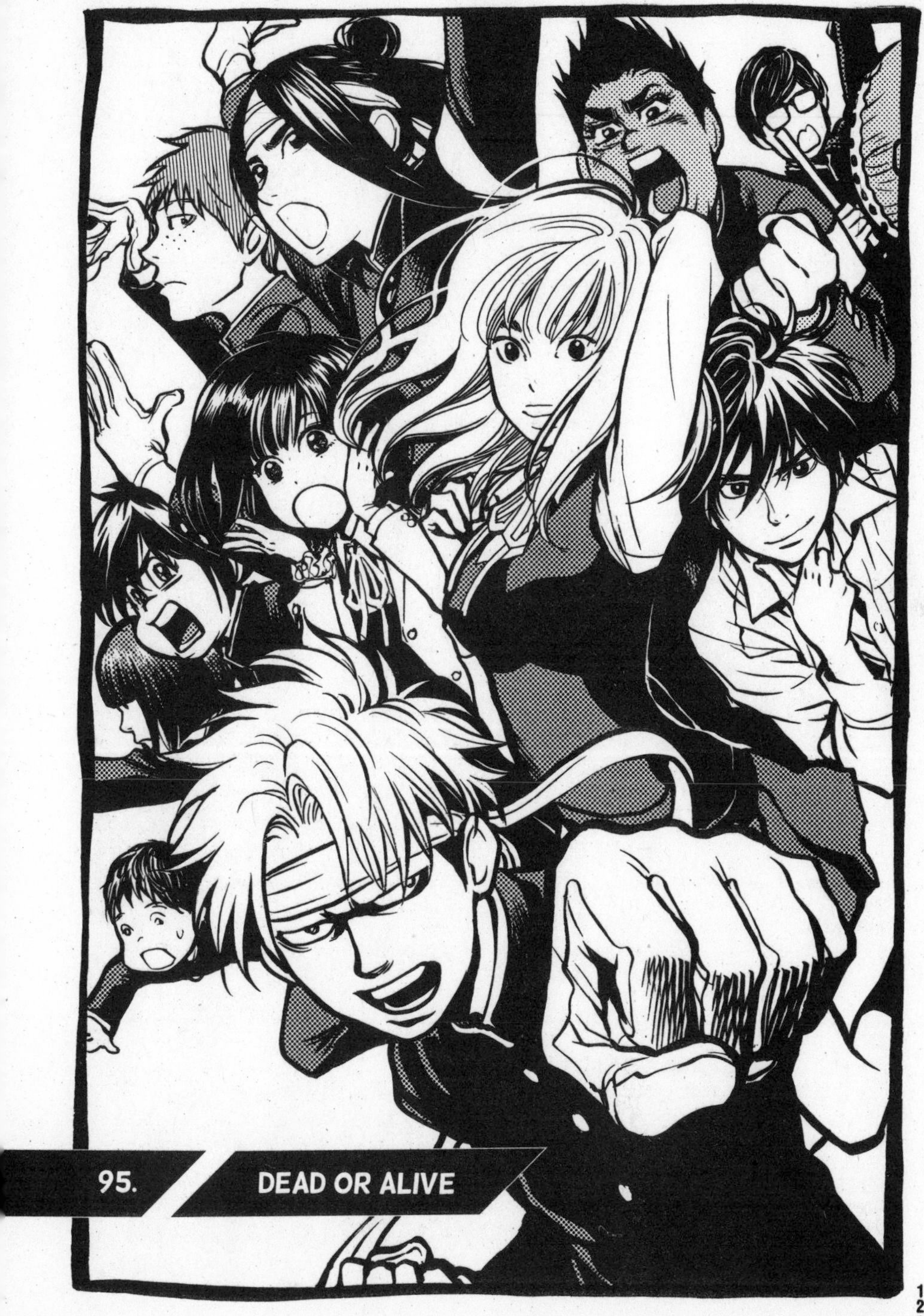
95.
DEAD OR ALIVE

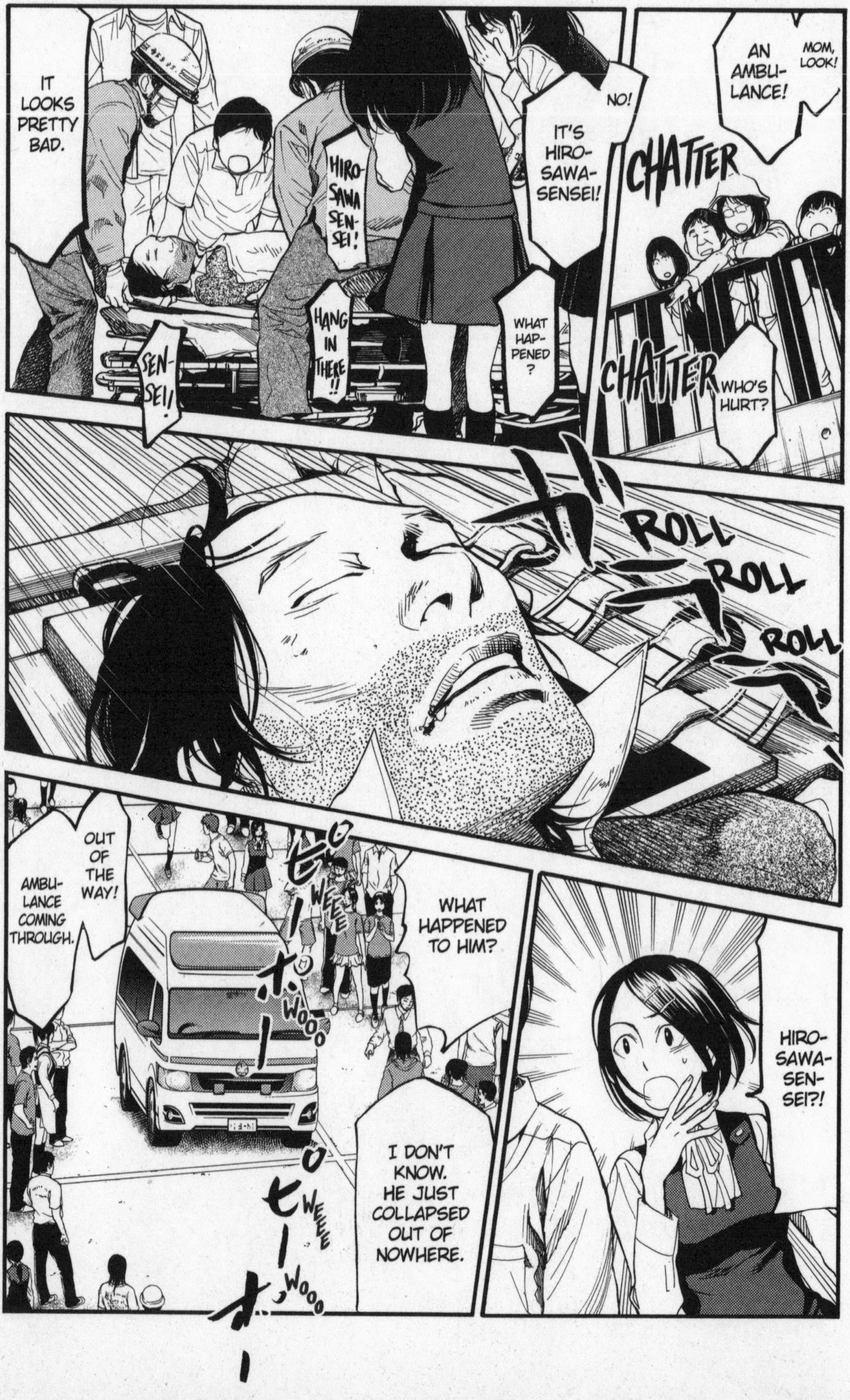
MOM, LOOK!
AN AMBU-LANCE!
CHATTER
CHATTER
WHO'S HURT?
NO!
IT'S HIRO-SAWA-SENSEI!
WHAT HAP-PENED?
HIRO-SAWA SEN-SEI!
HANG IN THERE!!
IT LOOKS PRETTY BAD.
SEN-SEI!
ROLL
ROLL
ROLL
HIRO-SAWA-SEN-SEI?!
WHAT HAPPENED TO HIM?
I DON'T KNOW. HE JUST COLLAPSED OUT OF NOWHERE.
WEEE
WOOO
WEEE
WOOO
OUT OF THE WAY!
AMBU-LANCE COMING THROUGH.

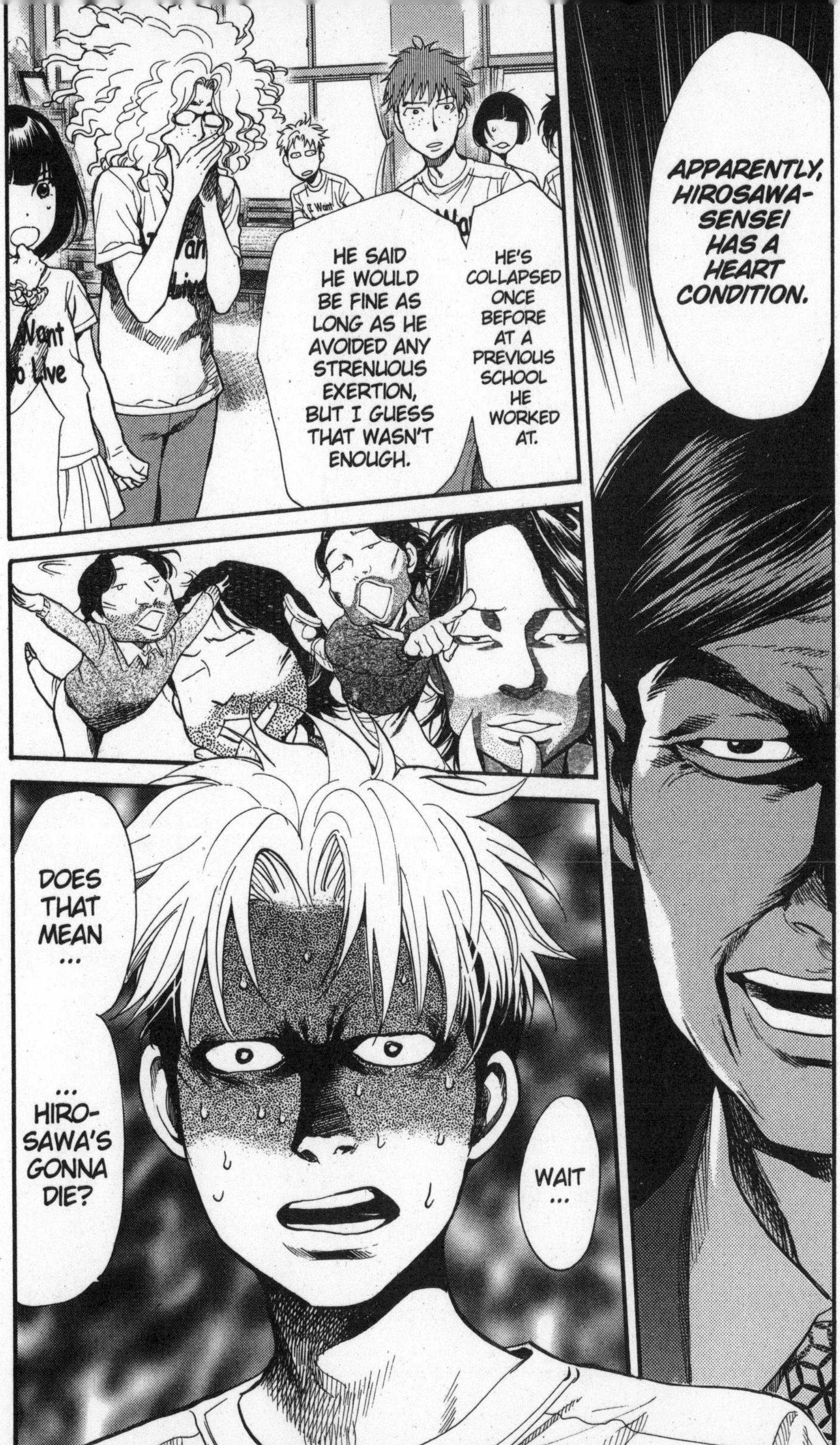
APPARENTLY, HIROSAWA-SENSEI HAS A HEART CONDITION.
HE'S COLLAPSED ONCE BEFORE AT A PREVIOUS SCHOOL HE WORKED AT.
HE SAID HE WOULD BE FINE AS LONG AS HE AVOIDED ANY STRENUOUS EXERTION, BUT I GUESS THAT WASN'T ENOUGH.
I Want to Live
WAIT ...
DOES THAT MEAN ...
... HIRO-SAWA'S GONNA DIE?

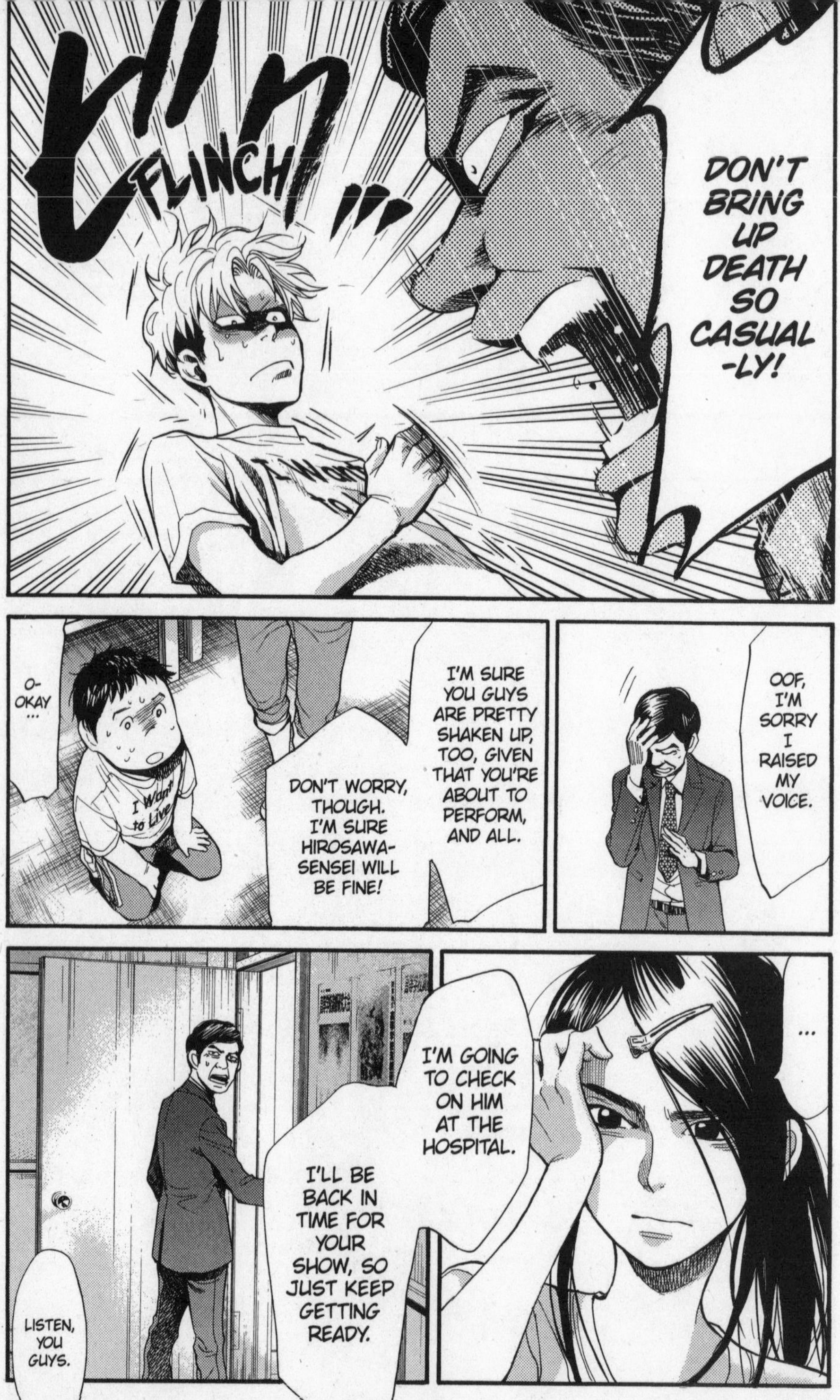
DON'T BRING UP DEATH SO CASUAL-LY!
FLINCH
OOF, I'M SORRY I RAISED MY VOICE.
I'M SURE YOU GUYS ARE PRETTY SHAKEN UP, TOO, GIVEN THAT YOU'RE ABOUT TO PERFORM, AND ALL.
DON'T WORRY, THOUGH. I'M SURE HIROSAWA-SENSEI WILL BE FINE!
O-OKAY...
I Want to Live
...
I'M GOING TO CHECK ON HIM AT THE HOSPITAL.
I'LL BE BACK IN TIME FOR YOUR SHOW, SO JUST KEEP GETTING READY.
LISTEN, YOU GUYS.

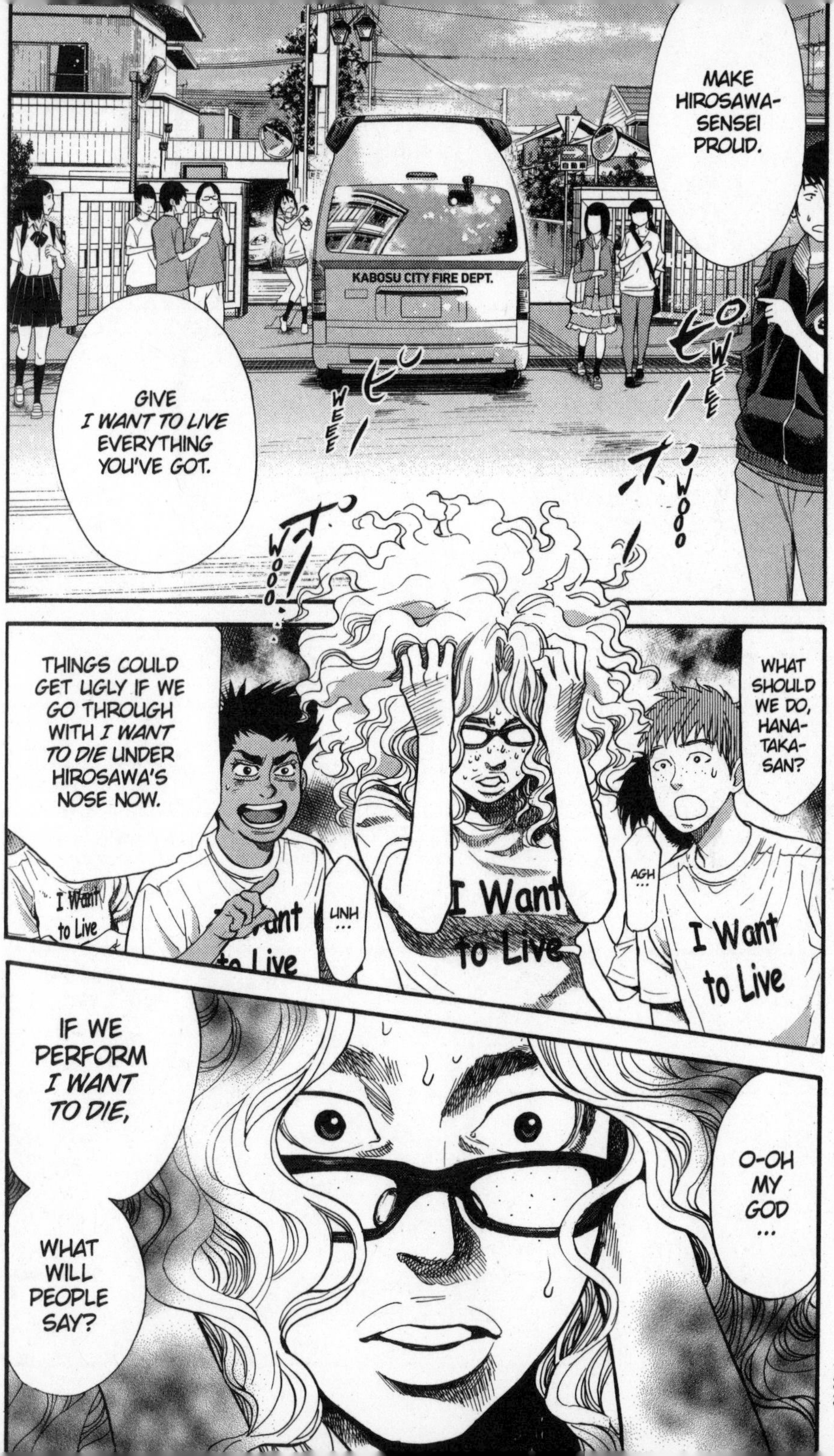
MAKE HIROSAWA-SENSEI PROUD.
WEEE
WOOO
KABOSU CITY FIRE DEPT.
WEEE
GIVE I WANT TO LIVE EVERYTHING YOU'VE GOT.
WOOO...
WHAT SHOULD WE DO, HANA-TAKA-SAN?
AGH...
I Want to Live
I Want to Live
UNH...
THINGS COULD GET UGLY IF WE GO THROUGH WITH I WANT TO DIE UNDER HIROSAWA'S NOSE NOW.
I Want to Live
I Want to Live
O-OH MY GOD...
IF WE PERFORM I WANT TO DIE,
WHAT WILL PEOPLE SAY?

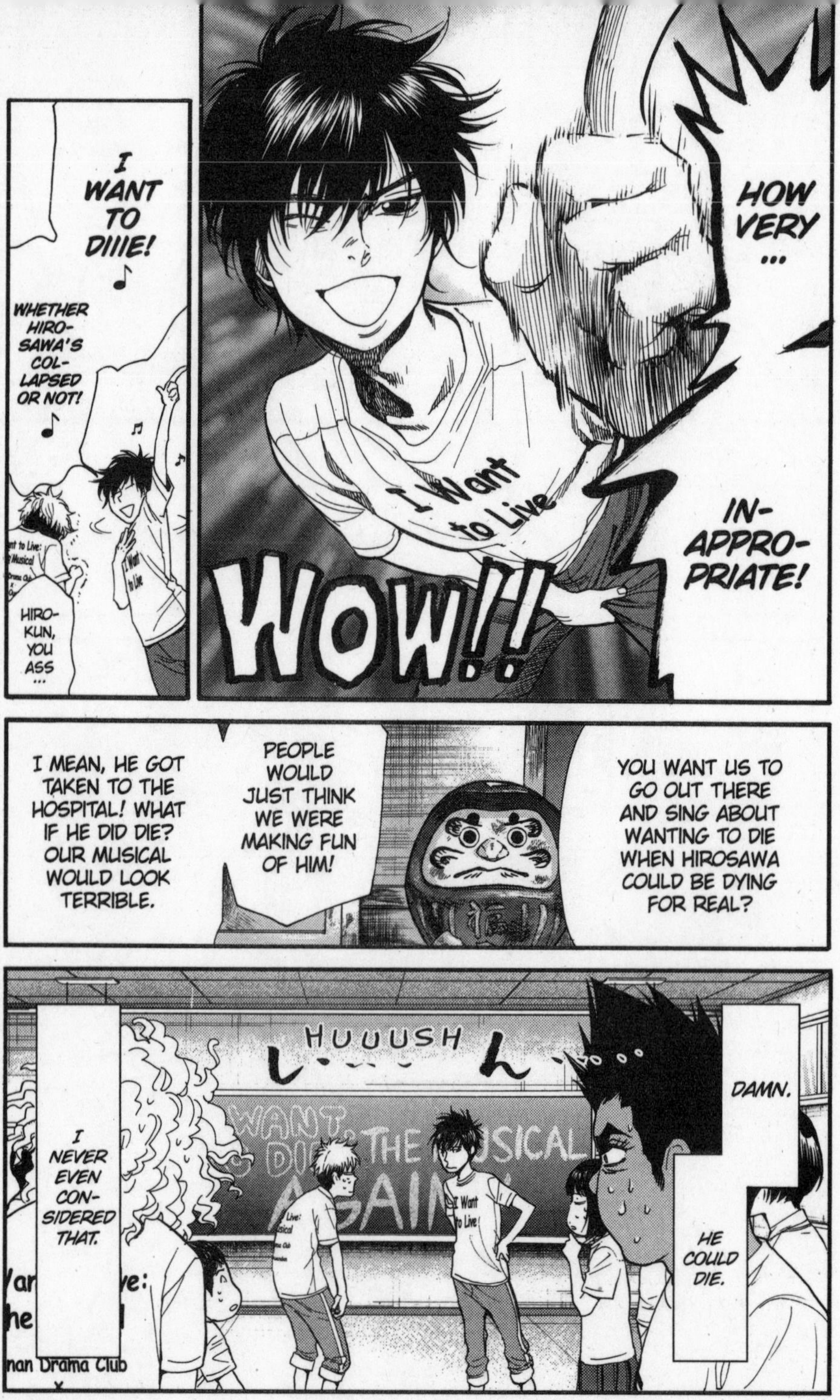
HOW VERY ...
IN-APPROPRIATE!
WOW!!
I Want to Live
I WANT TO DIIIE! ♪
WHETHER HIROSAWA'S COLLAPSED OR NOT! ♪
HIRO-KUN, YOU ASS ...
YOU WANT US TO GO OUT THERE AND SING ABOUT WANTING TO DIE WHEN HIROSAWA COULD BE DYING FOR REAL?
PEOPLE WOULD JUST THINK WE WERE MAKING FUN OF HIM!
I MEAN, HE GOT TAKEN TO THE HOSPITAL! WHAT IF HE DID DIE? OUR MUSICAL WOULD LOOK TERRIBLE.
DAMN.
HE COULD DIE.
HUUUSH
I NEVER EVEN CONSIDERED THAT.

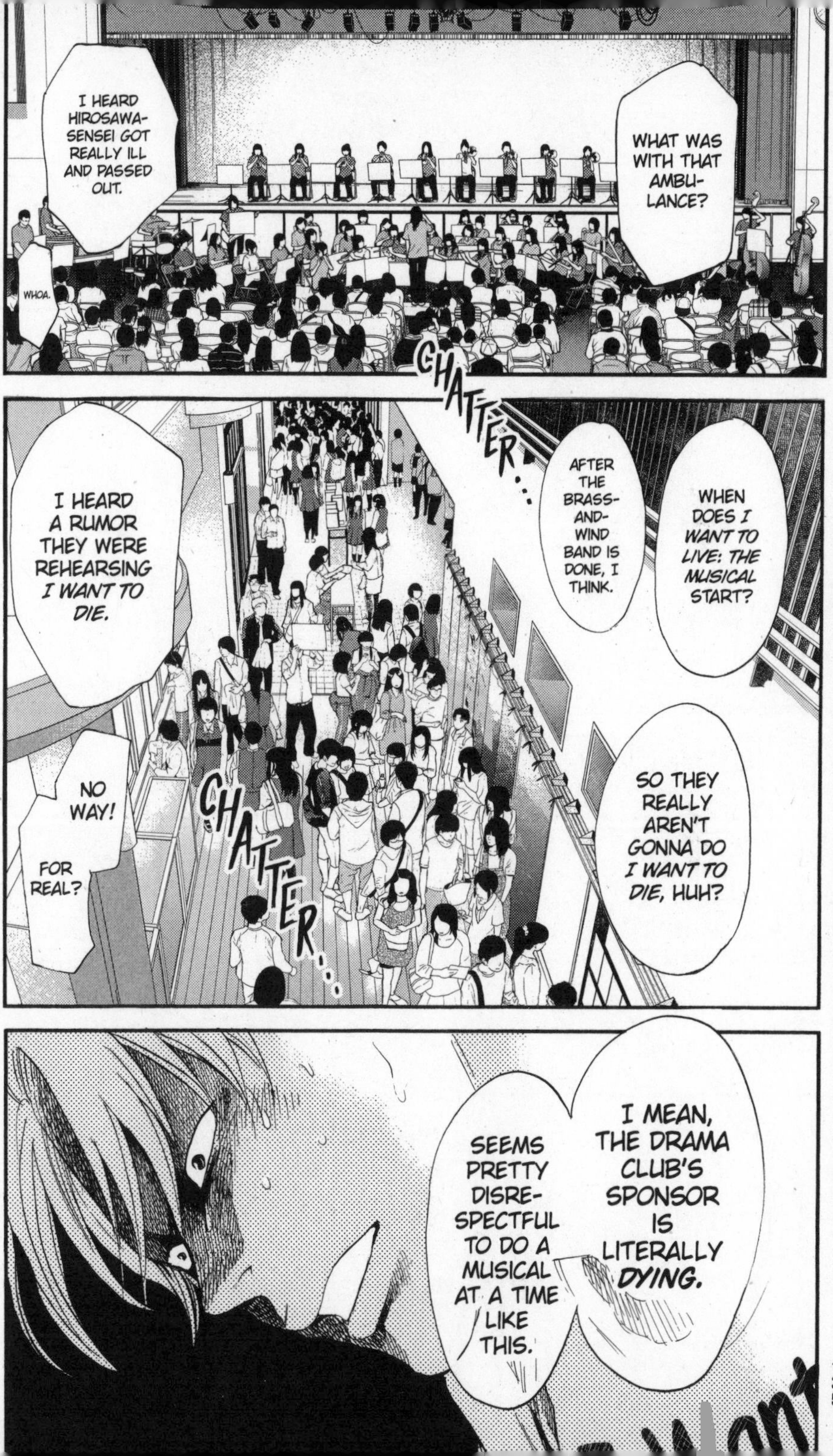
WHAT WAS WITH THAT AMBULANCE?
I HEARD HIROSAWA-SENSEI GOT REALLY ILL AND PASSED OUT.
WHOA.
CHATTER...
WHEN DOES *I WANT TO LIVE: THE MUSICAL* START?
AFTER THE BRASS-AND-WIND BAND IS DONE, I THINK.
I HEARD A RUMOR THEY WERE REHEARSING *I WANT TO DIE.*
SO THEY REALLY AREN'T GONNA DO *I WANT TO DIE*, HUH?
NO WAY!
FOR REAL?
CHATTER...
I MEAN, THE DRAMA CLUB'S SPONSOR IS LITERALLY **DYING.**
SEEMS PRETTY DISRESPECTFUL TO DO A MUSICAL AT A TIME LIKE THIS.

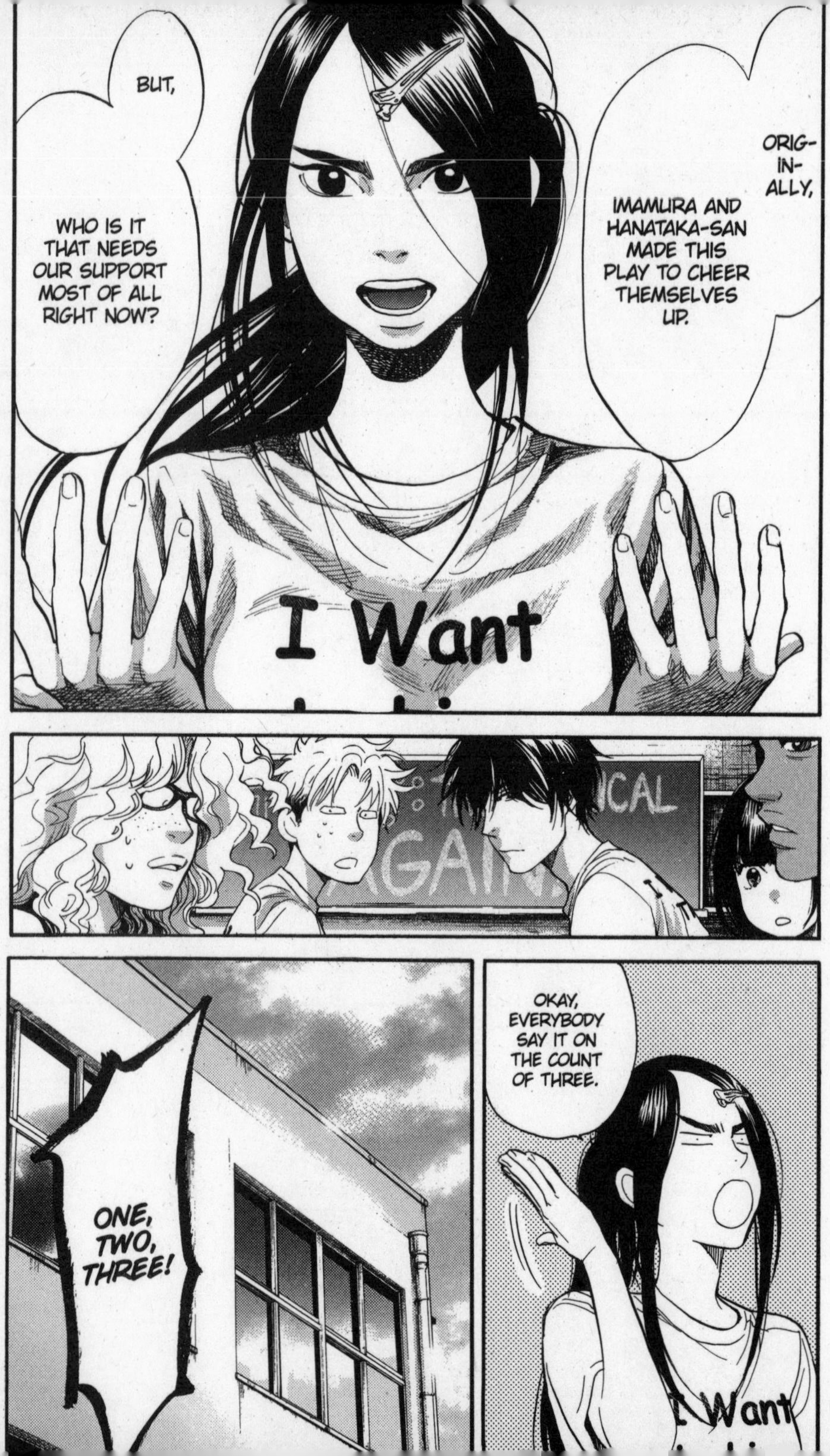
ORIG-IN-ALLY,
IMAMURA AND HANATAKA-SAN MADE THIS PLAY TO CHEER THEMSELVES UP.
BUT,
WHO IS IT THAT NEEDS OUR SUPPORT MOST OF ALL RIGHT NOW?
I Want
OKAY, EVERYBODY SAY IT ON THE COUNT OF THREE.
I Want
ONE, TWO, THREE!

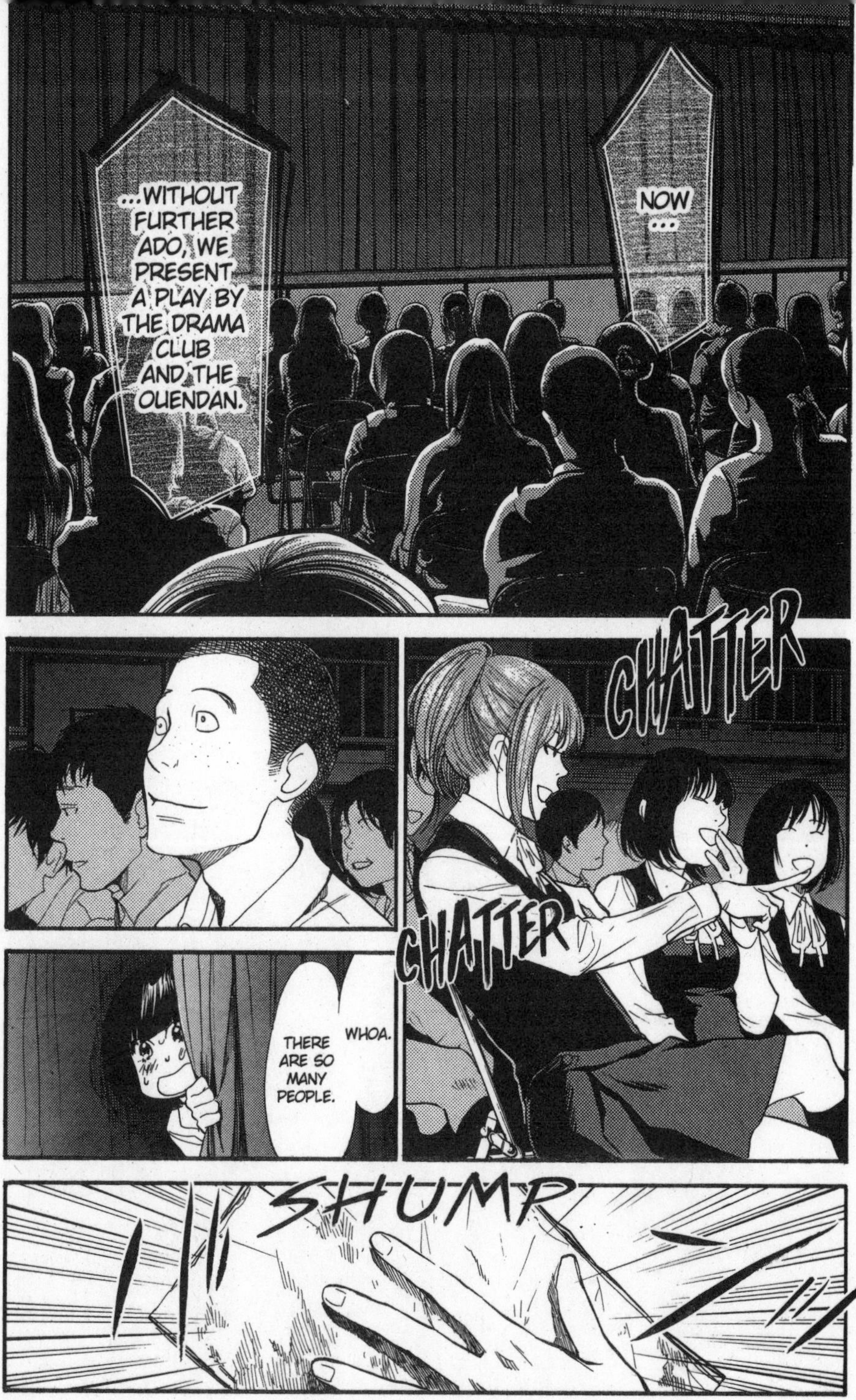
NOW...
...WITHOUT FURTHER ADO, WE PRESENT A PLAY BY THE DRAMA CLUB AND THE OUENDAN.
CHATTER
CHATTER
WHOA.
THERE ARE SO MANY PEOPLE.
SHUMP

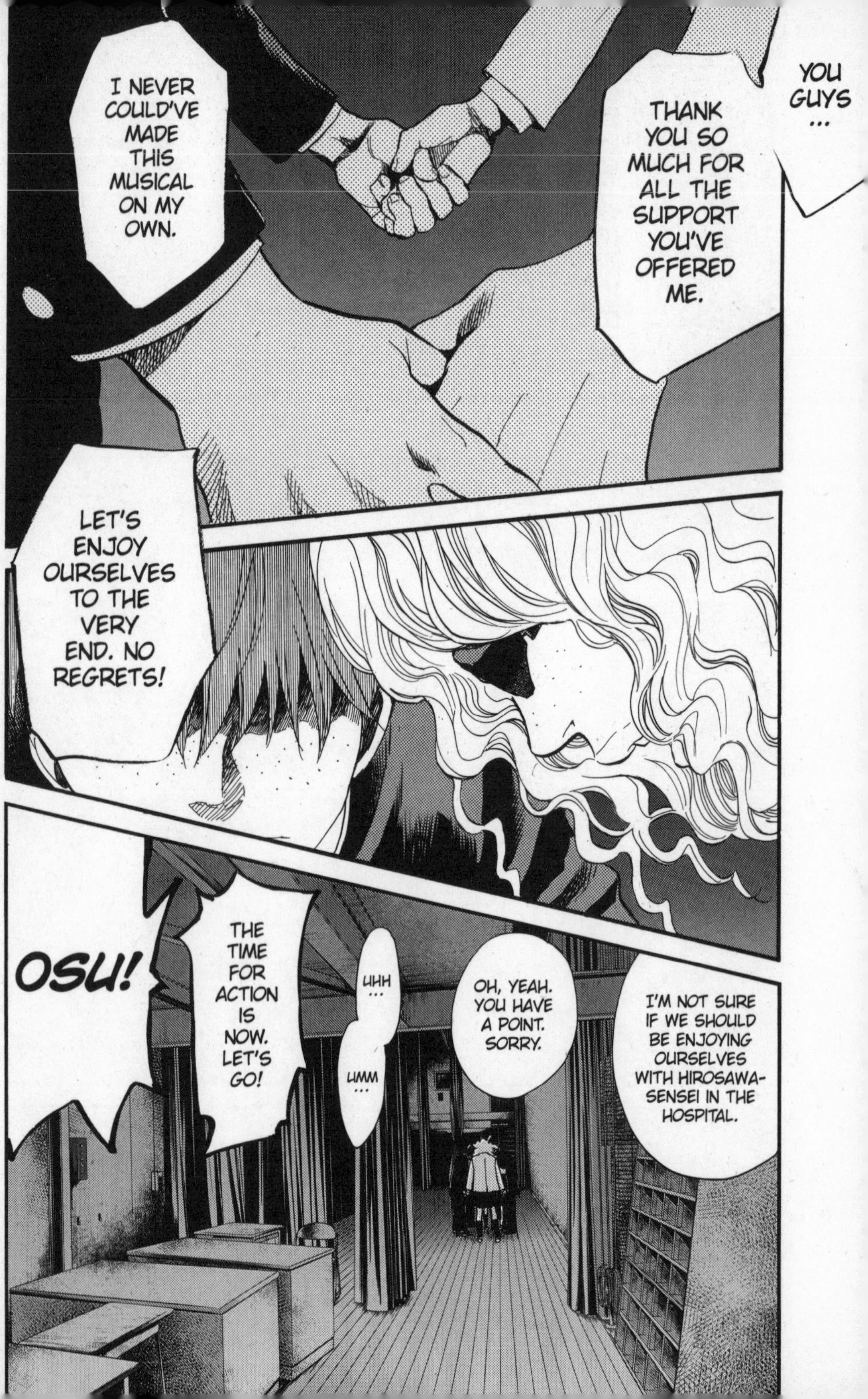

YOU GUYS...
THANK YOU SO MUCH FOR ALL THE SUPPORT YOU'VE OFFERED ME.
I NEVER COULD'VE MADE THIS MUSICAL ON MY OWN.
LET'S ENJOY OURSELVES TO THE VERY END. NO REGRETS!
I'M NOT SURE IF WE SHOULD BE ENJOYING OURSELVES WITH HIROSAWA-SENSEI IN THE HOSPITAL.
OH, YEAH. YOU HAVE A POINT. SORRY.
UHH...
UMM...
THE TIME FOR ACTION IS NOW. LET'S GO!
OSU!

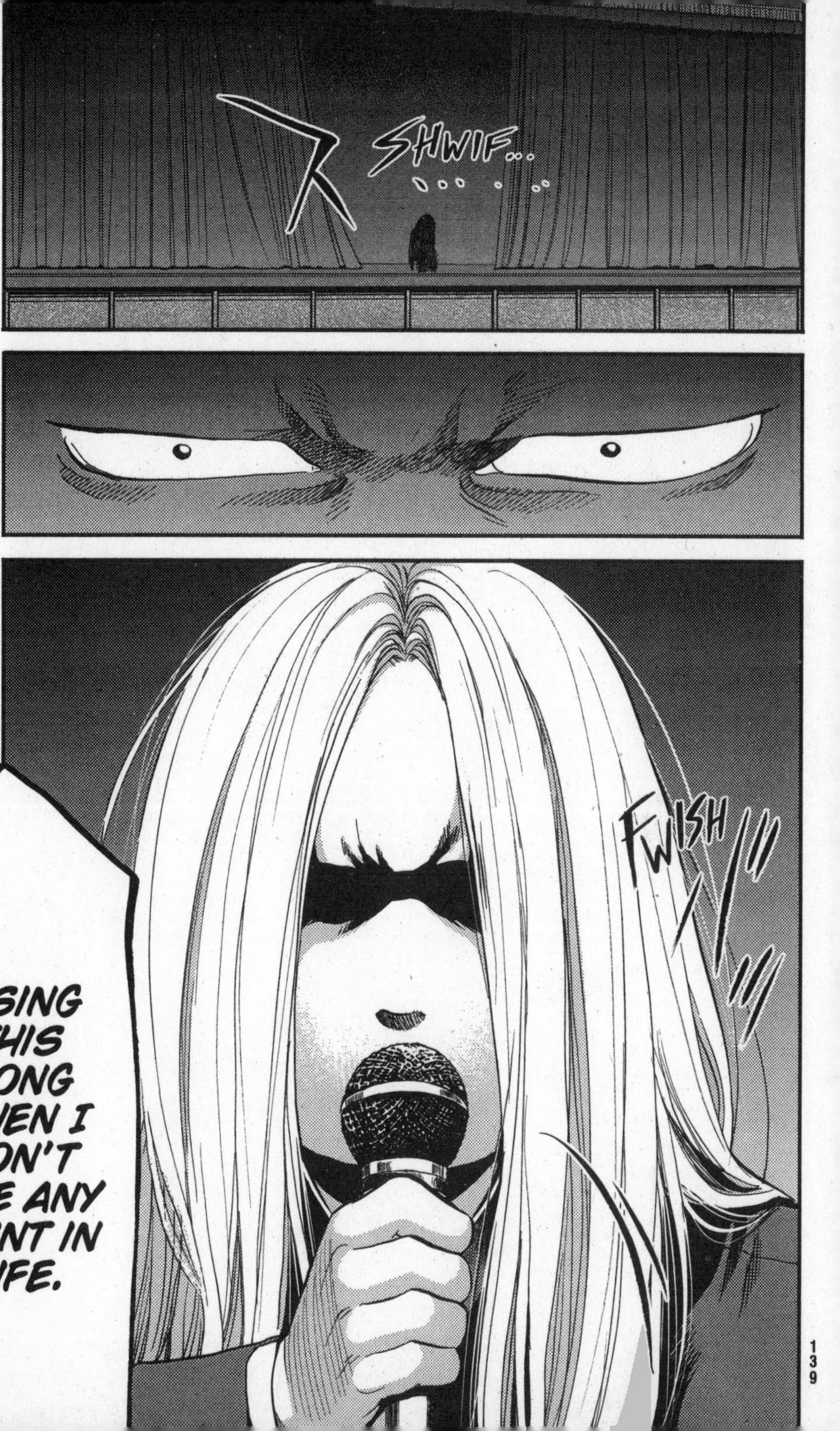
SHWIF...
FWISH
I SING THIS SONG WHEN I DON'T SEE ANY POINT IN LIFE.

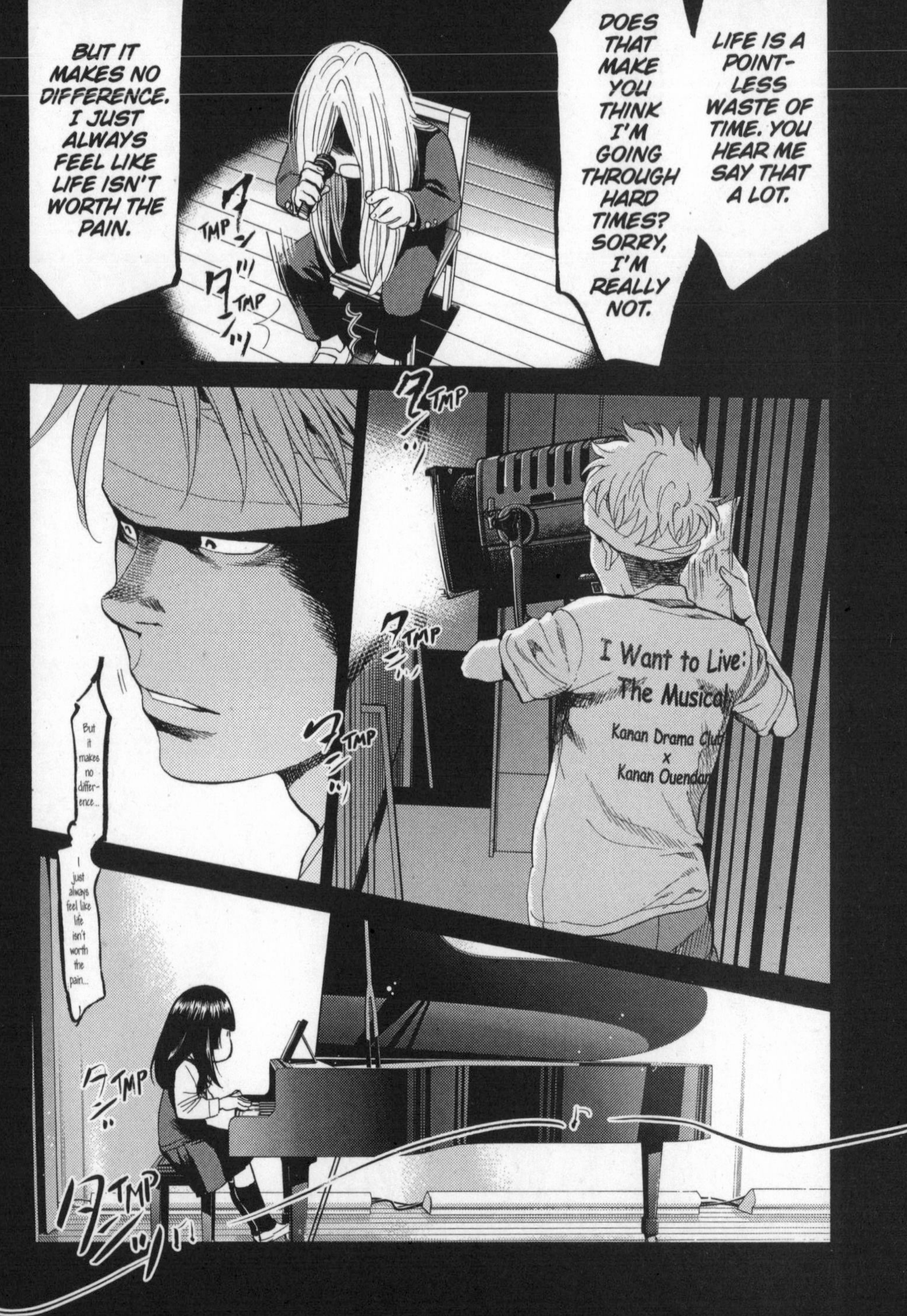
LIFE IS A POINTLESS WASTE OF TIME. YOU HEAR ME SAY THAT A LOT.
DOES THAT MAKE YOU THINK I'M GOING THROUGH HARD TIMES? SORRY, I'M REALLY NOT.
BUT IT MAKES NO DIFFERENCE. I JUST ALWAYS FEEL LIKE LIFE ISN'T WORTH THE PAIN.
TMP
TMP
TMP
I Want to Live: The Musical
Kanan Drama Club x Kanan Ouendan
TMP
TMP
But it makes no difference...
I just always feel like life isn't worth the pain...
TMP
TMP

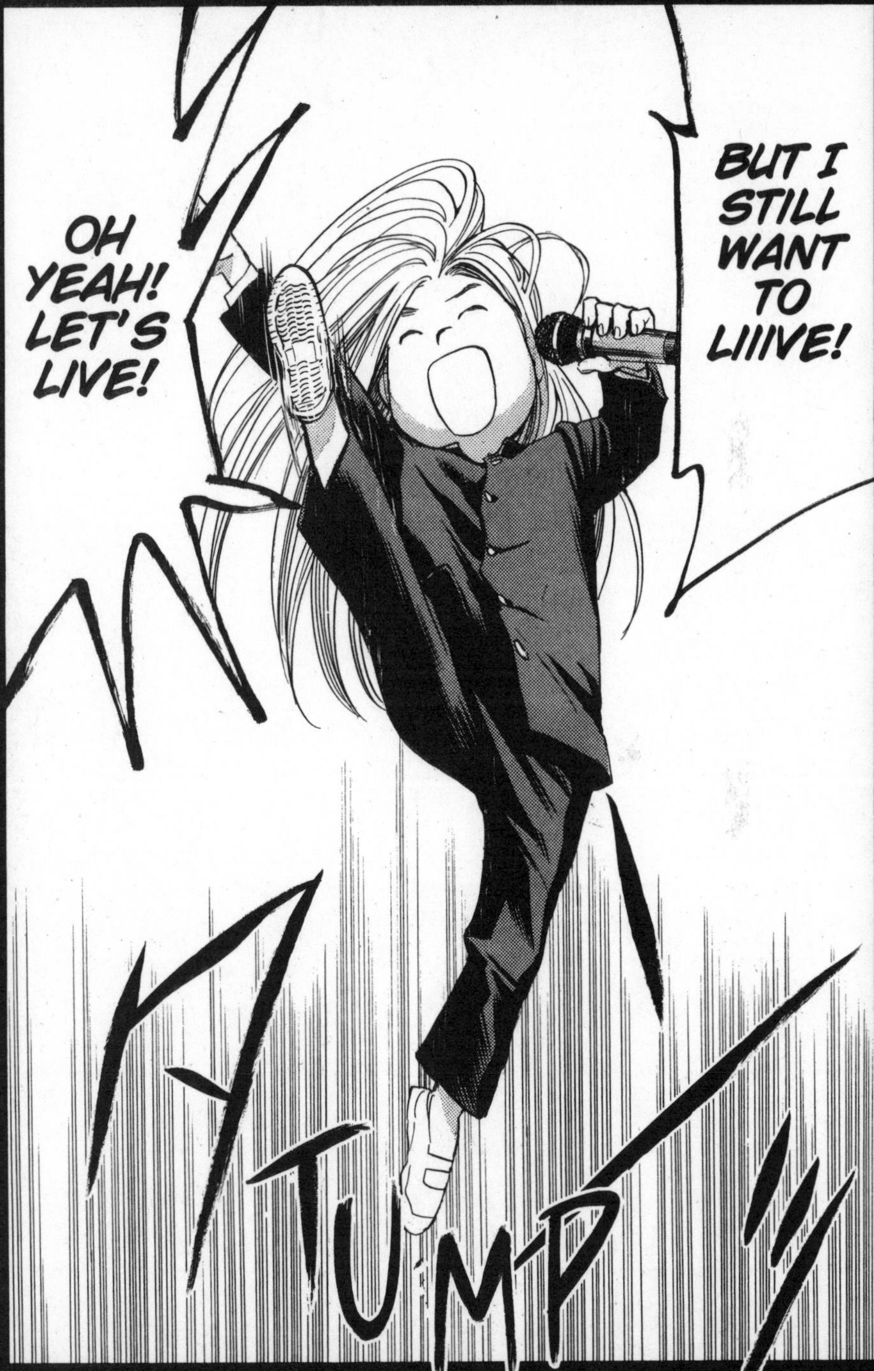
BUT I STILL WANT TO LIIIVE!
OH YEAH! LET'S LIVE!
TUMP

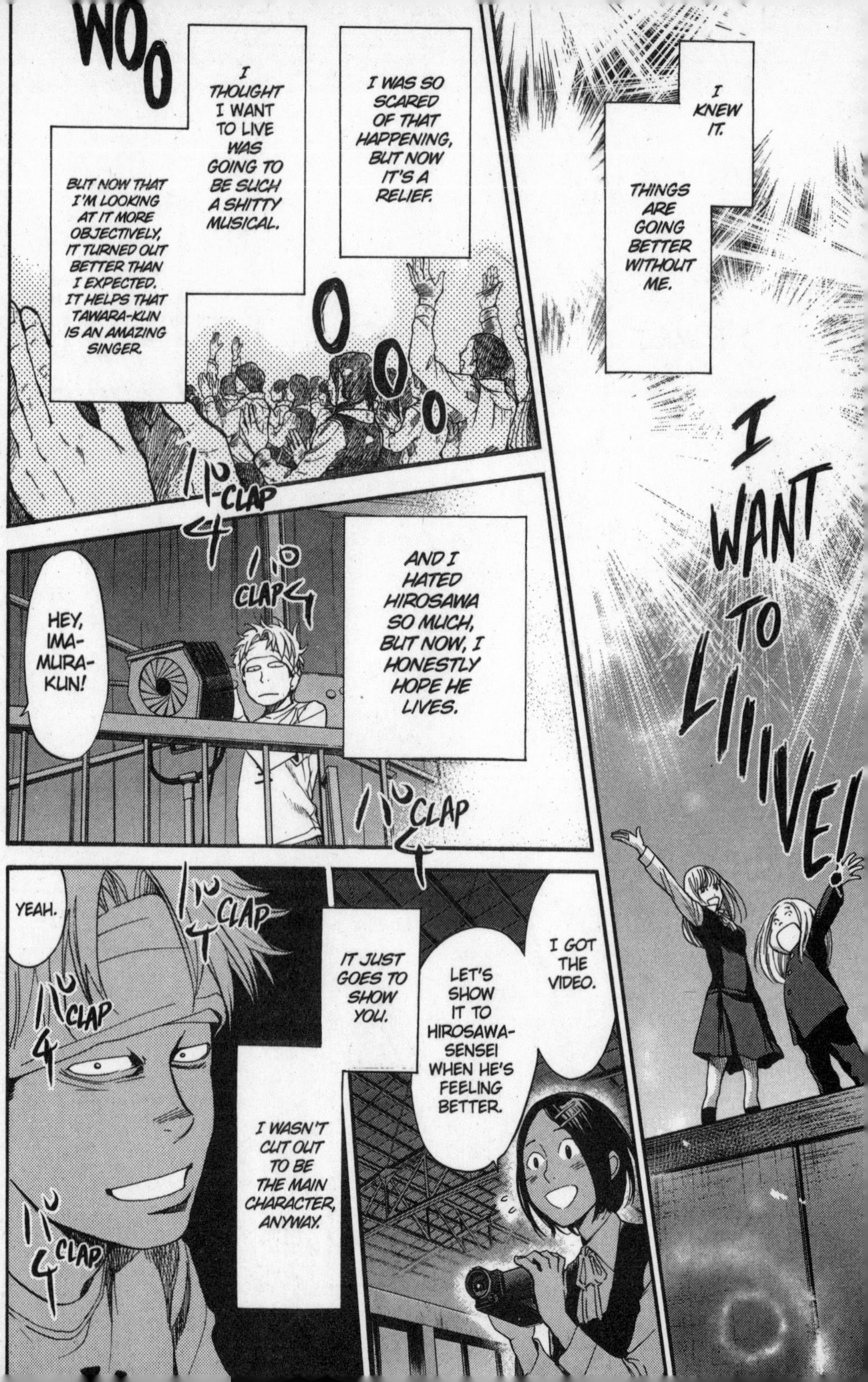
I KNEW IT.
THINGS ARE GOING BETTER WITHOUT ME.
I WANT TO LIIIIVE!
WOOOOOO
I WAS SO SCARED OF THAT HAPPENING, BUT NOW IT'S A RELIEF.
I THOUGHT I WANT TO LIVE WAS GOING TO BE SUCH A SHITTY MUSICAL.
BUT NOW THAT I'M LOOKING AT IT MORE OBJECTIVELY, IT TURNED OUT BETTER THAN I EXPECTED. IT HELPS THAT TAWARA-KUN IS AN AMAZING SINGER.
CLAP
CLAP
AND I HATED HIROSAWA SO MUCH, BUT NOW, I HONESTLY HOPE HE LIVES.
HEY, IMAMURA-KUN!
CLAP
I GOT THE VIDEO.
LET'S SHOW IT TO HIROSAWA-SENSEI WHEN HE'S FEELING BETTER.
YEAH.
CLAP
IT JUST GOES TO SHOW YOU.
I WASN'T CUT OUT TO BE THE MAIN CHARACTER, ANYWAY.
CLAP
CLAP

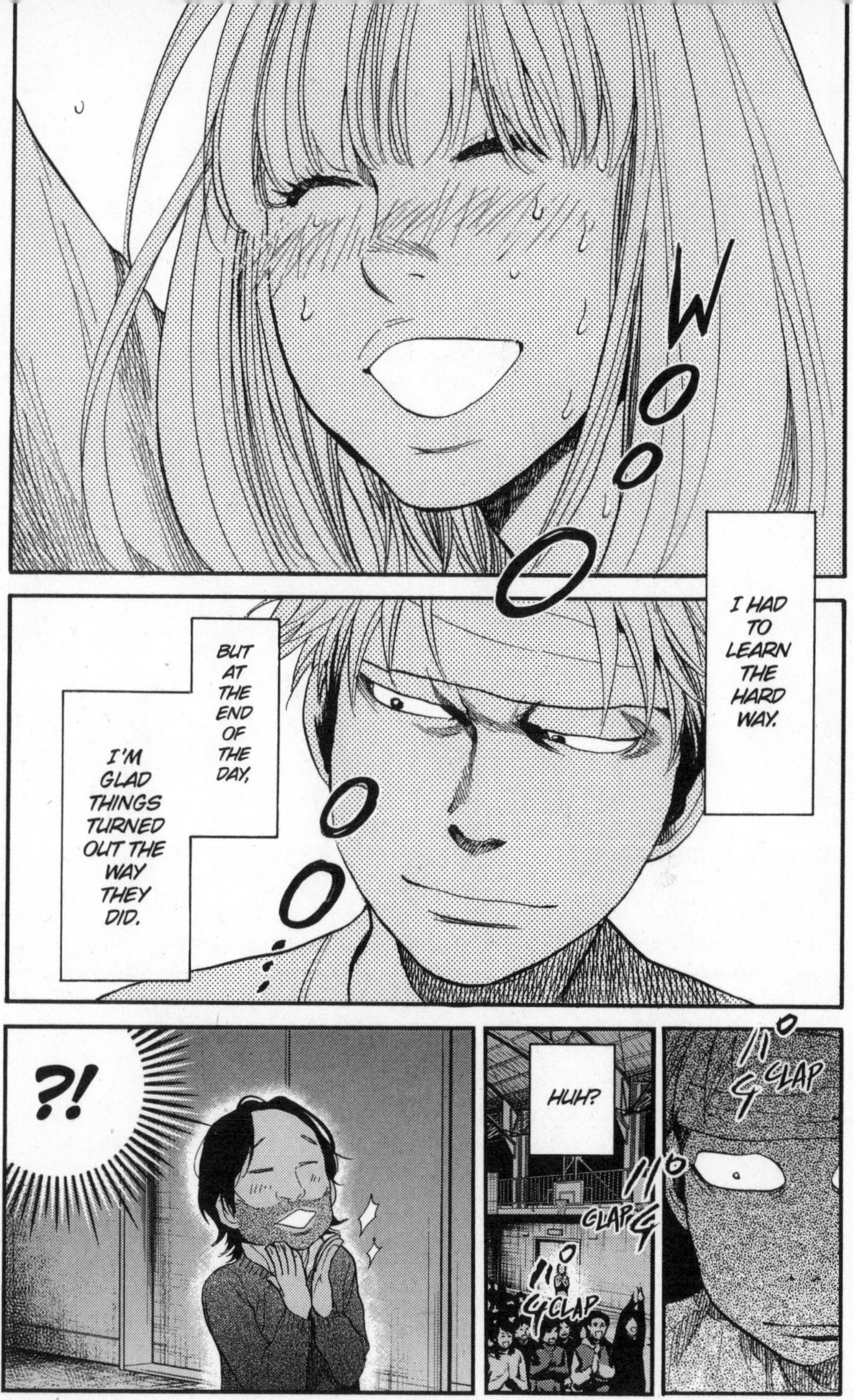

WOOOOO...
I HAD TO LEARN THE HARD WAY.
BUT AT THE END OF THE DAY,
I'M GLAD THINGS TURNED OUT THE WAY THEY DID.
CLAP
CLAP
HUH?
CLAP
CLAP
?!

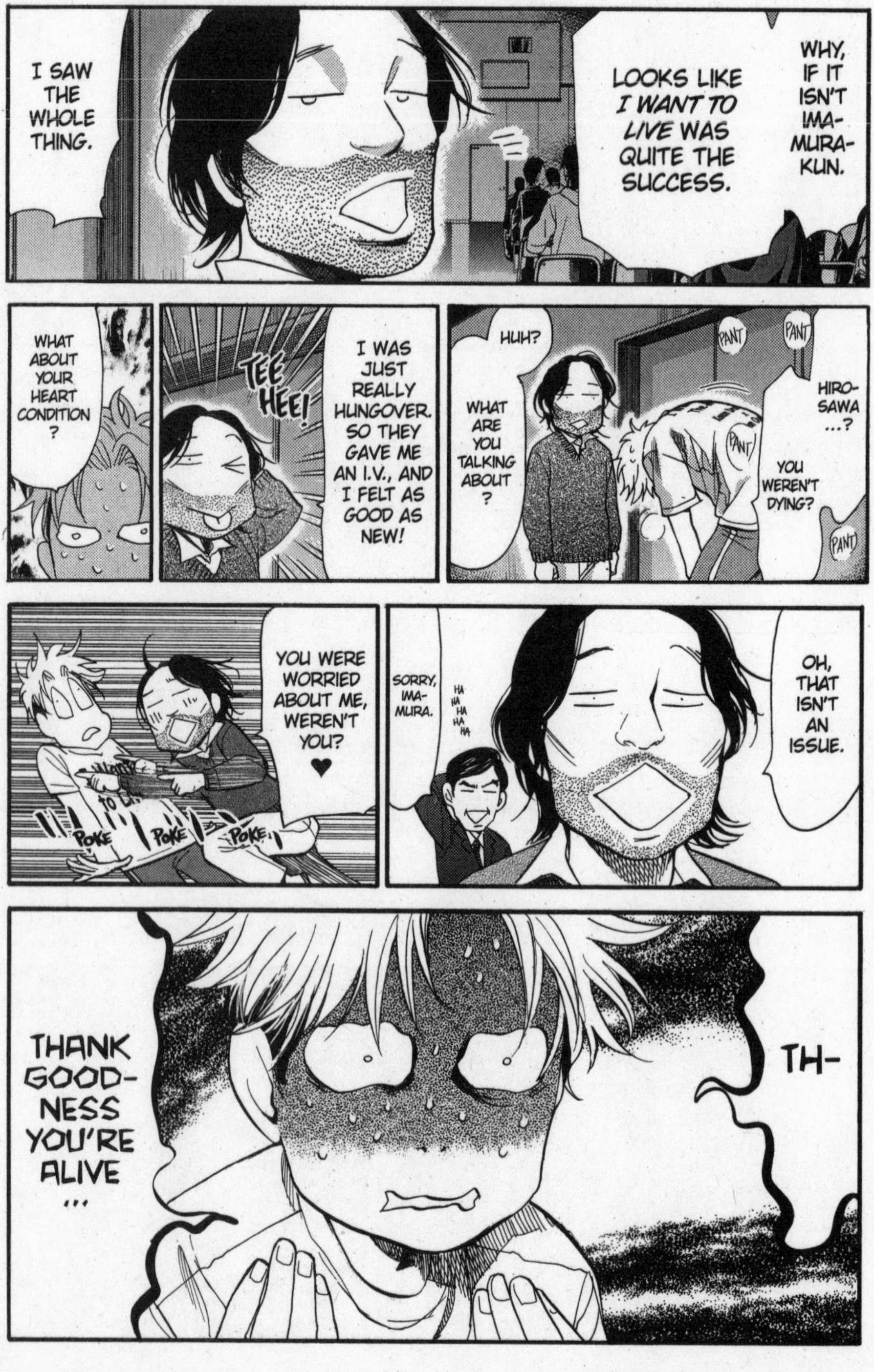

WHY, IF IT ISN'T IMA-MURA-KUN.
LOOKS LIKE *I WANT TO LIVE* WAS QUITE THE SUCCESS.
I SAW THE WHOLE THING.
PANT
PANT
HIRO-SAWA ...?
YOU WEREN'T DYING?
PANT
PANT
HUH?
WHAT ARE YOU TALKING ABOUT?
I WAS JUST REALLY HUNGOVER. SO THEY GAVE ME AN I.V., AND I FELT AS GOOD AS NEW!
TEE HEE!
WHAT ABOUT YOUR HEART CONDITION?
OH, THAT ISN'T AN ISSUE.
SORRY, IMA-MURA.
HA HA HA HA HA
YOU WERE WORRIED ABOUT ME, WEREN'T YOU? ♥
POKE
POKE
POKE
TH-
THANK GOOD-NESS YOU'RE ALIVE ...

96. DEATH WISH INFLATION

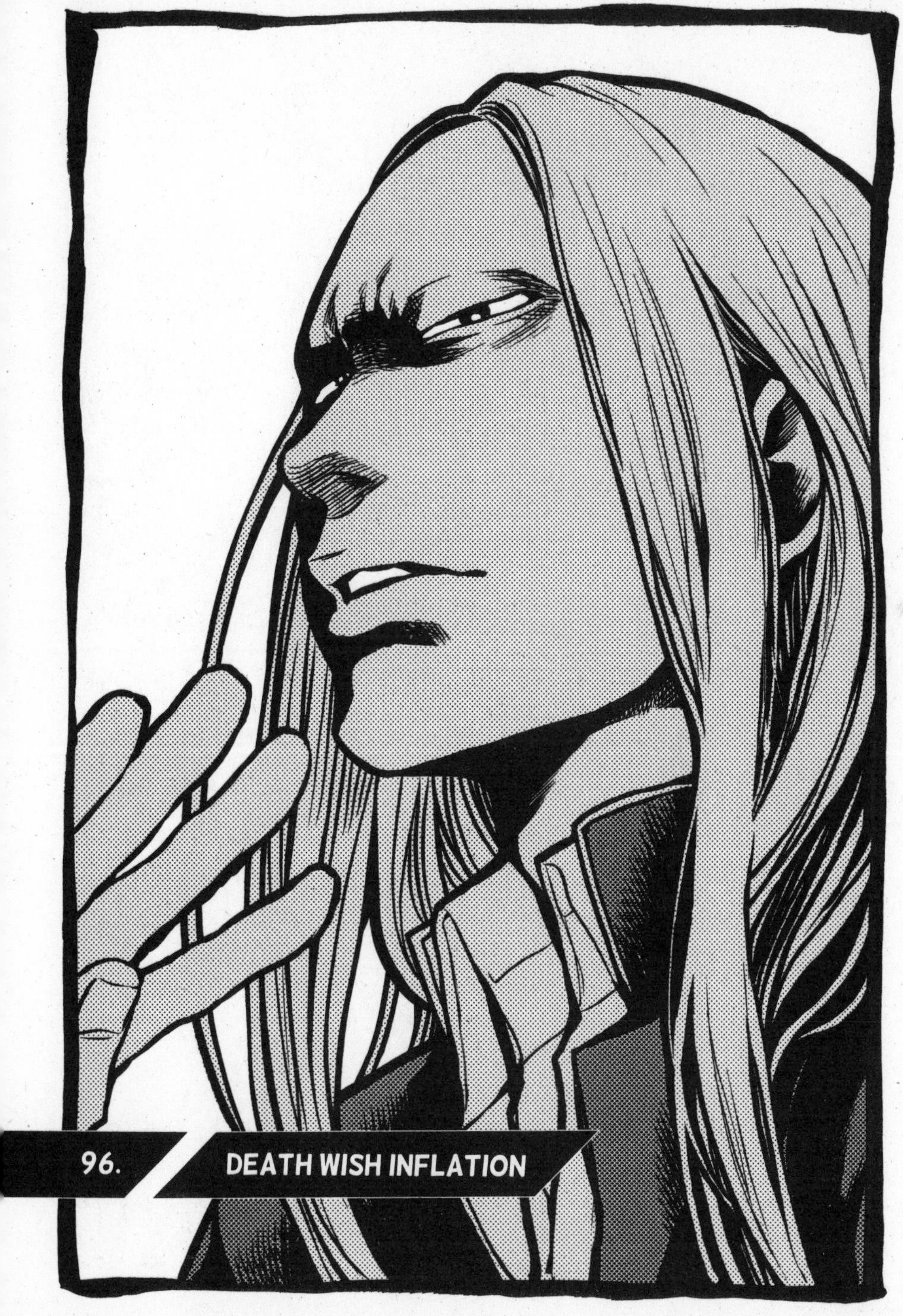

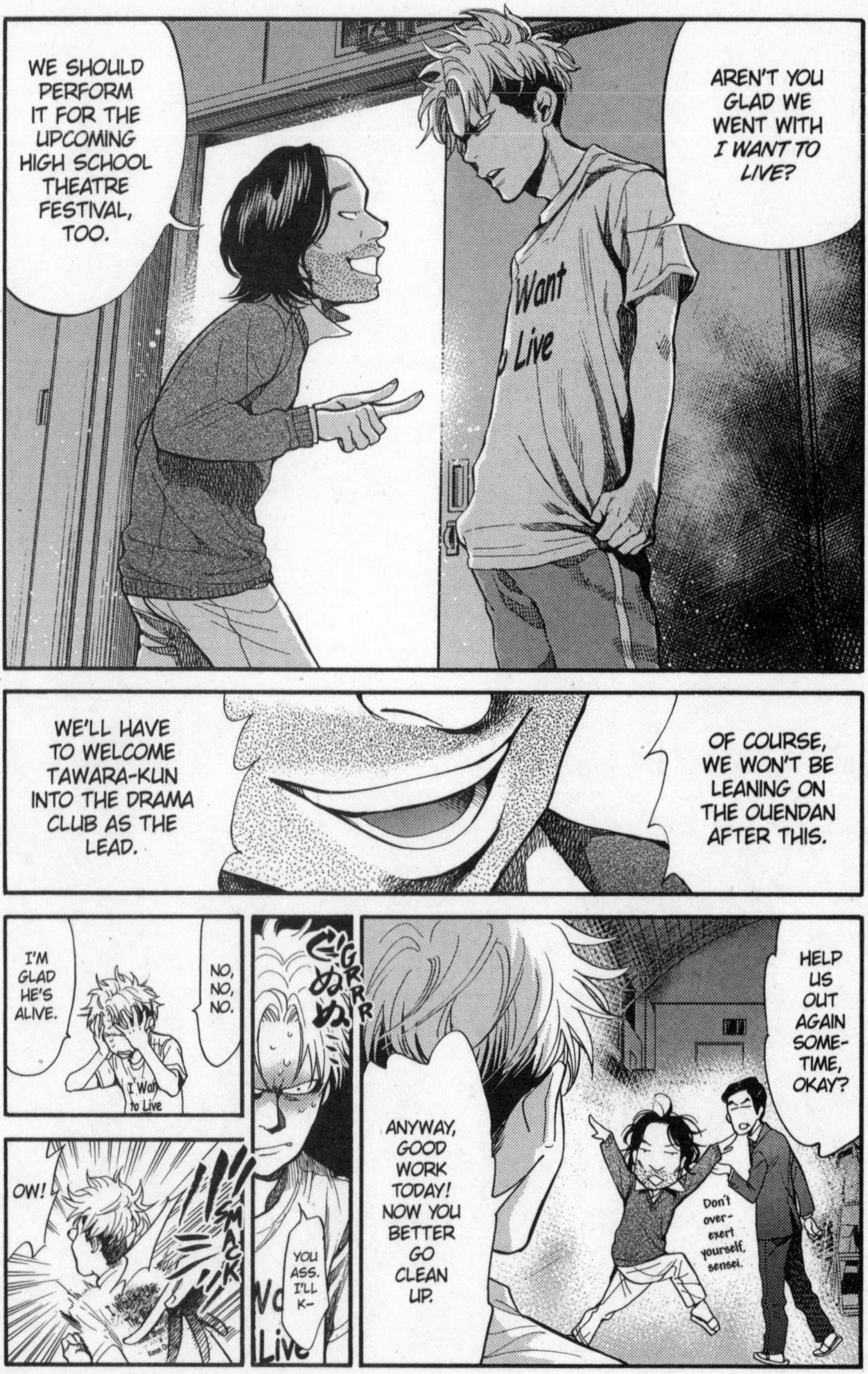
AREN'T YOU GLAD WE WENT WITH *I WANT TO LIVE?*
WE SHOULD PERFORM IT FOR THE UPCOMING HIGH SCHOOL THEATRE FESTIVAL, TOO.
OF COURSE, WE WON'T BE LEANING ON THE OUENDAN AFTER THIS.
WE'LL HAVE TO WELCOME TAWARA-KUN INTO THE DRAMA CLUB AS THE LEAD.
HELP US OUT AGAIN SOMETIME, OKAY?
Don't over-exert yourself, sensei.
ANYWAY, GOOD WORK TODAY! NOW YOU BETTER GO CLEAN UP.
ぐぬぬ GRRR
YOU ASS. I'LL K-
NO, NO, NO.
I'M GLAD HE'S ALIVE.
I Want to Live
SMACK
OW!

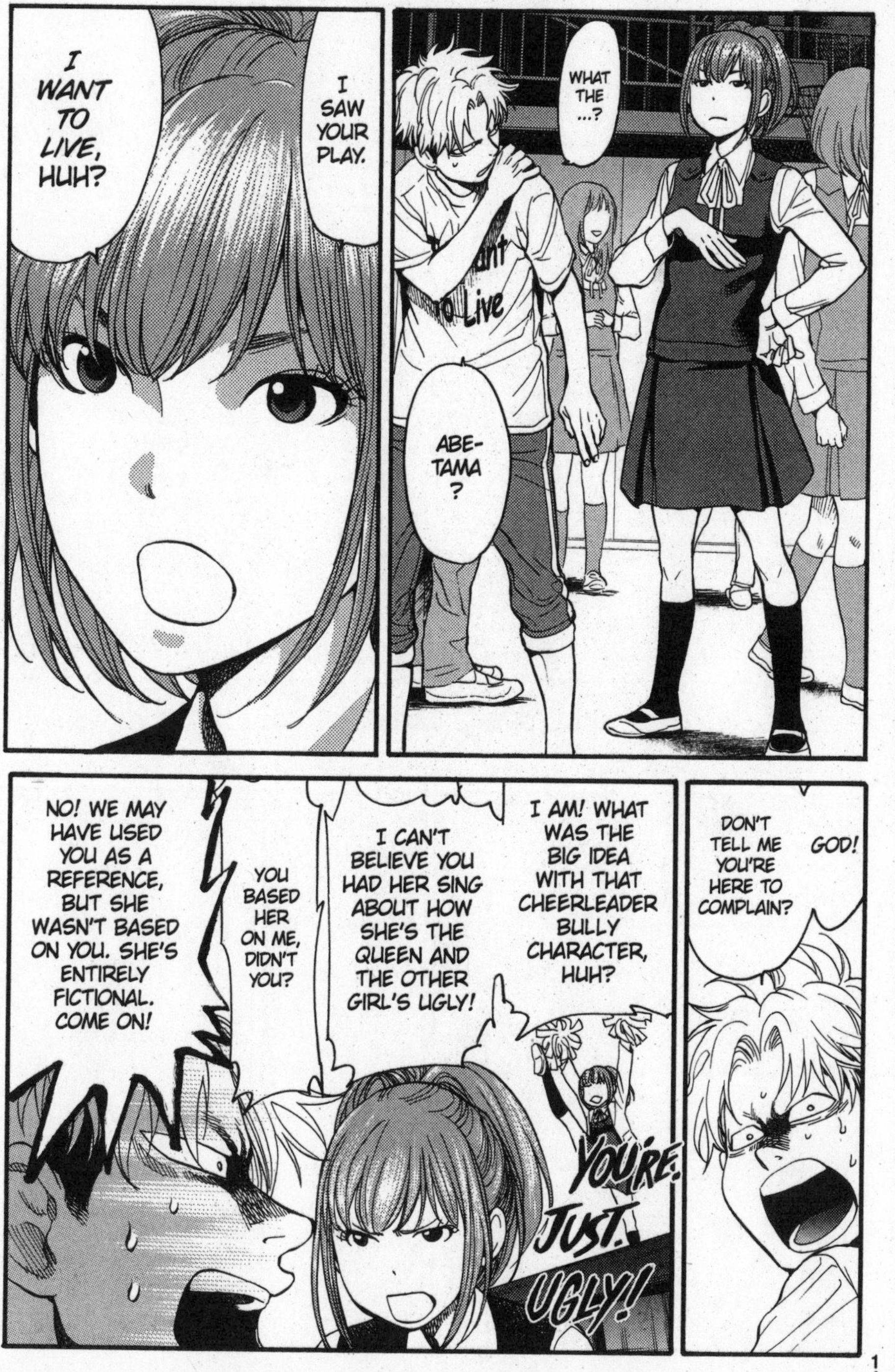
WHAT THE ...?
ABE-TAMA?
I SAW YOUR PLAY.
I WANT TO LIVE, HUH?
GOD!
DON'T TELL ME YOU'RE HERE TO COMPLAIN?
I AM! WHAT WAS THE BIG IDEA WITH THAT CHEERLEADER BULLY CHARACTER, HUH?
I CAN'T BELIEVE YOU HAD HER SING ABOUT HOW SHE'S THE QUEEN AND THE OTHER GIRL'S UGLY!
YOU'RE. JUST. UGLY!
YOU BASED HER ON ME, DIDN'T YOU?
NO! WE MAY HAVE USED YOU AS A REFERENCE, BUT SHE WASN'T BASED ON YOU. SHE'S ENTIRELY FICTIONAL. COME ON!

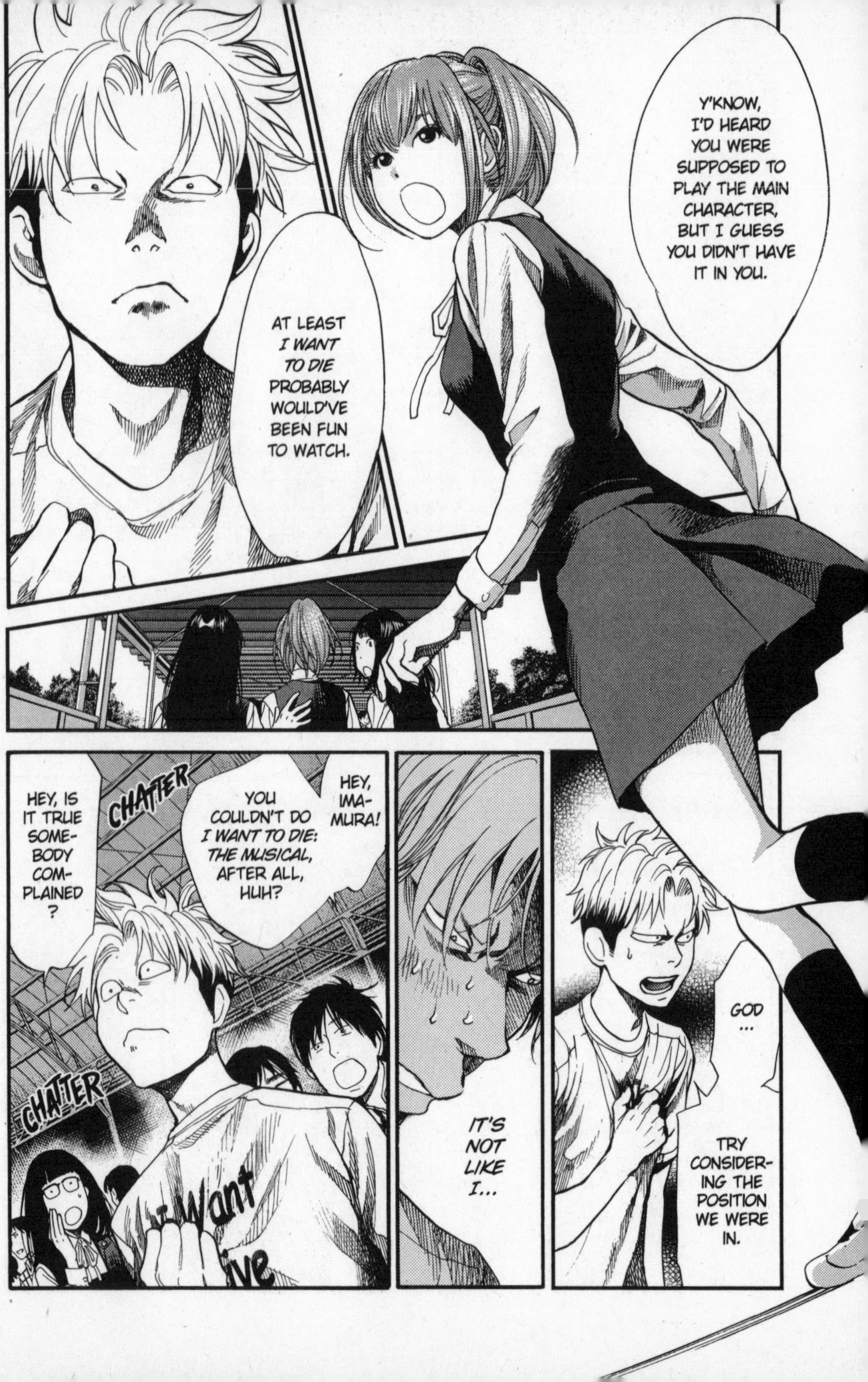
Y'KNOW, I'D HEARD YOU WERE SUPPOSED TO PLAY THE MAIN CHARACTER, BUT I GUESS YOU DIDN'T HAVE IT IN YOU.
AT LEAST *I WANT TO DIE* PROBABLY WOULD'VE BEEN FUN TO WATCH.
GOD ...
TRY CONSIDER-ING THE POSITION WE WERE IN.
IT'S NOT LIKE I...
HEY, IMA-MURA!
YOU COULDN'T DO *I WANT TO DIE: THE MUSICAL*, AFTER ALL, HUH?
CHATTER
HEY, IS IT TRUE SOME-BODY COM-PLAINED?
CHATTER

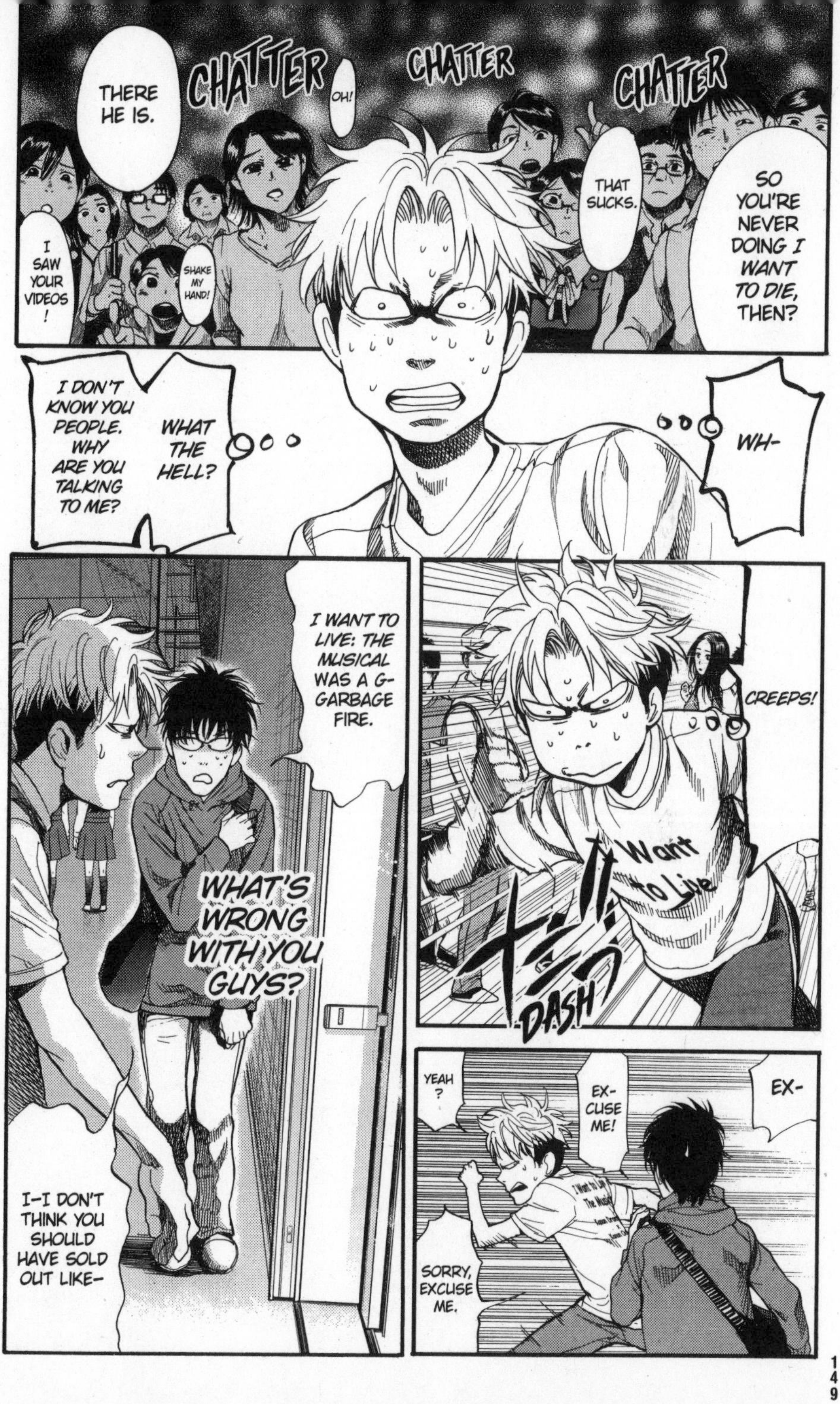
SO YOU'RE NEVER DOING *I WANT TO DIE*, THEN?
CHATTER
THAT SUCKS.
CHATTER
OH!
CHATTER
THERE HE IS.
SHAKE MY HAND!
I SAW YOUR VIDEOS!
WH-
WHAT THE HELL?
I DON'T KNOW YOU PEOPLE. WHY ARE YOU TALKING TO ME?
CREEPS!
Want to Live
DASH
EX-
EX-CUSE ME!
YEAH?
SORRY, EXCUSE ME.
I WANT TO LIVE: THE MUSICAL WAS A G-GARBAGE FIRE.
WHAT'S WRONG WITH YOU GUYS?
I-I DON'T THINK YOU SHOULD HAVE SOLD OUT LIKE-

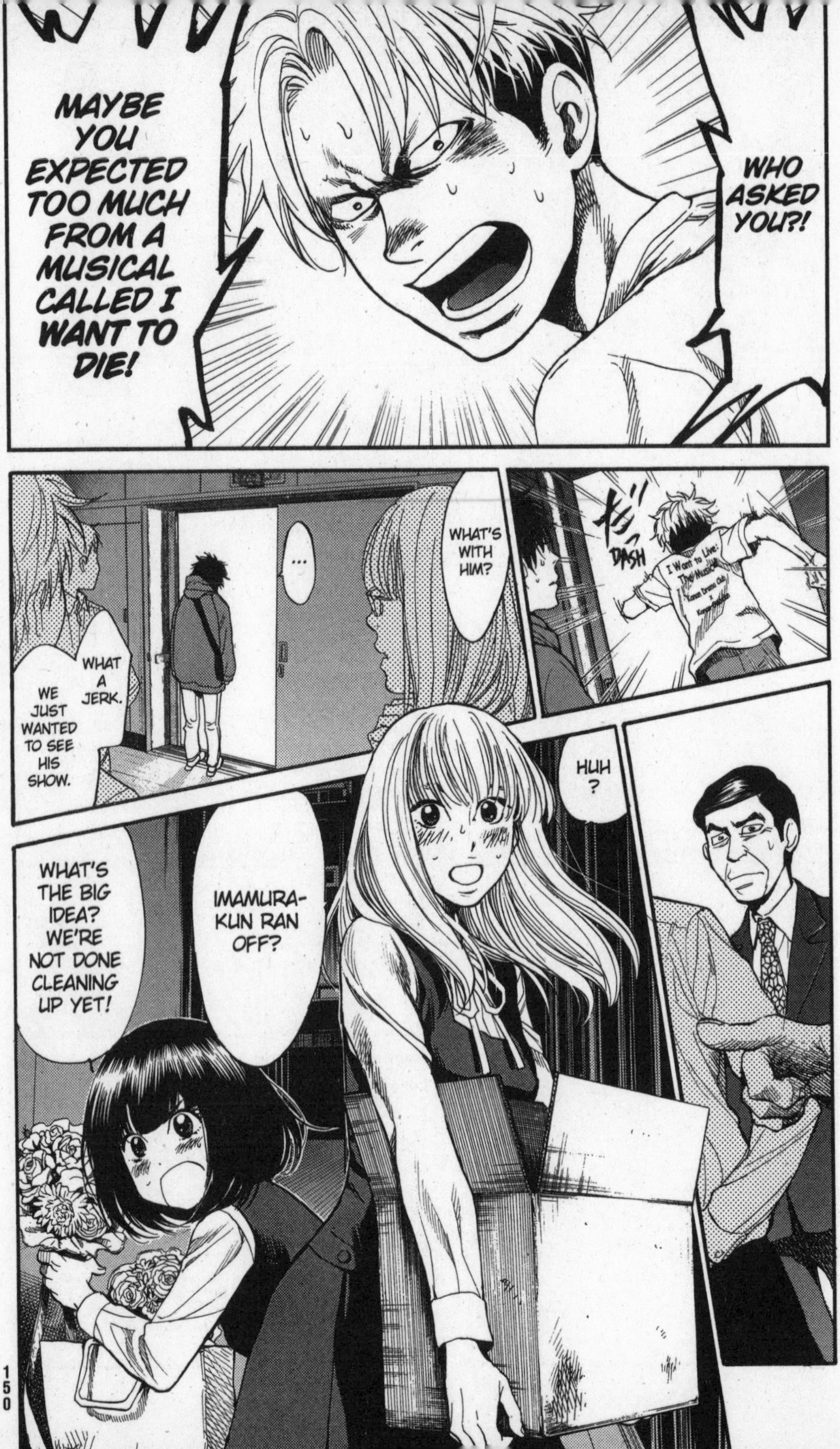
MAYBE YOU EXPECTED TOO MUCH FROM A MUSICAL CALLED I WANT TO DIE!
WHO ASKED YOU?!
DASH
I Want to Live: The Musical
WHAT'S WITH HIM?
...
WHAT A JERK.
WE JUST WANTED TO SEE HIS SHOW.
HUH?
IMAMURA-KUN RAN OFF?
WHAT'S THE BIG IDEA? WE'RE NOT DONE CLEANING UP YET!

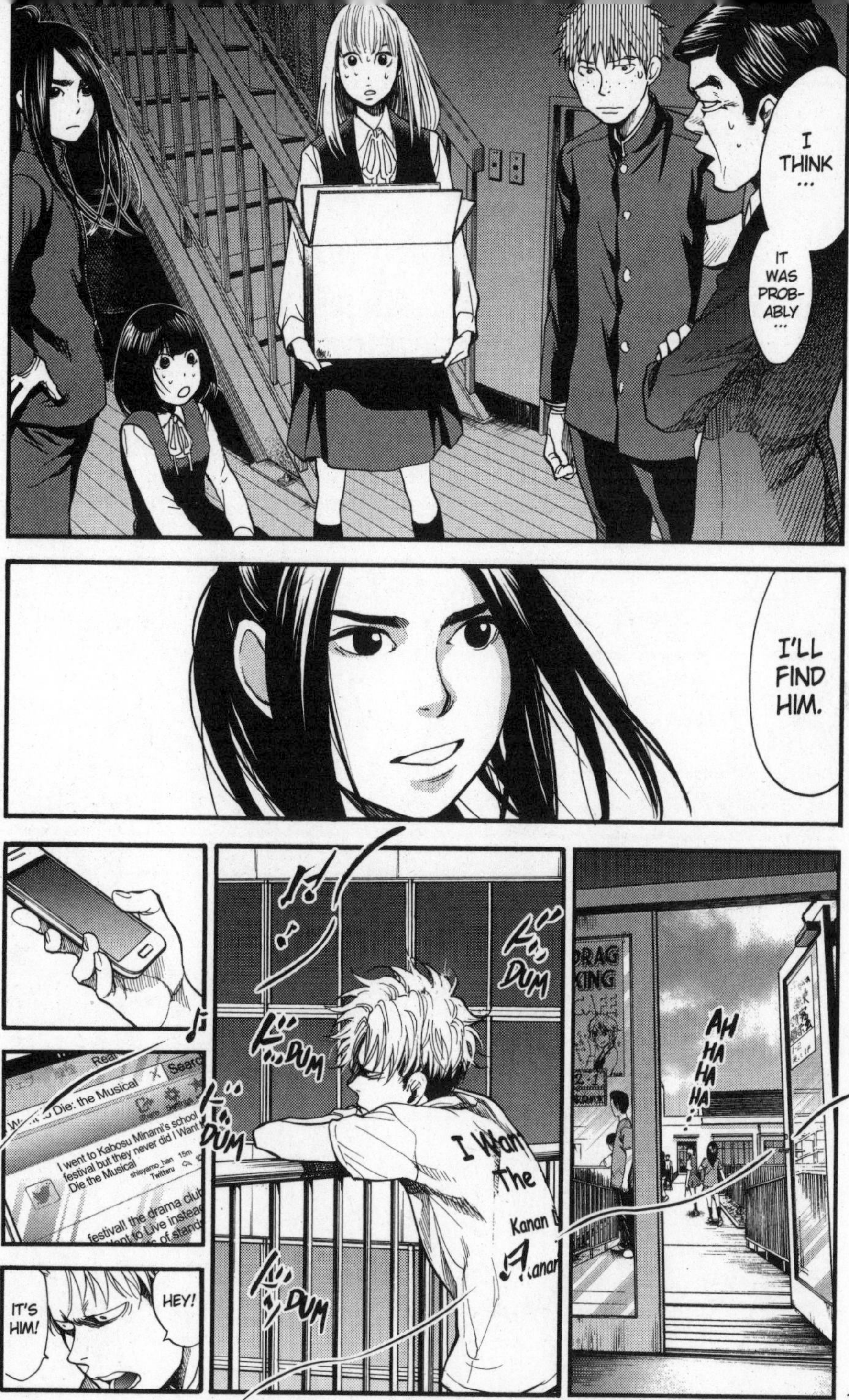
I THINK ...
IT WAS PROBABLY ...
I'LL FIND HIM.
AH HA HA HA HA!
DRAG KING
DUM
DUM
DUM
DUM
I Want The
Kanan
Die: the Musical
I went to Kabosu Minami's school festival but they never did I Want
Die the Musical
shisyamo_han 15m
Twitteru
HEY!
IT'S HIM!

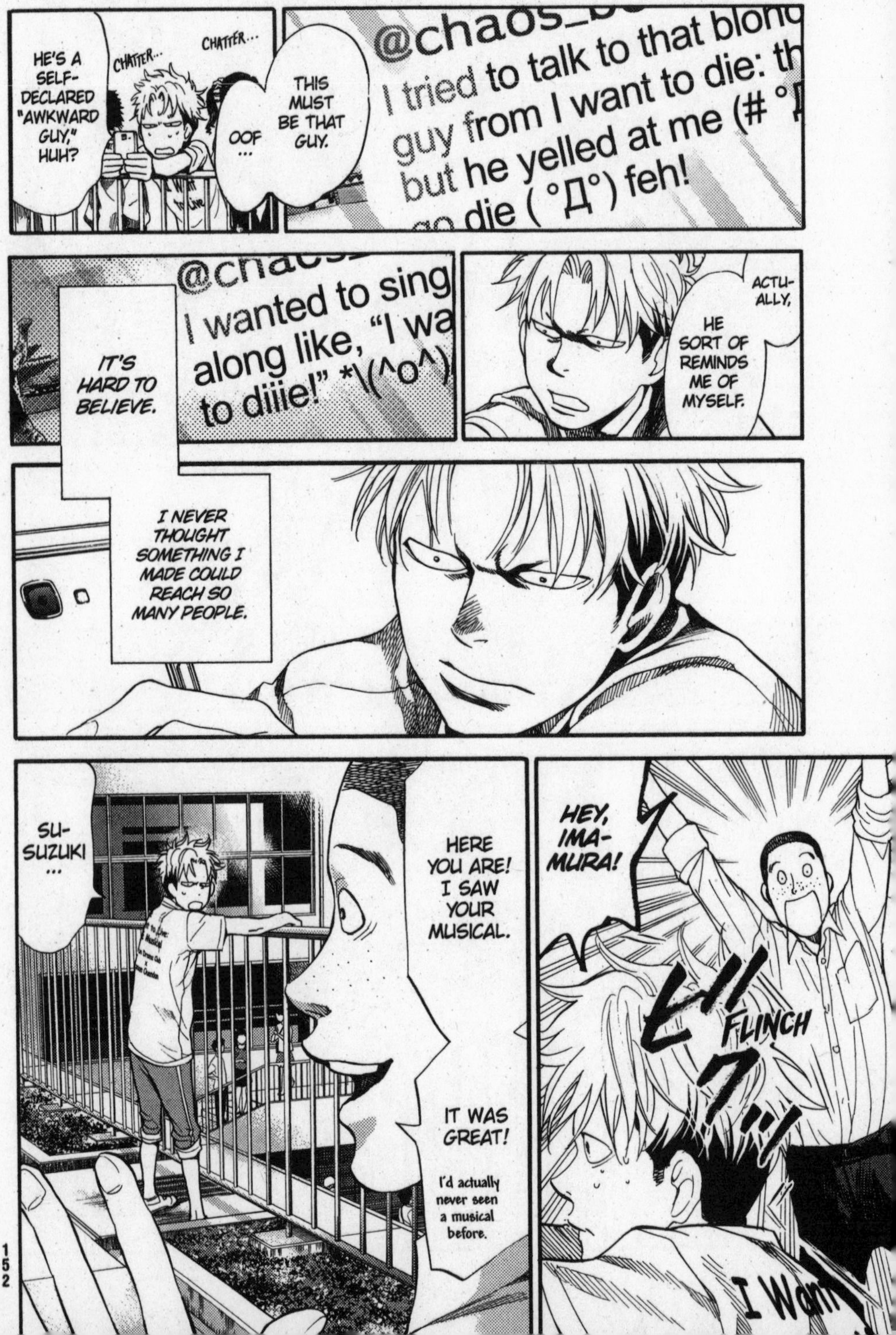

@chaos_b
I tried to talk to that blond
guy from I want to die: th
but he yelled at me (# °Д
go die (°Д°) feh!
THIS MUST BE THAT GUY.
OOF...
CHATTER...
CHATTER...
HE'S A SELF-DECLARED "AWKWARD GUY," HUH?
ACTU-ALLY, HE SORT OF REMINDS ME OF MYSELF.
@chaos
I wanted to sing
along like, "I wa
to diiie!" *\(^o^)
IT'S HARD TO BELIEVE.
I NEVER THOUGHT SOMETHING I MADE COULD REACH SO MANY PEOPLE.
HEY, IMA-MURA!
FLINCH
I Want
HERE YOU ARE! I SAW YOUR MUSICAL.
IT WAS GREAT!
I'd actually never seen a musical before.
SU-SUZUKI...

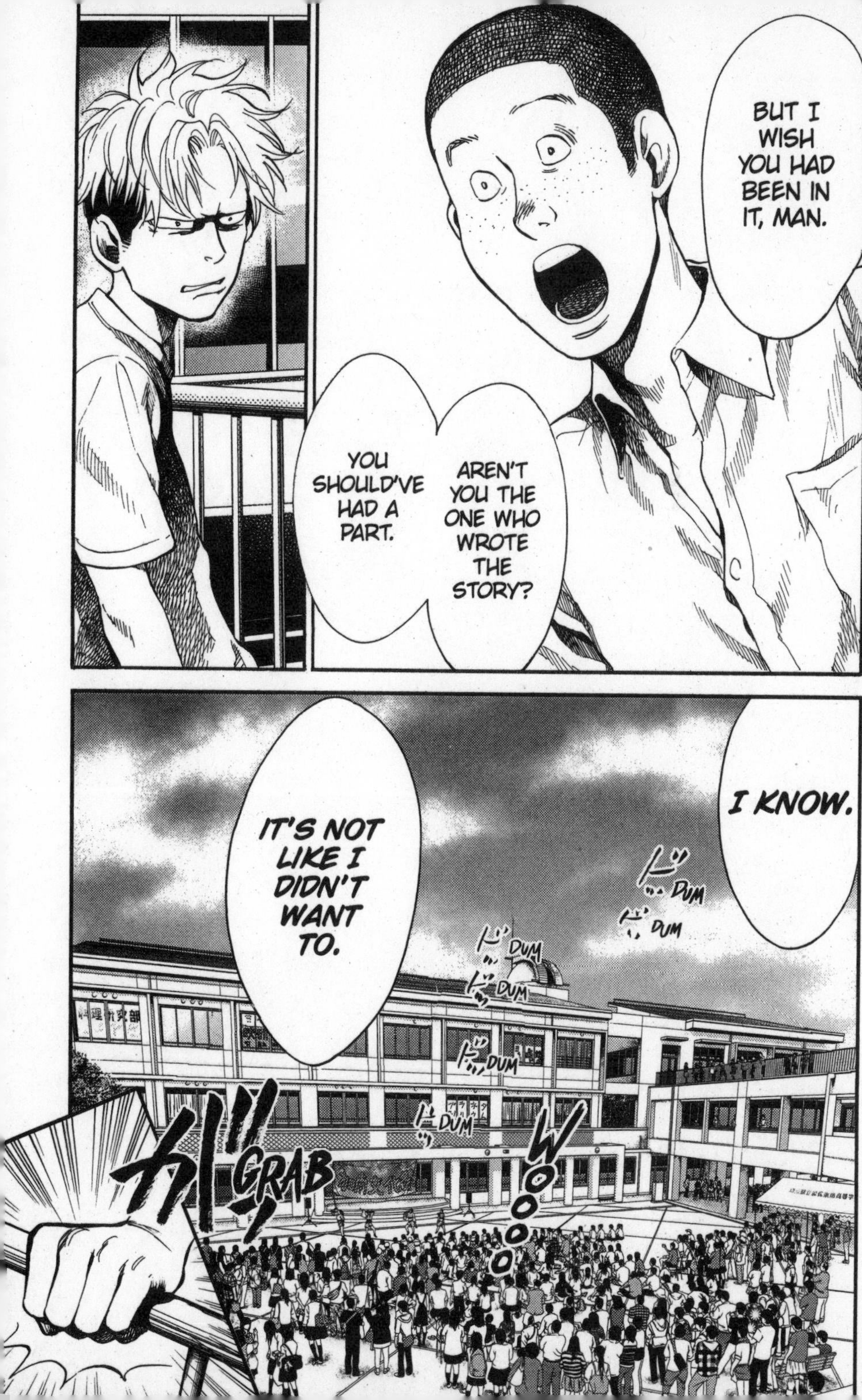
BUT I WISH YOU HAD BEEN IN IT, MAN.
AREN'T YOU THE ONE WHO WROTE THE STORY?
YOU SHOULD'VE HAD A PART.
I KNOW.
IT'S NOT LIKE I DIDN'T WANT TO.
DUM
DUM
DUM
DUM
DUM
DUM
WOOOOOO
GRAB

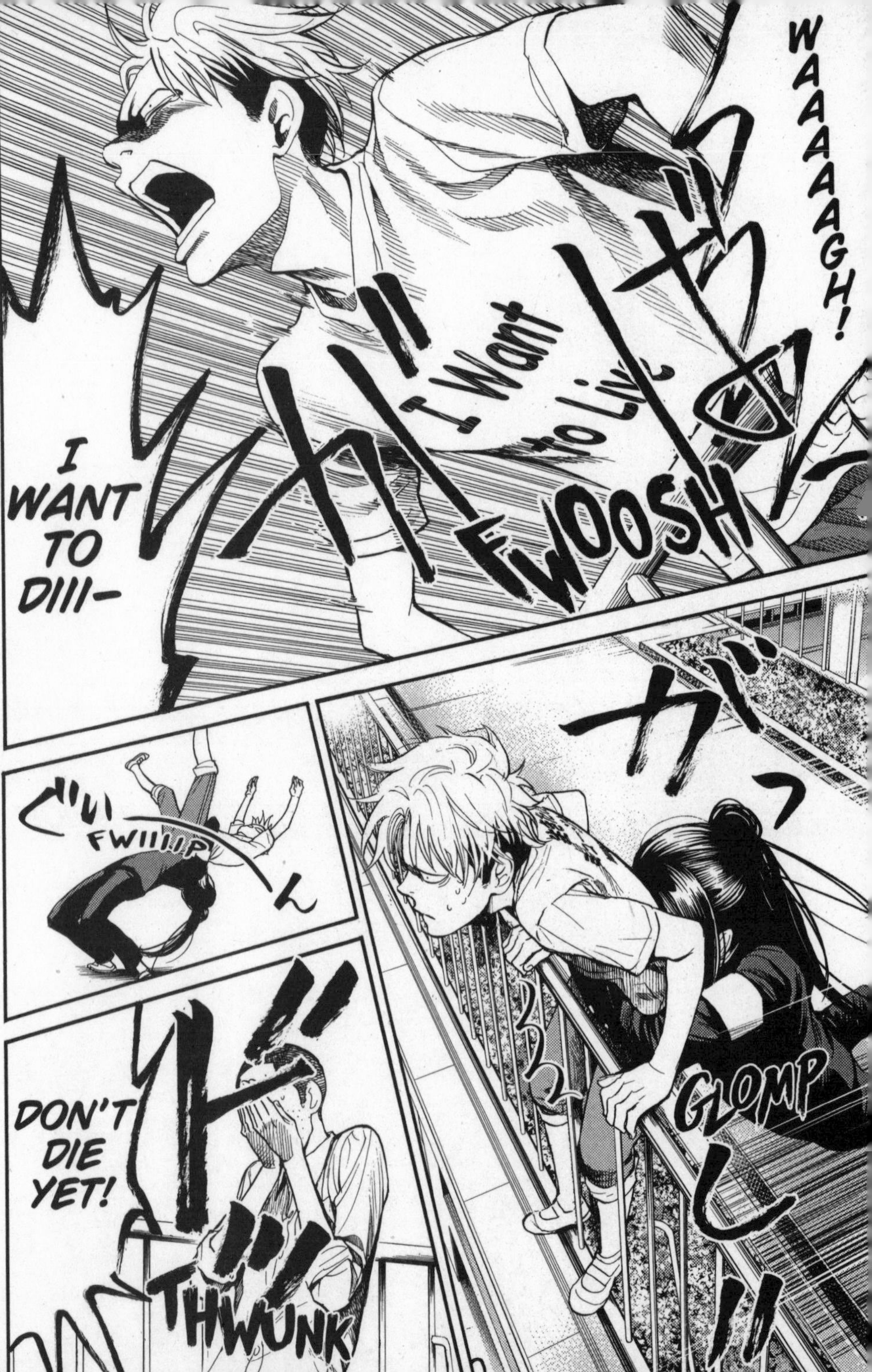

WAAAAAAGH!
I Want to Live
FWOOSH
I WANT TO DIII-
GLOMP
FWIIIIP
DON'T DIE YET!
THWUNK

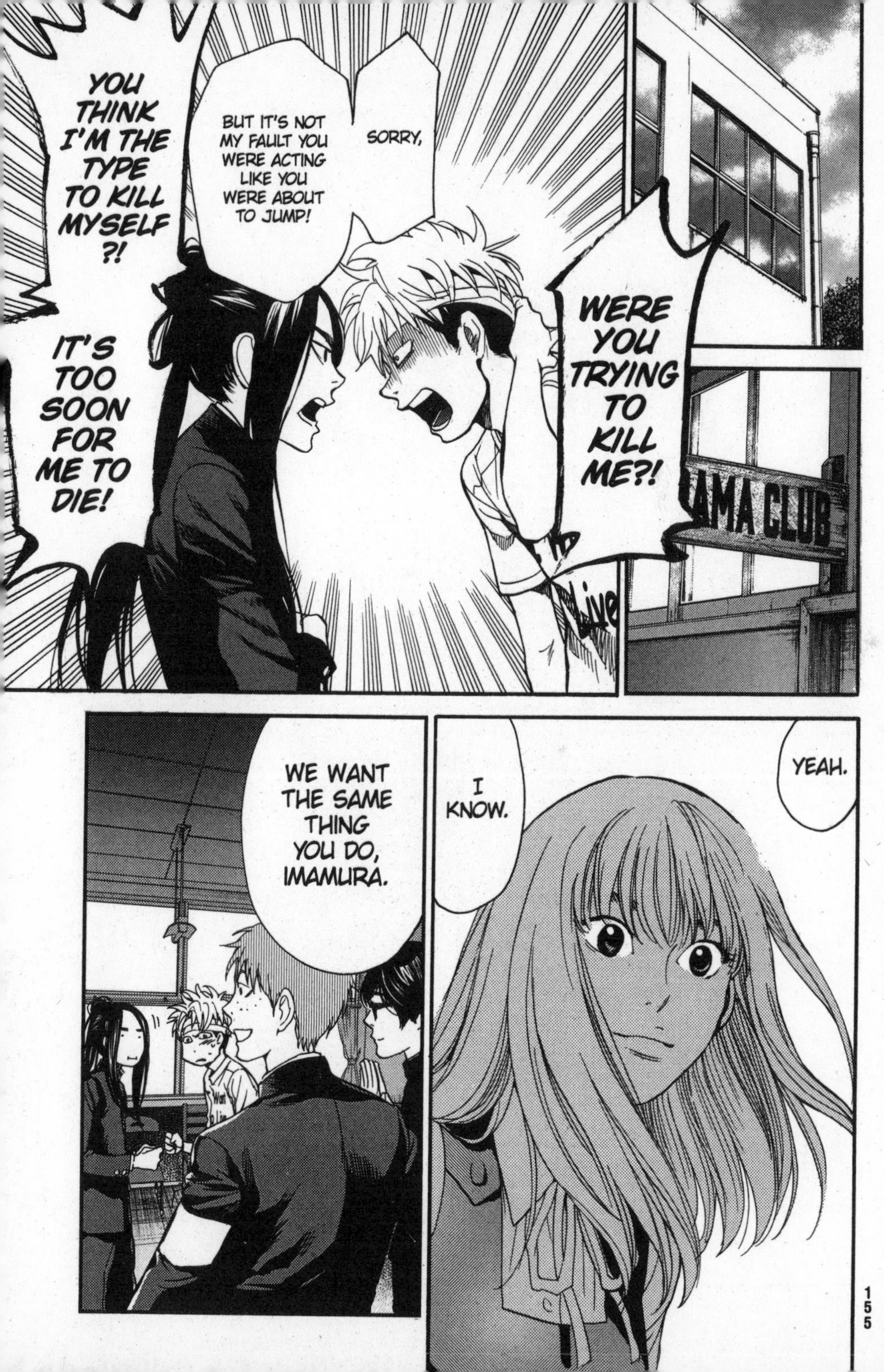
WERE YOU TRYING TO KILL ME?!
AMA CLUB
SORRY,
BUT IT'S NOT MY FAULT YOU WERE ACTING LIKE YOU WERE ABOUT TO JUMP!
YOU THINK I'M THE TYPE TO KILL MYSELF?!
IT'S TOO SOON FOR ME TO DIE!
YEAH.
I KNOW.
WE WANT THE SAME THING YOU DO, IMAMURA.

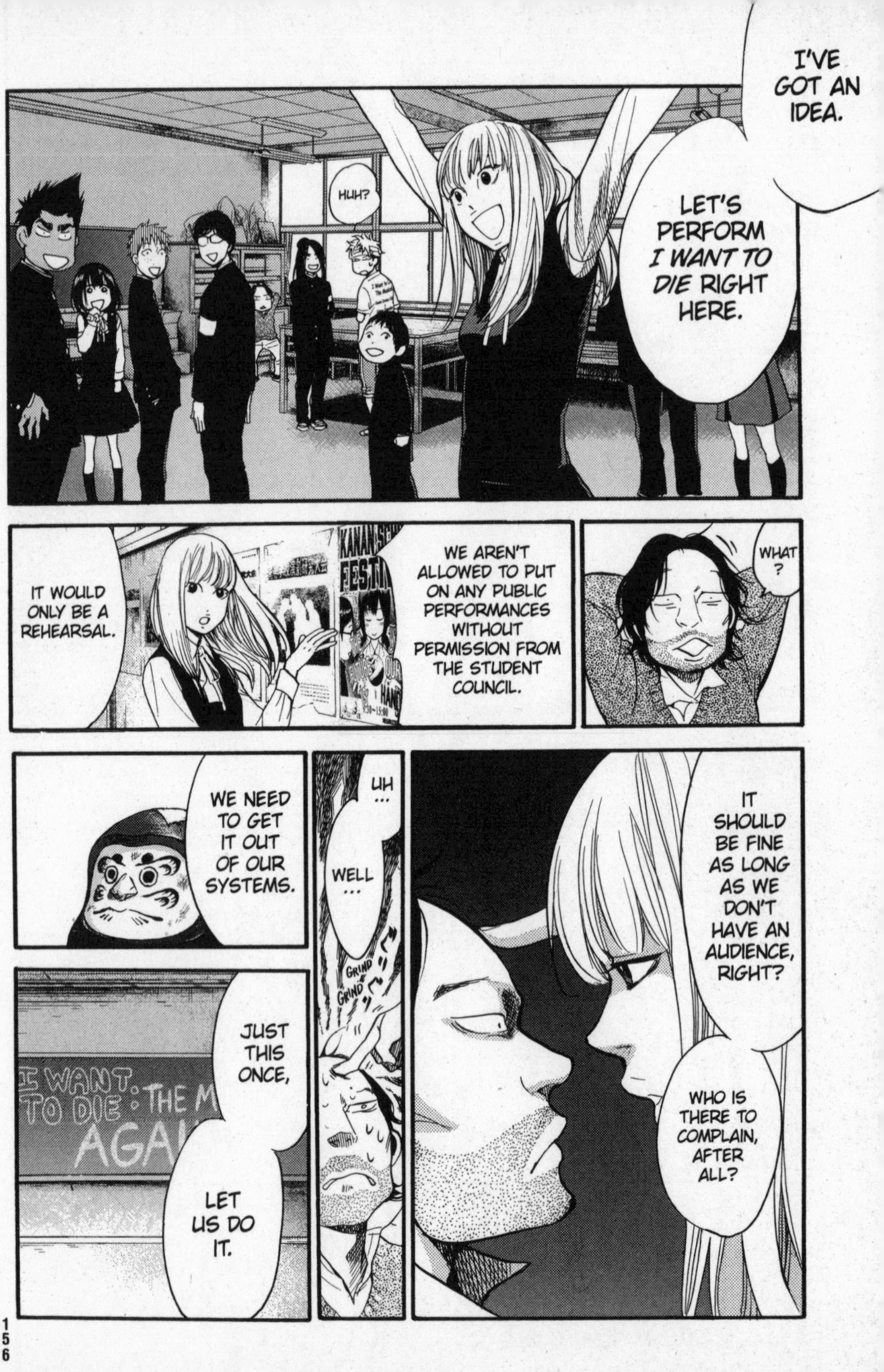
I'VE GOT AN IDEA.
LET'S PERFORM *I WANT TO DIE* RIGHT HERE.
HUH?
WHAT?
WE AREN'T ALLOWED TO PUT ON ANY PUBLIC PERFORMANCES WITHOUT PERMISSION FROM THE STUDENT COUNCIL.
IT WOULD ONLY BE A REHEARSAL.
IT SHOULD BE FINE AS LONG AS WE DON'T HAVE AN AUDIENCE, RIGHT?
WHO IS THERE TO COMPLAIN, AFTER ALL?
UH...
WELL...
GRIND GRIND
WE NEED TO GET IT OUT OF OUR SYSTEMS.
JUST THIS ONCE,
LET US DO IT.

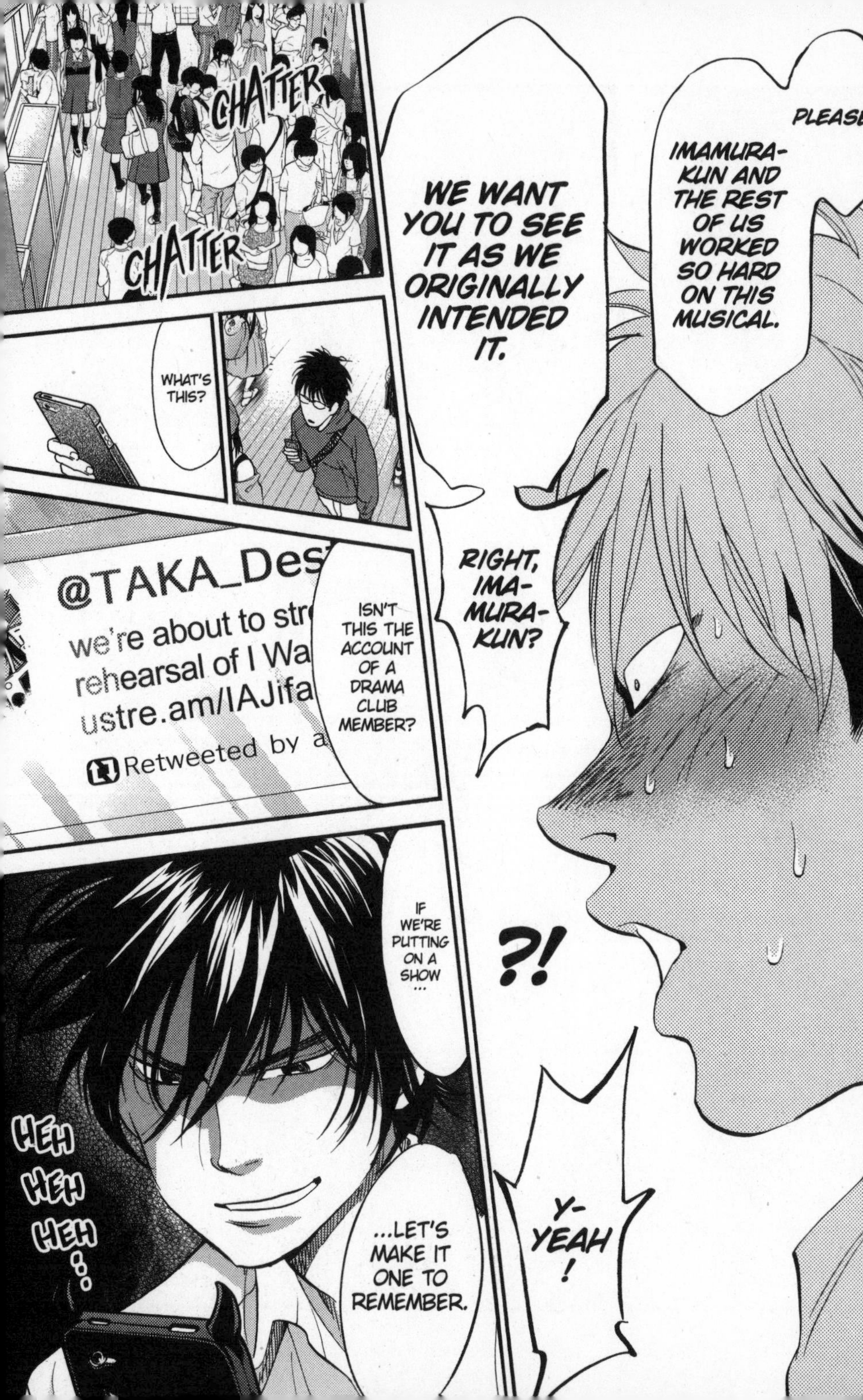
PLEASE.
IMAMURA-KUN AND THE REST OF US WORKED SO HARD ON THIS MUSICAL.
WE WANT YOU TO SEE IT AS WE ORIGINALLY INTENDED IT.
RIGHT, IMAMURA-KUN?
?!
Y-YEAH!
CHATTER
CHATTER
WHAT'S THIS?
@TAKA_Des
we're about to str
rehearsal of I Wa
ustre.am/IAJifa
Retweeted by a
ISN'T THIS THE ACCOUNT OF A DRAMA CLUB MEMBER?
IF WE'RE PUTTING ON A SHOW...
...LET'S MAKE IT ONE TO REMEMBER.
HEH HEH HEH...

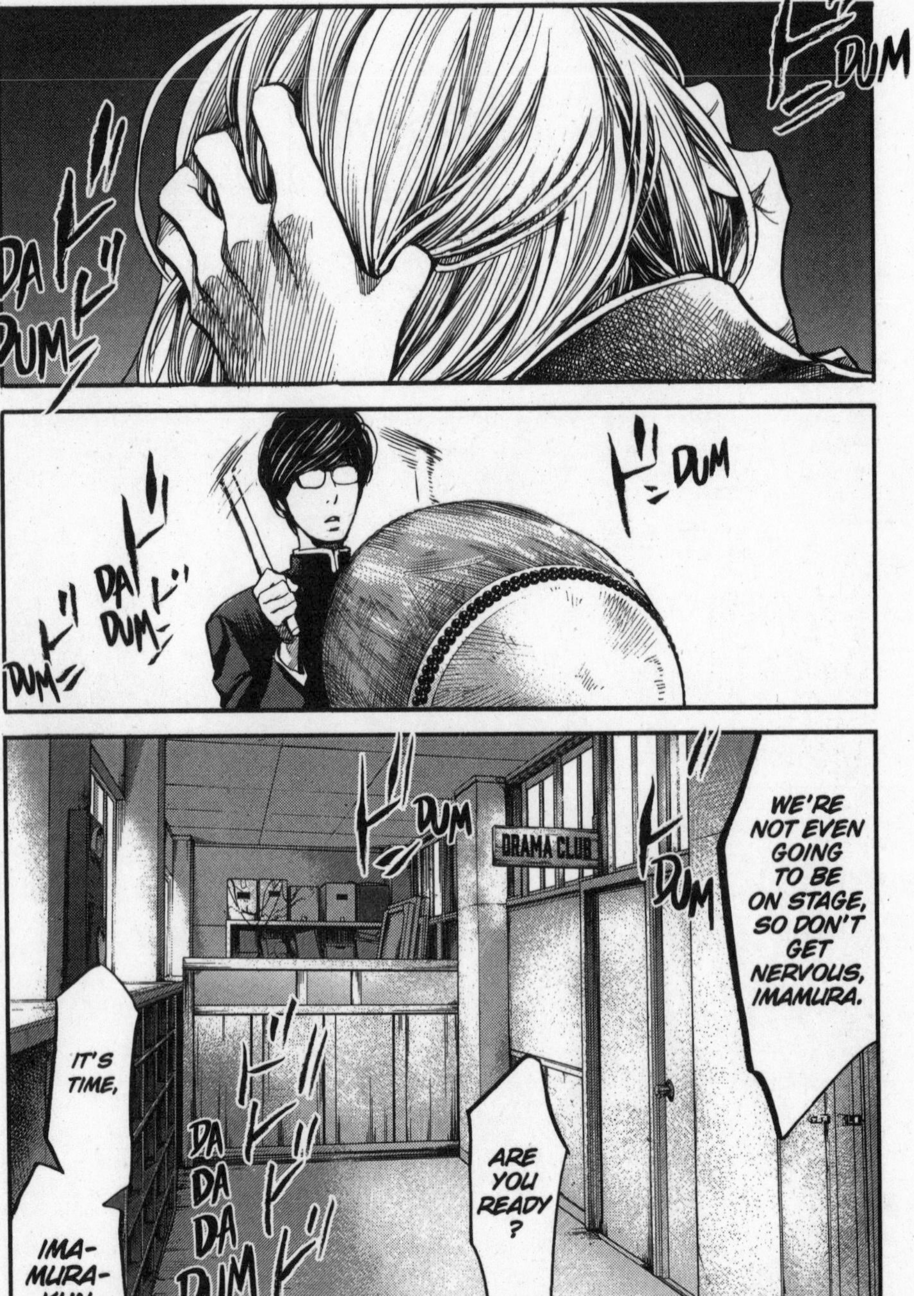
DUM
DA DUM
DUM
DA DUM
DUM
WE'RE NOT EVEN GOING TO BE ON STAGE, SO DON'T GET NERVOUS, IMAMURA.
DUM
DUM
DRAMA CLUB
ARE YOU READY?
DA DA DA DUM
IT'S TIME,
IMA-MURA-KUN.

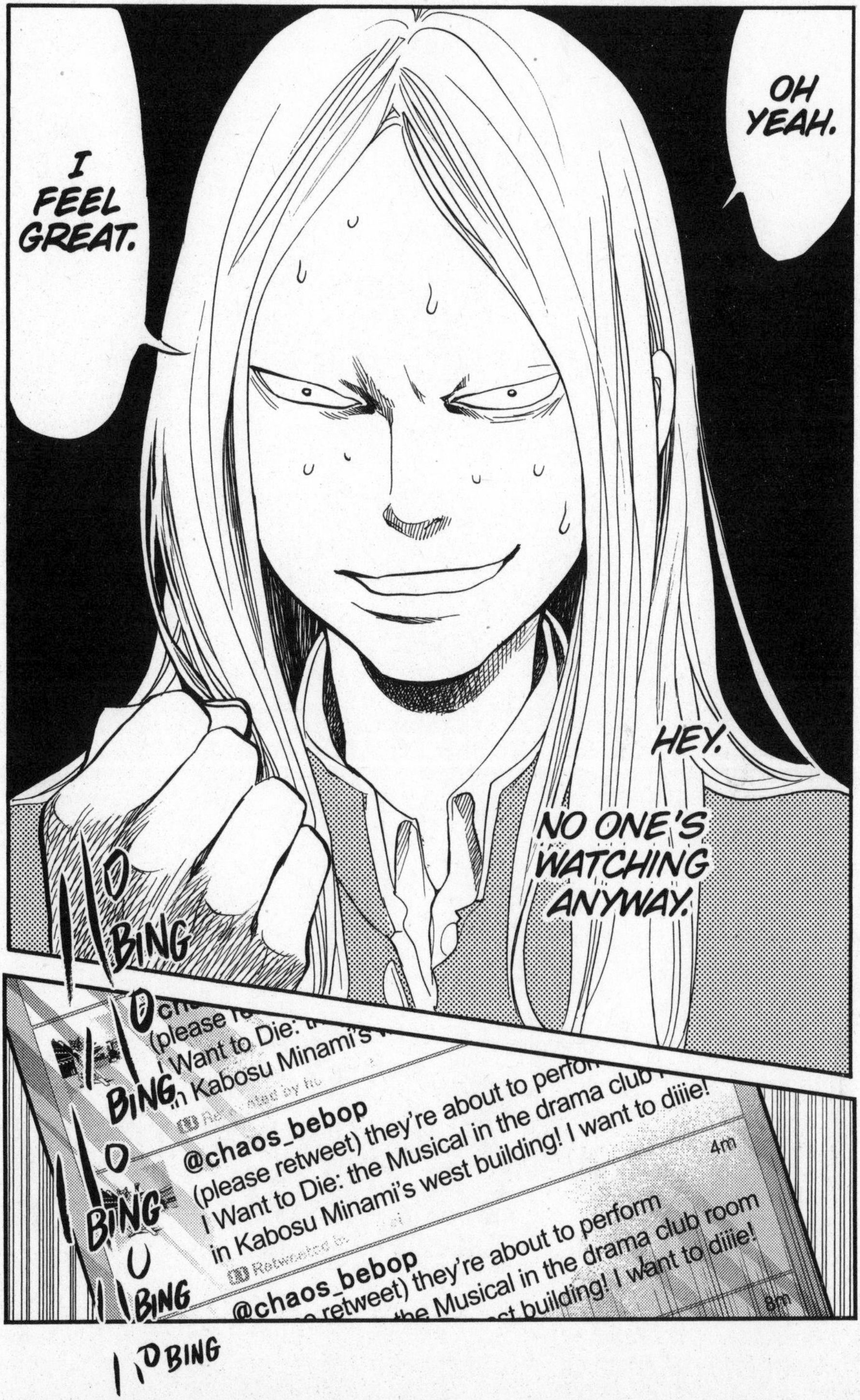
OH YEAH.
I FEEL GREAT.
HEY.
NO ONE'S WATCHING ANYWAY.
BING
BING
BING
BING
BING
@chaos_bebop
(please retweet) they're about to perform
I Want to Die: the Musical in the drama club room
in Kabosu Minami's west building! I want to diiie!
4m
@chaos_bebop
(please retweet) they're about to perform
I Want to Die: the Musical in the drama club room
in Kabosu Minami's west building! I want to diiie!

Again!!
アゲイン!!

97. THE EMPTY EVERYDAY

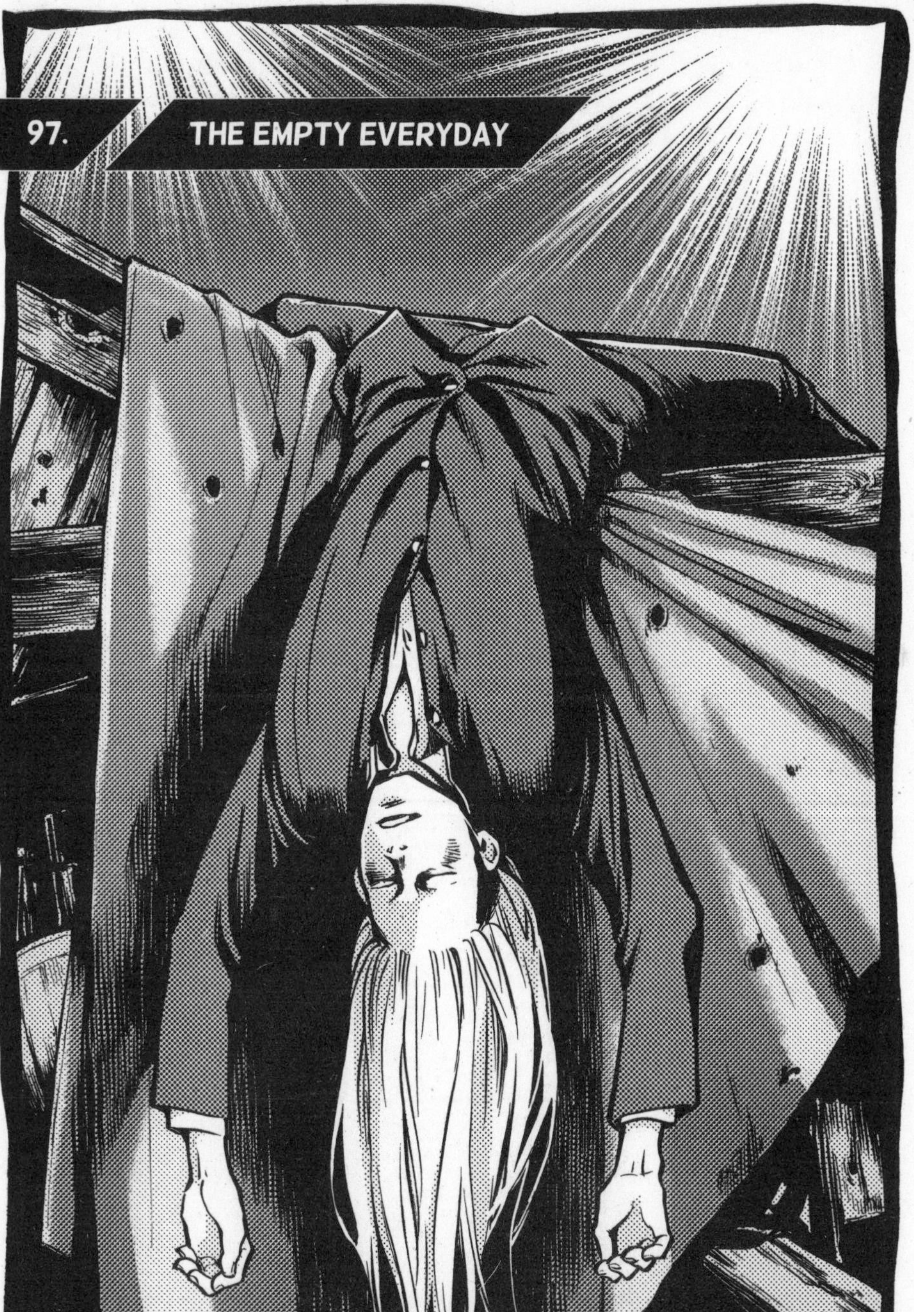

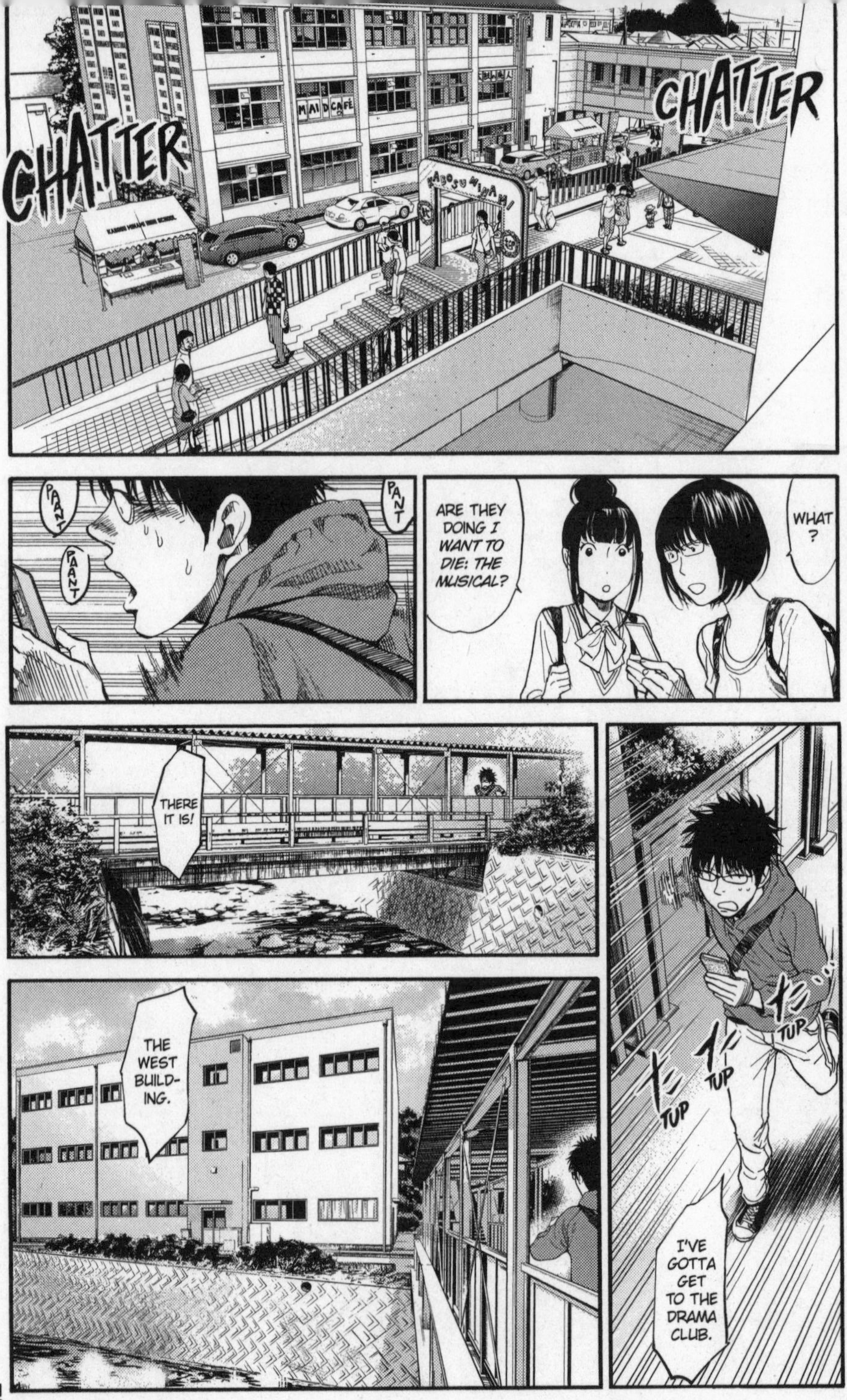
CHATTER
MAID CAFÉ
CHATTER
WHAT?
ARE THEY DOING I WANT TO DIE: THE MUSICAL?
PANT
PAANT
PAANT
TUP
TUP
TUP
I'VE GOTTA GET TO THE DRAMA CLUB.
THERE IT IS!
THE WEST BUILDING.

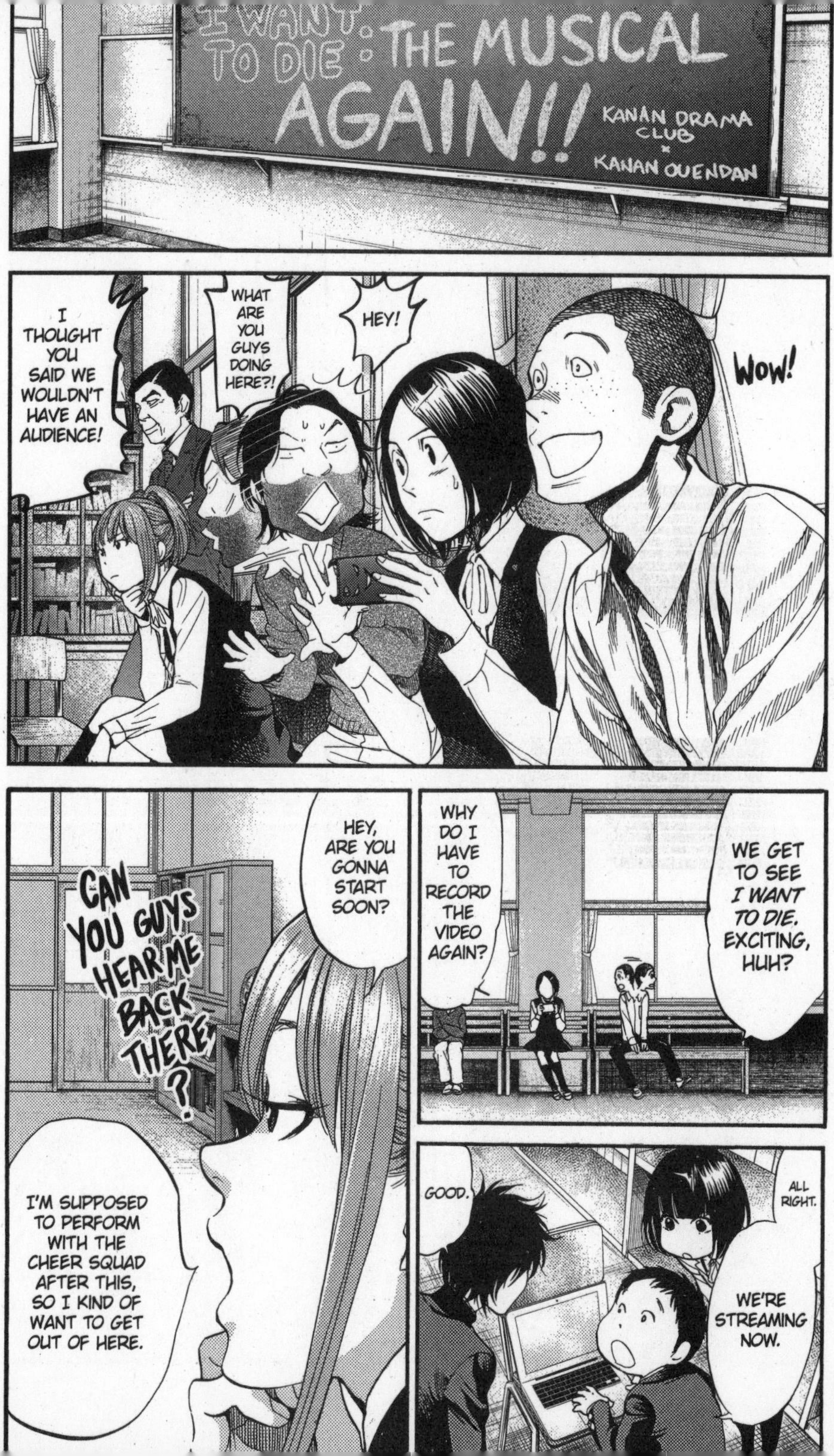
I WANT TO DIE: THE MUSICAL AGAIN!!
KANAN DRAMA CLUB × KANAN OUENDAN
WOW!
HEY!
WHAT ARE YOU GUYS DOING HERE?!
I THOUGHT YOU SAID WE WOULDN'T HAVE AN AUDIENCE!
WE GET TO SEE *I WANT TO DIE*. EXCITING, HUH?
WHY DO I HAVE TO RECORD THE VIDEO AGAIN?
ALL RIGHT.
WE'RE STREAMING NOW.
GOOD.
HEY, ARE YOU GONNA START SOON?
CAN YOU GUYS HEAR ME BACK THERE?
I'M SUPPOSED TO PERFORM WITH THE CHEER SQUAD AFTER THIS, SO I KIND OF WANT TO GET OUT OF HERE.

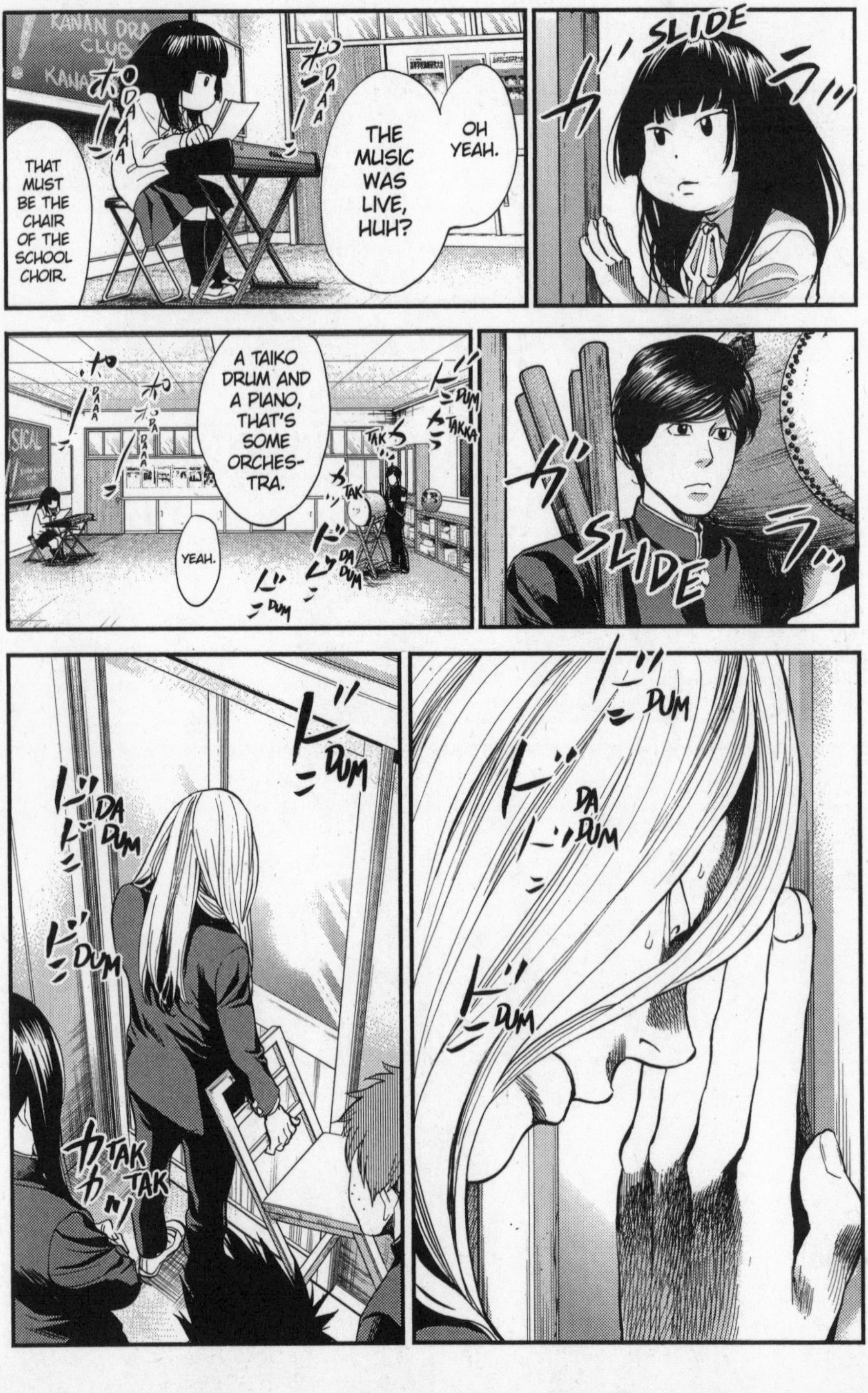
SLIDE
OH YEAH.
THE MUSIC WAS LIVE, HUH?
THAT MUST BE THE CHAIR OF THE SCHOOL CHOIR.
DAAA
DAAAA
SLIDE
A TAIKO DRUM AND A PIANO, THAT'S SOME ORCHESTRA.
YEAH.
DUM
TAKKA
TAK
TAK
DA DUM
DUM
DAAA
DAAA
DUM
DA DUM
DUM
DUM
DA DUM
DUM
TAK TAK

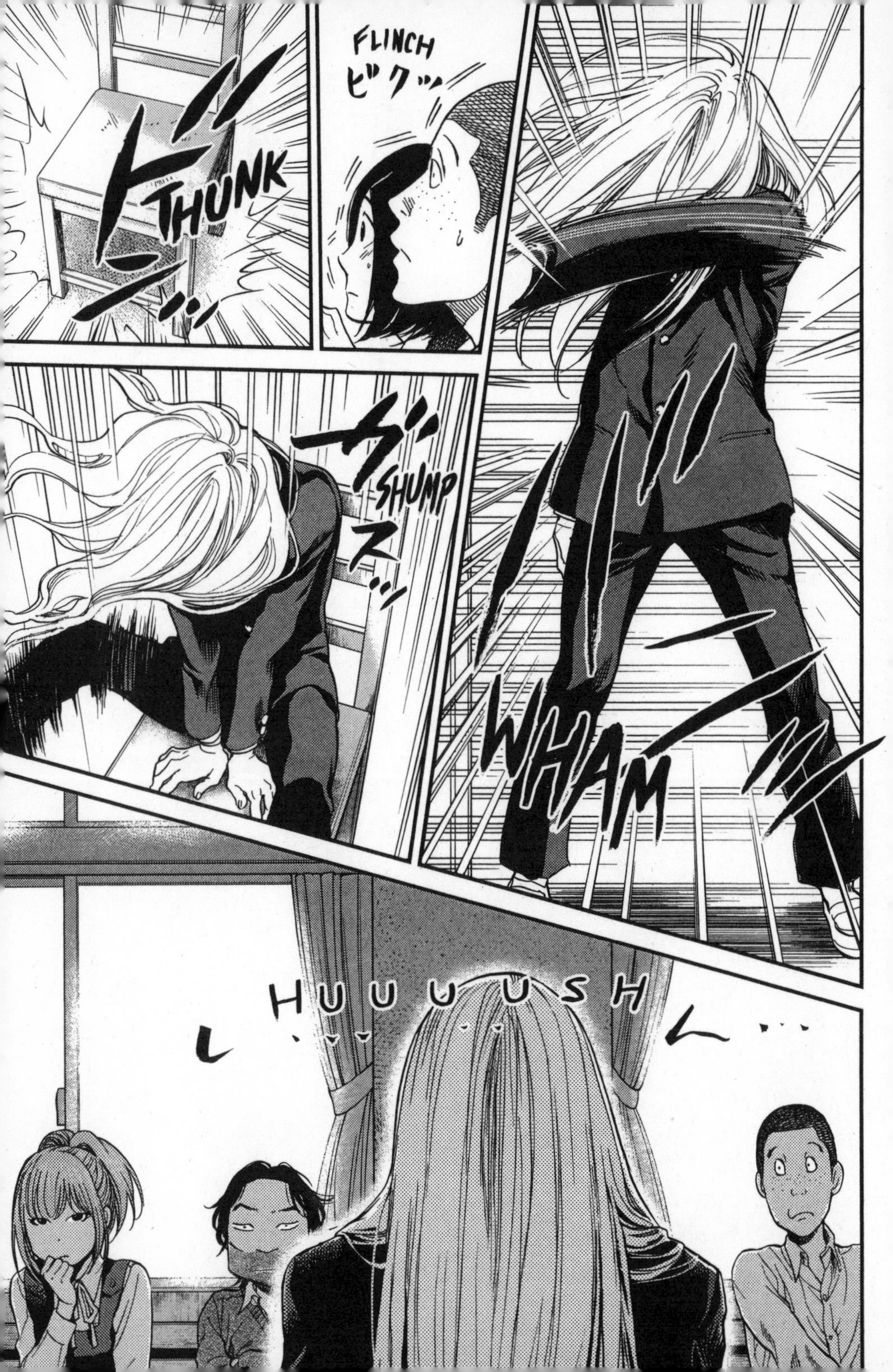

WHAM
FLINCH
ビクッ
THUNK
SHUMP
HUUUUSH
しーん…

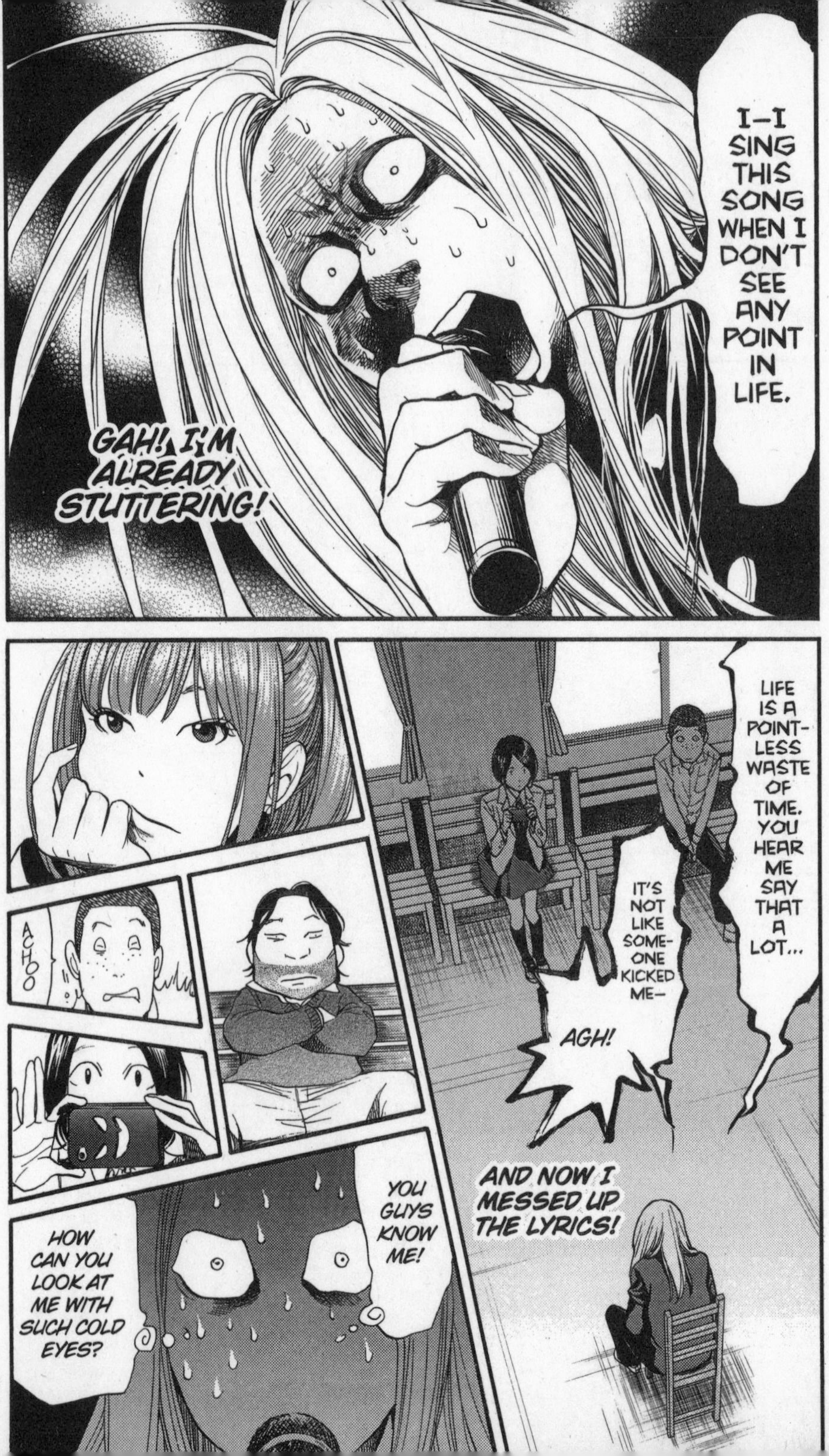
I-I SING THIS SONG WHEN I DON'T SEE ANY POINT IN LIFE.
GAH! I'M ALREADY STUTTERING!
LIFE IS A POINTLESS WASTE OF TIME. YOU HEAR ME SAY THAT A LOT...
IT'S NOT LIKE SOMEONE KICKED ME—
AGH!
AND NOW I MESSED UP THE LYRICS!
ACHOO
YOU GUYS KNOW ME!
HOW CAN YOU LOOK AT ME WITH SUCH COLD EYES?

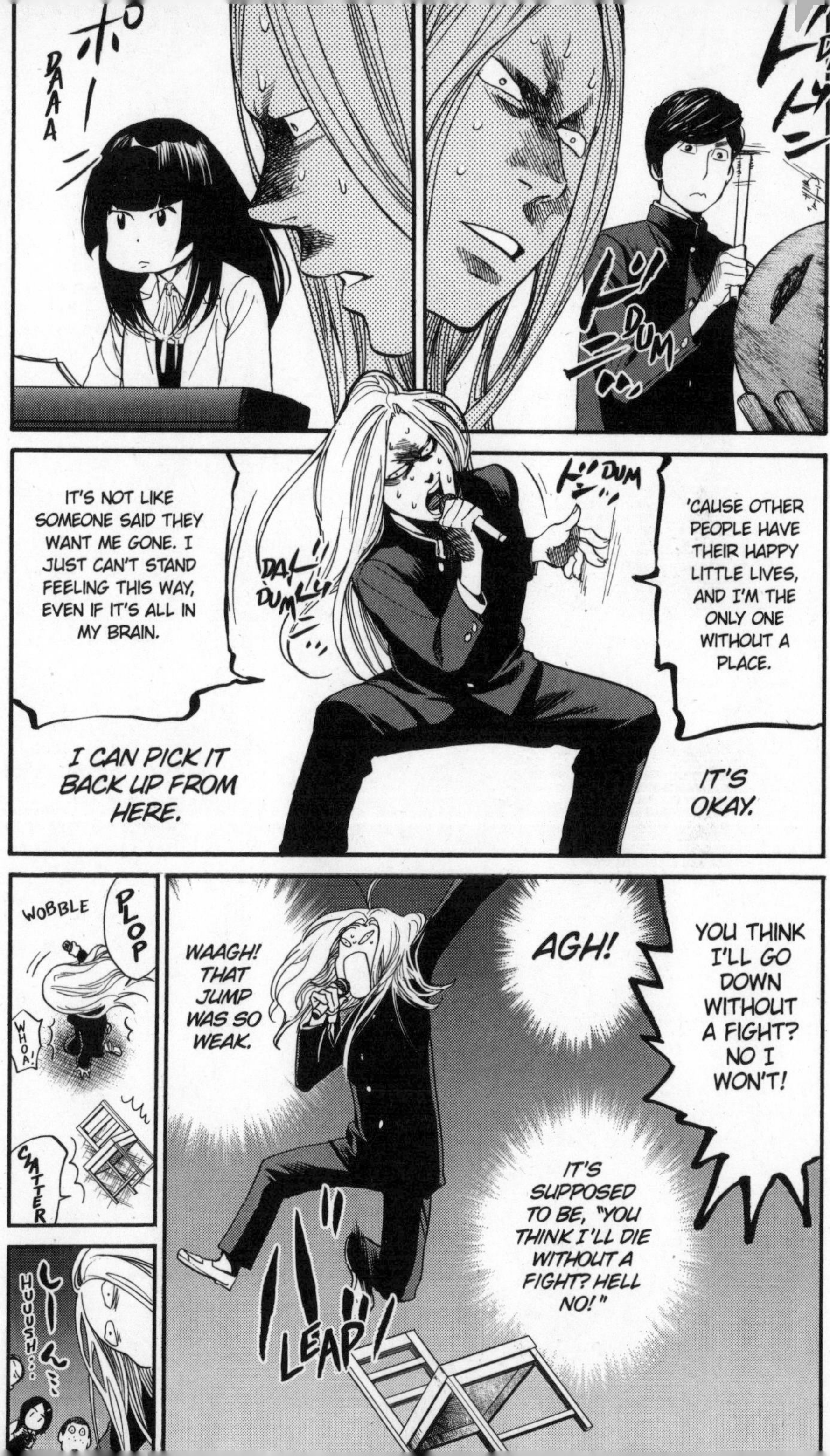
DA-DUN
DUM...
DAAAA
DUM
'CAUSE OTHER PEOPLE HAVE THEIR HAPPY LITTLE LIVES, AND I'M THE ONLY ONE WITHOUT A PLACE.
IT'S NOT LIKE SOMEONE SAID THEY WANT ME GONE. I JUST CAN'T STAND FEELING THIS WAY, EVEN IF IT'S ALL IN MY BRAIN.
DA DUM
IT'S OKAY.
I CAN PICK IT BACK UP FROM HERE.
YOU THINK I'LL GO DOWN WITHOUT A FIGHT? NO I WON'T!
AGH!
WAAGH! THAT JUMP WAS SO WEAK.
IT'S SUPPOSED TO BE, "YOU THINK I'LL DIE WITHOUT A FIGHT? HELL NO!"
LEAP
PLOP
WOBBLE
WHOA!
CLATTER
HUUUSH...

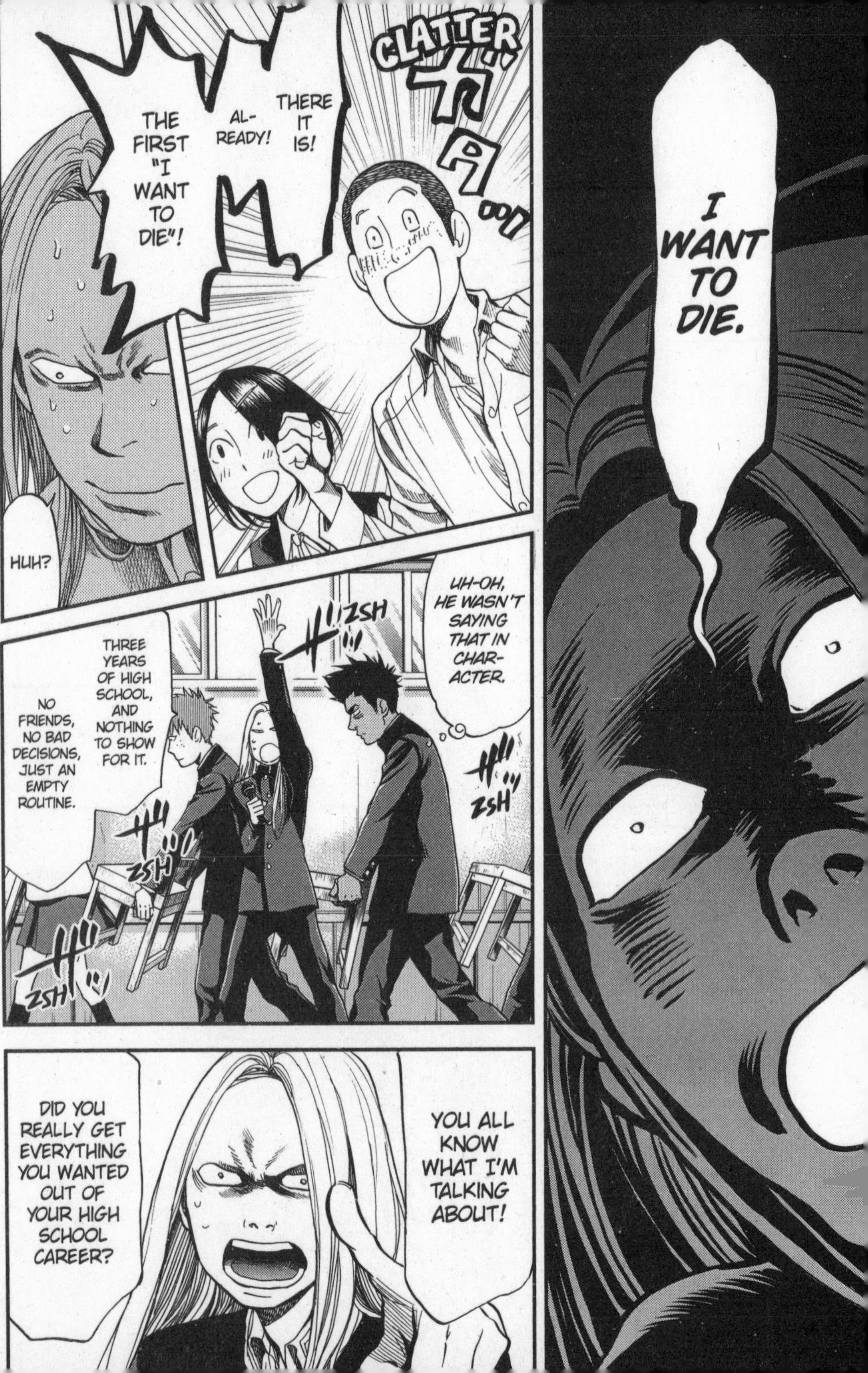
I WANT TO DIE.
CLATTER
THERE IT IS!
AL-READY!
THE FIRST "I WANT TO DIE"!
HUH?
UH-OH, HE WASN'T SAYING THAT IN CHAR-ACTER.
ZSH
ZSH
THREE YEARS OF HIGH SCHOOL, AND NOTHING TO SHOW FOR IT.
NO FRIENDS, NO BAD DECISIONS, JUST AN EMPTY ROUTINE.
ZSH
ZSH
YOU ALL KNOW WHAT I'M TALKING ABOUT!
DID YOU REALLY GET EVERYTHING YOU WANTED OUT OF YOUR HIGH SCHOOL CAREER?

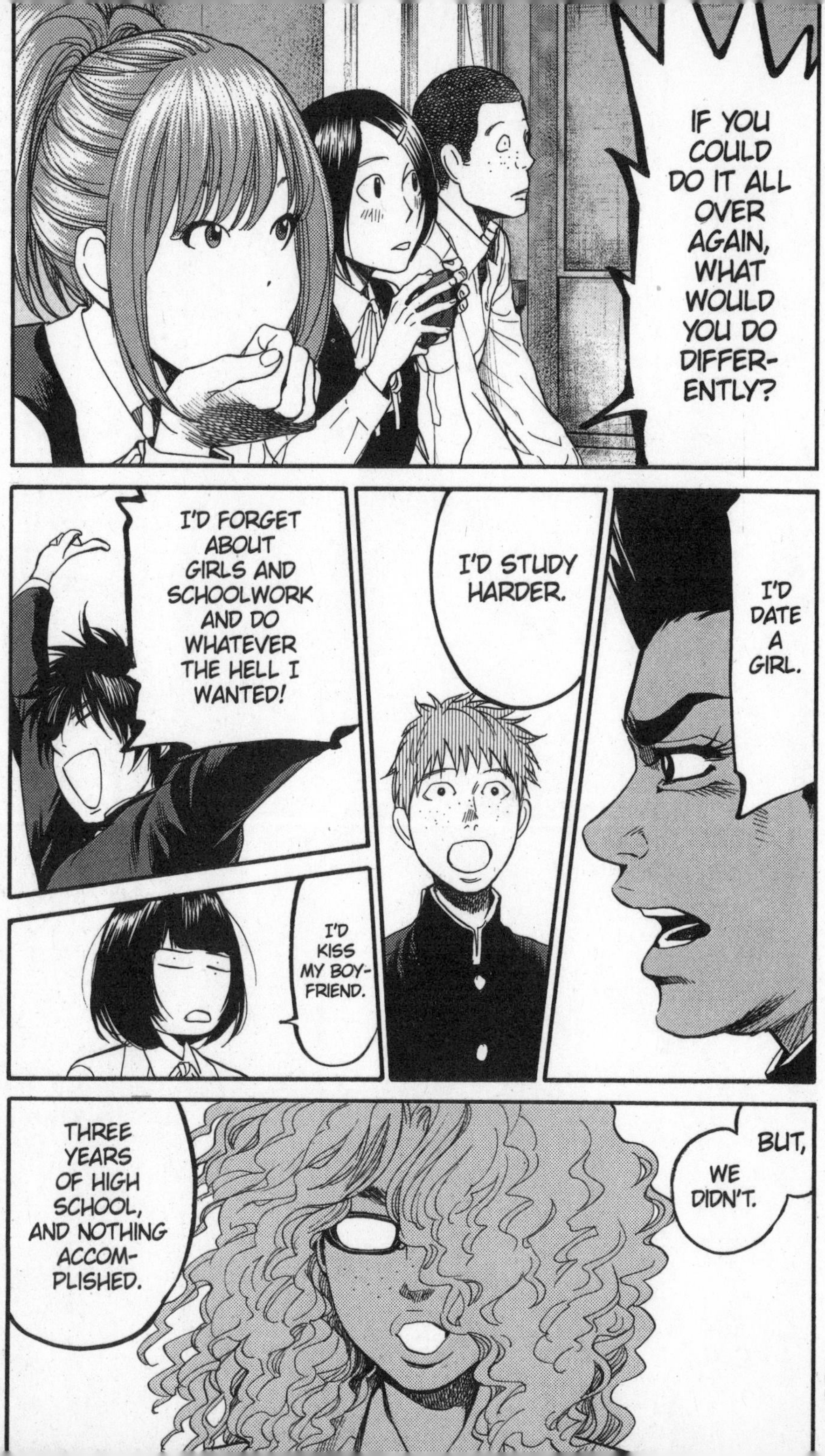
IF YOU COULD DO IT ALL OVER AGAIN, WHAT WOULD YOU DO DIFFER-ENTLY?
I'D DATE A GIRL.
I'D STUDY HARDER.
I'D FORGET ABOUT GIRLS AND SCHOOLWORK AND DO WHATEVER THE HELL I WANTED!
I'D KISS MY BOY-FRIEND.
BUT,
WE DIDN'T.
THREE YEARS OF HIGH SCHOOL, AND NOTHING ACCOM-PLISHED.

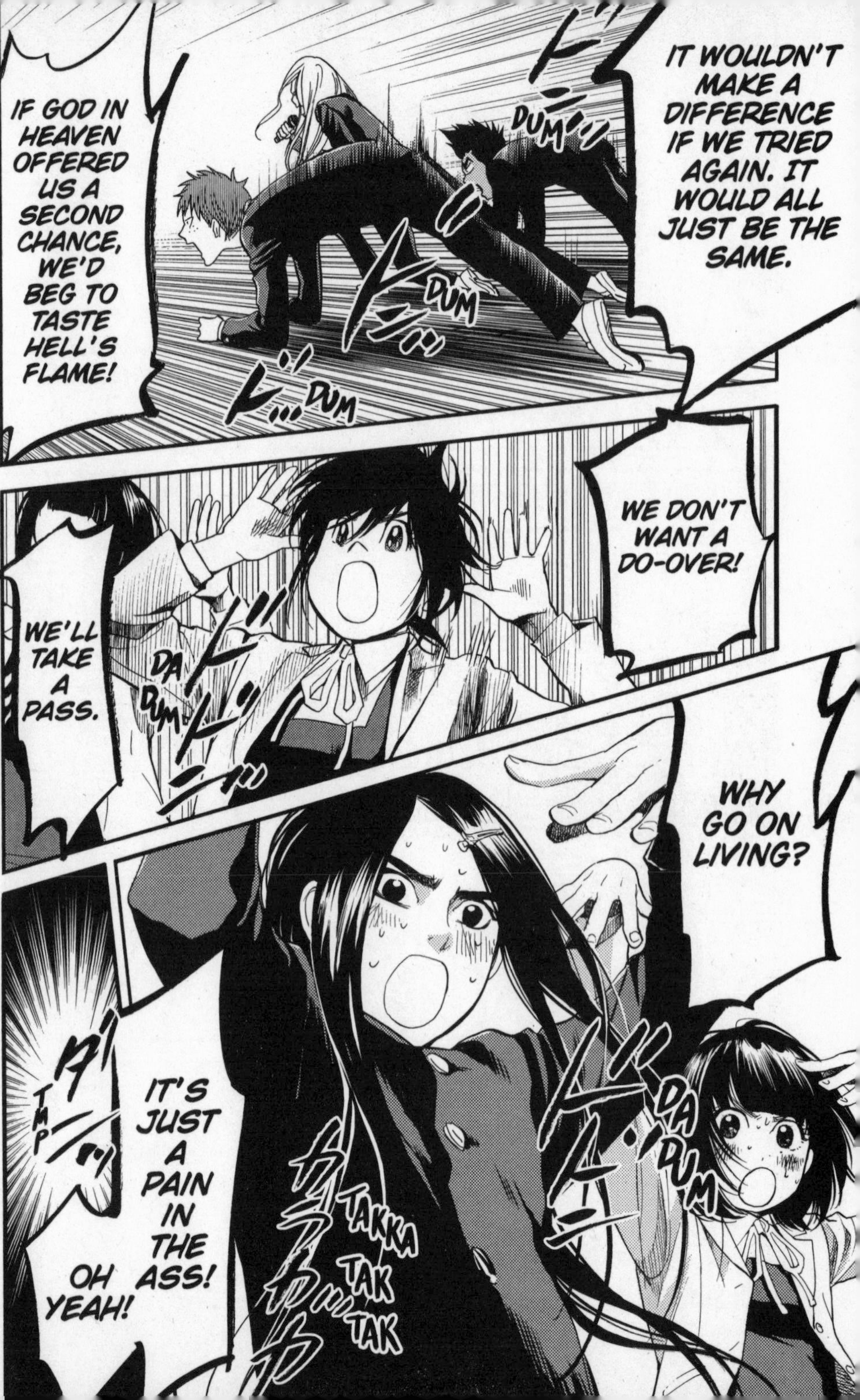
IT WOULDN'T MAKE A DIFFERENCE IF WE TRIED AGAIN. IT WOULD ALL JUST BE THE SAME.
DUM
DUM
IF GOD IN HEAVEN OFFERED US A SECOND CHANCE, WE'D BEG TO TASTE HELL'S FLAME!
DUM
WE DON'T WANT A DO-OVER!
DA DUM
WE'LL TAKE A PASS.
WHY GO ON LIVING?
DA DUM
TAKKA TAK TAK
IT'S JUST A PAIN IN THE ASS!
TMP
OH YEAH!

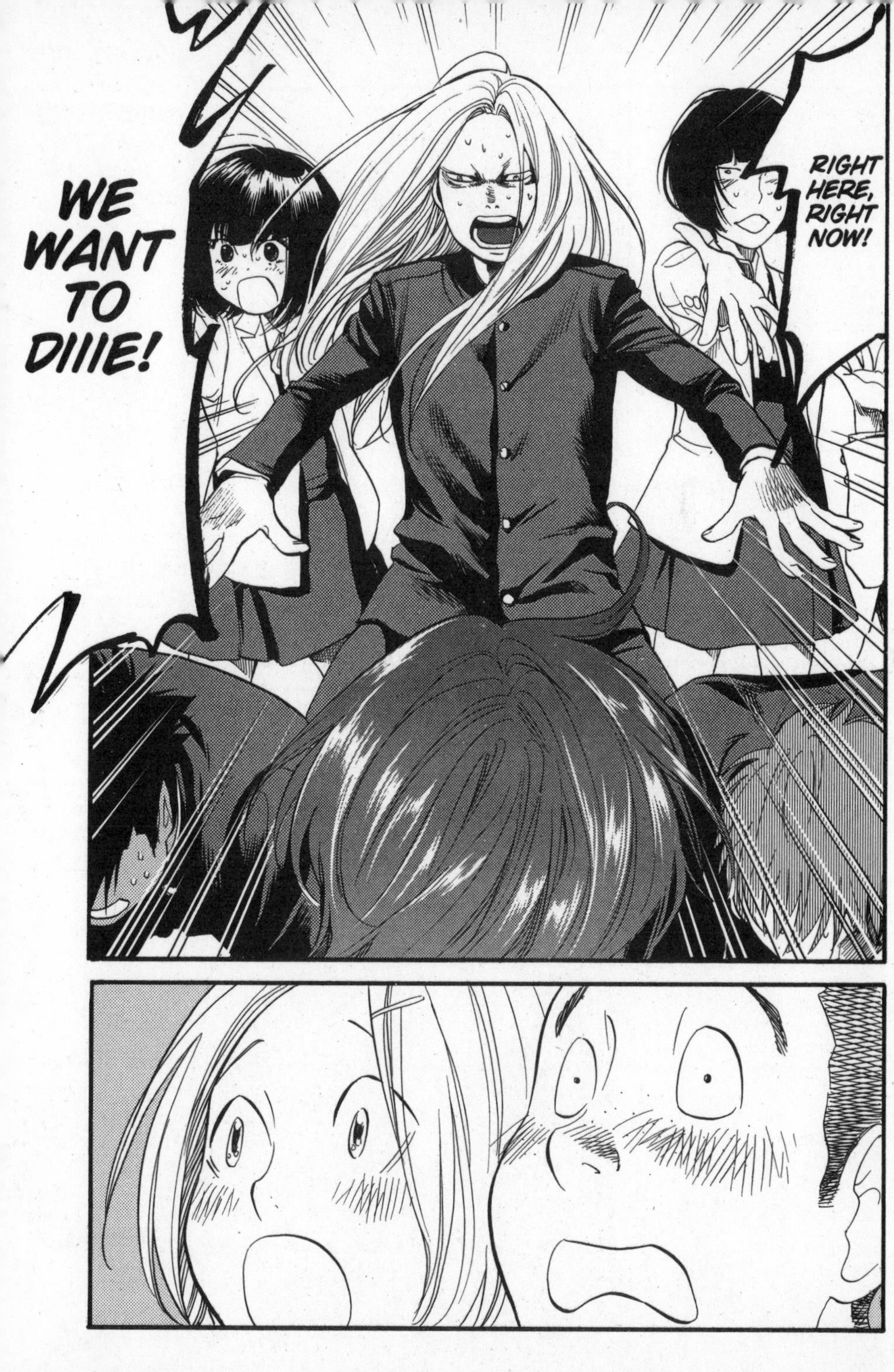
RIGHT HERE, RIGHT NOW!
WE WANT TO DIIIE!

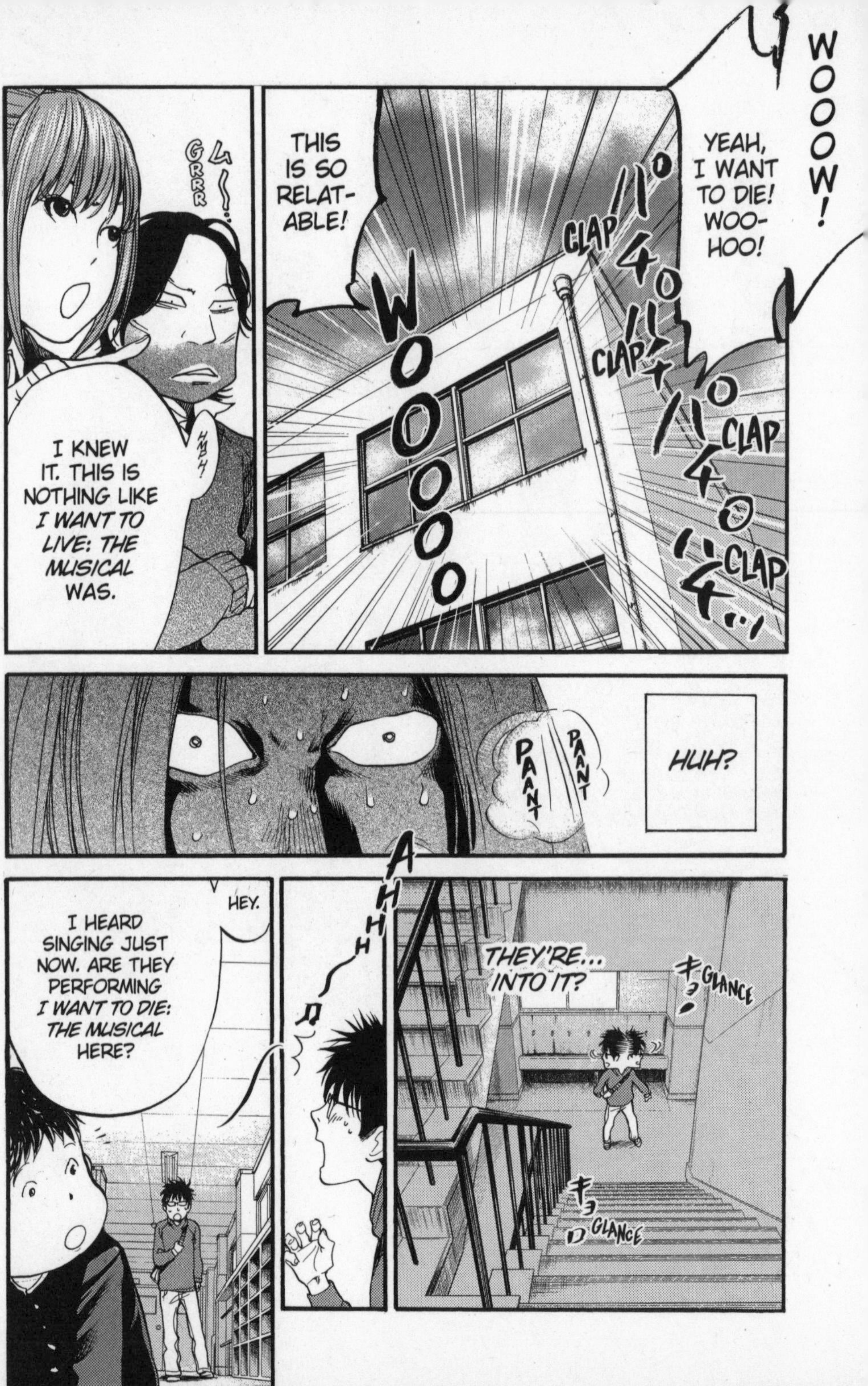
WOOOOW!
YEAH, I WANT TO DIE! WOO-HOO!
CLAP
CLAP
CLAP
CLAP
WOOOOO
THIS IS SO RELATABLE!
GRRR
I KNEW IT. THIS IS NOTHING LIKE *I WANT TO LIVE: THE MUSICAL* WAS.
HMPH
HUH?
PAANT
PAANT
AHHHH
GLANCE
THEY'RE... INTO IT?
GLANCE
HEY.
I HEARD SINGING JUST NOW. ARE THEY PERFORMING *I WANT TO DIE: THE MUSICAL* HERE?

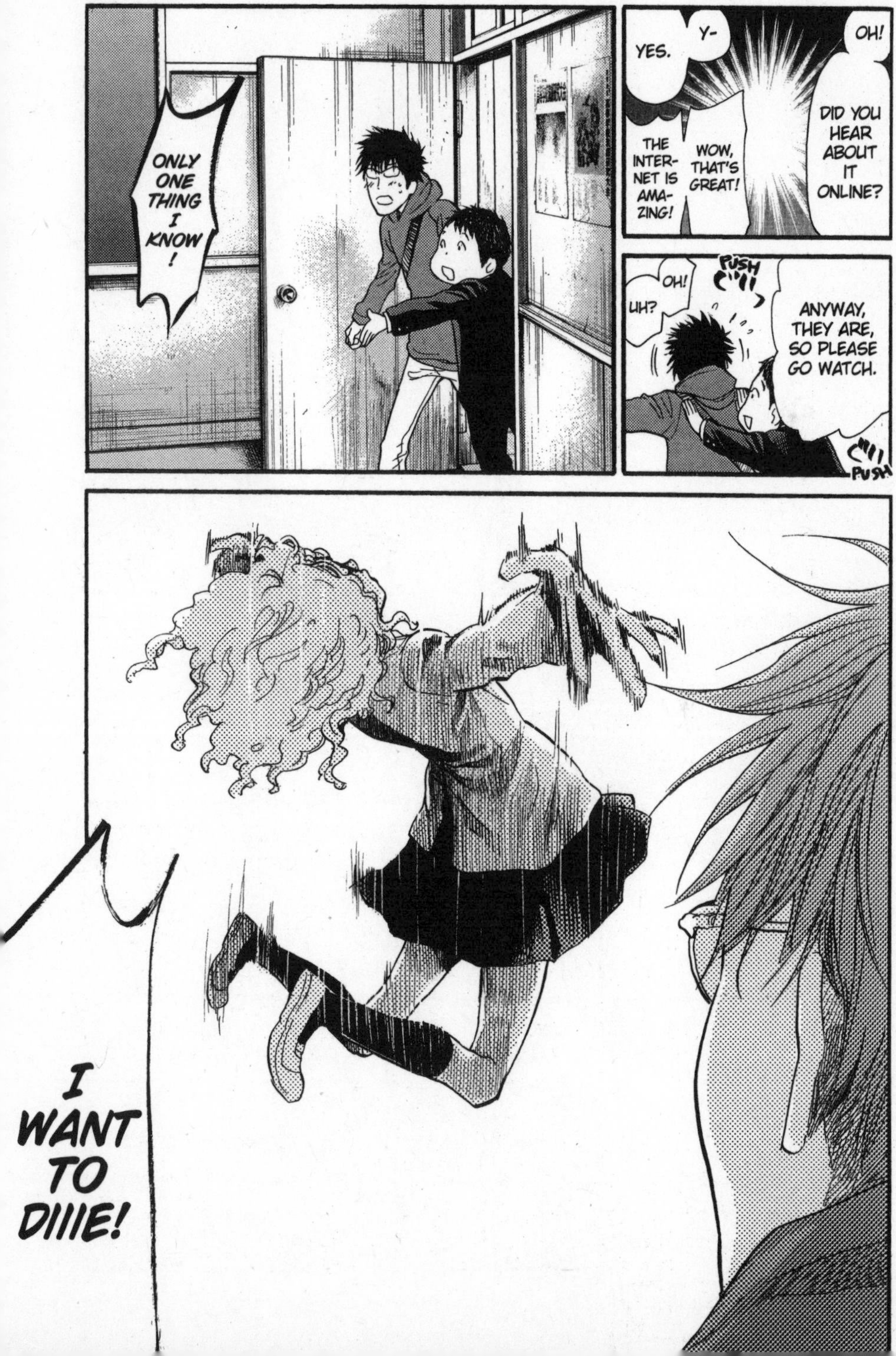
OH!
DID YOU HEAR ABOUT IT ONLINE?
Y-
YES.
WOW, THAT'S GREAT!
THE INTERNET IS AMAZING!
ANYWAY, THEY ARE, SO PLEASE GO WATCH.
PUSH
OH!
UH?
PUSH
ONLY ONE THING I KNOW!
I WANT TO DIIIE!

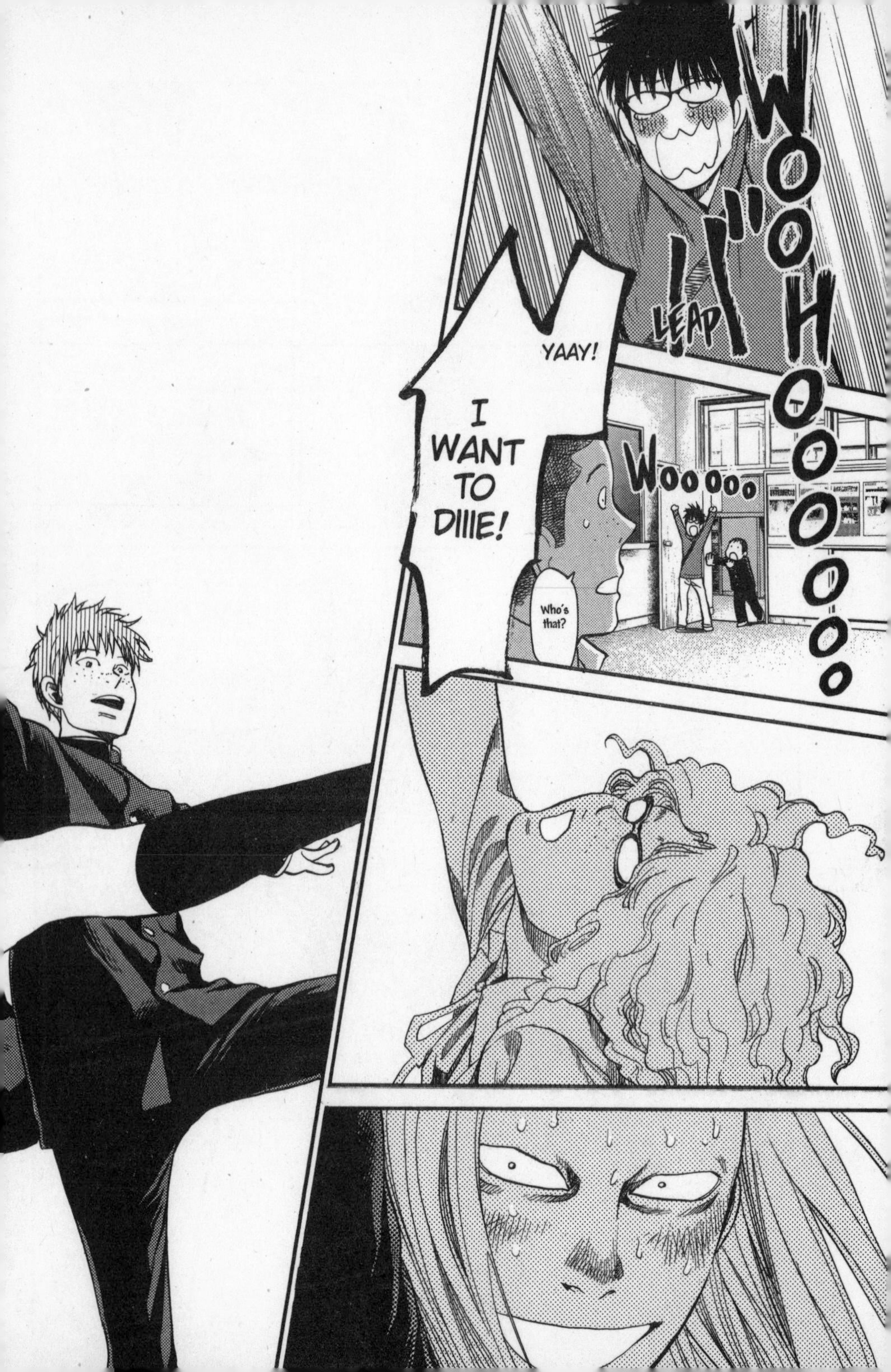
WOOOHOOOOOOOO
LEAP
YAAY!
I WANT TO DIIIE!
Woooooo
Who's that?

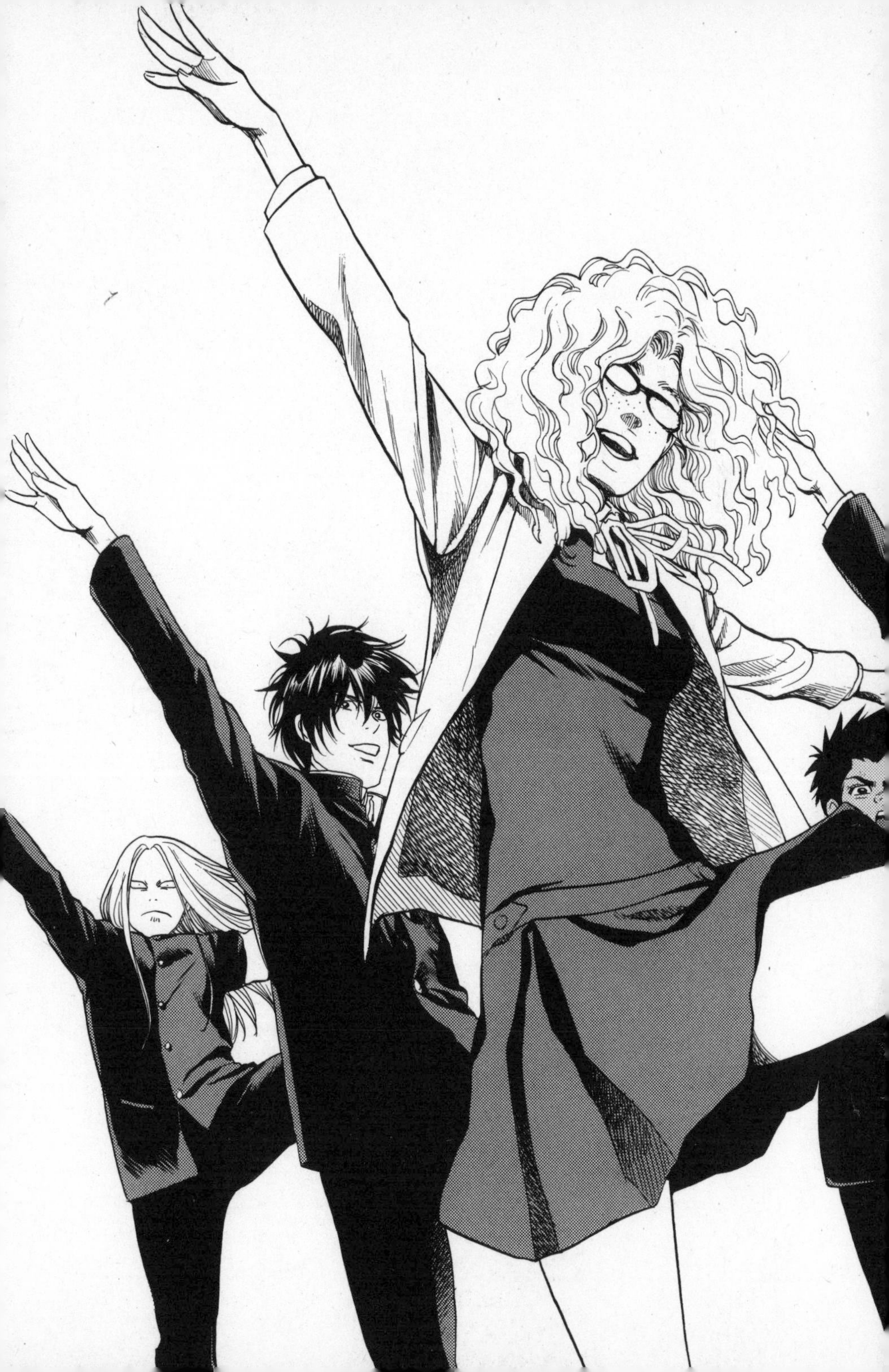

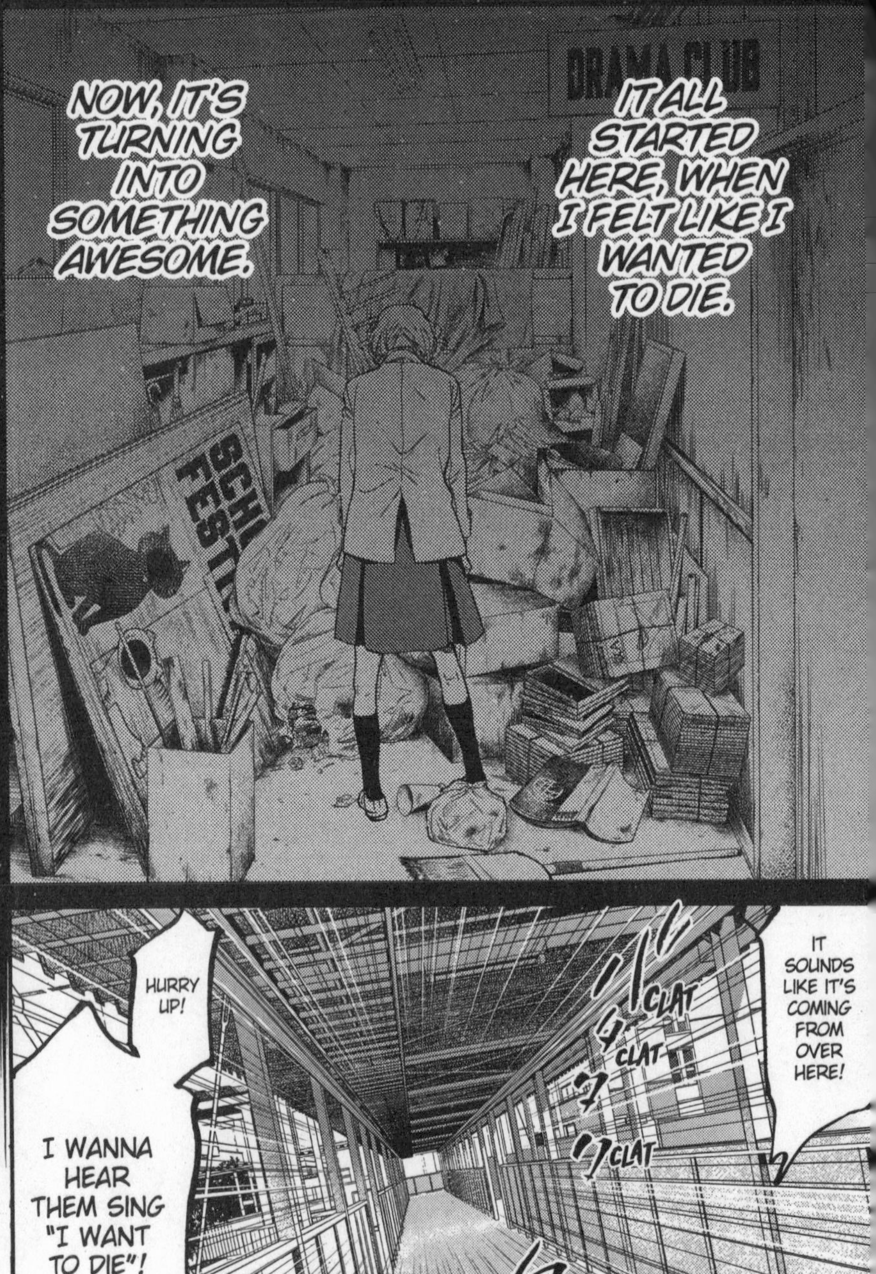
DRAMA CLUB
IT ALL STARTED HERE, WHEN I FELT LIKE I WANTED TO DIE.
NOW, IT'S TURNING INTO SOMETHING AWESOME.
IT SOUNDS LIKE IT'S COMING FROM OVER HERE!
CLAT
CLAT
CLAT
CLAT
HURRY UP!
I WANNA HEAR THEM SING "I WANT TO DIE"!

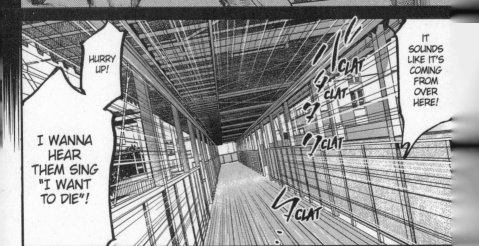

98. HAPPY SCARY

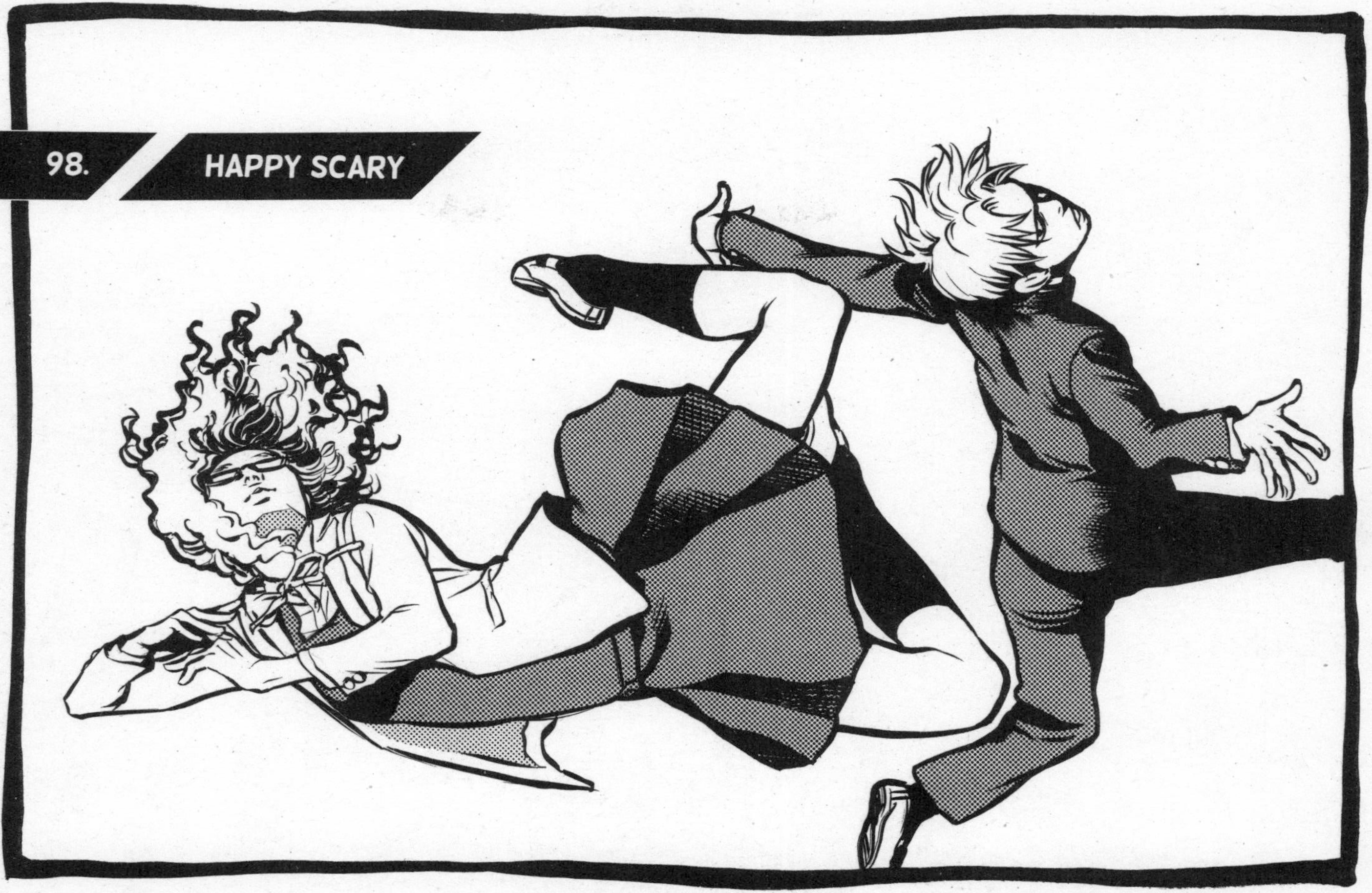

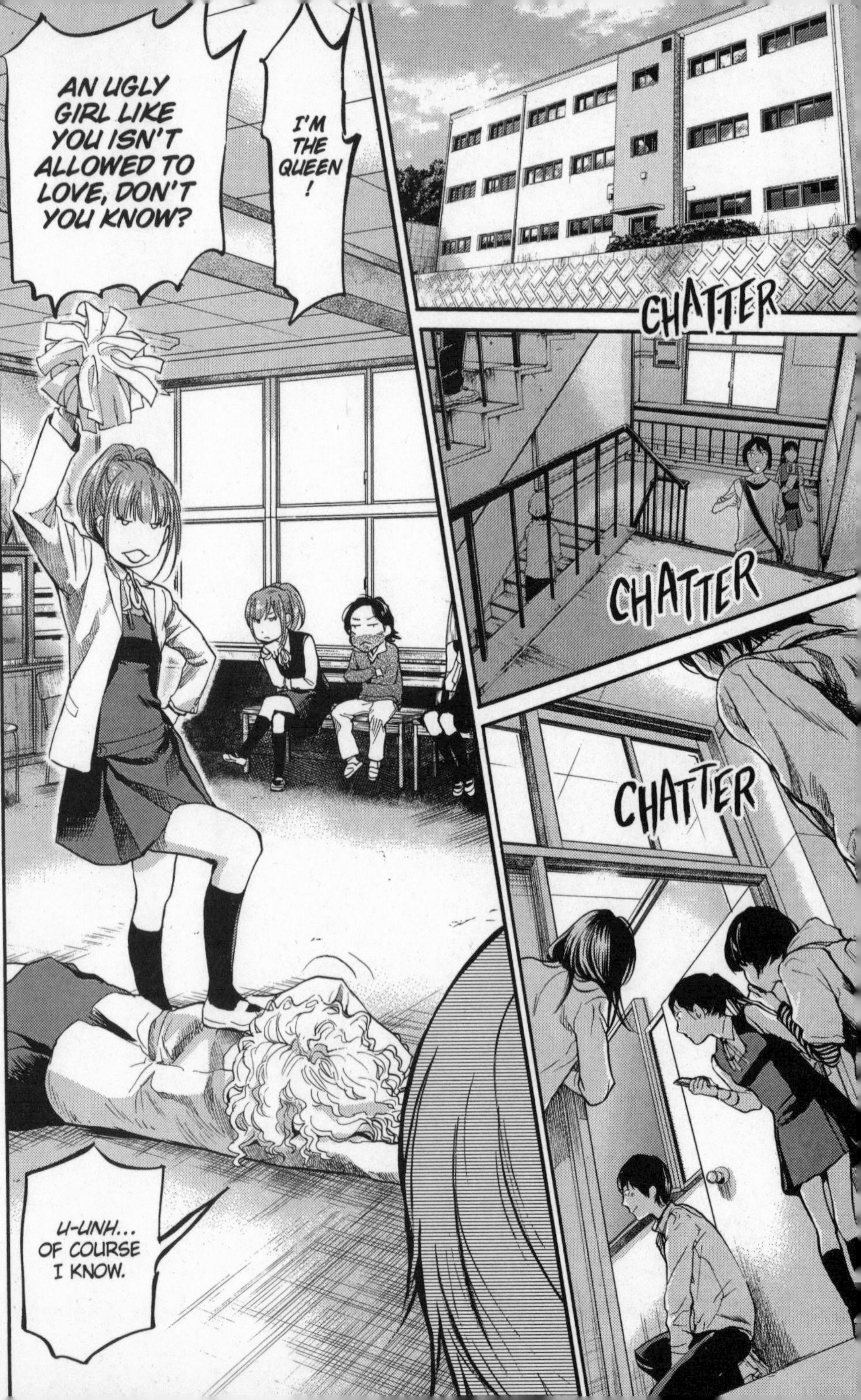
CHATTER
CHATTER
CHATTER
I'M THE QUEEN!
AN UGLY GIRL LIKE YOU ISN'T ALLOWED TO LOVE, DON'T YOU KNOW?
U-UNH... OF COURSE I KNOW.

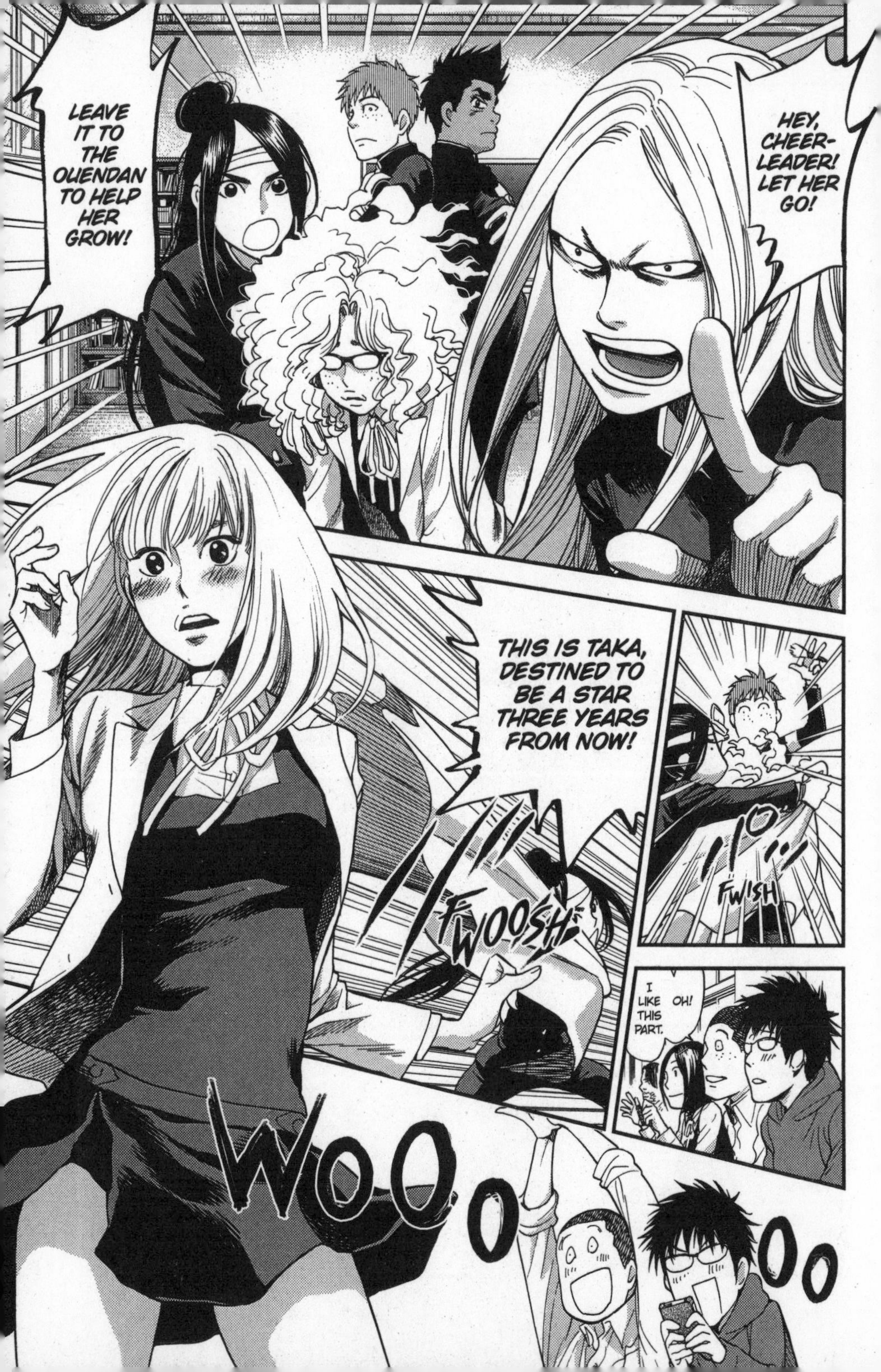
HEY, CHEER-LEADER! LET HER GO!
LEAVE IT TO THE OUENDAN TO HELP HER GROW!
FWISH
OH!
I LIKE THIS PART.
THIS IS TAKA, DESTINED TO BE A STAR THREE YEARS FROM NOW!
FWOOSH
WOOOOOOO

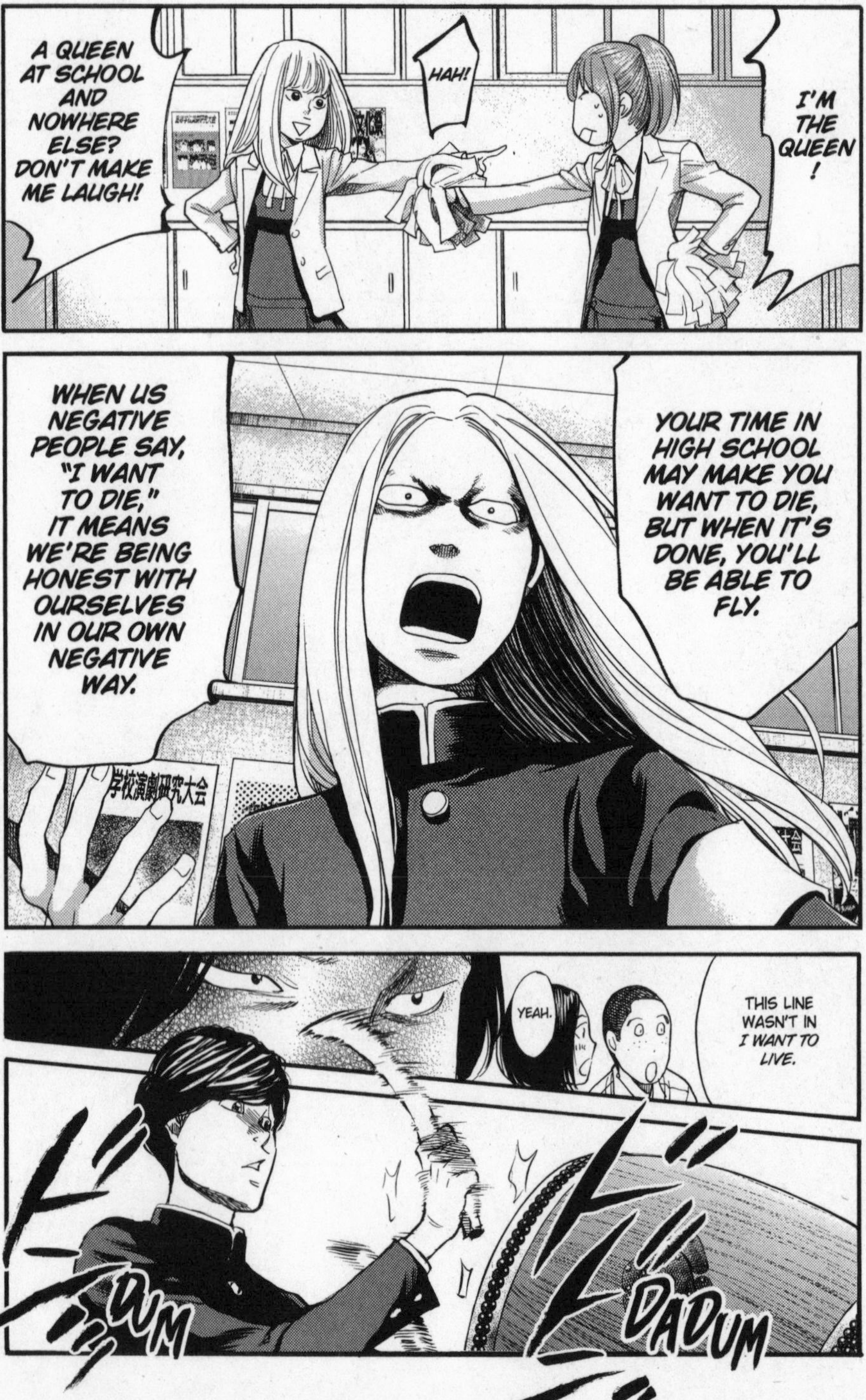
I'M THE QUEEN!
HAH!
A QUEEN AT SCHOOL AND NOWHERE ELSE? DON'T MAKE ME LAUGH!
YOUR TIME IN HIGH SCHOOL MAY MAKE YOU WANT TO DIE, BUT WHEN IT'S DONE, YOU'LL BE ABLE TO FLY.
WHEN US NEGATIVE PEOPLE SAY, "I WANT TO DIE," IT MEANS WE'RE BEING HONEST WITH OURSELVES IN OUR OWN NEGATIVE WAY.
学校演劇研究大会
THIS LINE WASN'T IN I WANT TO LIVE.
YEAH.
DADUM
DUM

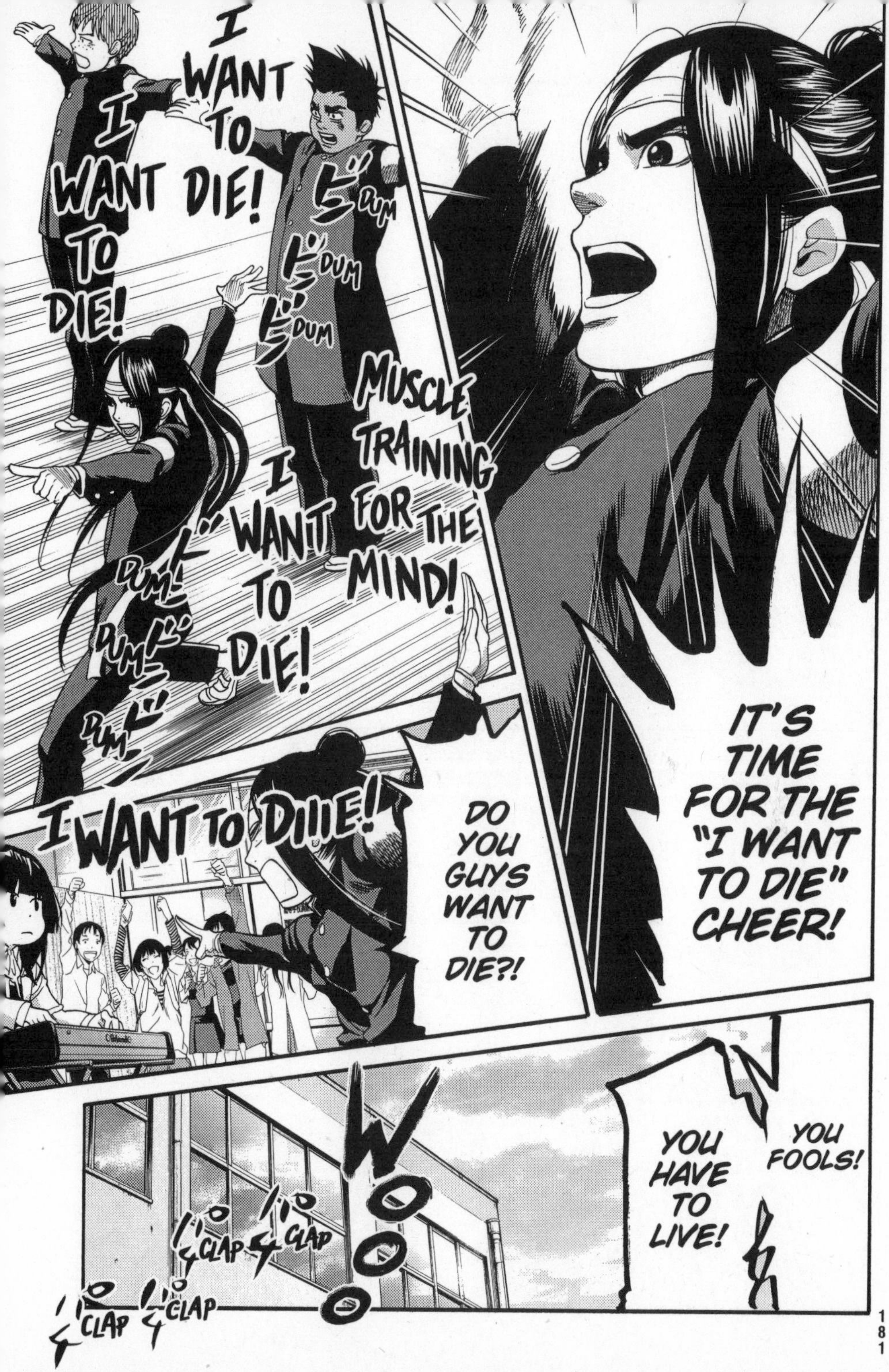
IT'S TIME FOR THE "I WANT TO DIE" CHEER!
I WANT TO DIE!
I WANT TO DIE!
DUM
DUM
DUM
MUSCLE TRAINING FOR THE MIND!
I WANT TO DIE!
DUM
DUM
DUM
DO YOU GUYS WANT TO DIE?!
I WANT TO DIIIE!
YOU FOOLS!
YOU HAVE TO LIVE!
WOOOO
CLAP
CLAP
CLAP
CLAP

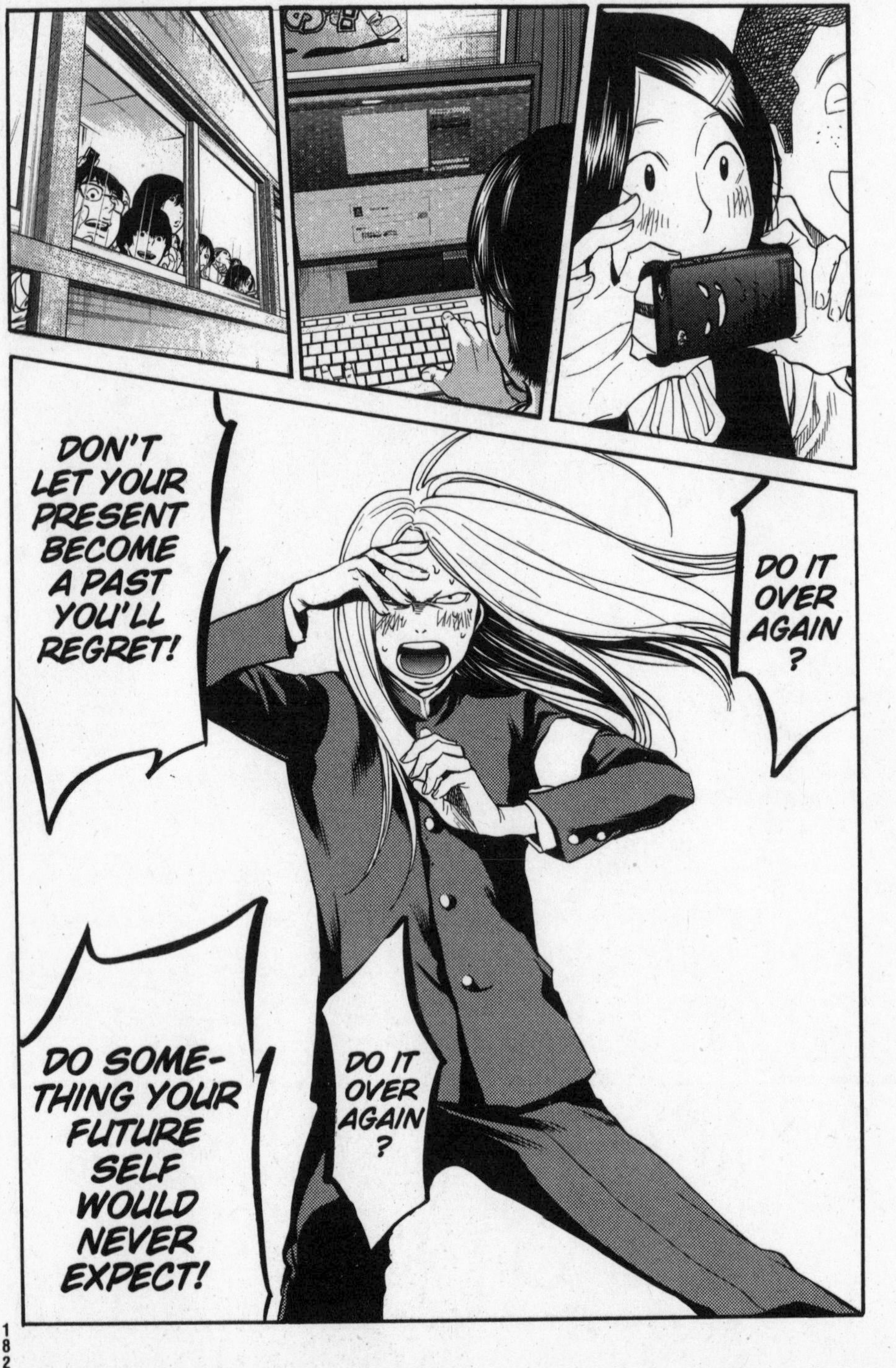
DO IT OVER AGAIN?
DON'T LET YOUR PRESENT BECOME A PAST YOU'LL REGRET!
DO IT OVER AGAIN?
DO SOME-THING YOUR FUTURE SELF WOULD NEVER EXPECT!

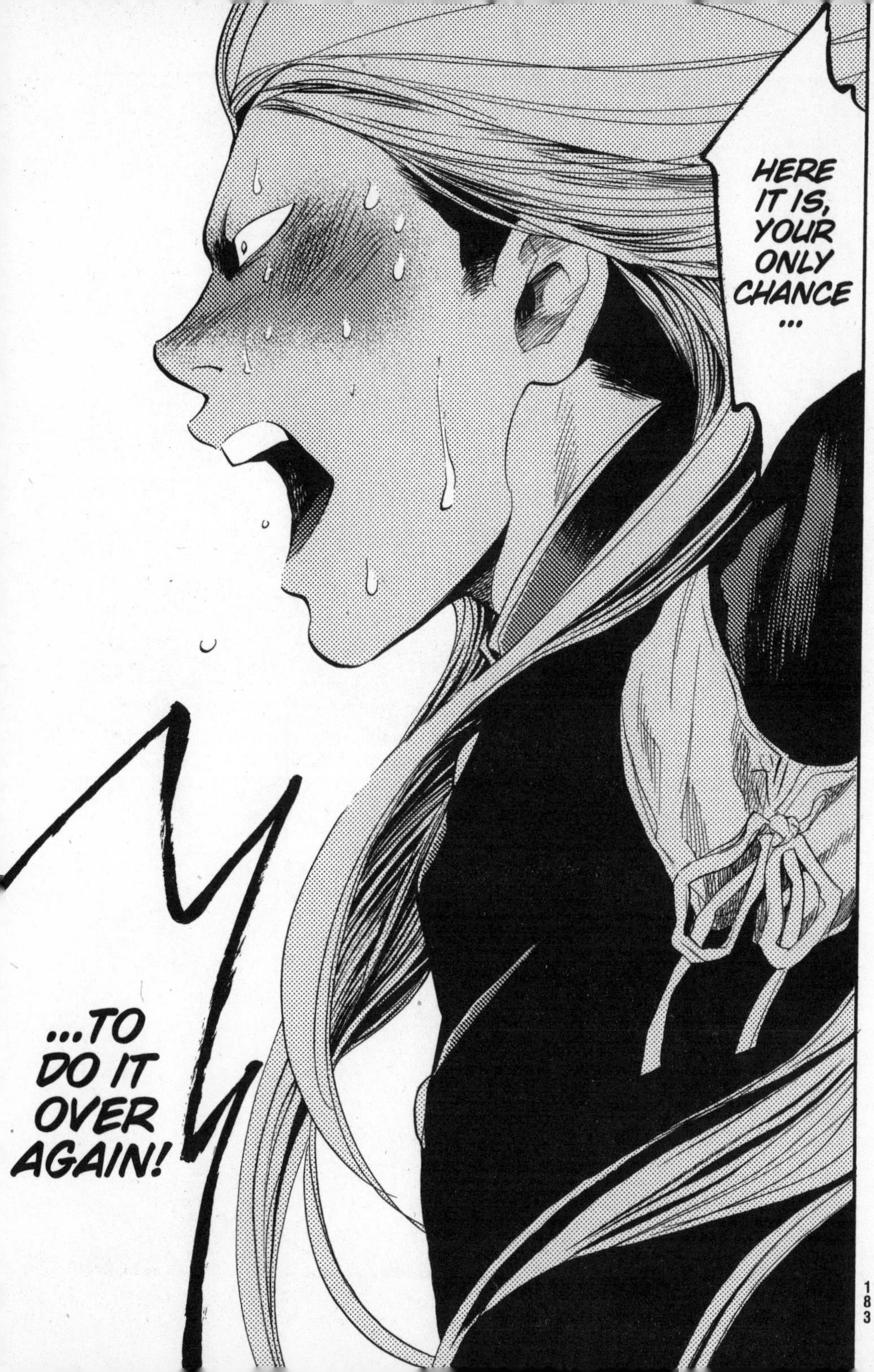
HERE IT IS, YOUR ONLY CHANCE ...
...TO DO IT OVER AGAIN!

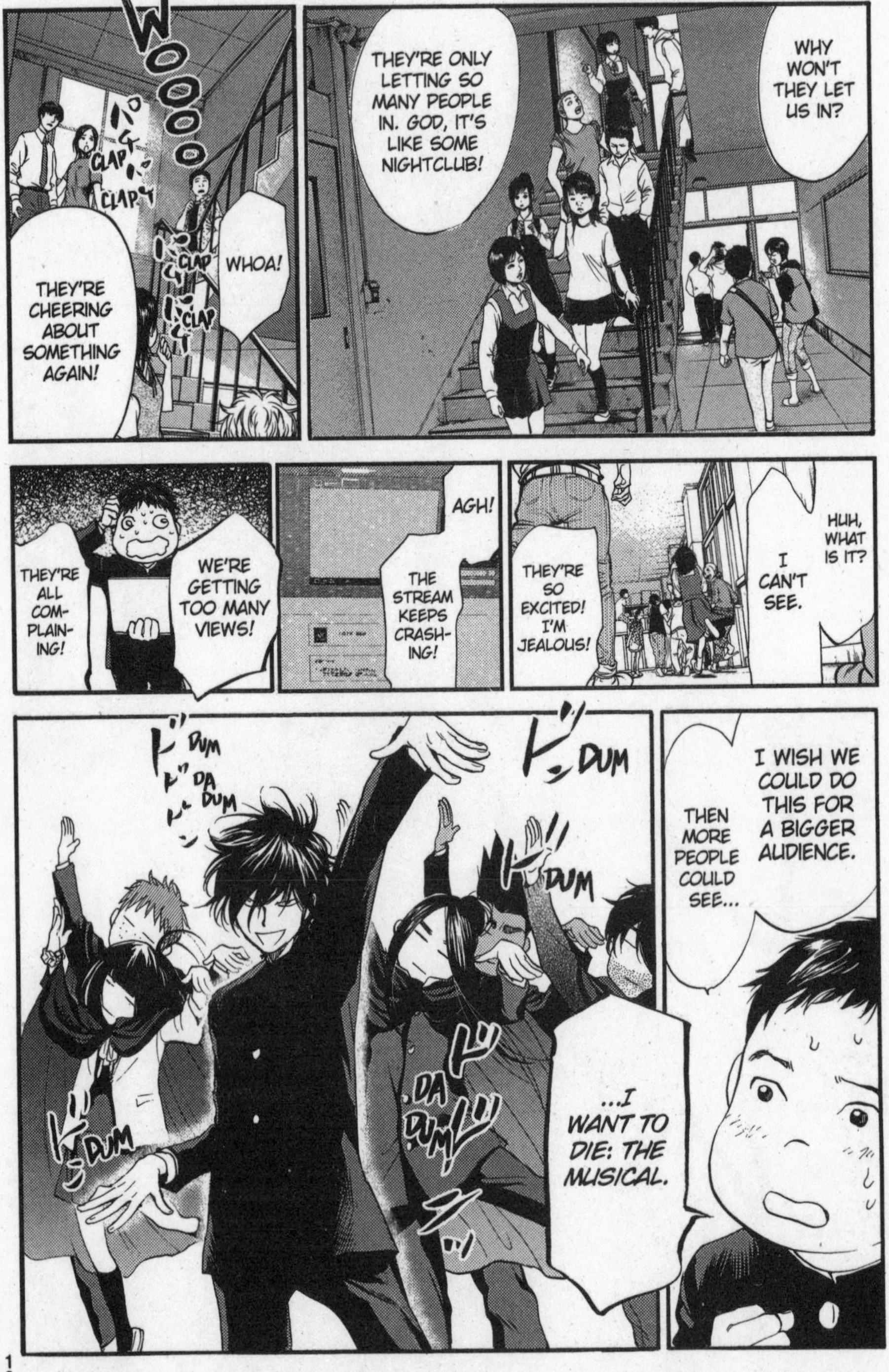
WHY WON'T THEY LET US IN?
THEY'RE ONLY LETTING SO MANY PEOPLE IN. GOD, IT'S LIKE SOME NIGHTCLUB!
WOOOOO
CLAP CLAP
WHOA!
CLAP CLAP
THEY'RE CHEERING ABOUT SOMETHING AGAIN!
HUH, WHAT IS IT?
I CAN'T SEE.
THEY'RE SO EXCITED! I'M JEALOUS!
AGH!
THE STREAM KEEPS CRASHING!
WE'RE GETTING TOO MANY VIEWS!
THEY'RE ALL COM-PLAIN-ING!
I WISH WE COULD DO THIS FOR A BIGGER AUDIENCE.
THEN MORE PEOPLE COULD SEE...
...I WANT TO DIE: THE MUSICAL.
DUM
DUM
DUM DA DUM
DA DUM
DUM
DUM

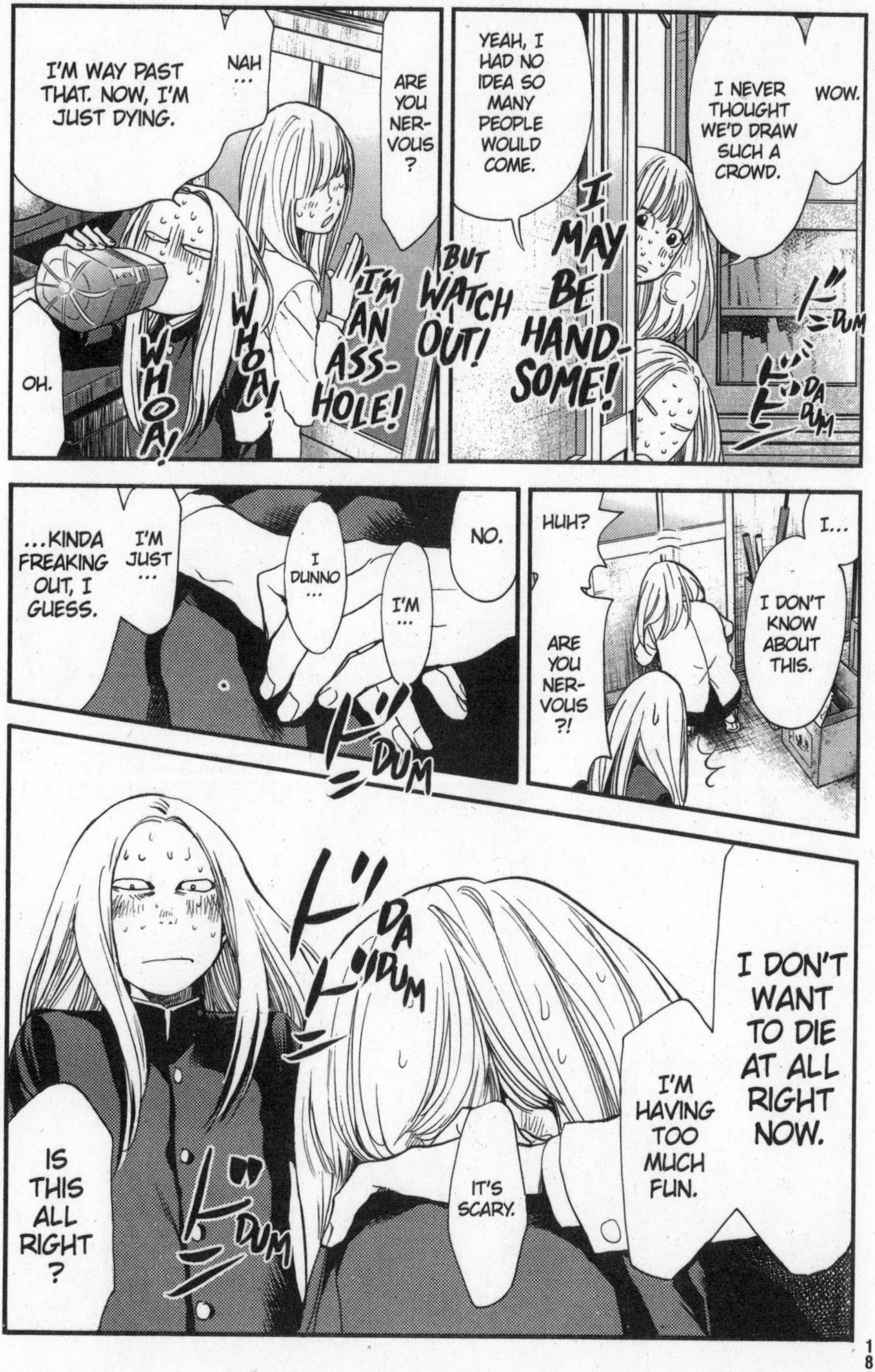
WOW.
I NEVER THOUGHT WE'D DRAW SUCH A CROWD.
YEAH, I HAD NO IDEA SO MANY PEOPLE WOULD COME.
DUM
DA DUM
I MAY BE HANDSOME!
BUT WATCH OUT!
I'M AN ASSHOLE!
ARE YOU NERVOUS?
NAH...
I'M WAY PAST THAT. NOW, I'M JUST DYING.
WHOA!
WHOA!
OH.
I...
I DON'T KNOW ABOUT THIS.
HUH?
ARE YOU NERVOUS?!
NO.
I'M...
I DUNNO...
I'M JUST...
...KINDA FREAKING OUT, I GUESS.
DUM
I DON'T WANT TO DIE AT ALL RIGHT NOW.
I'M HAVING TOO MUCH FUN.
IT'S SCARY.
DA DUM
DUM
IS THIS ALL RIGHT?

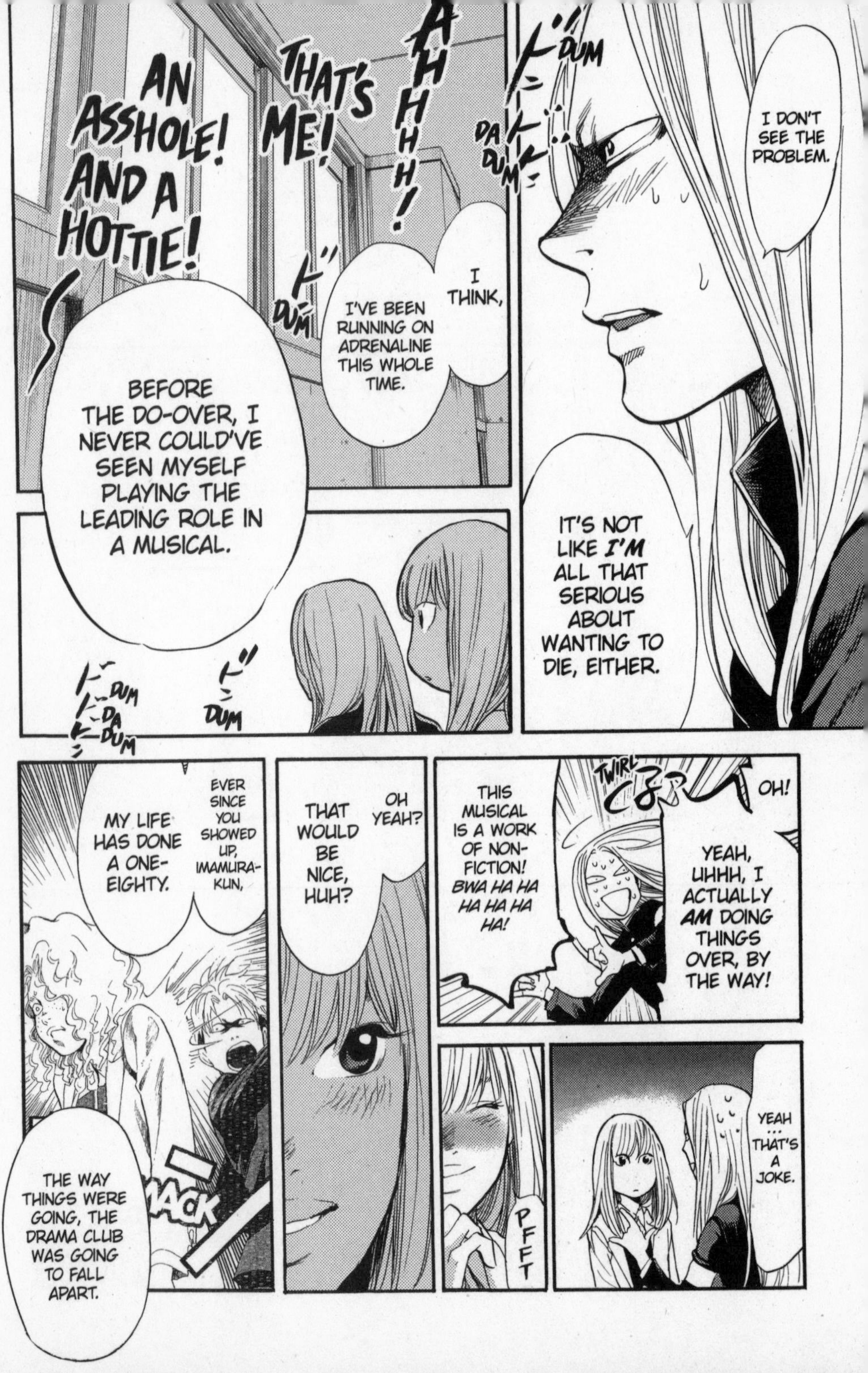
DUM
DA DUM
I DON'T SEE THE PROBLEM.
IT'S NOT LIKE I'M ALL THAT SERIOUS ABOUT WANTING TO DIE, EITHER.
AHHHHH!
THAT'S ME!
AN ASSHOLE! AND A HOTTIE!
I THINK,
I'VE BEEN RUNNING ON ADRENALINE THIS WHOLE TIME.
DUM
BEFORE THE DO-OVER, I NEVER COULD'VE SEEN MYSELF PLAYING THE LEADING ROLE IN A MUSICAL.
DUM
DUM DA DUM
OH!
TWIRL
YEAH, UHHH, I ACTUALLY AM DOING THINGS OVER, BY THE WAY!
THIS MUSICAL IS A WORK OF NON-FICTION! BWA HA HA HA HA HA HA!
YEAH... THAT'S A JOKE.
PFFT
OH YEAH?
THAT WOULD BE NICE, HUH?
EVER SINCE YOU SHOWED UP, IMAMURA-KUN,
MY LIFE HAS DONE A ONE-EIGHTY.
MACK
THE WAY THINGS WERE GOING, THE DRAMA CLUB WAS GOING TO FALL APART.

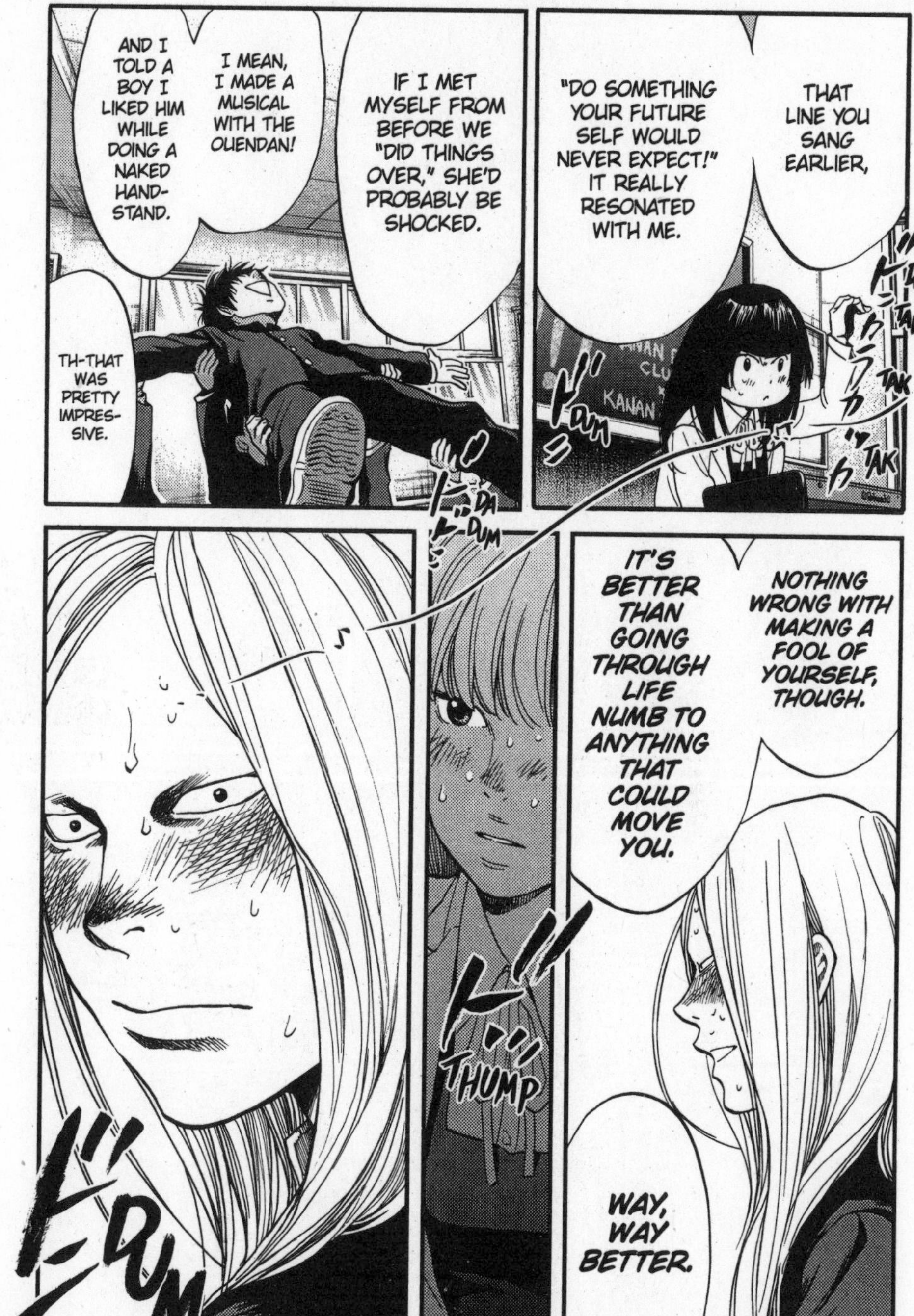
THAT LINE YOU SANG EARLIER,
"DO SOMETHING YOUR FUTURE SELF WOULD NEVER EXPECT!" IT REALLY RESONATED WITH ME.
DUM TAKKA TAK TAK
DUM
IF I MET MYSELF FROM BEFORE WE "DID THINGS OVER," SHE'D PROBABLY BE SHOCKED.
I MEAN, I MADE A MUSICAL WITH THE OUENDAN!
AND I TOLD A BOY I LIKED HIM WHILE DOING A NAKED HAND-STAND.
TH-THAT WAS PRETTY IMPRES-SIVE.
DA DUM
NOTHING WRONG WITH MAKING A FOOL OF YOURSELF, THOUGH.
IT'S BETTER THAN GOING THROUGH LIFE NUMB TO ANYTHING THAT COULD MOVE YOU.
WAY, WAY BETTER.
THUMP
DUM

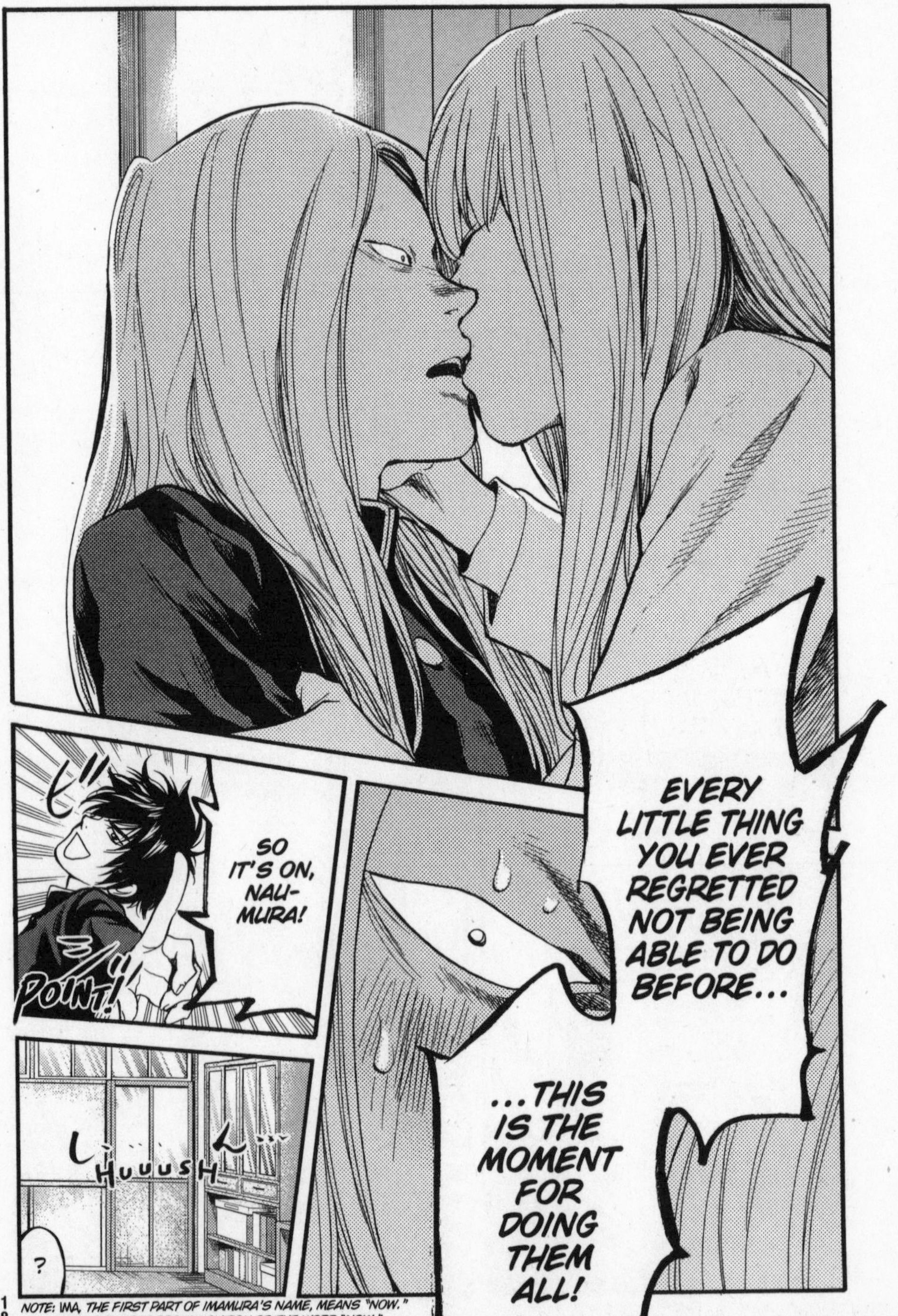
EVERY LITTLE THING YOU EVER REGRETTED NOT BEING ABLE TO DO BEFORE...
...THIS IS THE MOMENT FOR DOING THEM ALL!
SO IT'S ON, NAUMURA!
POINT!
HUUUSH
?

NOTE: IMA, THE FIRST PART OF IMAMURA'S NAME, MEANS "NOW." NAU IS THE JAPANESE PRONUNCIATION OF THE WORD "NOW," HENCE NAUMURA, THE NAME OF HIS THINLY-VEILED SELF-INSERT CHARACTER IN THE MUSICAL.

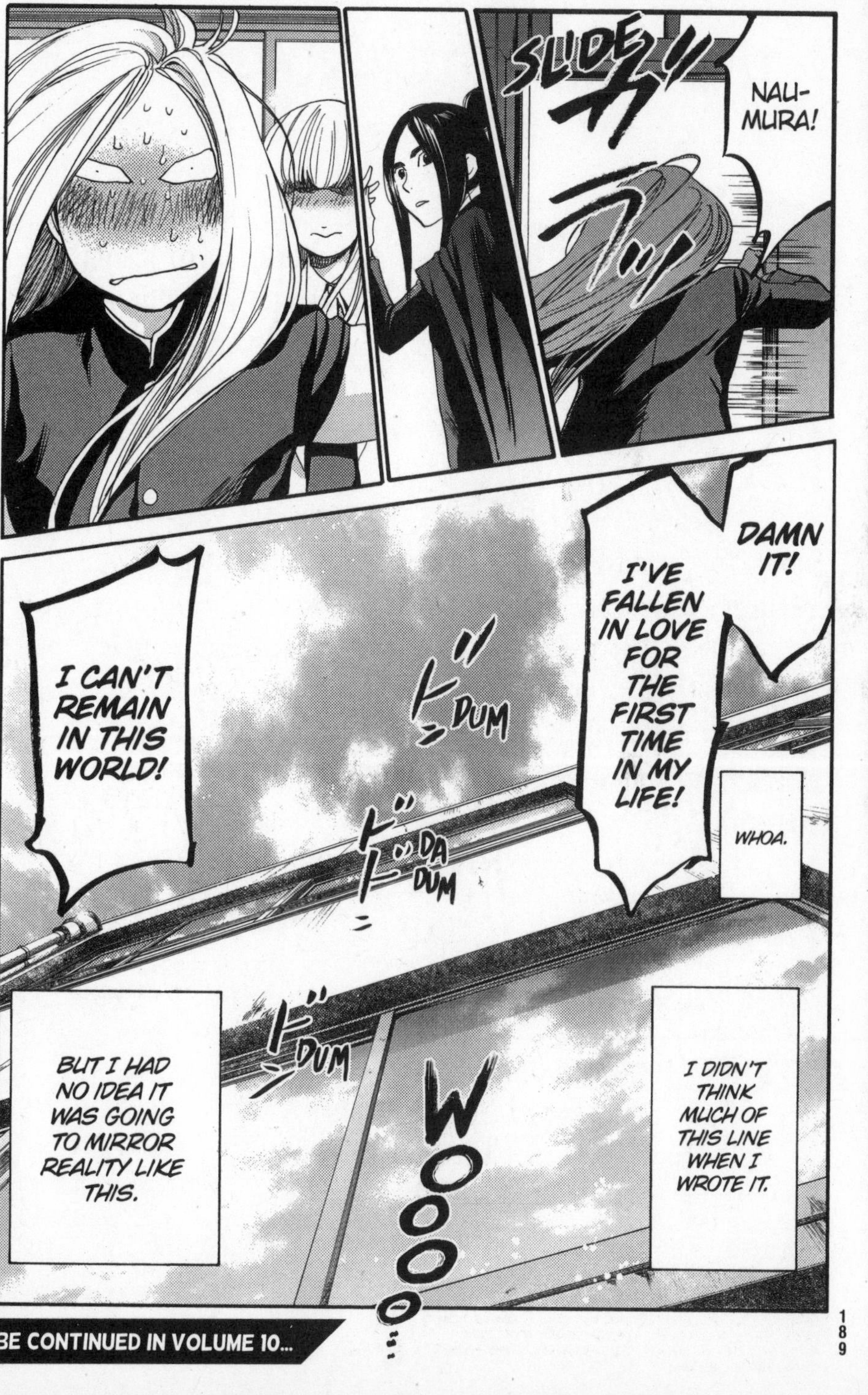
SLIDE
NAU-MURA!
DAMN IT!
I'VE FALLEN IN LOVE FOR THE FIRST TIME IN MY LIFE!
WHOA.
I CAN'T REMAIN IN THIS WORLD!
DUM
DA DUM
DUM
I DIDN'T THINK MUCH OF THIS LINE WHEN I WROTE IT.
WOOOOO...
BUT I HAD NO IDEA IT WAS GOING TO MIRROR REALITY LIKE THIS.

TO BE CONTINUED IN VOLUME 10...

This is the AFTERWORD!

When I was in my high school's drama club, we sometimes got help from the ouendan because we didn't have enough people of our own. They did voice-only parts they could play from backstage, and their deep, resonating voices made them very reliable.

Back then, I never had a boyfriend or anything, but in a way, I guess you could say my life was very fulfilling since I got the chance to make something together with people so different from myself.

Mitsurou Kubo, June 2013

2013. 6. 久保ミツロウ

 My Agent: Hiromi Sakitani

 My Assistants: Shunsuke Ono
Youko Mikuni
Hiromu Kitano
Koushi Tezuka
Rana Satou
Kouhei Mihara

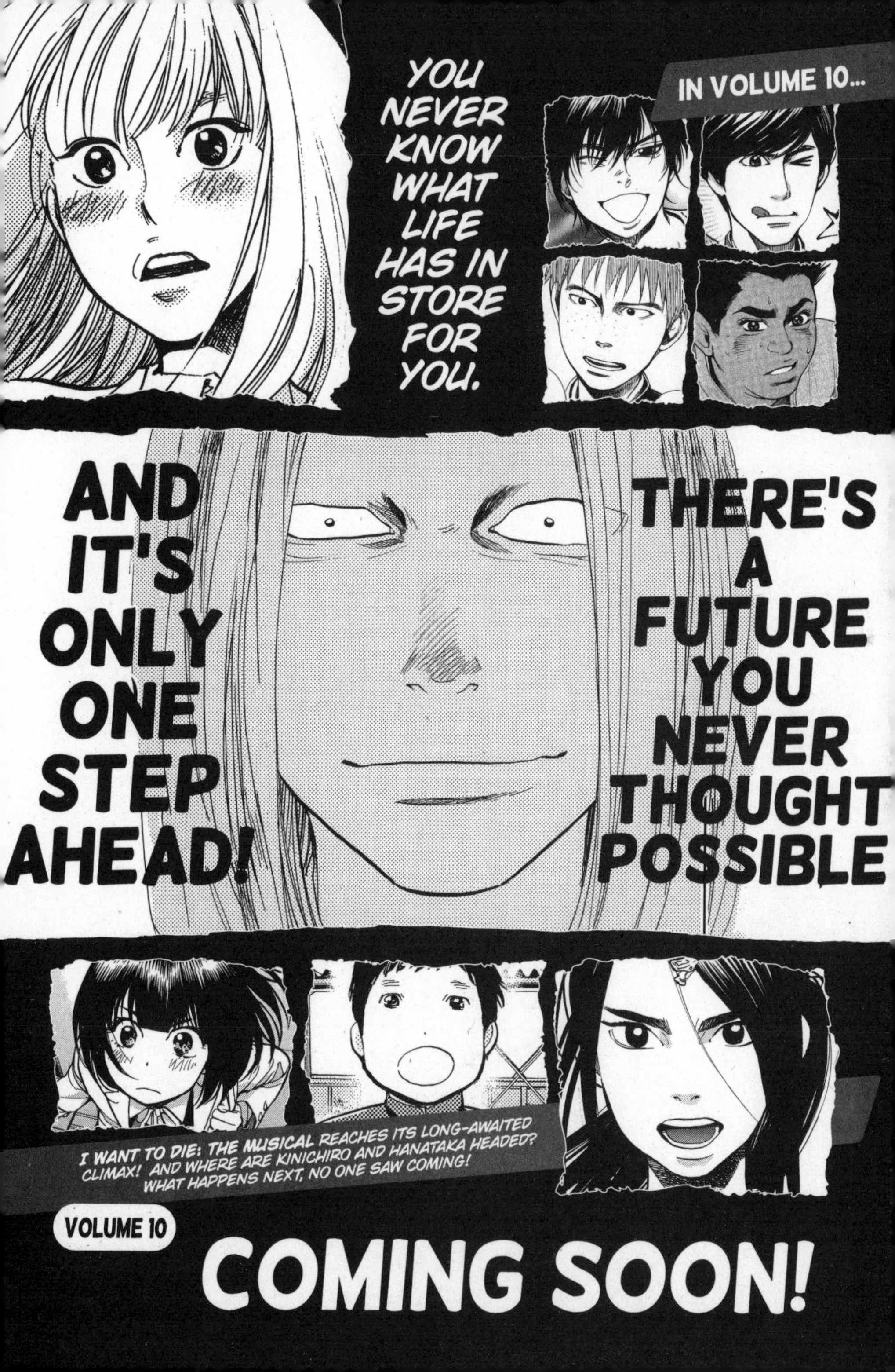

IN VOLUME 10...
YOU NEVER KNOW WHAT LIFE HAS IN STORE FOR YOU.
THERE'S A FUTURE YOU NEVER THOUGHT POSSIBLE
AND IT'S ONLY ONE STEP AHEAD!
I WANT TO DIE: THE MUSICAL REACHES ITS LONG-AWAITED
CLIMAX! AND WHERE ARE KINICHIRO AND HANATAKA HEADED?
WHAT HAPPENS NEXT, NO ONE SAW COMING!
VOLUME 10
COMING SOON!

A Kodansha Comics Trade Paperback Original.

Again!! volume 9 copyright © 2013 Mitsurou Kubo
English translation copyright © 2019 Mitsurou Kubo

Published in the United States by Kodansha Comics, an imprint of Kodansha USA Publishing, LLC, New York.

Publication rights for this English edition arranged through Kodansha Ltd., Tokyo.

First published in Japan in 2013 by Kodansha Ltd., Tokyo, as *Agein!!* volume 9.

ISBN 978-1-63236-781-5

Printed in the United States of America.

www.kodanshacomics.com

9 8 7 6 5 4 3 2 1

Translator: Rose Padgett
Lettering: E. K. Weaver
Editing: Paul Starr
Editorial Assistance: Tiff Ferentini
Kodansha Comics edition cover design by Phil Balsman